I0555205

This book belongs to

Name: _____

www.math-knots.com

Cover Design by :
MATH-KNOTS LLC

First Edition :
December, 2018

Author:
Gowri Vemuri

Questions: mathknots.help@gmail.com

This book is dedicated to:

My Mom, who is my best critic, guide and supporter.

To what I am today, and what I am going to become tomorrow,

is all because of your blessings, unconditional affection and support.

This book is dedicated to the

strongest women of my life ,

my dearest mom

and

to all those moms in this universe.

G.V.

www.math-knots.com

What is CoGAT ?

The Cognitive Ability Test® (CoGAT) test measures skills in young children from K-12, in various sections of Verbal, Quantitative and Non-Verbal, Thinking and Analytical. Many counties and states conduct this test to identify kids for CoGAT serves as one of the basic measures to identify the gifted and Talented pool for accelerated educational programs in many counties and states.

Cognitive skills are the skills the brain uses to think, learn, read, remember, pay attention, and solve problems. Kids develop these skills as part of their growing up. Our book helps kids, in channelizing their skills.

As Einstein said Education is not the learning of facts, but the training of minds to think. We want to bring joy of learning while channelizing the young minds thinking to reach their optimum potential. Students get familiarized with various strategies, tips and techniques thus improving their thinking abilities. All our tests are created in a multi-color, kid friendly format. For each test is based on theme for the students to have a little fun as they learn. As the students get familiarize with testing format, their vocabulary also builds up.

Our tests give an edge and simulate the testing pattern, in such a way that child feels very comfortable when they take the test in their schools.

Various counties and states apply multiple criteria for selecting kids for gifted or Advanced Academic programs and CogAT is one of the basic criteria. CogAT comprises of the following three main categories

- Verbal Section
- Quantitative Aptitude
- Non-Verbal Section.

Our Practice tests are based on the following:

Verbal Section:

Students are tested in the areas of vocabulary, comprehension of ideas, and the relation between various words. The test comprises of the below three sub sections/tests.

1. **Verbal Classification**

Three words that are alike in some way and form a group are given to the students, along with four choices to choose. One of the four choices don't belong to the group. Student has to identify the odd man and bubbles the correct option in the bubble sheet.

2. Sentence Completion

A sentence is given to the student with four picture options. Student uses the vocabulary and comprehension skills and choses the right picture that makes the best sense in the sentence. Student Bubbles the correct option in the bubble sheet.

3. Verbal Analogies

The student is given three words. The first two words go together. The third word goes with one of the answer choices. The student is asked to choose the word that goes with the third word the same way that the second word goes with the first. Student Bubbles the correct option in the bubble sheet.

Quantitative Aptitude Section:

The Quantitative Aptitude sub sections tests the student's abstract reasoning, quantitative reasoning, analytical and problem-solving skills. The test comprises of the below three sub sections/tests.

1. Quantitative Relations/Number Analogies

Figures in the first row belong to each other in a certain way. Student is expected to identify the number analogy in the first row. The figures in the second row follow the same analogy as the first row. Student analyzes and thinks through to find the right choice from the given four options. Student Bubbles the correct option in the bubble sheet.

2. Number Series

Series of beads are given on various strings /rods. Student identifies the number series and figures out the beads on missing rod/string. Student Bubbles the correct option in the bubble sheet.

3. Equation Building /Number Puzzles

A number equation is given in a kid friendly format. Student solves for the number that goes in the place of the question mark. Student Bubbles the correct option in the bubble sheet.

Non-Verbal Section (Spatial Reasoning):

The Nonverbal Battery comprises of the most unique problems to students. The questions on these tests are based on geometric shapes and figures. The tests require visualization, thinking and analytical abilities. The test comprises of the below three sub tests.

1. Figure Classification

The student is given three figures that are a like in some way. Four answer choices are given to choose from and one of the choices belong to the given group in a certain way. Students analyzes the figures to choose the right option and bubbles the correct option in the bubble sheet.

2. Figure Analogies/ Figure Matrices

Figures in the first row belong to each other in a certain way. Student is expected to identify the figure analogy between figures in the first row. The figures in the second row follow the same analogy as the first row. Student analyzes and thinks through to find the right choice from the given four options and bubbles the correct option in the bubble sheet.

3. Figure Analysis/Paper Folding

A Square, Rectangle or any shape figure is folded once or more as shown in the figure. Holes are punched to the folded figure and opened completely. Students are expected to think through on how the figure will look like after opening it up and bubbles the correct option in the bubble sheet.

Book Includes, detailed solutions and tips, that will help kids do well in the **CoGAT test.**

Do Visit our website www.math-knots.com for more products and also for our online subscription.

Math-Knots ------- Joy of Learning

INDEX

Test Strategies 10

    How to Bubble?

    Preparation for the test.

Test 1 Verbal Section: 13

    1. Verbal Classification

    2. Sentence Completion

    3. Verbal Analogies

Test 1 Quantitative Aptitude Section: 47

    4. Quantitative Relations/Number Analogies

    5. Number Series

    6. Equation Building /Number Puzzles

Test 1 Non-Verbal Section(Spatial Reasoning): 89

    7. Figure Classification

    8. Figure Analogies/ Figure Matrices

    9. Figure Analysis/Paper Folding

Test 2 Verbal Section : 131

    1. Verbal Classification

    2. Sentence Completion

    3. Verbal Analogies

Test 2 Quantitative Aptitude Section : 165

    4. Quantitative Relations/Number Analogies

    5. Number Series

    6. Equation Building/Number Puzzles

Test 2 Non-Verbal Section(Spatial Reasoning) : 207

    7. Figure Classification

    8. Figure Analogies/Figure Matrices

    9. Figure Analysis/Paper Folding

www.math-knots.com

INDEX

Answer Key Test 1 Verbal Section: 251

1. Verbal Classification

2. Sentence Completion

3. Verbal Analogies

Answer Key Test 1 : Quantitative Aptitude Section:................................ 255

4. Quantitative Relations/Number Analogies

5. Number Series

6. Equation Building /Number Puzzles

Answer Key Test 1: Non-Verbal Section
(Spatial Reasoning): 262

7. Figure Classification

8. Figure Analogies/ Figure Matrices

9. Figure Analysis/Paper Folding

Answer Key Test 2 : Verbal Section : 267

1. Verbal Classification

2. Sentence Completion

3. Verbal Analogies

Answer Key Test 2 : Quantitative Aptitude Section :................................ 271

4. Quantitative Relations/Number Analogies

5. Number Series

6. Equation Building/Number Puzzles

Answer Key Test 1: Non-Verbal Section
(Spatial Reasoning): 277

7. Figure Classification

8. Figure Analogies/ Figure Matrices

9. Figure Analysis/Paper Folding

Paper Folding Practice figures 283

16 figures

Bubble Sheet 287

Start from the middle of right choice and fully fill the bubble completely.

Wrong

A    B ◯   C ◯   D ◯

Wrong

A ◯   B ◯   C   D ◯

Wrong

A ◯   B ◯   C   D ◯

Partial Filled Bubble is not correct.

Correct

A ◯   B ◯   C ⬤   D ◯

www.math-knots.com

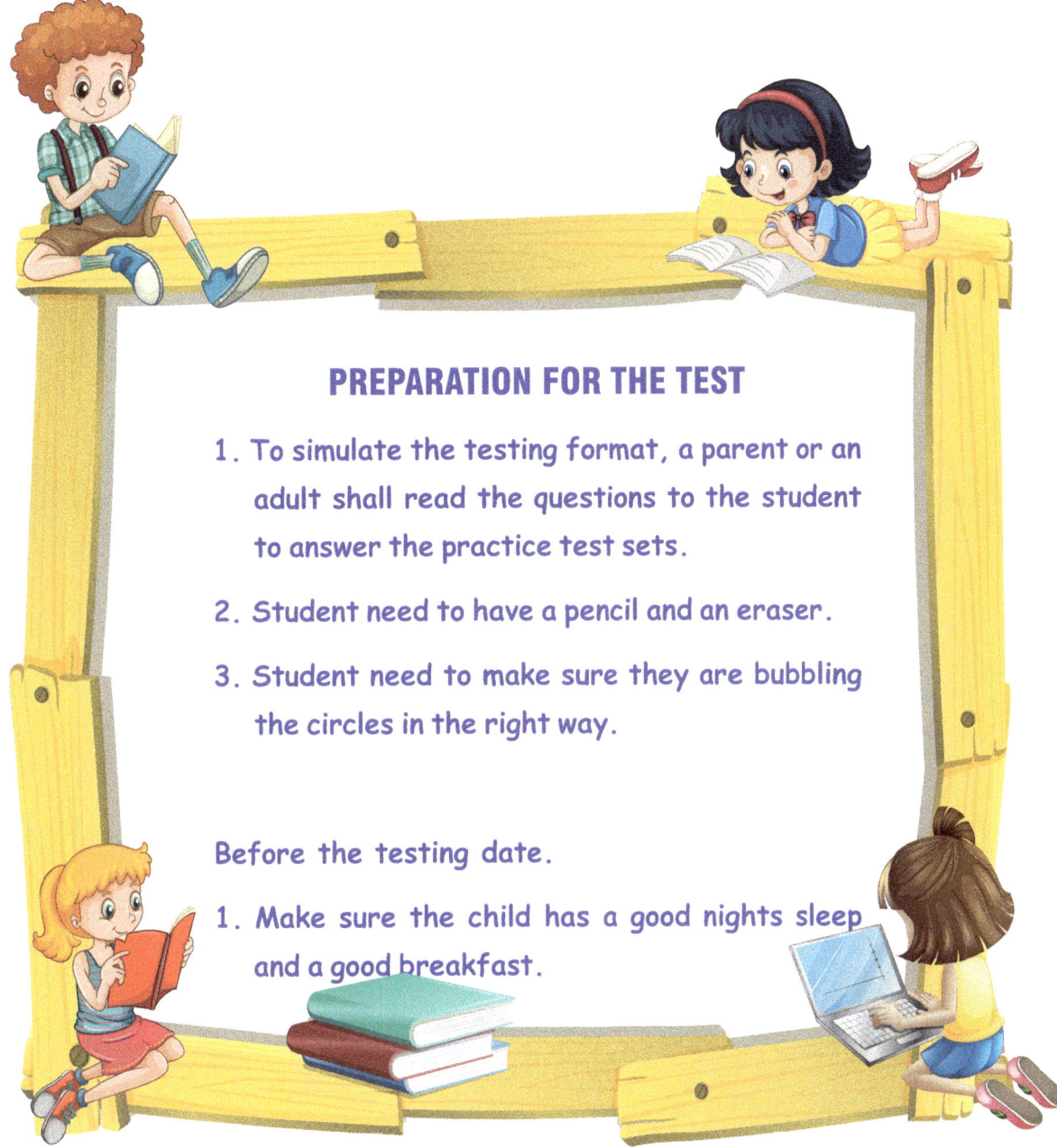

PREPARATION FOR THE TEST

1. To simulate the testing format, a parent or an adult shall read the questions to the student to answer the practice test sets.

2. Student need to have a pencil and an eraser.

3. Student need to make sure they are bubbling the circles in the right way.

Before the testing date.

1. Make sure the child has a good nights sleep and a good breakfast.

www.math-knots.com

TEST - 1

VERBAL SECTION

VERBAL CLASSIFICATION

Lets Start the Test...

www.math-knots.com

Sample Three words are related in a certain way. Four options are given. Identify the choice that does not belong to the group ?

One	Two	Three	
Six	Eight	Five	Gate
A ◯	B ◯	C ◯	D ◯

Solution : D

Three words in the question belong to one group. One of the four choices doesn't belong to the same group. Identify and bubble the correct choice. In the given question all three in first row are words as well as numbers in words. Lets take a look at the answers. All choices are words but three are numbers in words and one other word gate, which is incorrect.

All the questions in verbal classification test 1 are to be answered following the below question (instruction).

Three words are related in a certain way. Four options are given. Identify the choice that <u>does not belong</u> to the group ?

www.math-knots.com

www.math-knots.com

1. **Dress**   **Shorts**   **Tie**

    Umbrella   Pant   Socks   Shirt

    A ◯   B ◯   C ◯   D ◯

2. **Earthquakes**   **Hurricane**   **Catastrophe**

    War   Tornado   Blizzard   Floods

    A ◯   B ◯   C ◯   D ◯

3. **Yellow**   **Orange**   **Green**

    Red   Blue   Color   Orange

    A ◯   B ◯   C ◯   D ◯

4. **Eyes**   **Nose**   **Hearing**

    Skin   Tongue   Sound   Teeth

    A ◯   B ◯   C ◯   D ◯

5. **Nitrogen**   **Helium**   **Oxygen**

    Carbon dioxide   Zone   Hydrogen   Ozone

    A ◯   B ◯   C ◯   D ◯

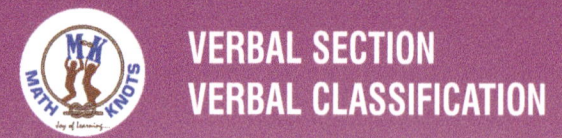
6. **Awesome**   **Fantastic**   **Happy**

   Lively   Ecstatic   Joy   Gloomy

   A ◯   B ◯   C ◯   D ◯

7. **Gold**   **Bronze**   **Iron**

   Mercury   Copper   Steel   Tin

   A ◯   B ◯   C ◯   D ◯

8. **Shoulder**   **Hip**   **Fingers**

   Knee   Palm   Ankle   Elbow

   A ◯   B ◯   C ◯   D ◯

9. **Lawyer**   **Professor**   **Doctor**

   Engineer   Fire Fighter   Journalist   Learner

   A ◯   B ◯   C ◯   D ◯

10. **Mentor**   **Coach**   **Principal**

    Professor   Teacher   Student   Tutor

    A ◯   B ◯   C ◯   D ◯

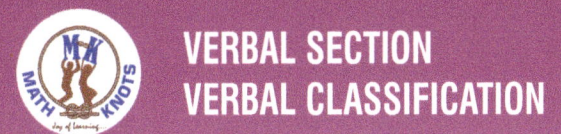

11. **Viola**   **Guitar**   **Sitar**

   Violin   Tabla   Cello   Harp

   A ◯   B ◯   C ◯   D ◯

12. **Creek**   **River**   **Brook**

   Runnel   Pond   Stream   Spring

   A ◯   B ◯   C ◯   D ◯

13. **Twig**   **Branch**   **Flower**

   Trunk   Tree   Fruit   Root

   A ◯   B ◯   C ◯   D ◯

14. **Train**   **Helicopter**   **Bus**

   Transport   Airplane   Cab   Ferry

   A ◯   B ◯   C ◯   D ◯

15. **Skiers**   **Wrestler**   **Jockey**

   Archers   Boxers   Player   Rowers

   A ◯   B ◯   C ◯   D ◯

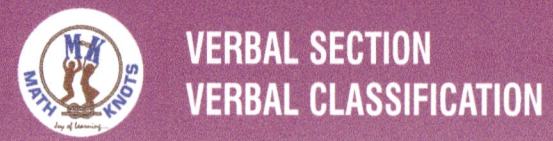
16. **Freedom** **Admission** **Sanction**

    Permit   Agree   Consent   Confess

    A ◯   B ◯   C ◯   D ◯

17. **Fence**   **Door**   **Desk**

    Firewood   Wood   Tooth Picks   Deck

    A ◯   B ◯   C ◯   D ◯

18. **Climax**   **Vertex**   **Zenith**

    Pack   Acme   Crest   Peak

    A ◯   B ◯   C ◯   D ◯

TEST - 1

VERBAL SECTION

SENTENCE COMPLETION

Lets Start the Test...

Sample

Look at the question with the Tennis Ball. Maya is trying to solve the below brain teaser. "Rik has more stamps then Ryan. Ryan has more stamps than Luke. Who has more stamps?" Bubble the correct option.

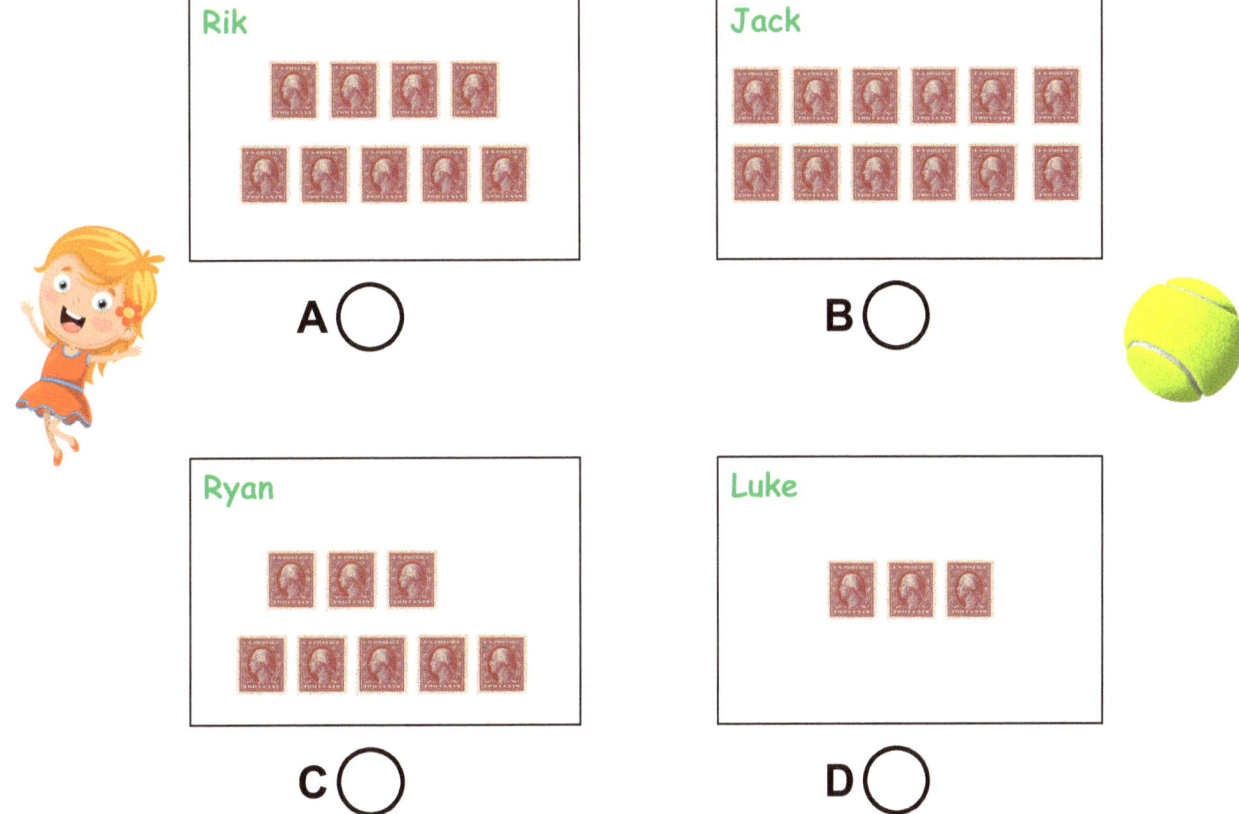

Solution : A

The Correct choice is A. The question doesn't compare with what Jack has.

Rik has the most stamps.

Rik >   Ryan >   Luke

www.math-knots.com

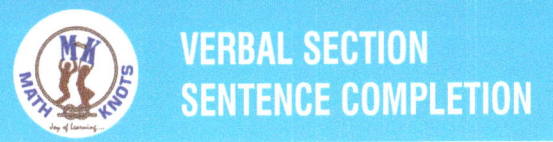

Q-1

Look at the question with the Ice Cream. Ben and Fred are at a camping site. They together made a tent and are looking at it . A strong wing blew. What could have happened to the tent? Identify the correct picture and help them to bubble the correct option.

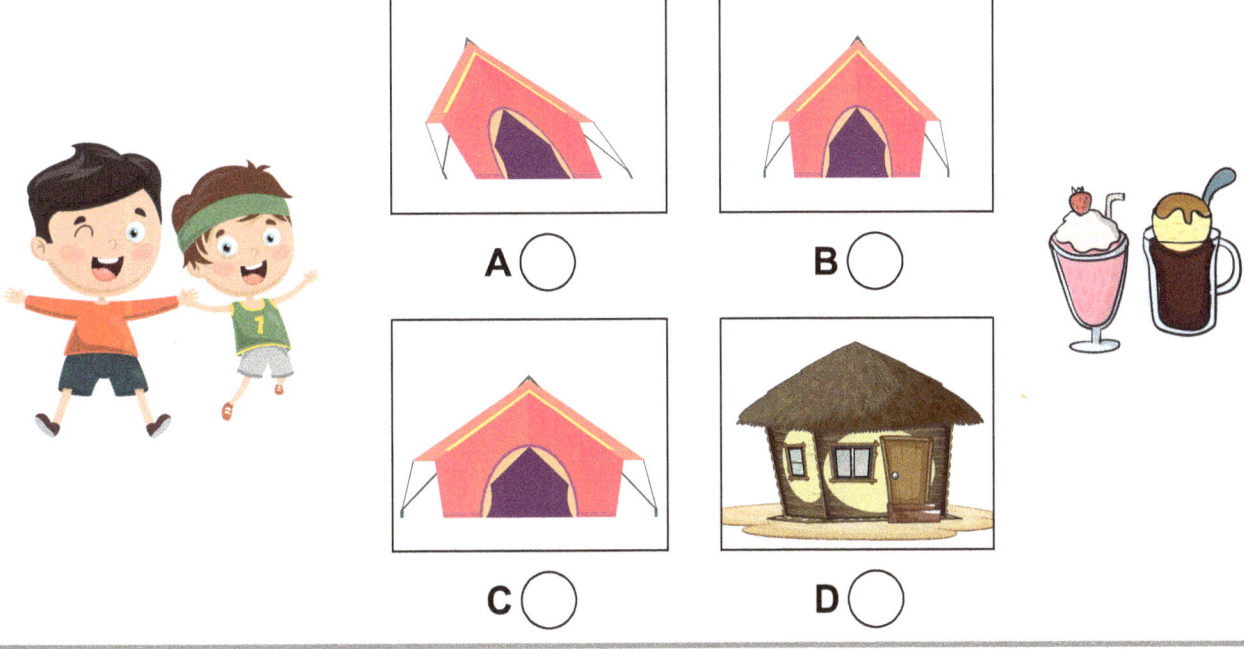

A ◯   B ◯

C ◯   D ◯

Q-2

Look at the question with the Bread. Mrs. Kim's father lives thousands of miles away and is admitted in hospital. She wants to visit her father. Which is the fastest way to travel? Identify the correct picture from the given choices below. Help her to bubble the correct option.

A ◯   B ◯

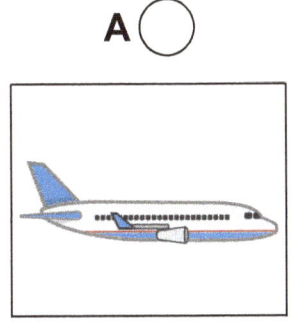

C ◯   D ◯

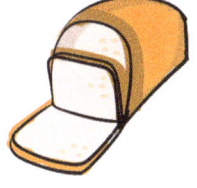

www.math-knots.com

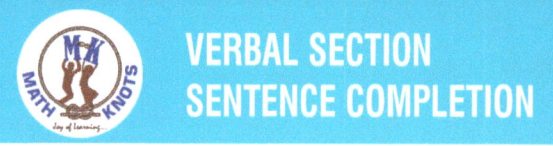
Q-3

Look at the question with the Milk Bottle. Liam wants to cross the river and reach the other shore. Help him to choose the right transportation from the below choices. Bubble the correct option.

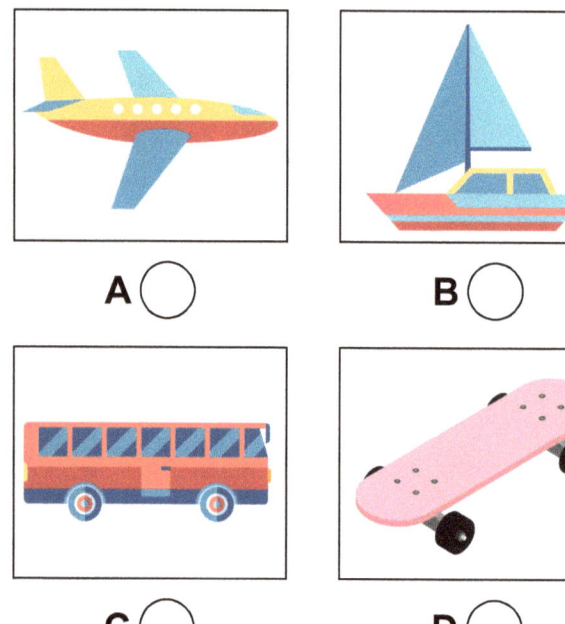

A ○   B ○

C ○   D ○

Q-4

Look at the question with the Coffee Mug. Lucy wants to go out for shopping in her new car. What do you think she should take with her along from the below choices? Bubble the correct option.

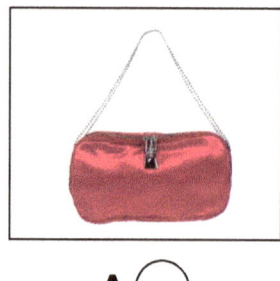   

A ○   B ○

C ○   D ○

www.math-knots.com

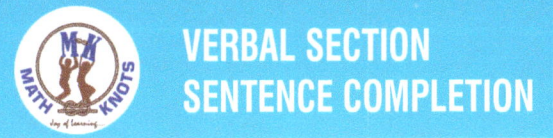
Q-5 Look at the question with the Muffin. Schools have a snow day off today. Rita wants to go out and play in snow. What do you think she shall choose from the below choices? Bubble the correct option.

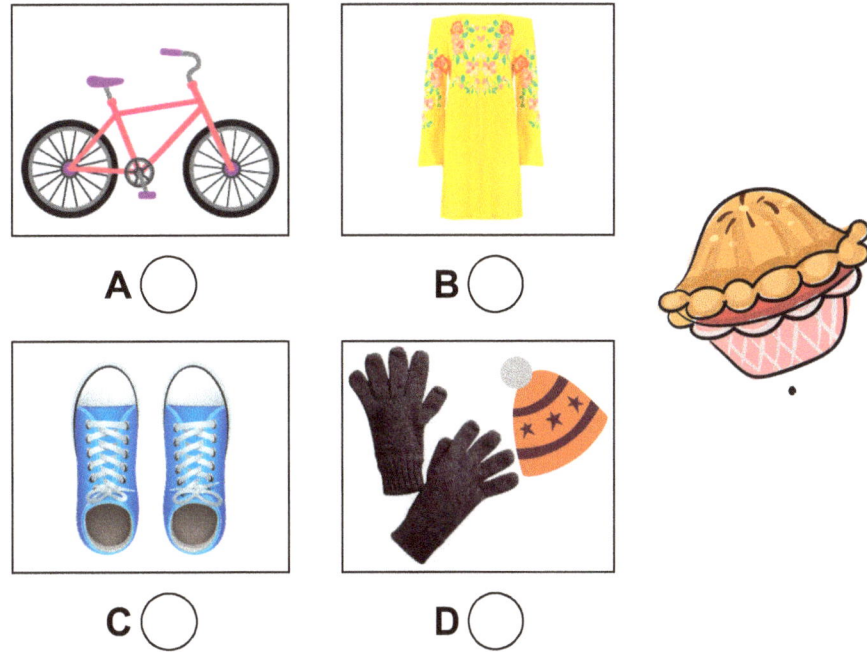

A ◯   B ◯

C ◯   D ◯

Q-6 Look at the question with the Jell-O. While Emily is reading a book, she comes across the word "Enclosed". She wondering what not enclosed means? What do you think she shall choose from the below choices? Bubble the correct option.

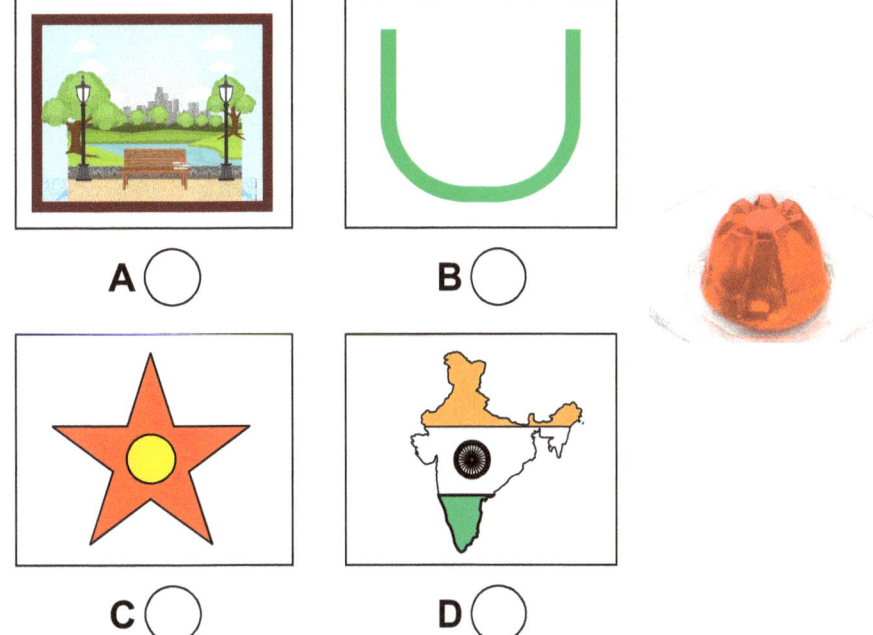

A ◯   B ◯

C ◯   D ◯

www.math-knots.com

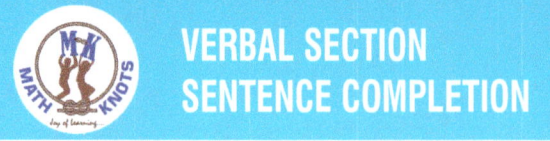
Q-7

Look at the question with the Oil Jar. Noah is trying to find a single object? What do you think he shall choose from the below choices? Bubble the correct option.

A ◯

B ◯

C ◯

D ◯

Q-8

Look at the question with the French Fries. Henry is trying to find the nine planets? What do you think he shall choose from the below choices? Bubble the correct option.

A ◯

B ◯

C ◯

D ◯

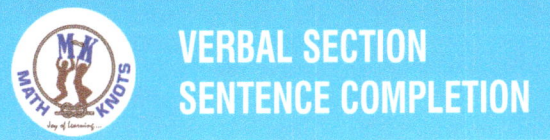
Q-9 Look at the question with the House. Raksha is trying to find which of the below can Fly? What do you think she shall choose from the below choices? Bubble the correct option.

A ◯

B ◯

C ◯

D ◯

Q-10 Look at the question with the Turkey. Aiden is trying to find three pairs of objects? What do you think he shall choose from the below choices? Bubble the correct option.

A ◯

B ◯

C ◯

D ◯

www.math-knots.com

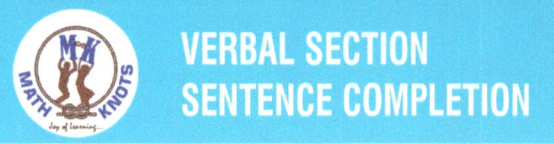
Q-11 Look at the question with the Cake. Carl wants to charge his cell phone and laptop? What do you think he shall choose from the below choices? Bubble the correct option.

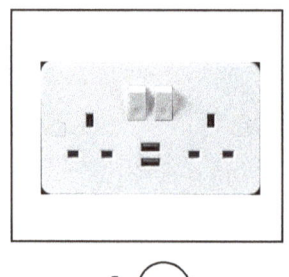

A ◯

B ◯

C ◯

D ◯

Q-12 Look at the question with the Tea Kettle. Aria is looking around for her hair band. What do you think she shall choose from the below choices? Bubble the correct option.

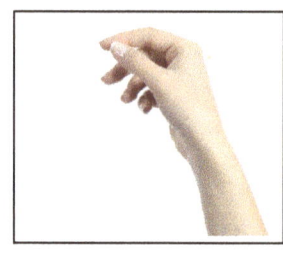

A ◯

B ◯

C ◯

D ◯

www.math-knots.com

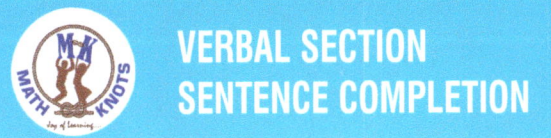
Q-13 Look at the question with the Pan Cakes. Xavier wants to know the meaning of pack. What do you think he shall choose from the below choices resembling pack? Bubble the correct option.

A ◯

B ◯

C ◯

D ◯

Q-14 Look at the question with the Bread Toast. Rosy bought a Soccer Post and wanted to fix it immediately for her kids to play. She is looking into her tool box. What do you think she will find in her tool box from the choices below? Bubble the correct option.

A ◯

B ◯

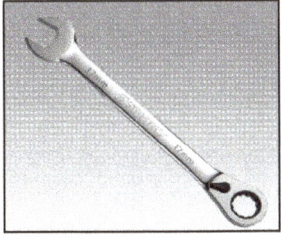

C ◯

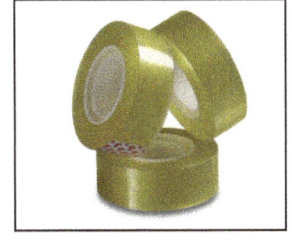

D ◯

www.math-knots.com

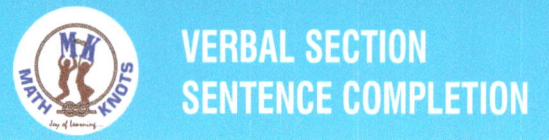
Q-15

Look at the question with the Sandwich. Karen is sitting in the garden and hears a croak sound. Which of the below choices made the sound? Bubble the correct option.

A ◯ B ◯

C ◯ D ◯

Q-16

Look at the question with the Soup Bowl. Sriyan, who is turning one year soon is playing with toys. Which of the below choices will he have trouble opeing? Bubble the correct option.

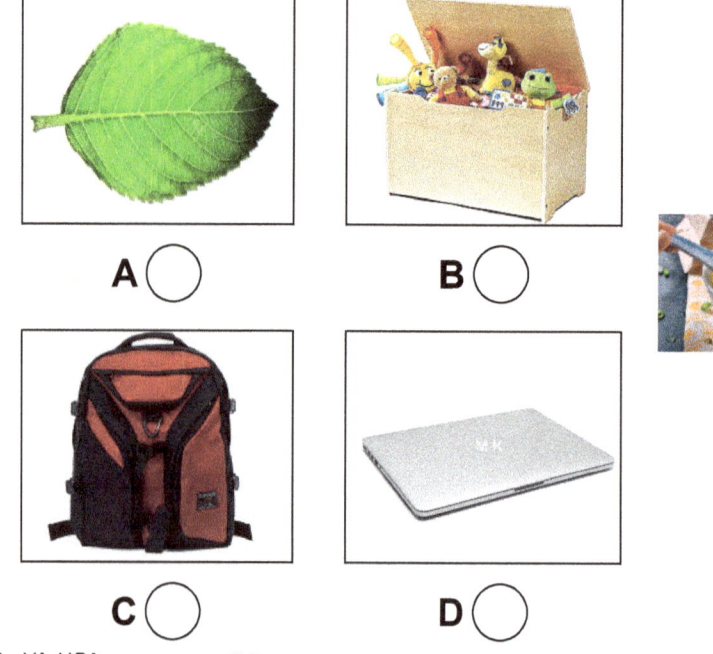

A ◯ B ◯

C ◯ D ◯

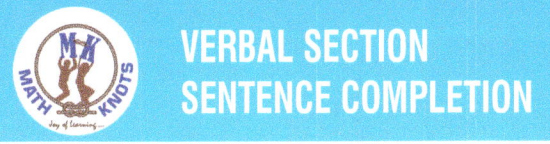
Q-17 Look at the question with the Ketchup Bottle. Ian is a member of his high school strings club. He goes to the music store to buy a new instrument. Which of the below could be his choice? Bubble the correct option.

A ◯   B ◯

C ◯   D ◯

Q-18 Look at the question with the Fried eggs. Samantha knows that Tomatoes are red in color. She is wondering which of the below choices are of the same color. Help her bubble the correct option.

A ◯   B ◯

C ◯   D ◯

www.math-knots.com

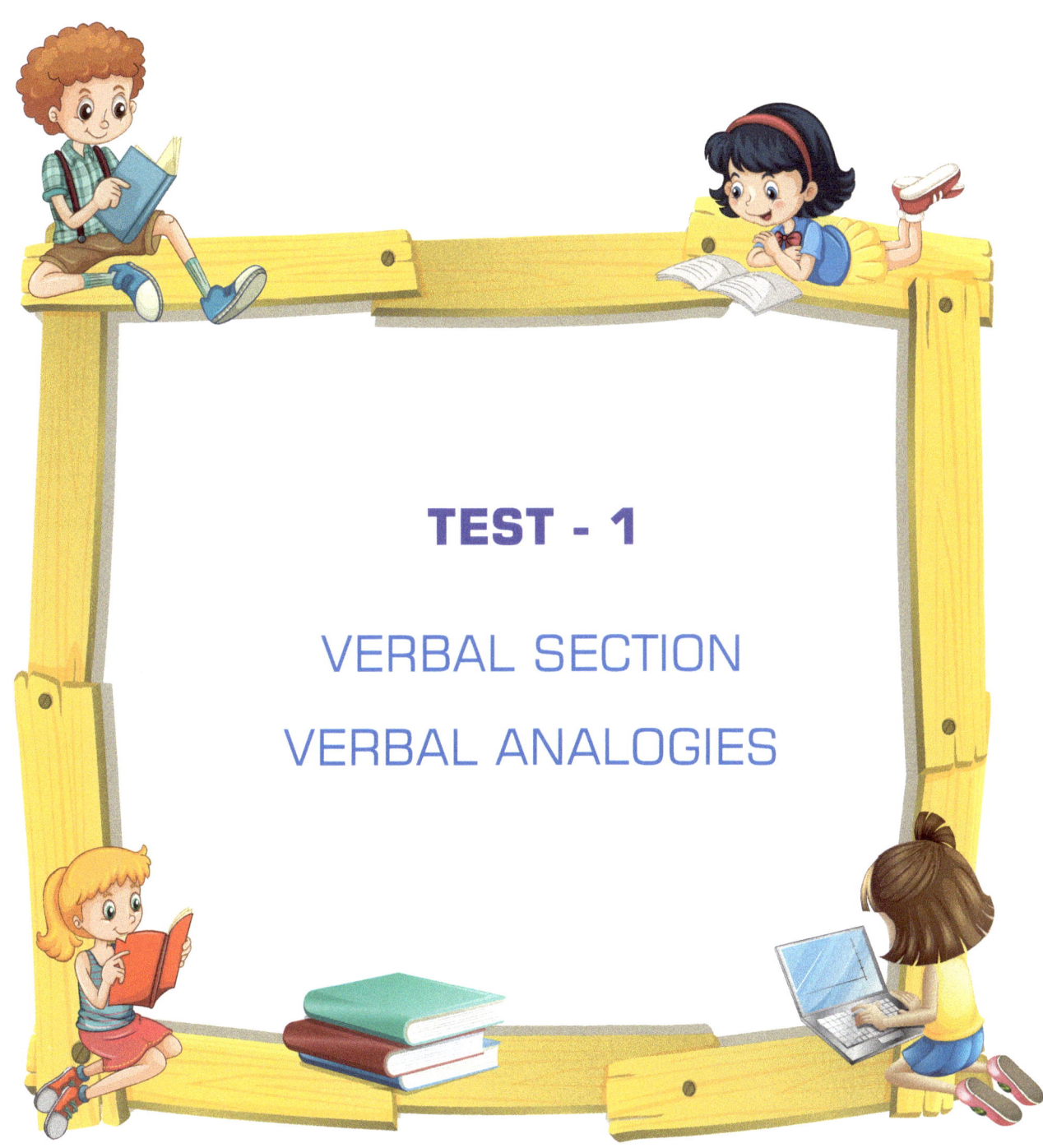

TEST - 1

VERBAL SECTION

VERBAL ANALOGIES

Lets Start the Test...

Sample The first two words are related in a certain way as the next two words. Identify the missing word.

Clouds : White :: Sky : ?

Bold   Blue   Silver   Yellow

A ◯   B ◯   C ◯   D ◯

Solution : B

First analogy is color of the clouds which is white. Color of sky is blue.

Right choice is B.

Student needs to think through how the first two are related and then relate it to next analogy in the same way. Bubble the correct option.

All the questions in verbal analogies test 1 are to be answered following the below question (instruction).

The first two words are related in a certain way as the next two words. Identify the missing word.

1.   Ship : Water :: Airplane : ?

   Sky   Road   Travel   Gate

   A◯   B◯   C◯   D◯

2.   Deer : Grass lands :: Bull : ?

   Den   Kennel   Stable   Cattle Shed

   A◯   B◯   C◯   D◯

3.   Hand : Fingers :: ? : Toes

   Ankle   Knee   Feet   Arm

   A◯   B◯   C◯   D◯

4.   Ocean : Surfing :: Sand : ?

   Soccer Ball   Basket Ball   Bricks   Castles

   A◯   B◯   C◯   D◯

5.   Trees : Green :: Sky : ?

   Blue   Plane   Clouds   Rain

   A◯   B◯   C◯   D◯

43

6.   Shorts : Summer :: Fur Coat :   ?

Miami   Spring   Winter   Snow man

A◯   B◯   C◯   D◯

7.   Summer : June :: Spring :   ?

April   June   September   December

A◯   B◯   C◯   D◯

8.   Mosquito : Blood :: Termites :   ?

Bees   Metal   Leaves   Wood

A◯   B◯   C◯   D◯

9.   Numbers : Math :: Alphabets :   ?

Vowels   Consonants   Reading   Briley

A◯   B◯   C◯   D◯

10.   Camera : Pictures :: Paintbrush :   ?

Pixel   Painting   Draw   Frame

A◯   B◯   C◯   D◯

11.   Spring : Leaves Grow :: Fall :   ?

Leaves   Flowers Bloom   Harvesting   Leaves Fall

A◯   B◯   C◯   D◯

12.   Sun : Day :: Moon :   ?

Night   Afternoon   Dusk   Morning

A◯   B◯   C◯   D◯

13.   Owl : Owlet :: Deer :   ?

Calf   Moan   Fawn   Cub

A◯   B◯   C◯   D◯

14.   Solo : One :: Duet :   ?

Five   Two   Triplet   One

A◯   B◯   C◯   D◯

15.   Echinoderms : 5 legs :: Deco pods :   ?

Six legs   Four legs   Two legs   Ten legs

A◯   B◯   C◯   D◯

16.   Bank : Money :: Library : ?

      Computers   Books   Food   Service

      A ◯   B ◯   C ◯   D ◯

17.   Bury : Cover :: Dig : ?

      Hide   Open   Uncover   Close

      A ◯   B ◯   C ◯   D ◯

18.   Decade : 10 Years :: Century : ?

      One Hundred Years   A ◯

      One Million Years   B ◯

      Five Hundred Years   C ◯

      Thousand years   D ◯

www.math-knots.com

TEST - 1

QUANTITATIVE APTITUDE

NUMBER ANALOGIES

Lets Start the Test...

Sample

Look at the question with the Parrot. Two boxes in the first row are related in a certain way which is similar to two boxes in the second row. Ken is trying to fill the bubble under the correct option. Help him to select from options A, B, C, and D.

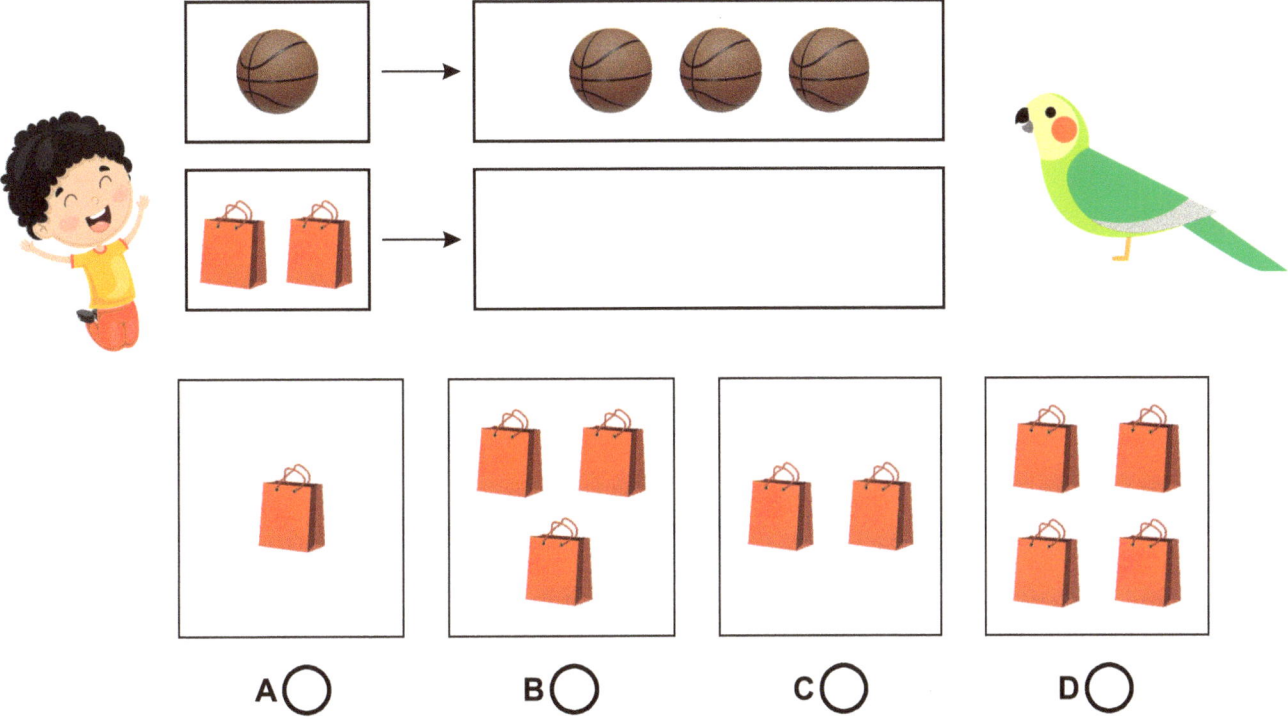

A◯   B◯   C◯   D◯

Solution : D

In first row, one ball to three balls [(1+2) adding two more]

In second row, two bags by adding two more will become four bags.

The analogies can be formed by adding or subtracting a certain number meaning increasing or decreasing by a certain quantity. Students needs to understand the right analogy and bubble the correct option.

www.math-knots.com

www.math-knots.com

Q-1

Look at the question with the Soccer Ball. Two boxes in the first row are related in a certain way which is similar to two boxes in the second row. Sam is trying to fill the bubble under the correct option. Help him to select from options A, B, C, and D.

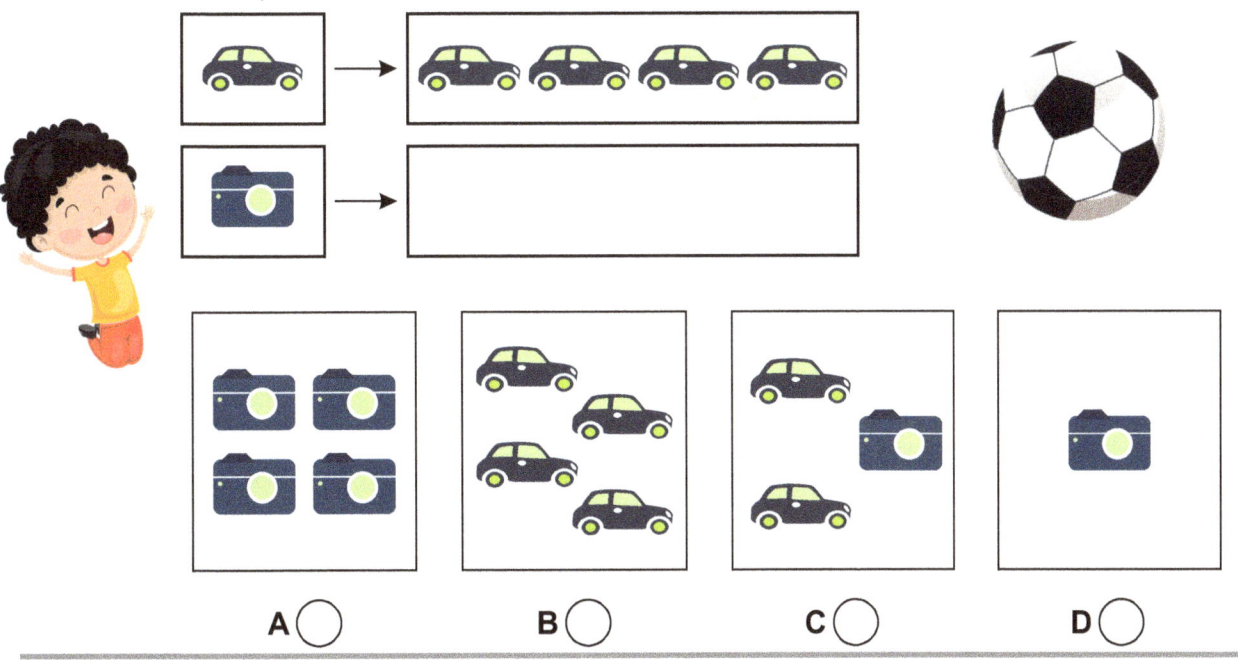

A ◯   B ◯   C ◯   D ◯

Q-2

Look at the question with the Foot Ball. Two boxes in the first row are related in a certain way which is similar to two boxes in the second row. Mary is trying to to fill the bubble under the correct option. Help her to select from options A, B, C, and D.

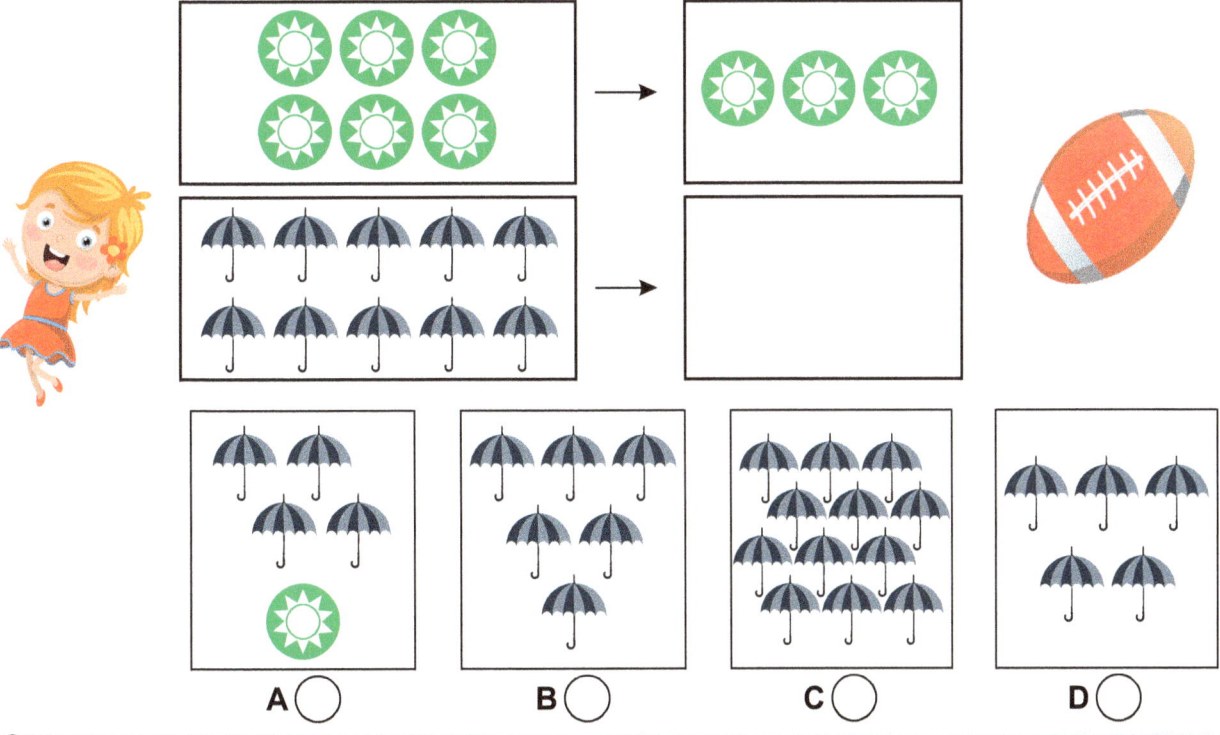

A ◯   B ◯   C ◯   D ◯

www.math-knots.com

Q-3 Look at the question with the Basket Ball. Two boxes in the first row are related in a certain way which is similar to two boxes in the second row. Sri is trying to fill the bubble under the correct option. Help her to select from options A, B, C, and D.

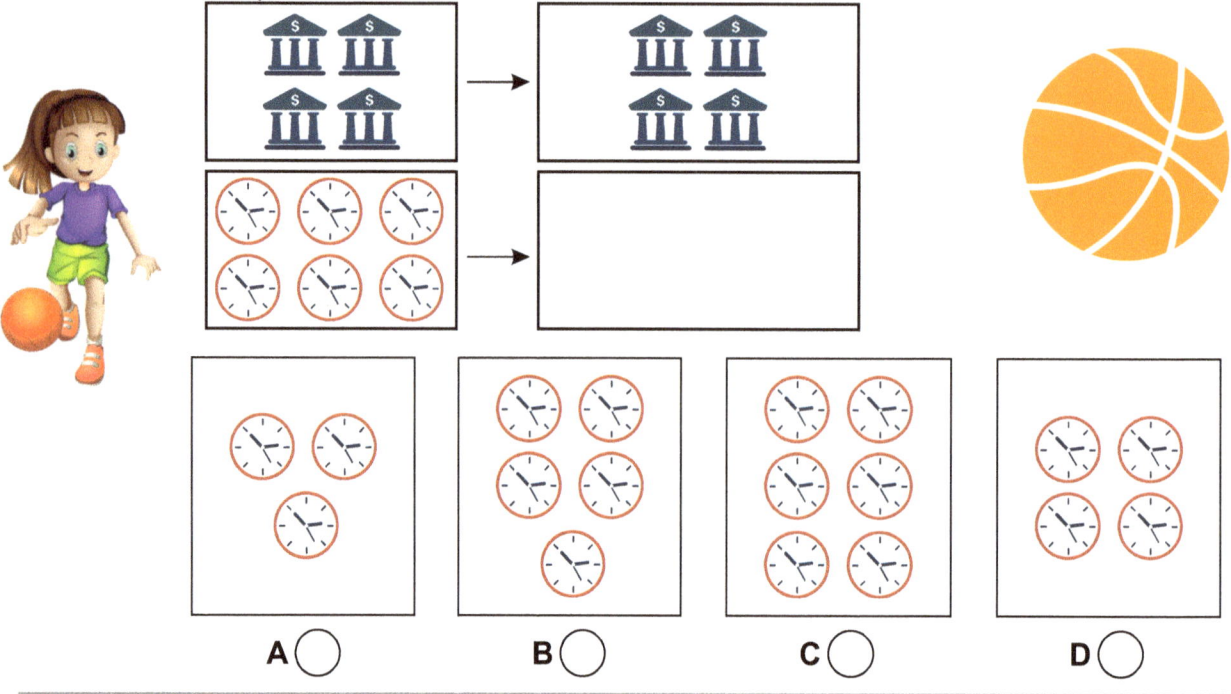

A ◯   B ◯   C ◯   D ◯

Q-4 Look at the question with the Shuttlecock. Two boxes in the first row are related in a certain way which is similar to two boxes in the second row. Robert is trying to fill the bubble under the correct option. Help him to select from options A, B, C, and D.

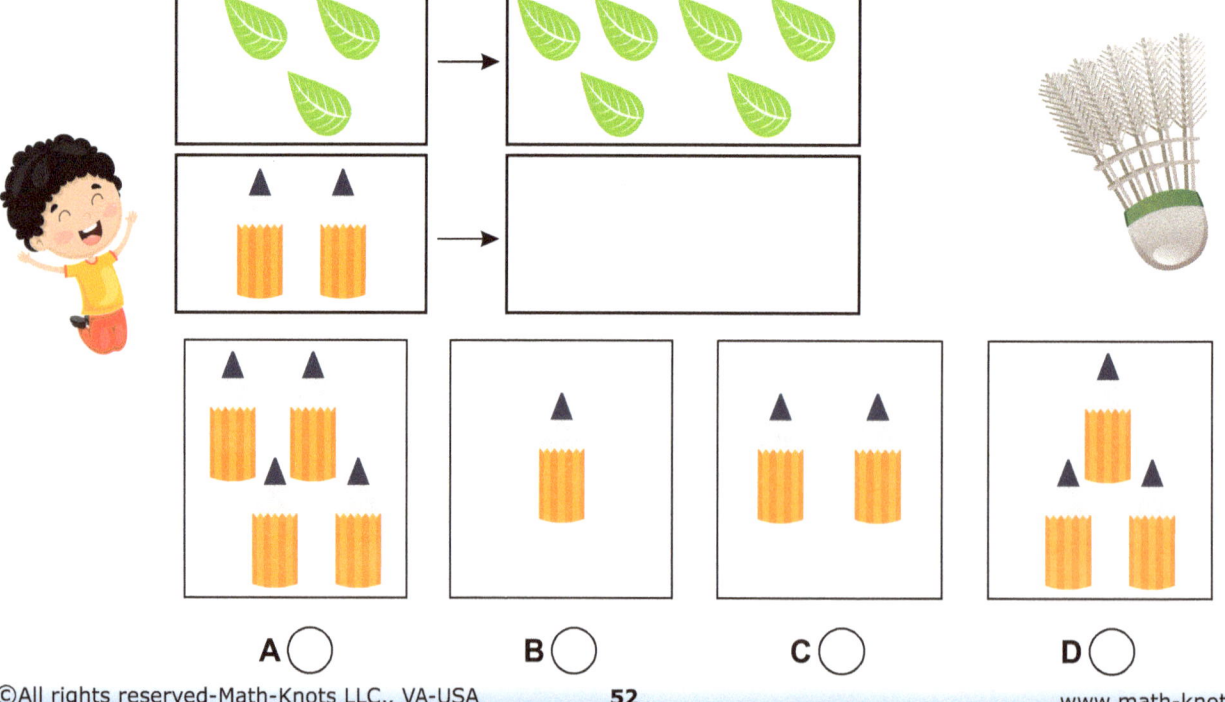

A ◯   B ◯   C ◯   D ◯

www.math-knots.com

Q-5

Look at the question with the Bowling Pin. Two boxes in the first row are related in a certain way which is similar to two boxes in the second row. Sreya is trying to fill the bubble under the correct option. Help her to select from options A, B, C, and D.

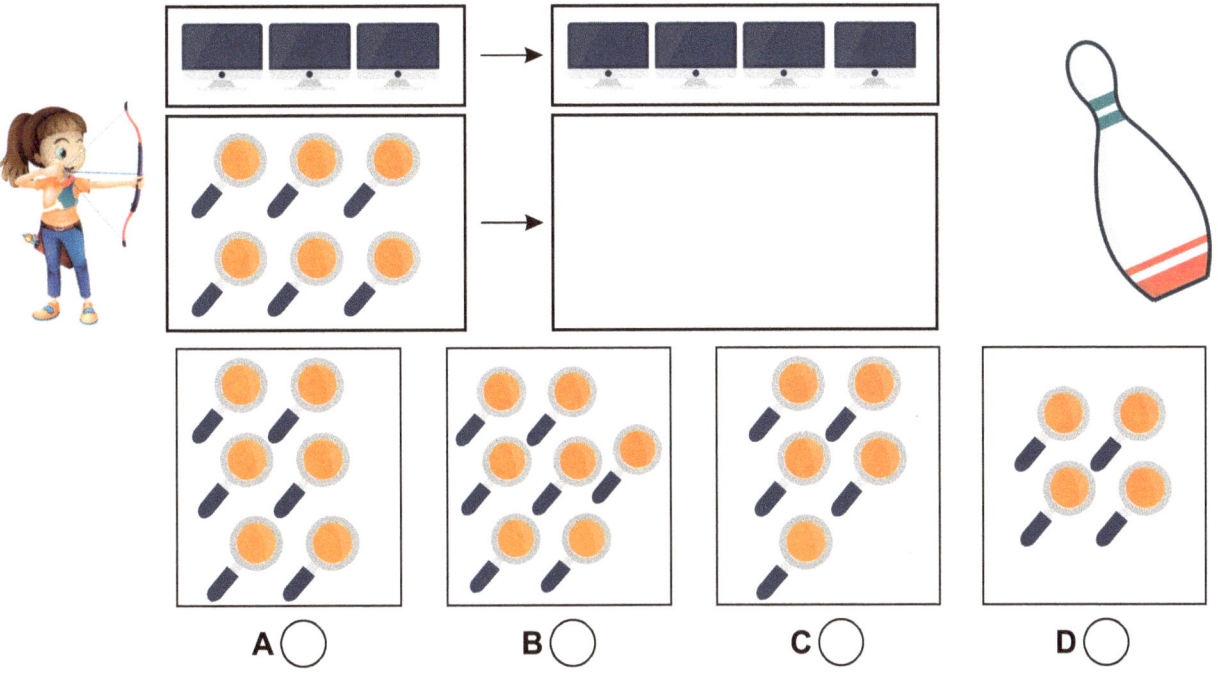

A ◯   B ◯   C ◯   D ◯

Q-6

Look at the question with the Hockey Stick. Two boxes in the first row are related in a certain way which is similar to two boxes in the second row. Sofia is trying to fill the bubble under the correct option. Help her to select from options A, B, C, and D.

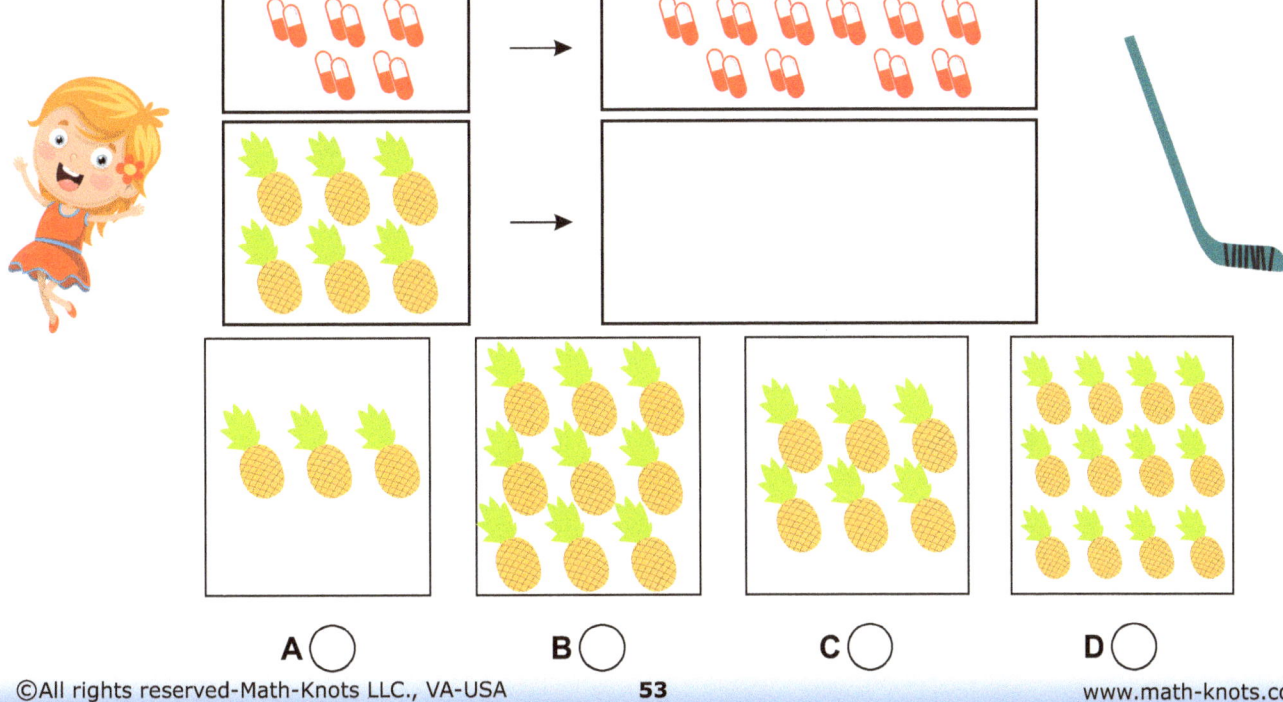

A ◯   B ◯   C ◯   D ◯

Q-7

Look at the question with the Tennis Ball. Two boxes in the first row are related in a certain way which is similar to two boxes in the second row. Ava is trying to fill the bubble under the correct option. Help her to select from options A, B, C, and D.

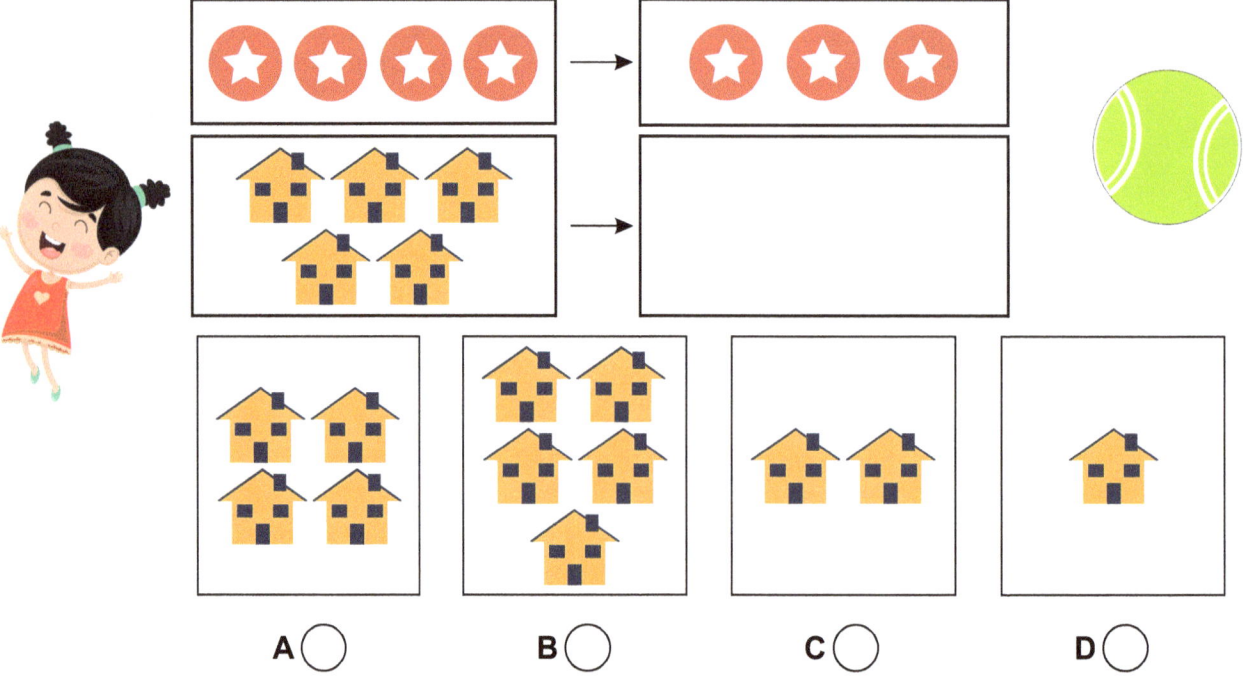

A◯   B◯   C◯   D◯

Q-8

Look at the question with the Cricket Bat. Two boxes in the first row are related in a certain way which is similar to two boxes in the second row. Johnson is trying to fill the bubble under the correct option. Help him to select from options A, B, C, and D.

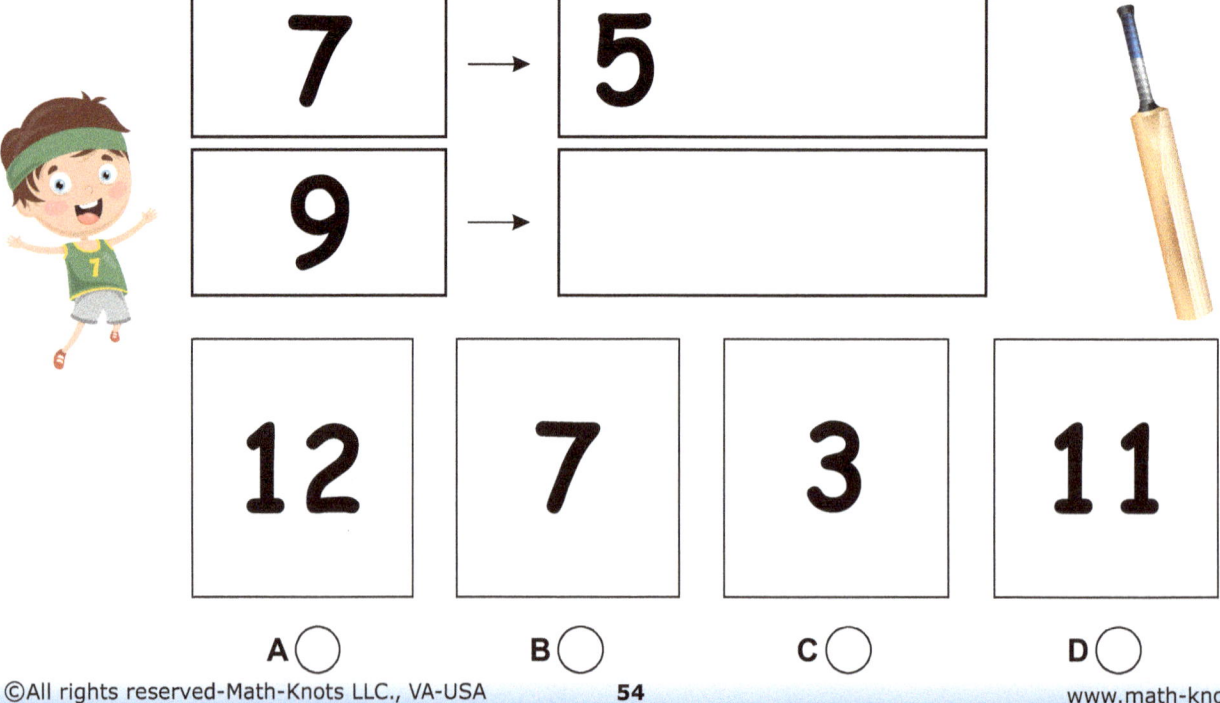

A◯   B◯   C◯   D◯

Q-9 Look at the question with the Boat. Two boxes in the first row are related in a certain way which is similar to two boxes in the second row. Alexander is trying to fill the bubble under the correct option. Help him to select from options A, B, C, and D.

A	B	C	D
6	4	12	2

Q-10 Look at the question with the Ping-Pong bat. Two boxes in the first row are related in a certain way which is similar to two boxes in the second row. Lucas is trying to fill the bubble under the correct option. Help him to select from options A, B, C, and D.

www.math-knots.com

Q-11 Look at the question with the Bicycle. Two boxes in the first row are related in a certain way which is similar to two boxes in the second row. Ella is trying to fill the bubble under the correct option. Help her to select from options A, B, C, and D.

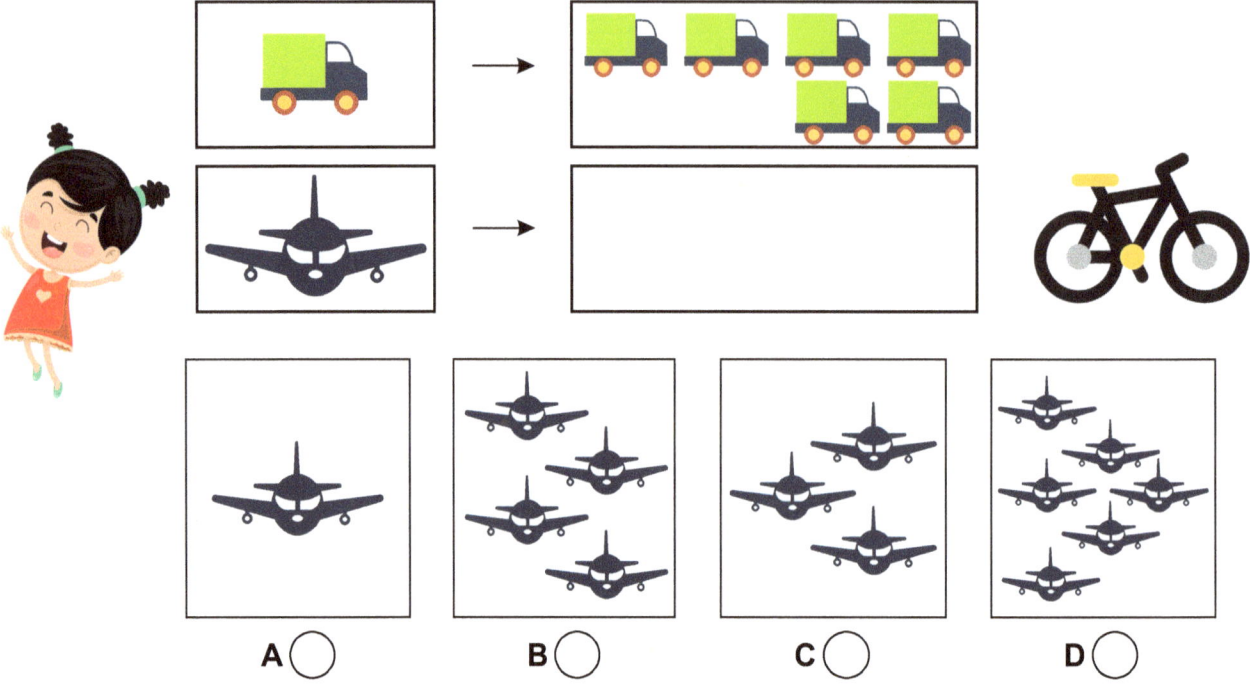

A ◯   B ◯   C ◯   D ◯

Q-12 Look at the question with the Dart Board. Two boxes in the first row are related in a certain way which is similar to two boxes in the second row. Samuel is trying to fill the bubble under the correct option. Help him to select from options A, B, C, and D.

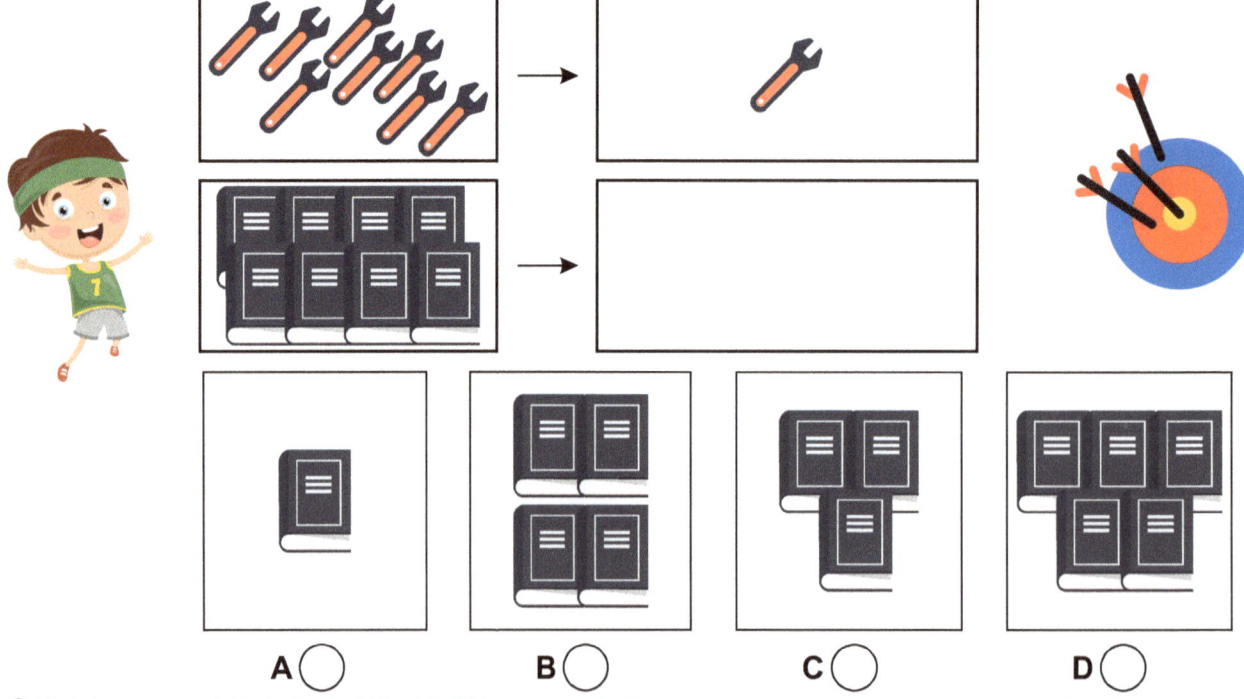

A ◯   B ◯   C ◯   D ◯

Q-13 Look at the question with the Weights. Two boxes in the first row are related in a certain way which is similar to two boxes in the second row. Anthony is trying to fill the bubble under the correct option. Help him to select from options A, B, C, and D.

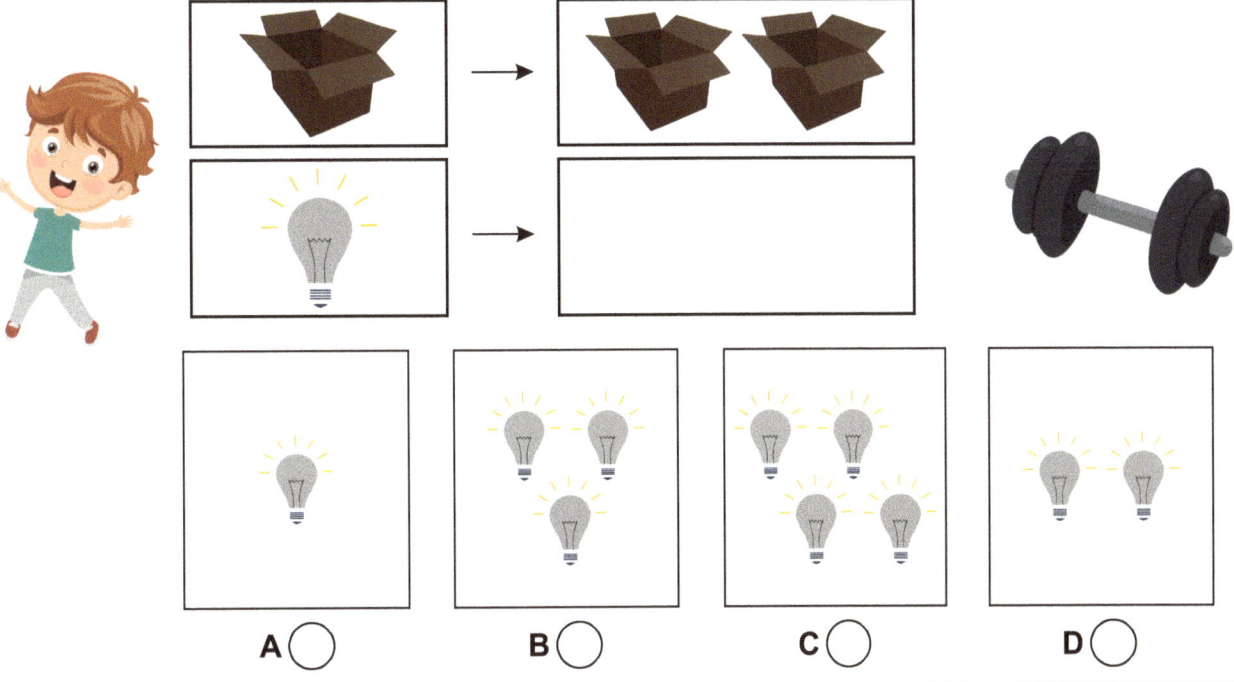

Q-14 Look at the question with the Skateboard. Two boxes in the first row are related in a certain way which is similar to two boxes in the second row. Skylar is trying to fill the bubble under the correct option. Help her to select from options A, B, C, and D.

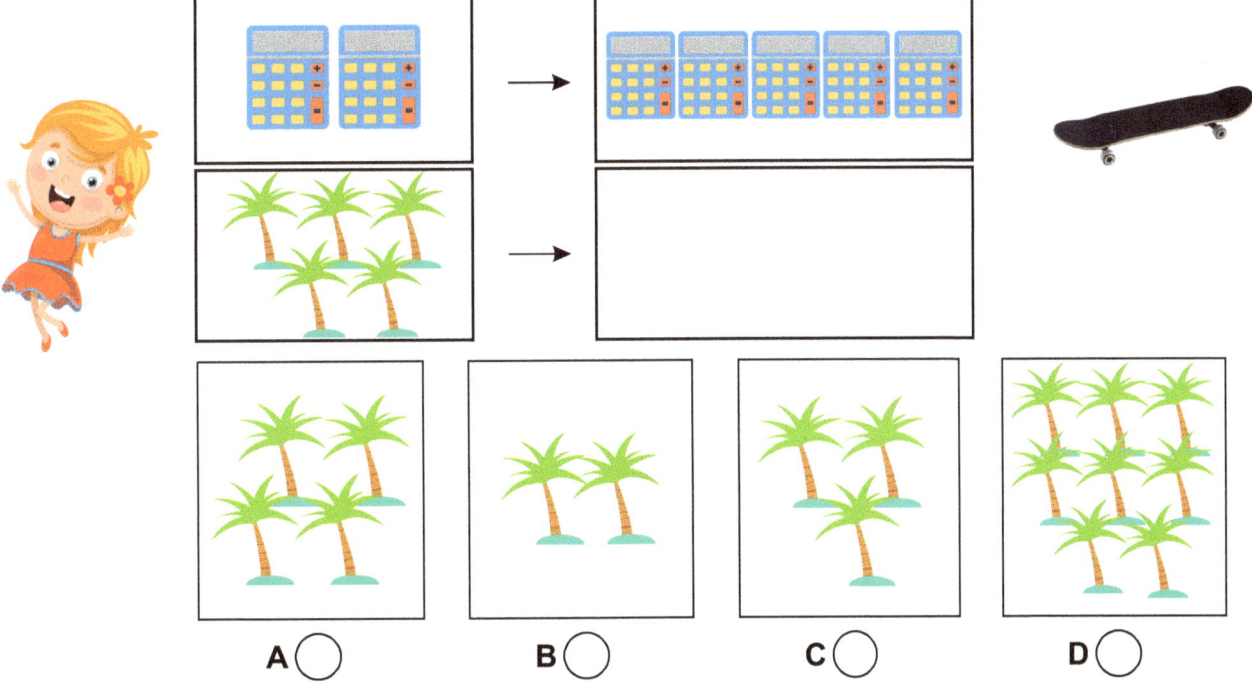

Q-15 Look at the question with the Karate Dress. Two boxes in the first row are related in a certain way which is similar to two boxes in the second row. Hannah is trying to fill the bubble under the correct option. Help her to select from options A, B, C, and D.

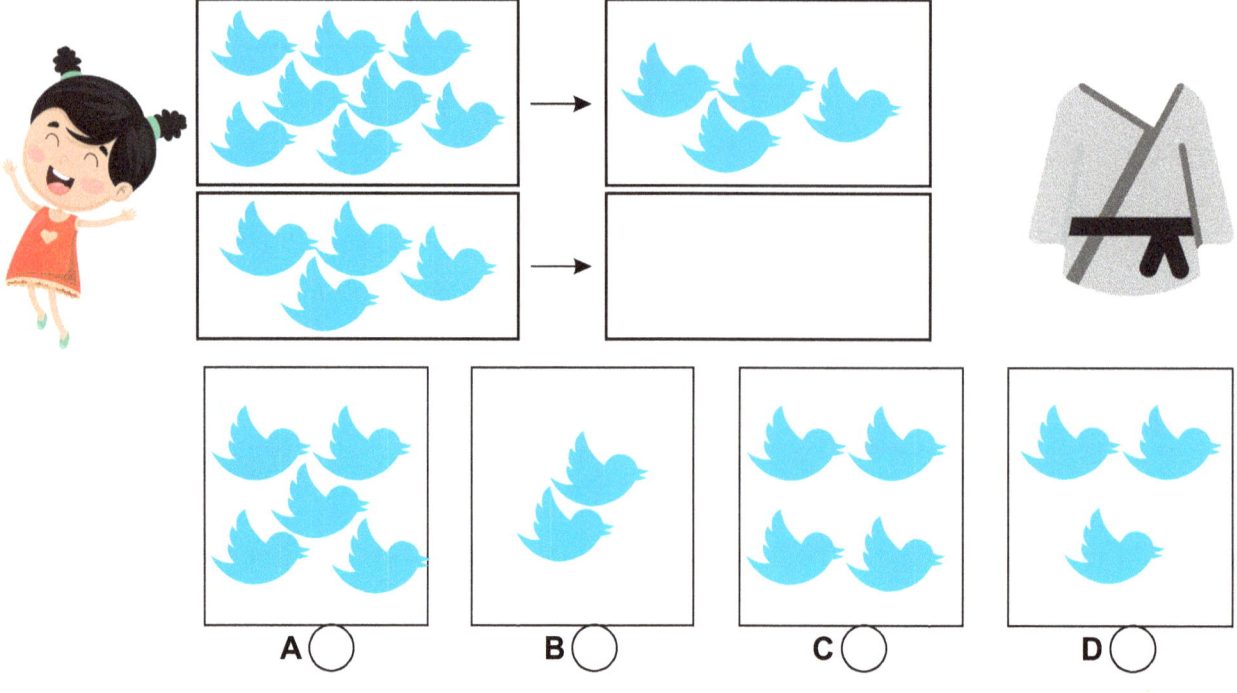

A ◯   B ◯   C ◯   D ◯

Q-16 Look at the question with the Swords. Two boxes in the first row are related in a certain way which is similar to two boxes in the second row. Mathew is trying to fill the bubble under the correct option. Help him to select from options A, B,C, and D.

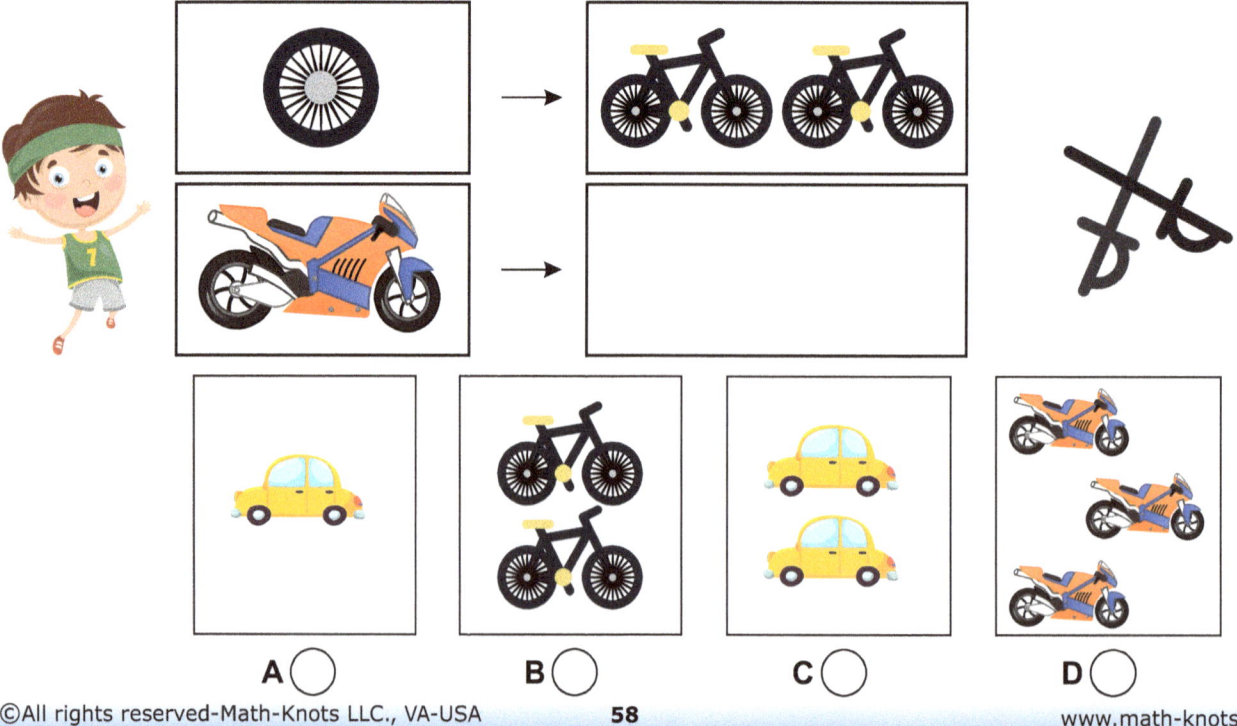

A ◯   B ◯   C ◯   D ◯

www.math-knots.com

Q-17

Look at the question with the Boxing Gloves. Two boxes in the first row are related in a certain way which is similar to two boxes in the second row. Joseph is trying to fill the bubble under the correct option. Help him to select from options A, B, C, and D.

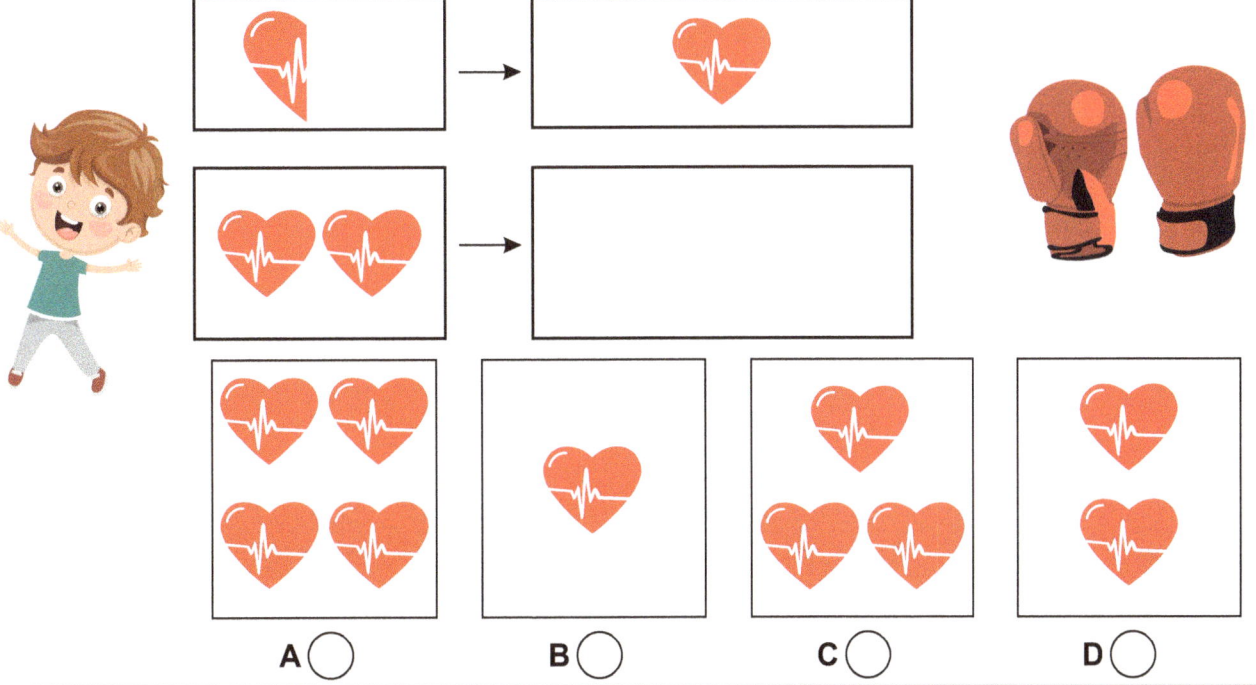

Q-18

Look at the question with the Racket. Two boxes in the first row are related in a certain way which is similar to two boxes in the second row. Chloe is trying to fill the bubble under the correct option. Help her to select from options A, B, C, and D.

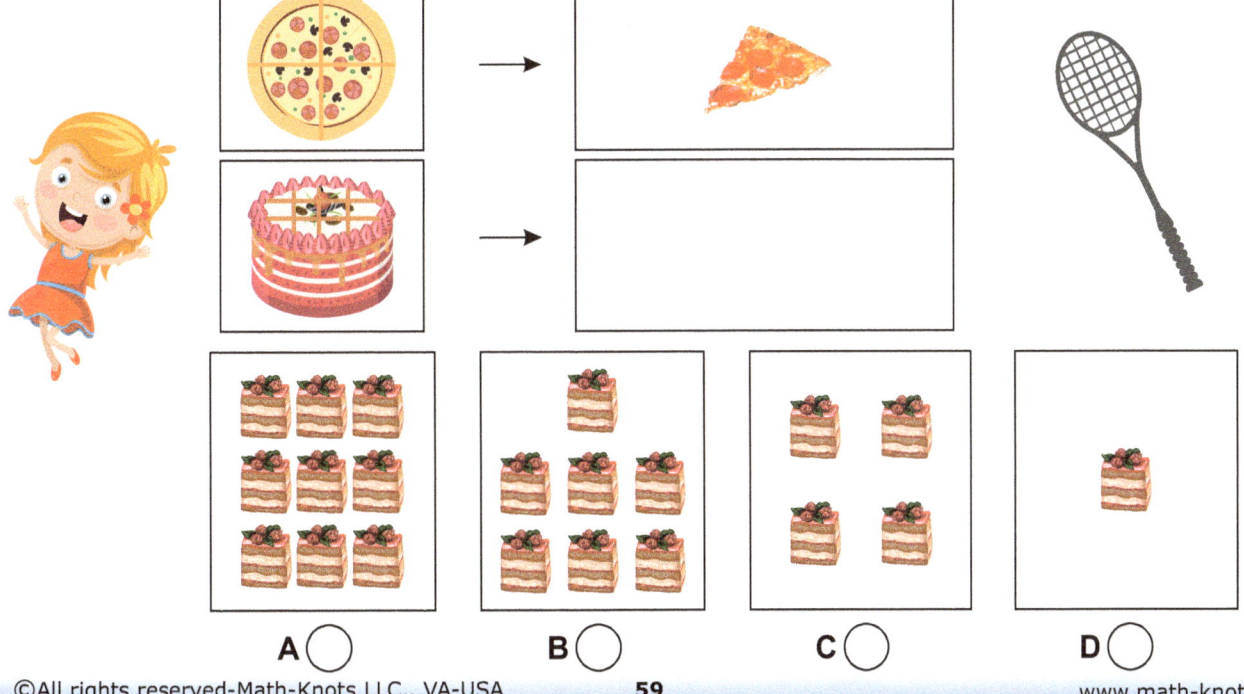

TEST - 1

QUANTITATIVE APTITUDE

NUMBER SERIES

Lets Start the Test...

Sample

Look at the question with the Triangle. Cathy is making a pattern with her hexagon shaped beads. Can you help her to identify what goes in the empty string from the given four options A,B,C, and D.

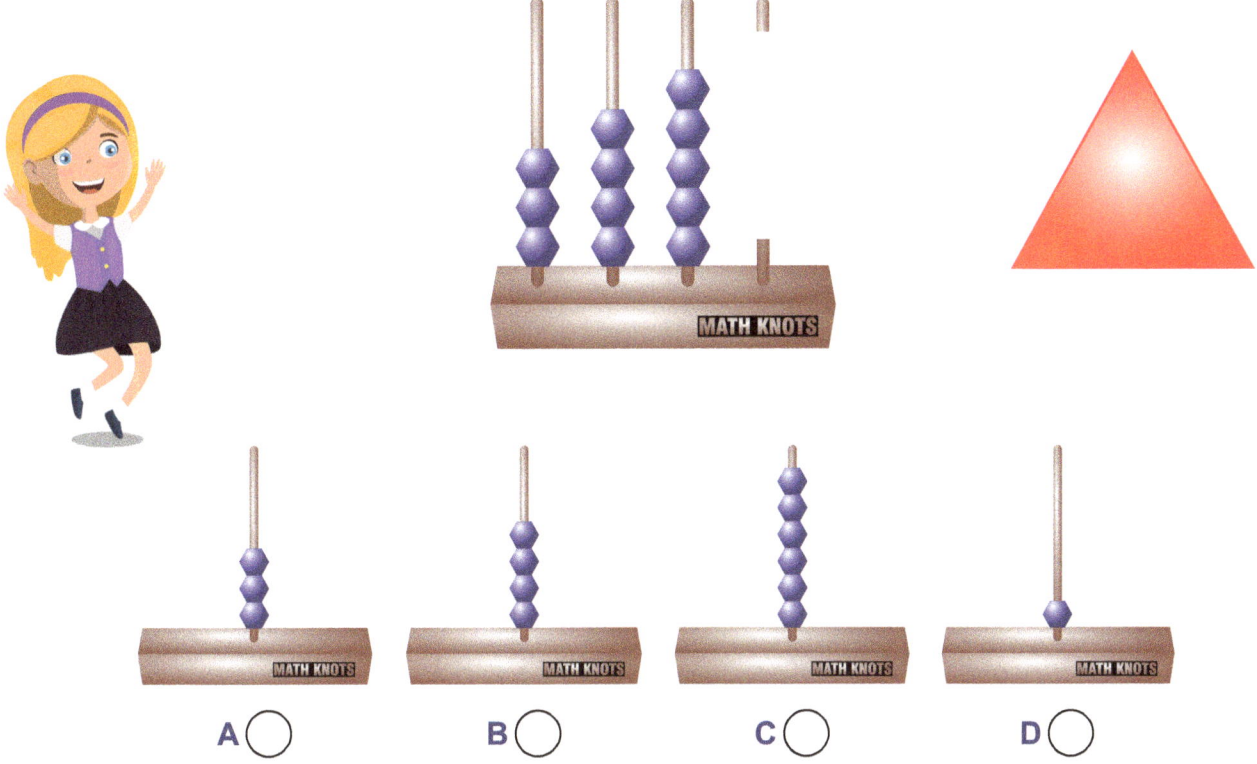

A ◯   B ◯   C ◯   D ◯

Solution : C

3,4,5.....

The beads are increasing by 1. So next string should have six beads. Option C is the correct choice. The patterns can increase or decrease by a certain number of beads. Students are supposed to identify the correct pattern and answer the correct choice.

Q-1 Look at the question with the Soccer Ball. Sam is making a pattern with his hexagon shaped beads. Can you help him to identify what goes in the empty string from the given four options A, B, C, and D.

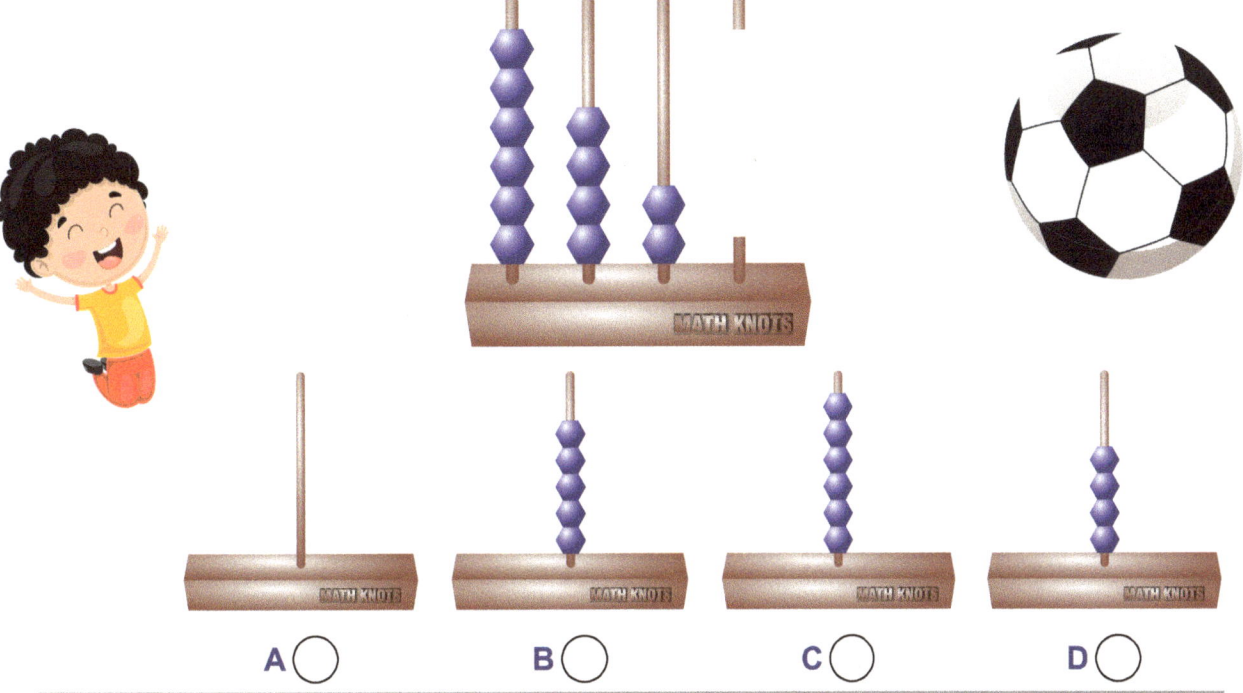

Q-2 Look at the question with the Foot Ball. Mary is making a pattern with her hexagon shaped beads. Can you help her to identify what goes in the empty string from the given four options A, B, C, and D.

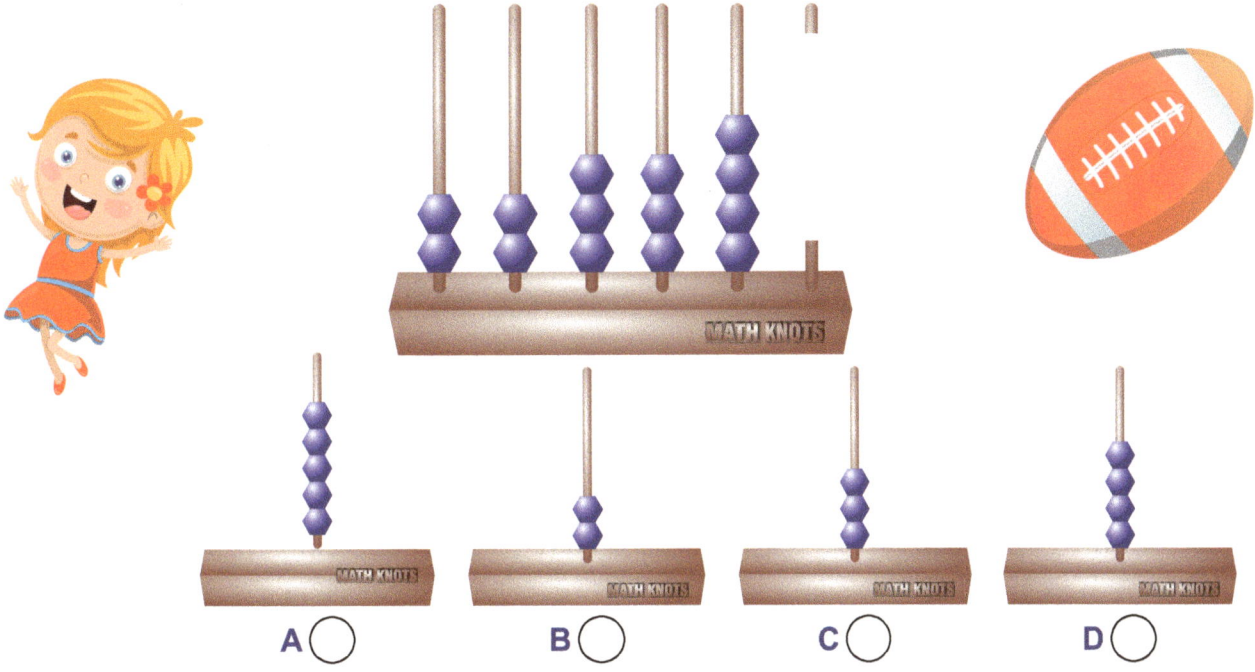

www.math-knots.com

Q-3

Look at the question with the Basket Ball. Maria is making a pattern with her hexagon shaped beads. Can you help her to identify what goes in the empty string from the given four options A, B, C, and D.

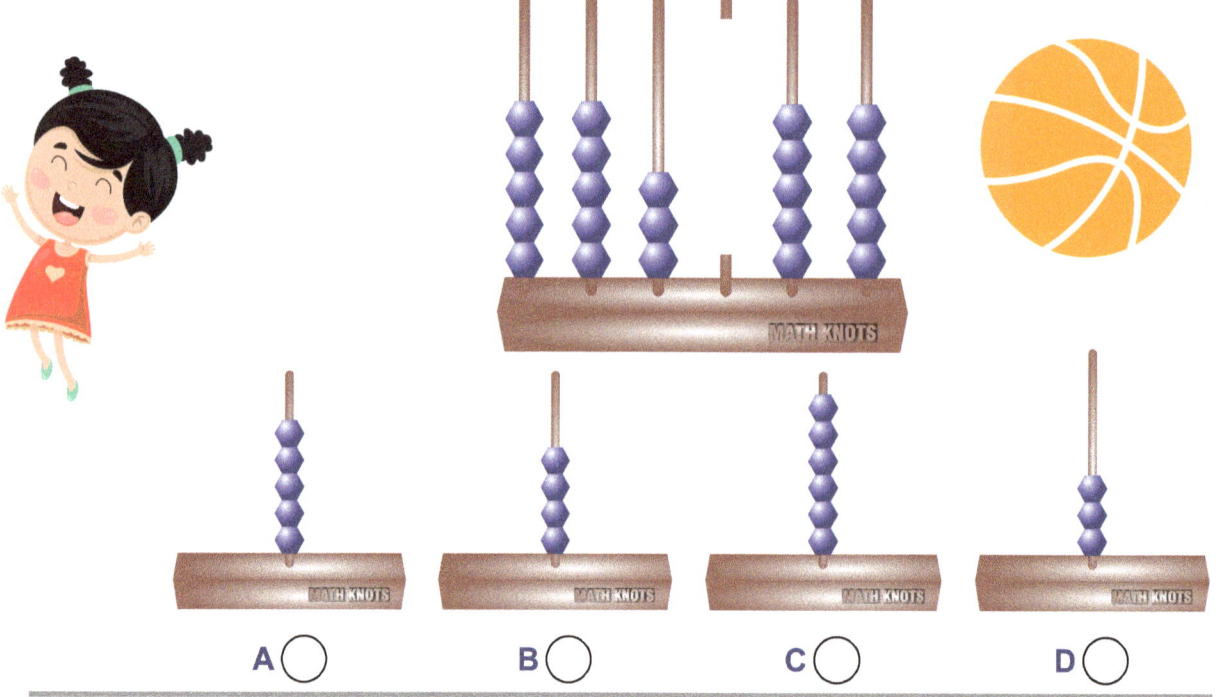

A ◯   B ◯   C ◯   D ◯

Q-4

Look at the question with the Shuttlecock. Dan is making a pattern with his hexagon shaped beads. Can you help him to identify what goes in the empty string from the given four options A, B, C, and D.

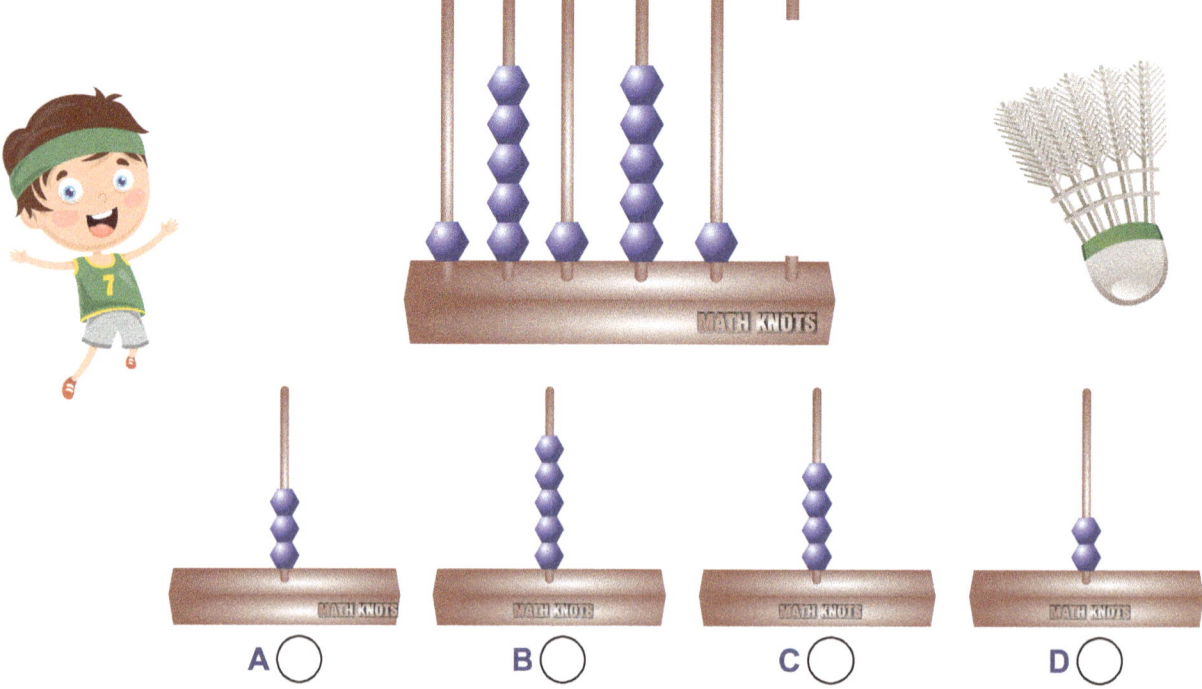

A ◯   B ◯   C ◯   D ◯

www.math-knots.com

Q-5 Look at the question with the Bowling Pin. Robert is making a pattern with his hexagon shaped beads. Can you help him to identify what goes in the empty string from the given four options A, B, C, and D.

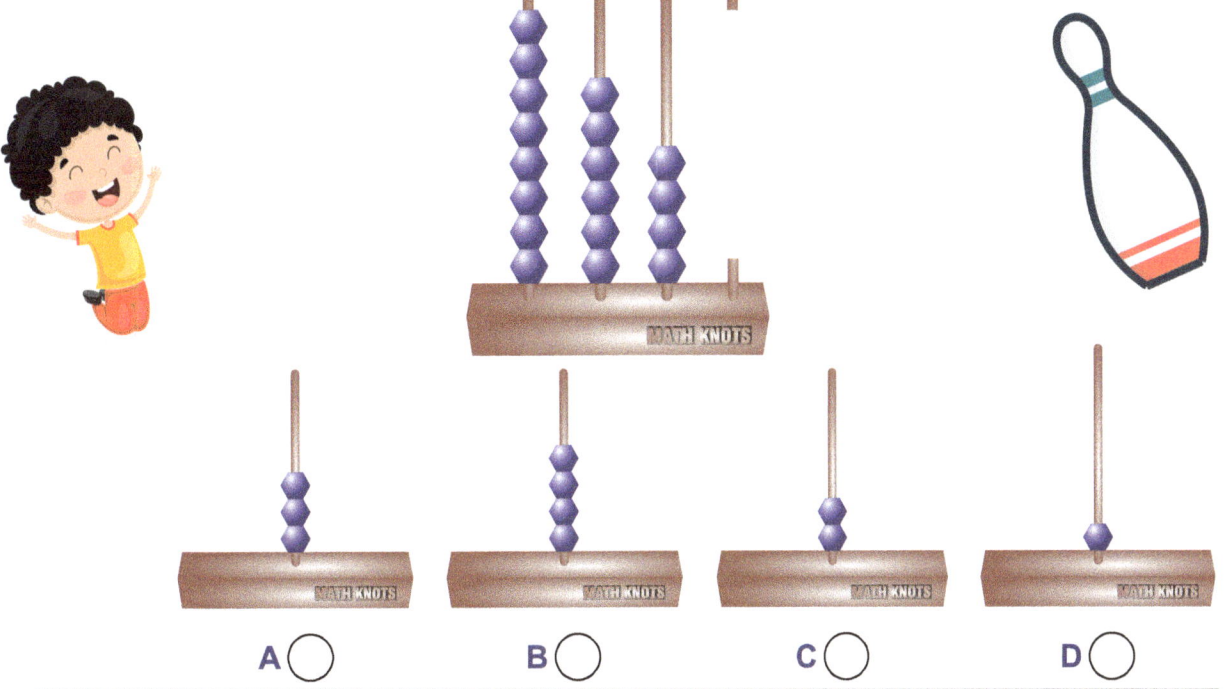

A ◯   B ◯   C ◯   D ◯

Q-6 Look at the question with the Hockey Stick. Kate is making a pattern with her hexagon shaped beads. Can you help her to identify what goes in the empty string from the given four options A, B, C, and D.

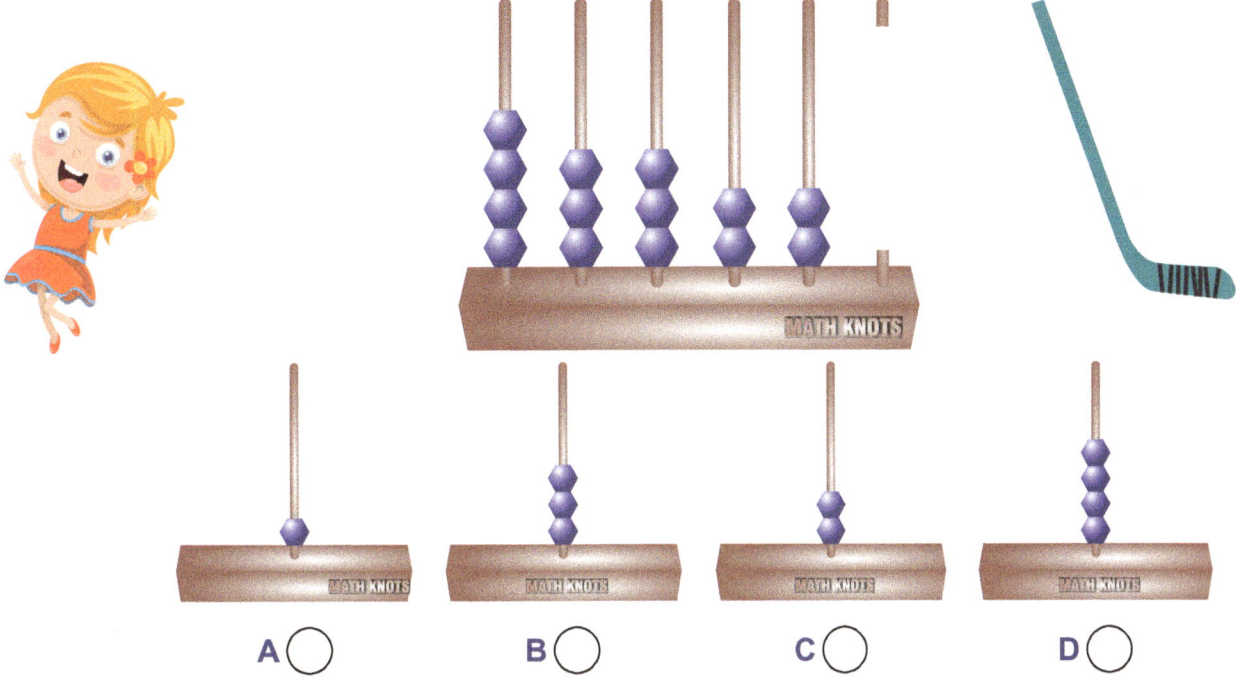

A ◯   B ◯   C ◯   D ◯

www.math-knots.com

Q-7

Look at the question with the Tennis Ball. Jane is making a pattern with her hexagon shaped beads. Can you help her to identify what goes in the empty string from the given four options A,B,C, and D.

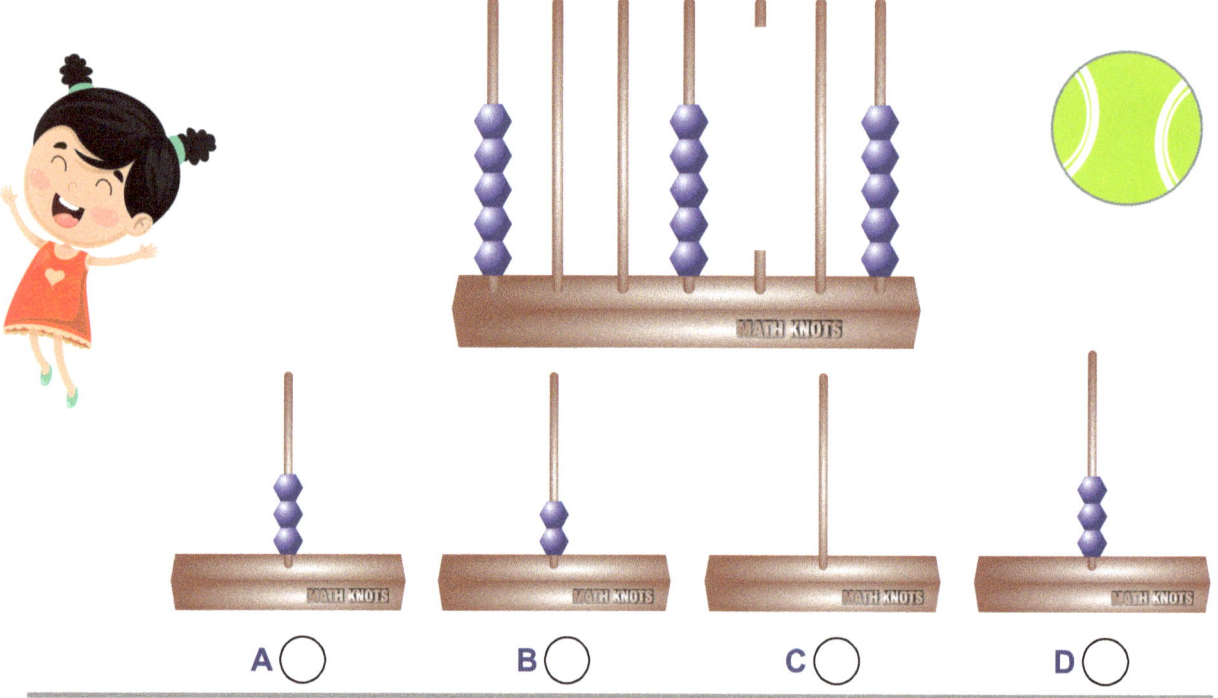

A ◯   B ◯   C ◯   D ◯

Q-8

Look at the question with the Cricket Bat. Johnson is making a pattern with his hexagon shaped beads. Can you help him to identify what goes in the empty string from the given four options A,B,C, and D.

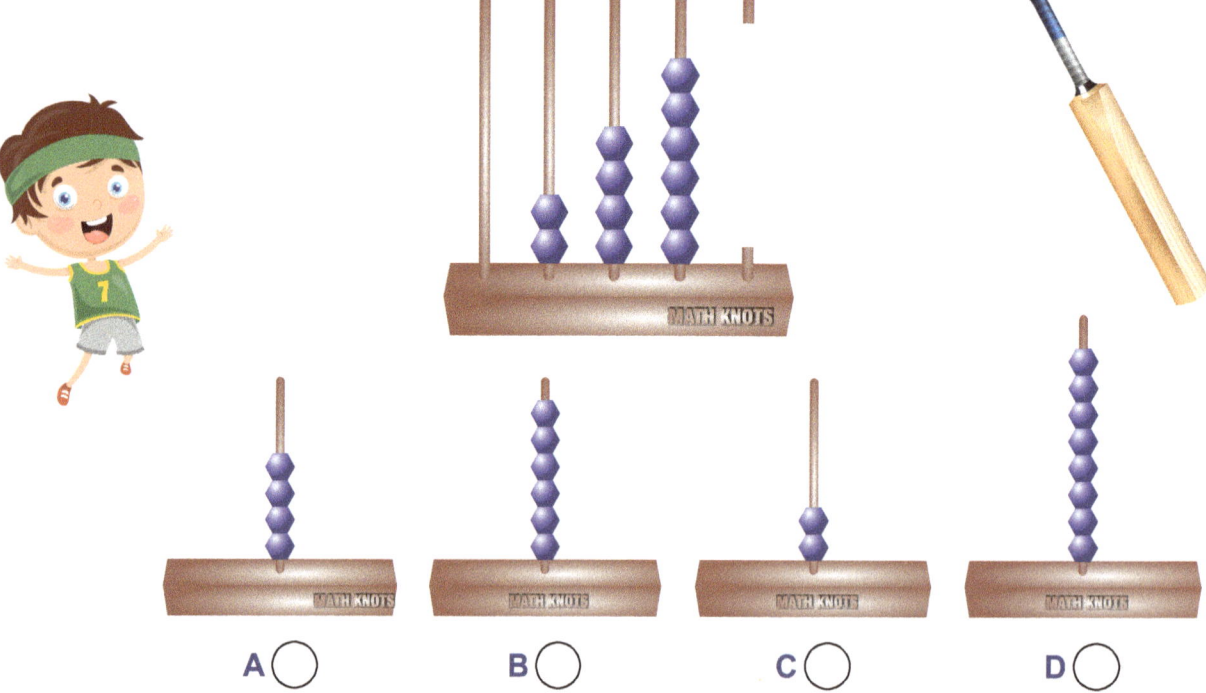

A ◯   B ◯   C ◯   D ◯

www.math-knots.com

Q-9

Look at the question with the Boat. Smitha, is making a pattern with her hexagon shaped beads. Can you help her to identify what goes in the empty string from the given four options A,B,C, and D.

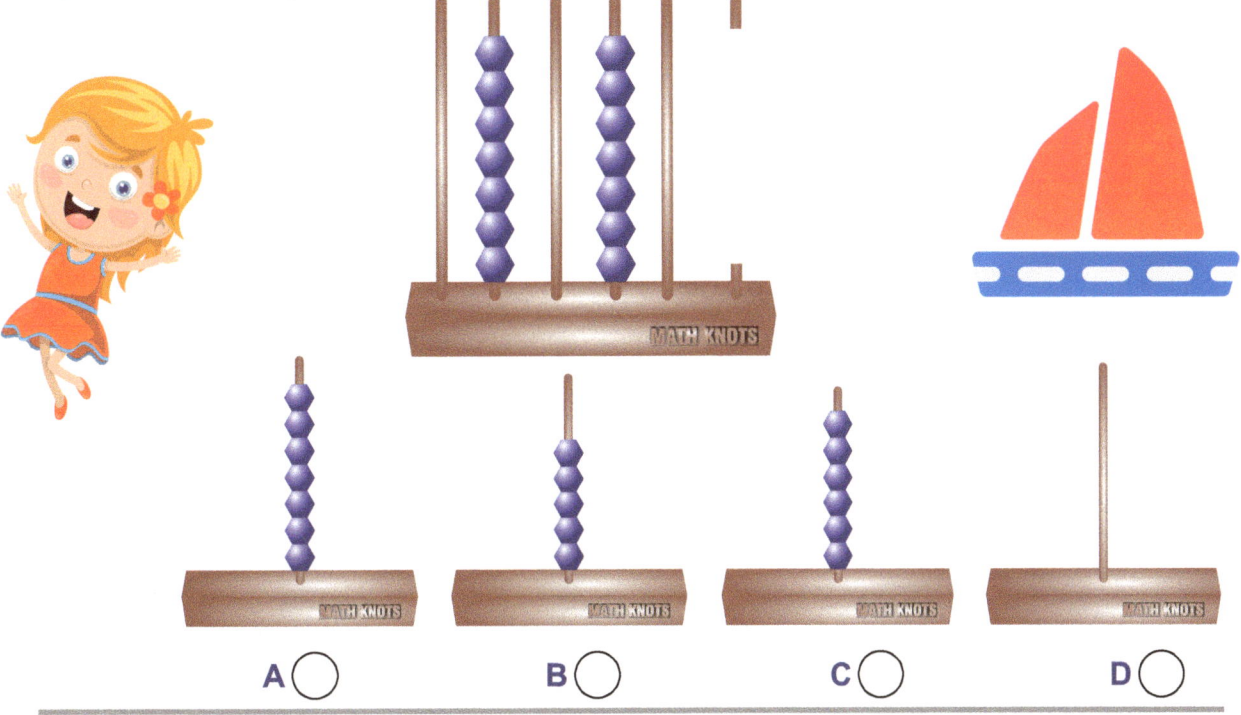

A ◯   B ◯   C ◯   D ◯

Q-10

Look at the question with the Baseball Bat. Adam is making a pattern with his hexagon shaped beads. Can you help him to identify what goes in the empty string from the given four options A,B,C, and D.

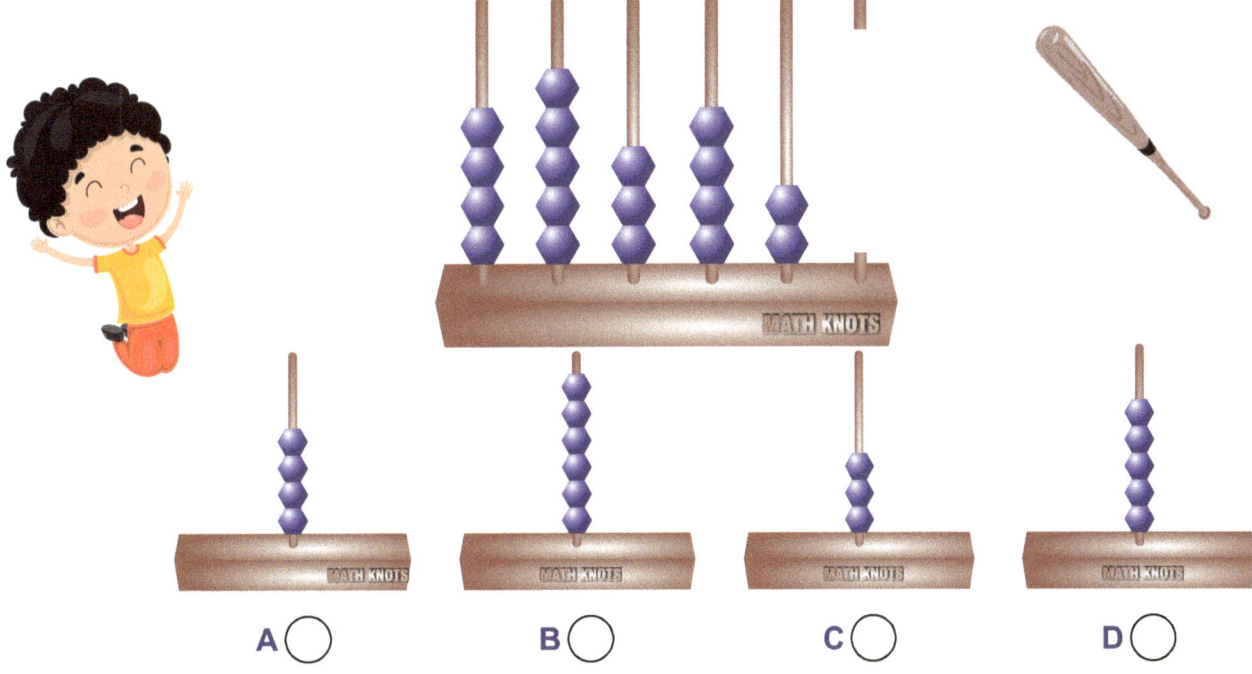

A ◯   B ◯   C ◯   D ◯

www.math-knots.com

Q-11 Look at the question with the Bicycle. Alvin is making a pattern with her hexagon shaped beads. Can you help her to identify what goes in the empty string from the given four options A, B, C, and D.

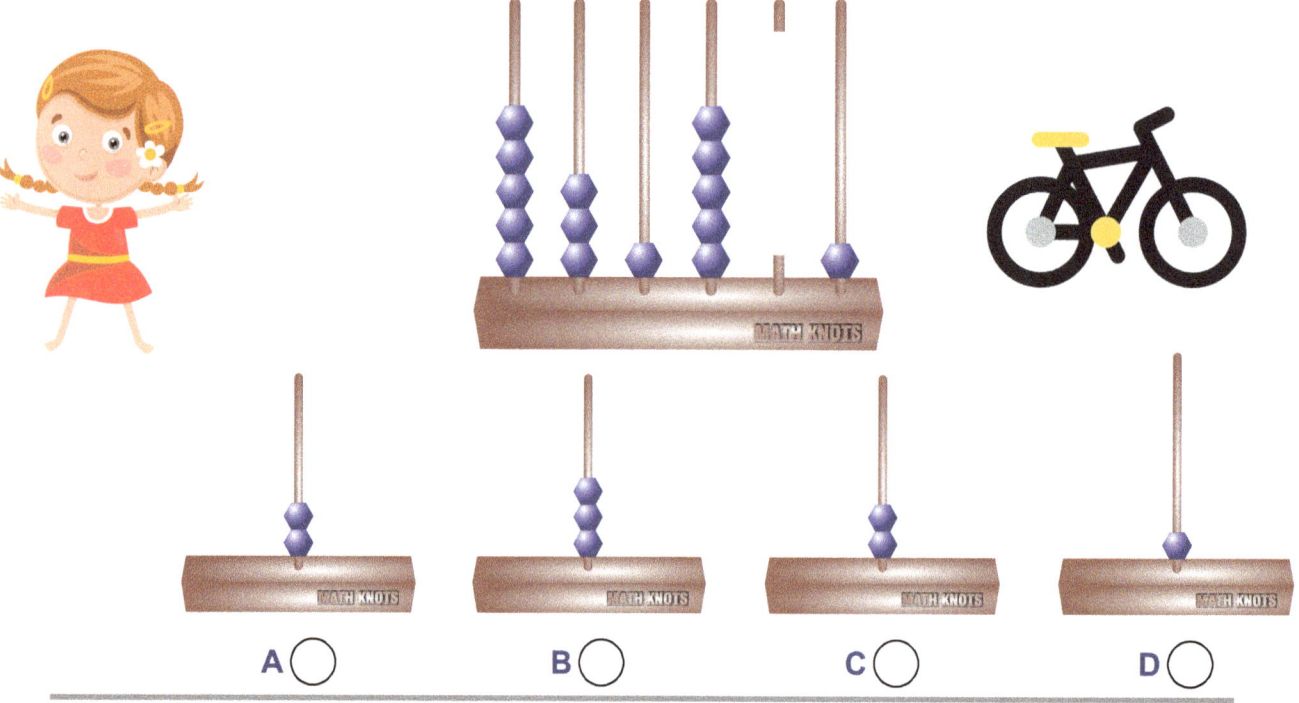

A ◯　　B ◯　　C ◯　　D ◯

Q-12 Look at the question with the Dart Board. John is making a pattern with his hexagon shaped beads. Can you help him to identify what goes in the empty string from the given four options A, B, C, and D.

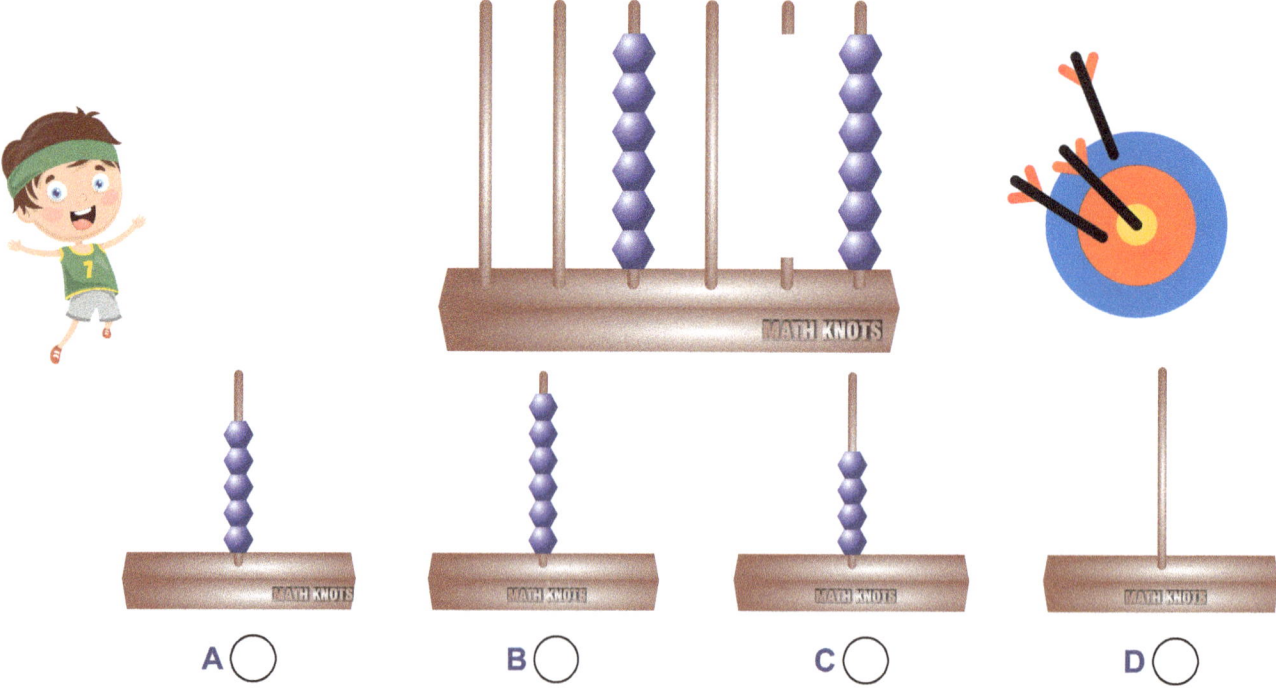

A ◯　　B ◯　　C ◯　　D ◯

www.math-knots.com

Q-13 Look at the question with the Weights. Lisa is making a pattern with her hexagon shaped beads. Can you help her to identify what goes in the empty string from the given four options A,B,C, and D.

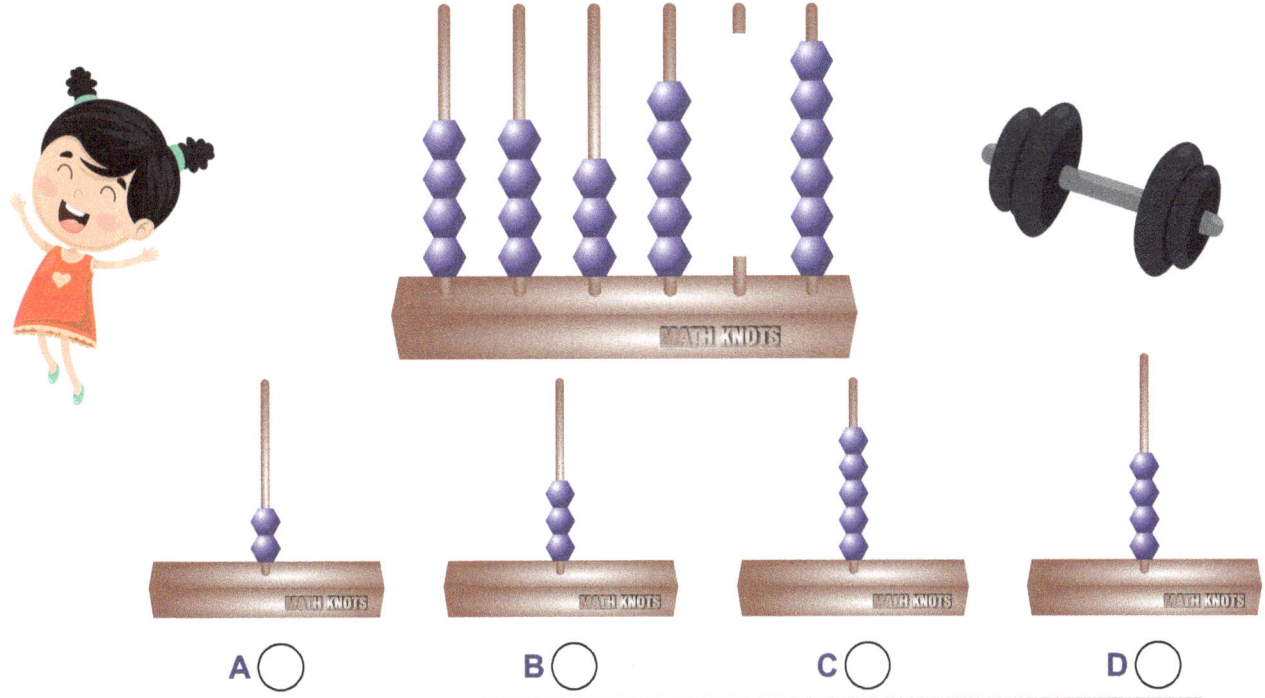

A ⃝   B ⃝   C ⃝   D ⃝

Q-14 Look at the question with the Ping-Pong Bats. Emma is making a pattern with her hexagon shaped beads. Can you help her to identify what goes in the empty string from the given four options A B,C ,and D.

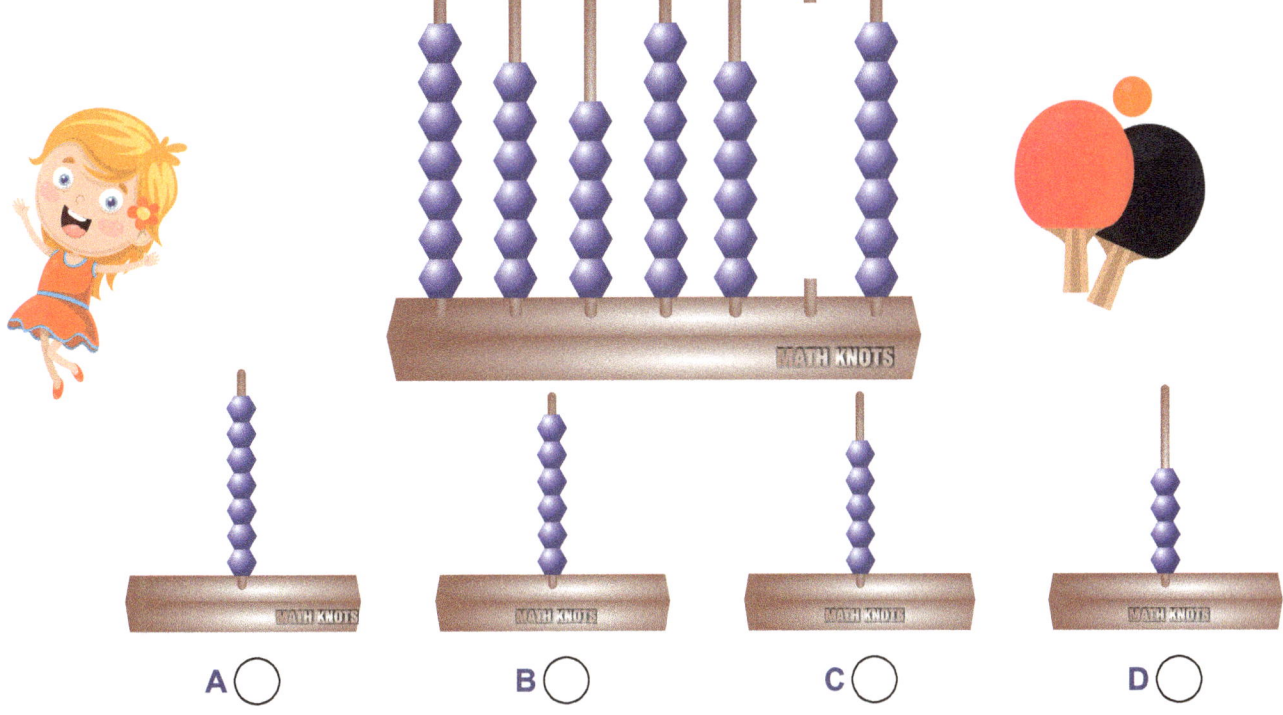

A ⃝   B ⃝   C ⃝   D ⃝

Q-15

Look at the question with the Karate Dress. Kathy is making a pattern with her hexagon shaped beads. Can you help her to identify what goes in the empty string from the given four options A,B,C, and D.

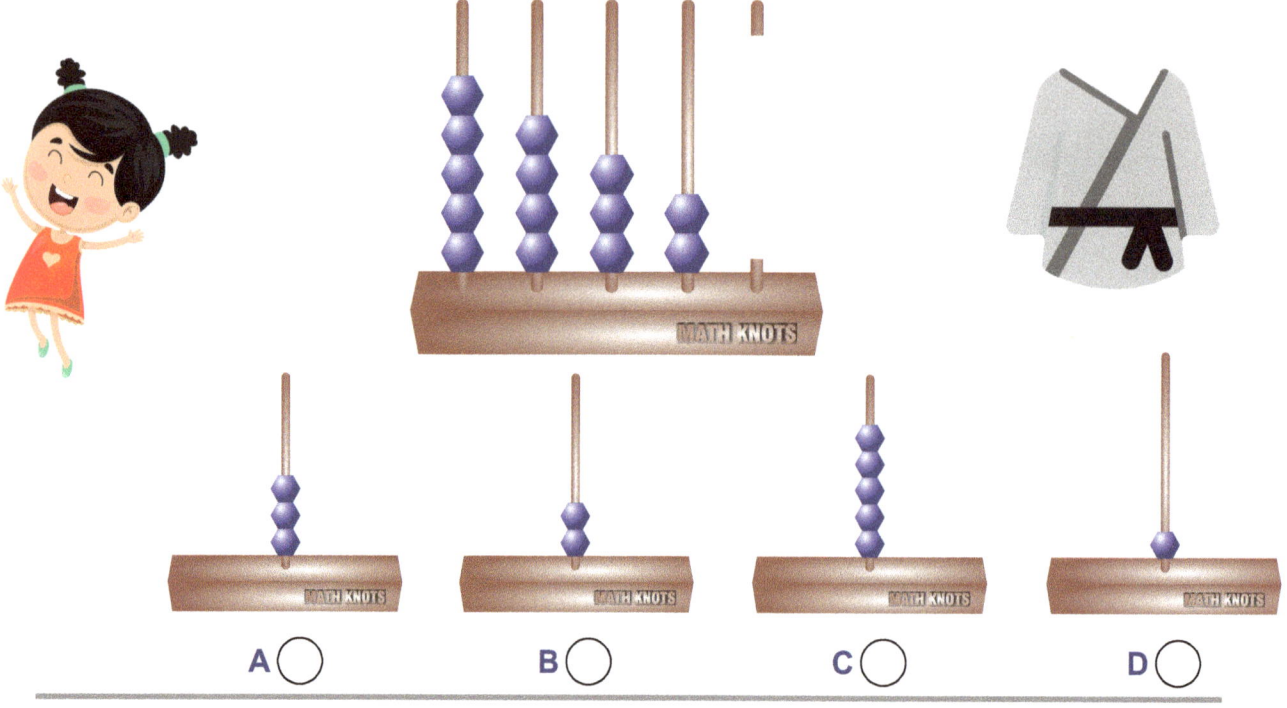

A◯   B◯   C◯   D◯

Q-16

Look at the question with the Swords. Berry is making a pattern with his hexagon shaped beads. Can you help him to identify what goes in the empty string from the given four options A,B,C, and D.

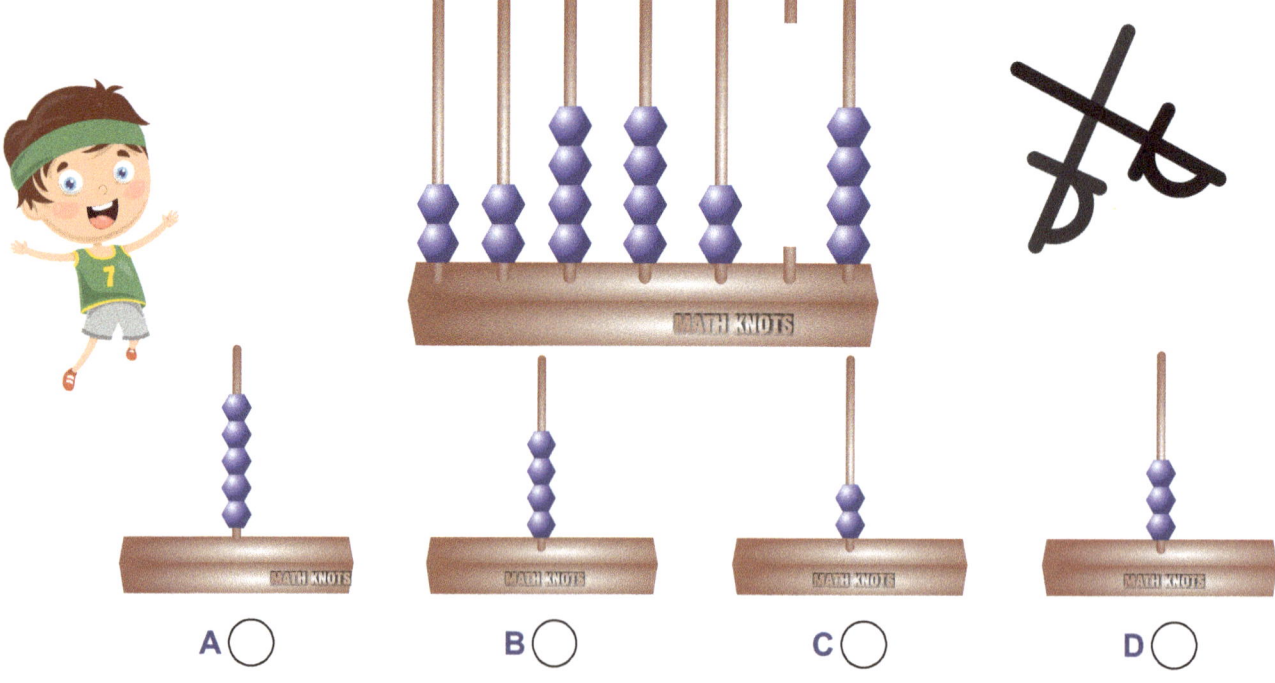

A◯   B◯   C◯   D◯

Q-17 Look at the question with the Boxing Gloves. Charles is making a pattern with his hexagon shaped beads. Can you help him to identify what goes in the empty string from the given four options A, B, C, and D.

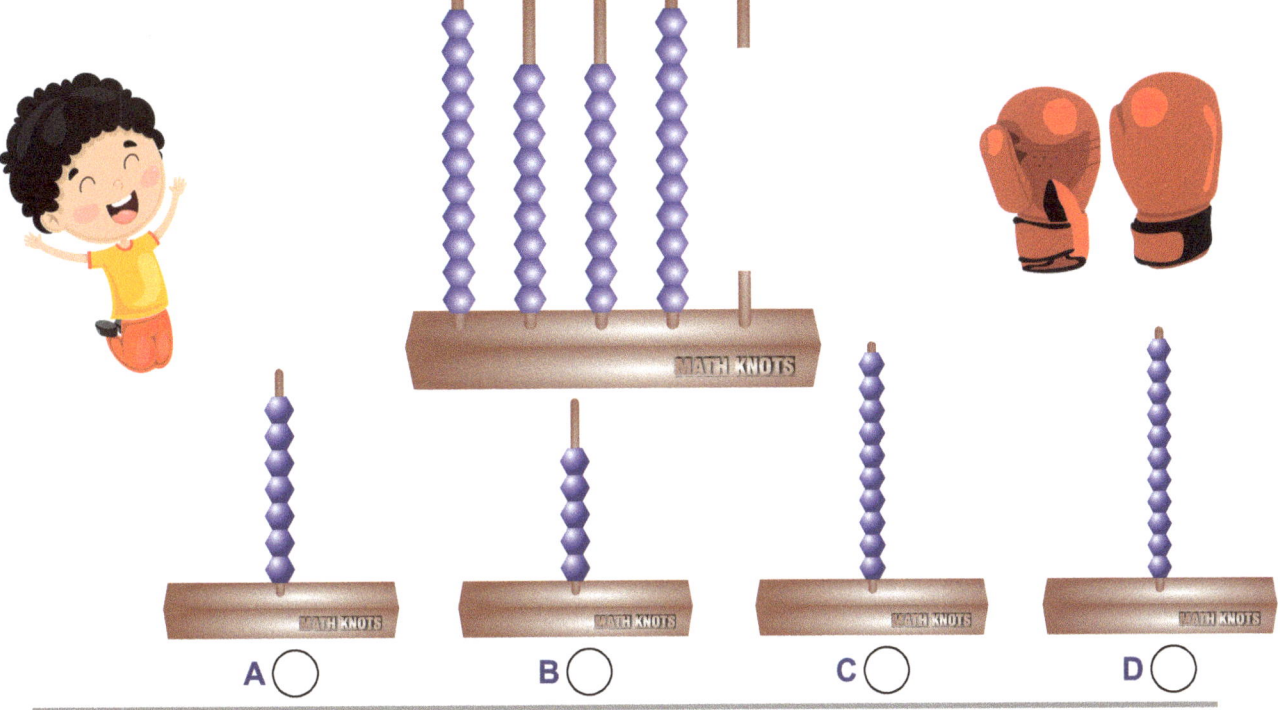

A ◯   B ◯   C ◯   D ◯

Q-18 Look at the question with the Racket. Claud is making a pattern with her hexagon shaped beads. Can you help her to identify what goes in the empty string from the given four options A, B, C, and D.

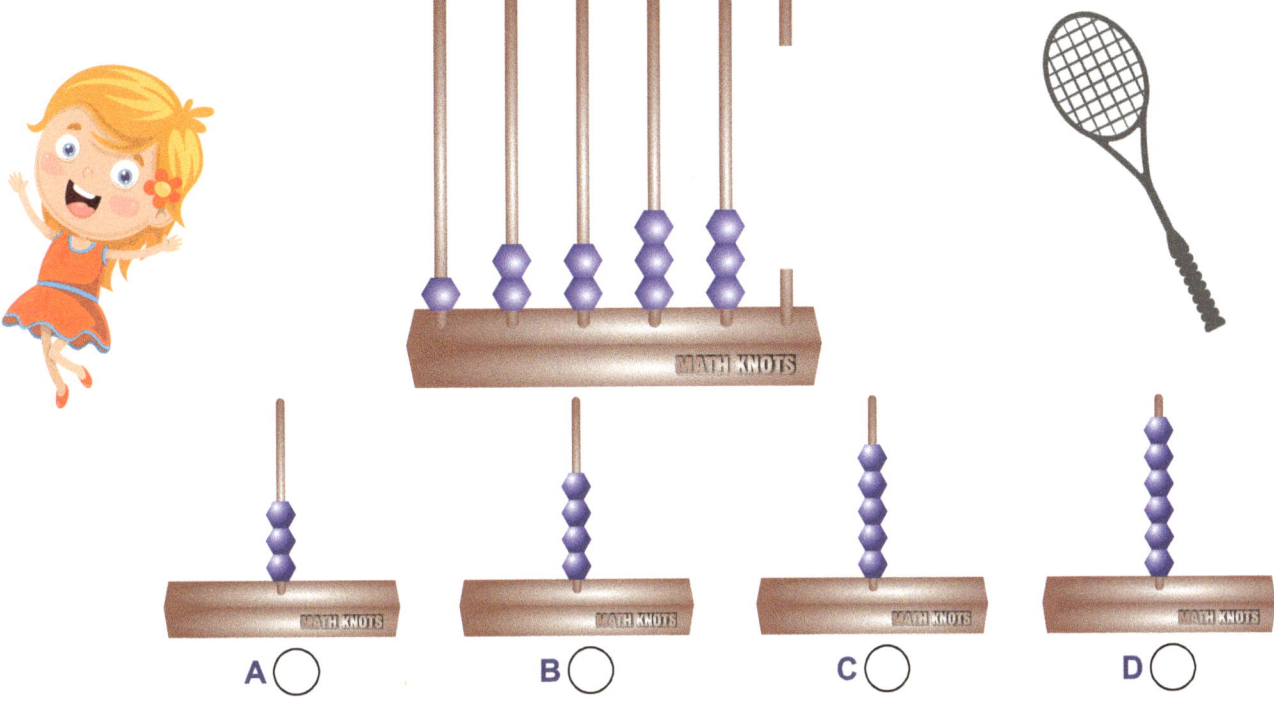

A ◯   B ◯   C ◯   D ◯

www.math-knots.com

TEST - 1

QUANTITATIVE APTITUDE

NUMBER PUZZLES

Lets Start the Test...

www.math-knots.com

Sample

Look at the question and put your finger on the Guitar. Ryan is wondering what is the missing number under the question mark ? Help him to find the missing number under the question mark and fill in the bubble.

$$2 + ? = 3$$

1	0	5	2
A○	B○	C○	D○

Solution : A

How much should be added to 2 to make it 3

3 - 2 = 1

Meaning if we add 1 to 2 we get a total of three

Q-1 Look at the question with Soccer Ball. Fred is wondering what is the missing number under the question mark ? Help him to find the missing number under the question mark and fill in the bubble.

5	**6**	**1**	**0**
A ◯	B ◯	C ◯	D ◯

Q-2 Look at the question with Foot Ball. Mary is wondering what is the missing number under the question mark ? Help her to find the missing number under the question mark and fill in the bubble.

5	**4**	**1**	**6**
A ◯	B ◯	C ◯	D ◯

www.math-knots.com

Q-3

Look at the question with Basket Ball. James is wondering what is the missing number under the question mark ? Help him to find the missing number under the question mark and fill in the bubble.

7	2	6	4
A ○	B ○	C ○	D ○

Q-4

Look at the question with Shuttlecock. Alfred is wondering what is the missing number under the question mark ? Help him to find the missing number under the question mark and fill in the bubble.

4	0	3	2
A ○	B ○	C ○	D ○

www.math-knots.com

Q-5 Look at the question with Bowling Pin. Jason is wondering what is the missing number under the question mark ? Help him to find the missing number under the question mark and fill in the bubble.

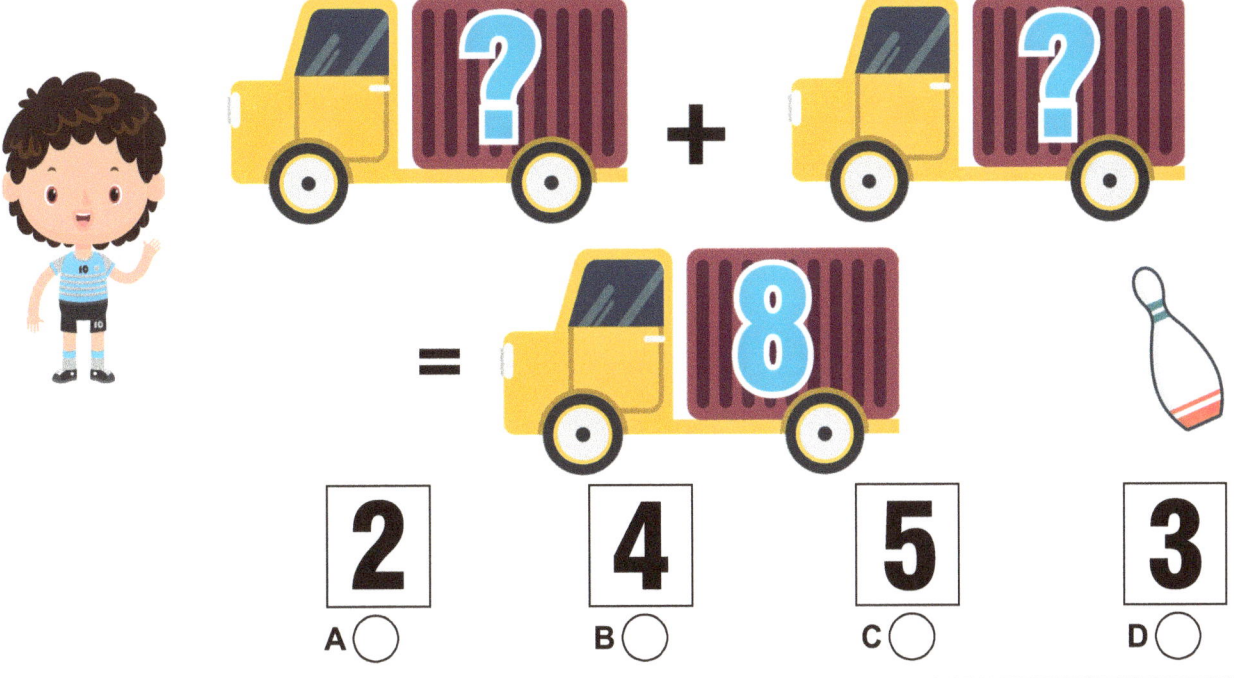

A 2   B 4   C 5   D 3

Q-6 Look at the question with Hockey Stick. Jia is wondering what is the missing number under the question mark ? Help her to find the missing number under the question mark and fill in the bubble.

A 3   B 0   C 5   D 2

www.math-knots.com

Q-7 Look at the question with Tennis Ball. Olivia is wondering what is the missing number under the question mark ? Help her to find the missing number under the question mark and fill in the bubble.

1	3	4	0
A○	B○	C○	D○

Q-8 Look at the question with Cricket Bat. Michael is wondering what is the missing number under the question mark ? Help him to find the missing number under the question mark and fill in the bubble.

10	11	12	14
A○	B○	C○	D○

www.math-knots.com

Q-9

Look at the question with Boat. Hope is wondering what is the missing number under the question mark ? Help her to find the missing number under the question mark and fill in the bubble.

A ○ 4   B ○ 6   C ○ 5   D ○ 10

Q-10

Look at the question with Pin-Pong Bat. Ethen is wondering what is the missing number under the question mark ? Help him to find the missing number under the question mark and fill in the bubble.

A ○ 0   B ○ 3   C ○ 2   D ○ 4

www.math-knots.com

Q-11

Look at the question with Bicycle. Elizabeth is wondering what is the missing number under the question mark ? Help her to find the missing number under the question mark and fill in the bubble.

5	0	1	8
A ◯	B ◯	C ◯	D ◯

Q-12

Look at the question with Dart Board. Logan is wondering what is the missing number under the question mark ? Help him to find the missing number under the question mark and fill in the bubble.

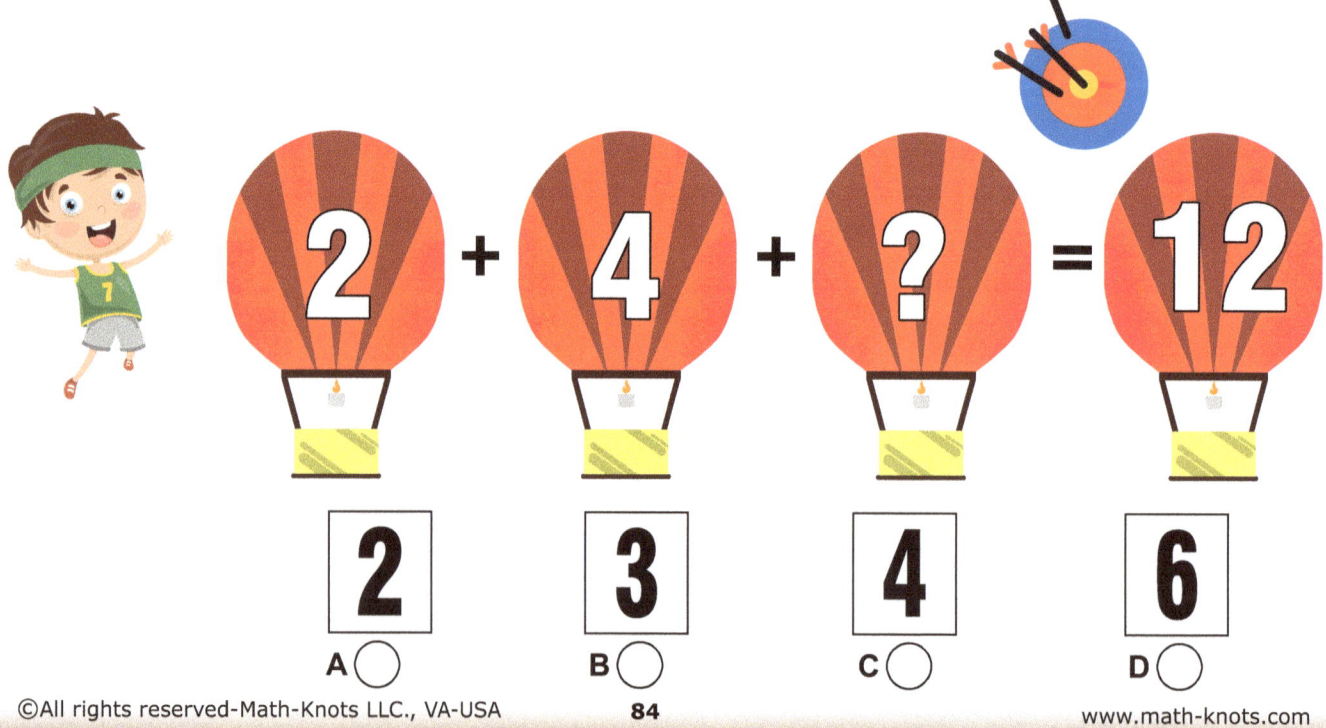

2	3	4	6
A ◯	B ◯	C ◯	D ◯

www.math-knots.com

Q-13 Look at the question with Weights. Olivia is wondering what is the missing number under the question mark ? Help her to find the missing number under the question mark and fill in the bubble.

A	B	C	D
0	6	7	9

Q-14 Look at the question with Skate Board. Grace is wondering what is the missing number under the question mark ? Help her to find the missing number under the question mark and fill in the bubble.

A	B	C	D
11	0	3	10

www.math-knots.com

Q-15

Look at the question with Karate Dress. Sophia is wondering what is the missing number under the question mark ? Help her to find the missing number under the question mark and fill in the bubble.

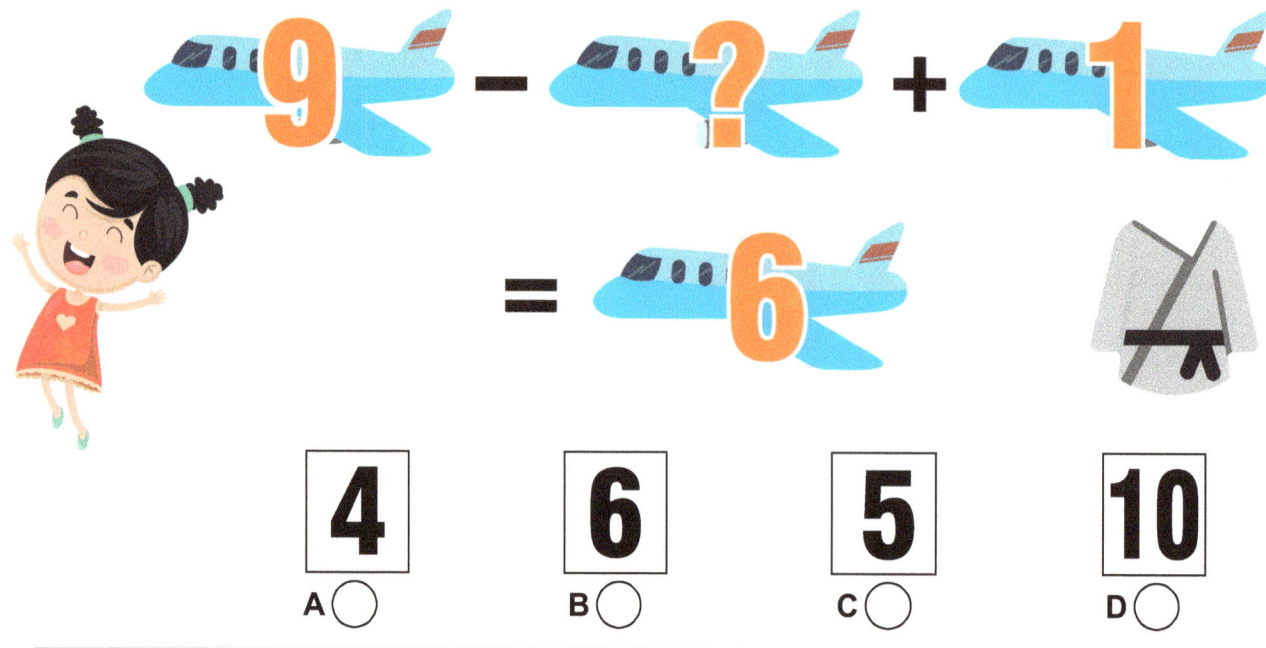

A ⃝ 4   B ⃝ 6   C ⃝ 5   D ⃝ 10

Q-16

Look at the question with Swords. Jackson is wondering what is the missing number under the question mark ? Help him to find the missing number under the question mark and fill in the bubble.

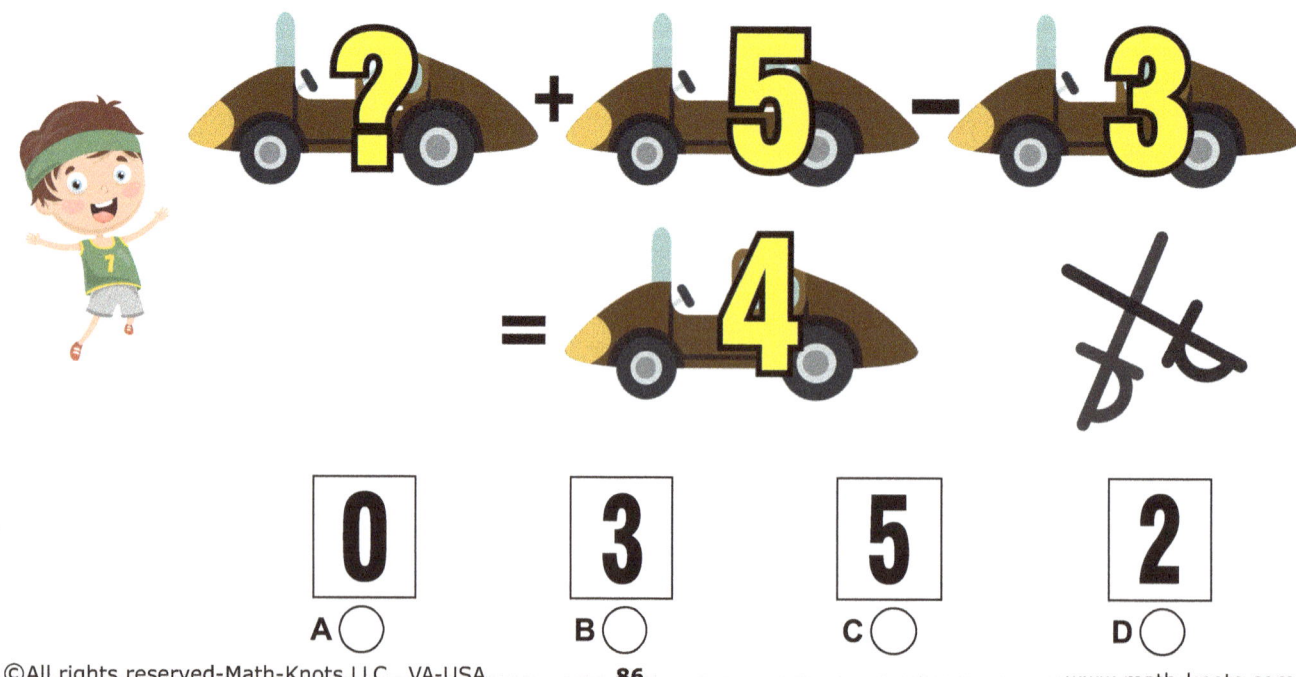

A ⃝ 0   B ⃝ 3   C ⃝ 5   D ⃝ 2

Q-17 Look at the question with Boxing gloves. Mathew is wondering what is the missing number under the question mark ? Help him to find the missing number under the question mark and fill in the bubble.

5	0	1	8
A○	B○	C○	D○

Q-18 Look at the question with Racket. Sofia is wondering what is the missing number under the question mark ? Help her to find the missing number under the question mark and fill in the bubble.

2	11	1	0
A○	B○	C○	D○

www.math-knots.com

Q-19

Look at the question with Skate Board. Benjamin is wondering what is the missing number under the question mark ? Help him to find the missing number under the question mark and fill in the bubble.

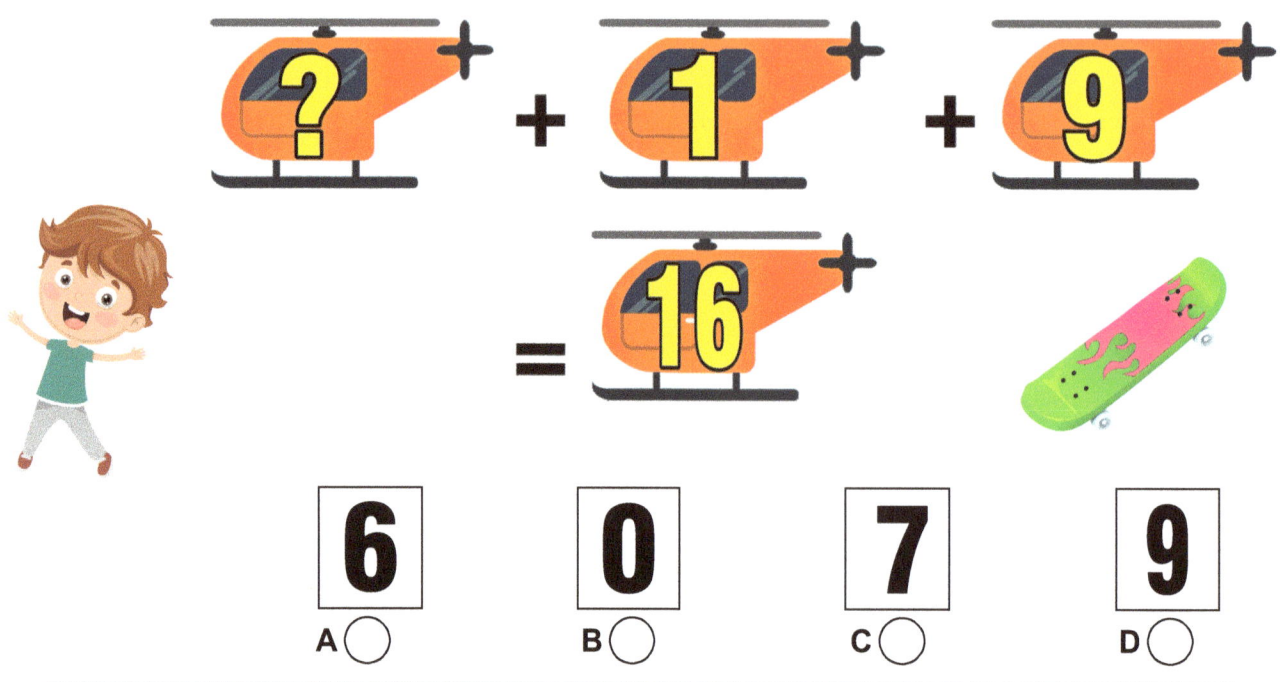

6	**0**	**7**	**9**
A ◯	B ◯	C ◯	D ◯

Q-20

Look at the question with Baseball Bat. Carol is wondering what is the missing number under the question mark ? Help her to find the missing number under the question mark and fill in the bubble.

0	**3**	**5**	**12**
A ◯	B ◯	C ◯	D ◯

 www.math-knots.com

TEST - 1

NON VERBAL SECTION

FIGURE MATRICES

Lets Start the Test...

www.math-knots.com

Sample Look at the question with the Tree. The first three pictures belong to one group in a common way. Help Bob to find out which of the below options belong to the same group. Identify the correct picture and help him to bubble the right choice.

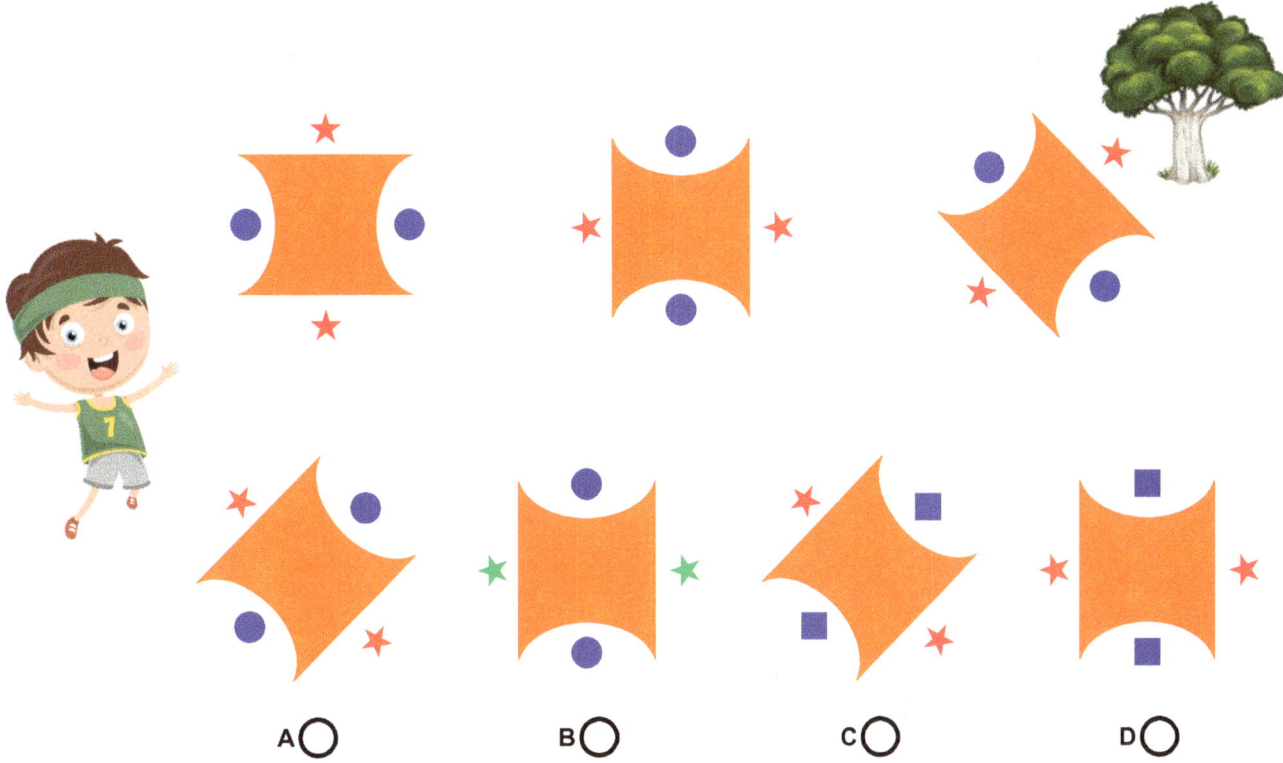

A○   B○   C○   D○

Solution : A

Option A is the only right choice. Option A matches the rest of the figure group in

the same way. The other option vary in some way. Pay attention to all options before answering the right choice.

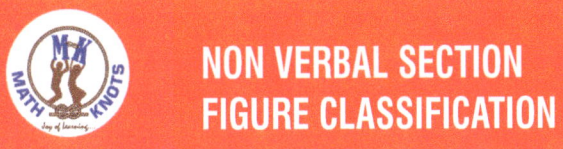

Q-1 Look at the question with the Raccoon. The first three pictures belong to one group in a common way. Help Jacob to find out which of the below options belong to the same group. Identify the correct picture and help him to bubble the right choice.

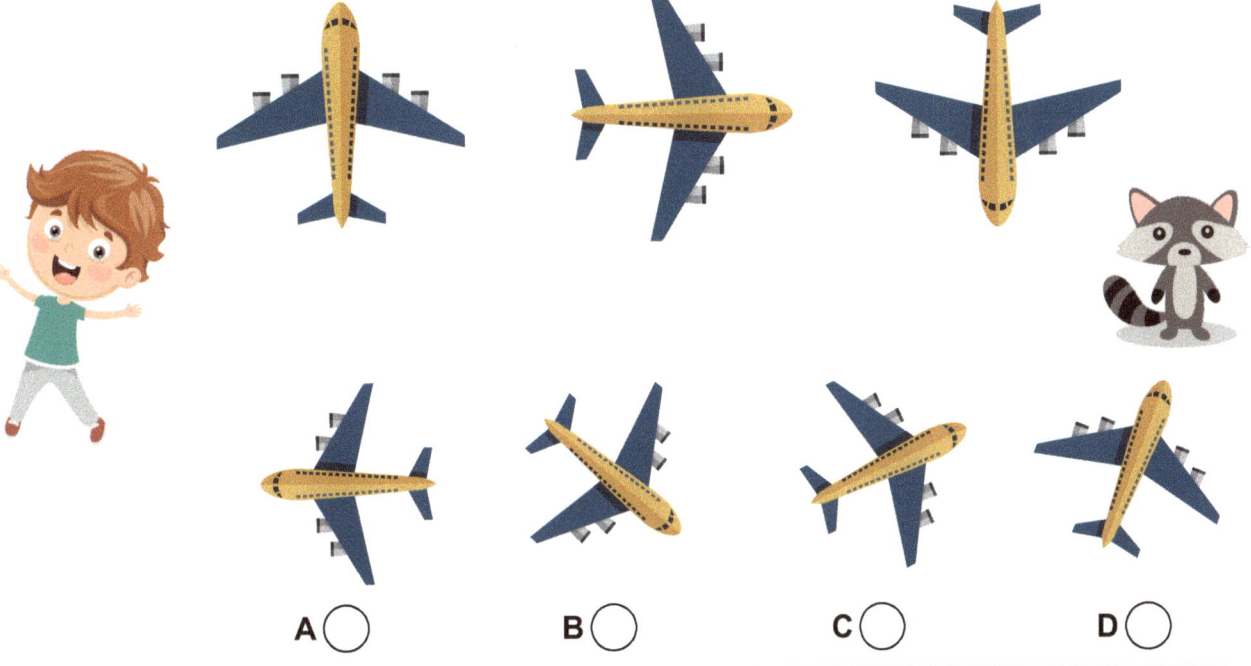

A ◯   B ◯   C ◯   D ◯

Q-2 Look at the question with the Walrus. The first three pictures belong to one group in a common way. Help Emma to find out which of the below options belong to the same group. Identify the correct picture and help her to bubble the right choice.

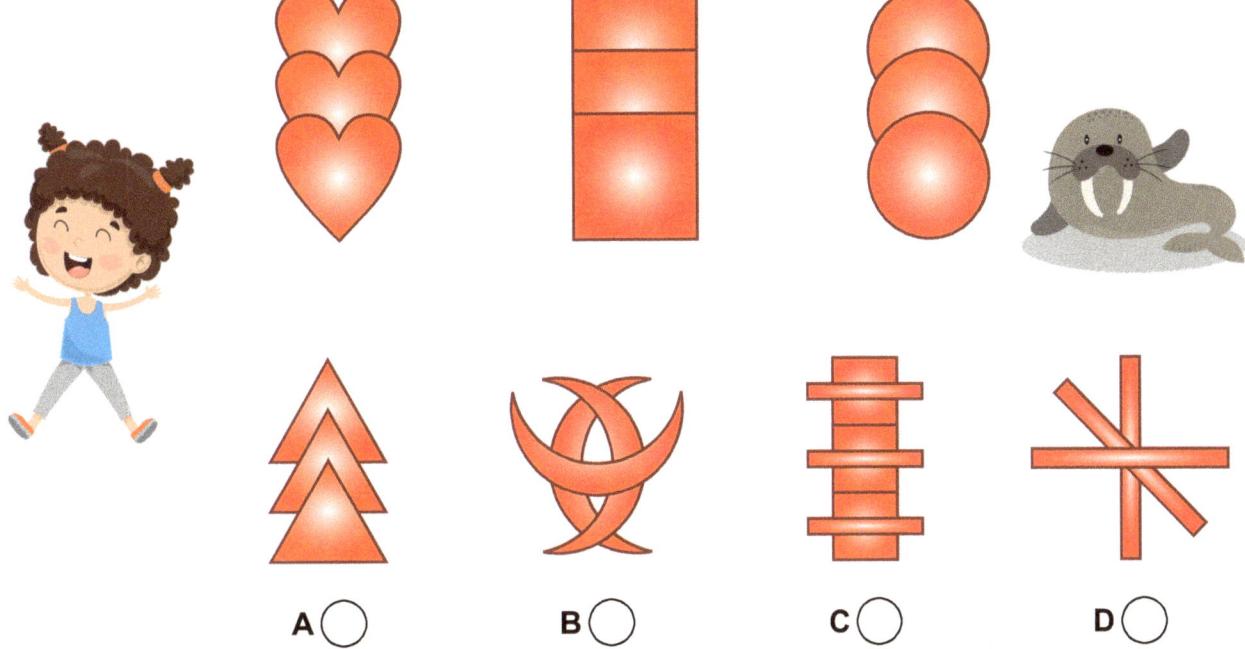

A ◯   B ◯   C ◯   D ◯

www.math-knots.com

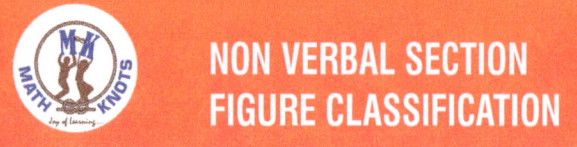

Q-3

Look at the question with the Quail. The first three pictures belong to one group in a common way. Help Michael to find out which of the below options belong to the same group. Identify the correct picture and help him to bubble the right choice.

A ◯   B ◯   C ◯   D ◯

Q-4

Look at the question with the Jellyfish. The first three pictures belong to one group in a common way. Help Olivia to find out which of the below options belong to the same group. Identify the correct picture and help her to bubble the right choice.

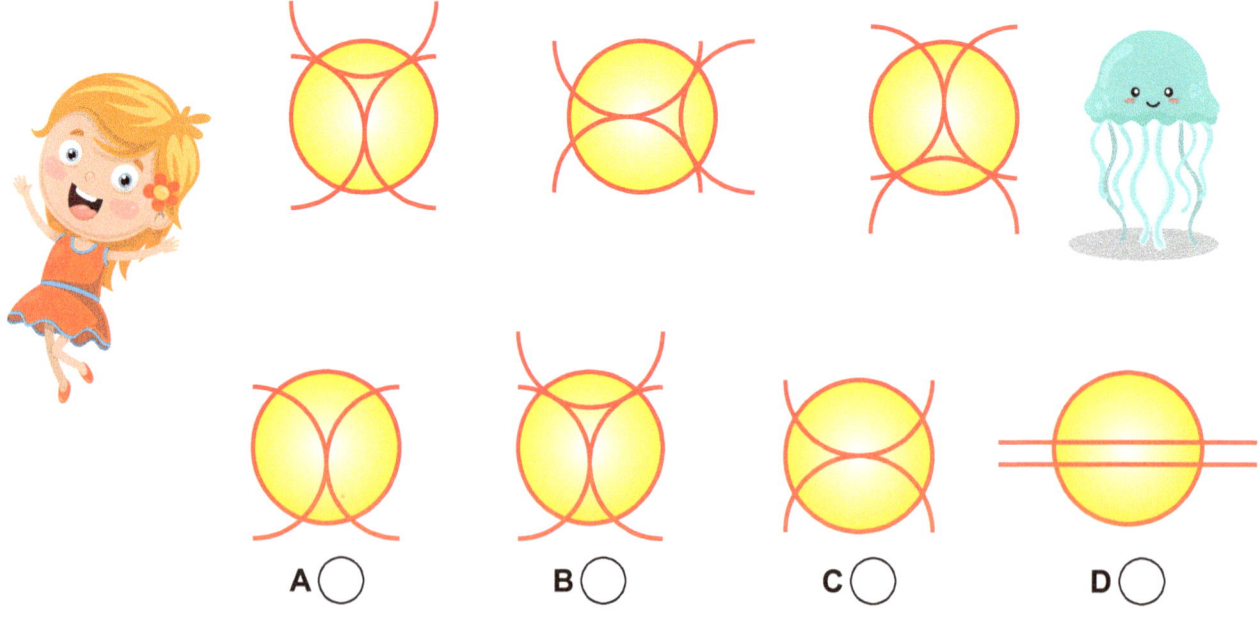

A ◯   B ◯   C ◯   D ◯

www.math-knots.com

Q-5

Look at the question with the Elephant. The first three pictures belong to one group in a common way. Help Matthew to find out which of the below options belong to the same group. Identify the correct picture and help him to bubble the right choice.

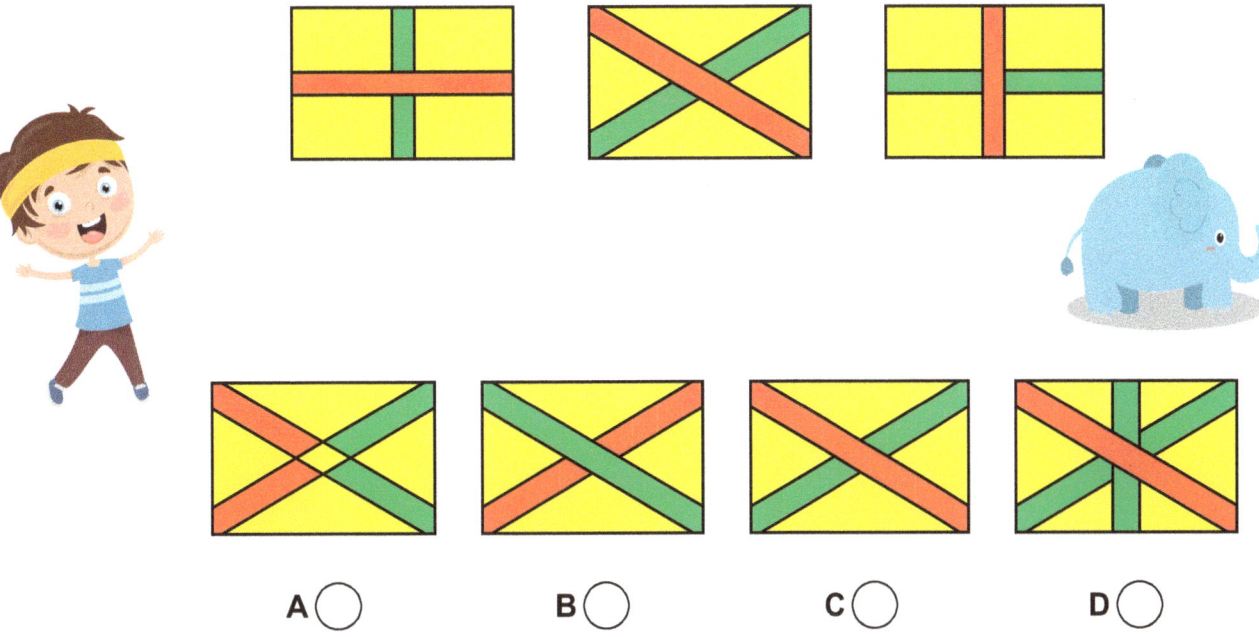

A◯ B◯ C◯ D◯

Q-6

Look at the question with the Turtle. The first three pictures belong to one group in a common way. Help Sophia to find out which of the below options belong to the same group. Identify the correct picture and help her to bubble the right choice.

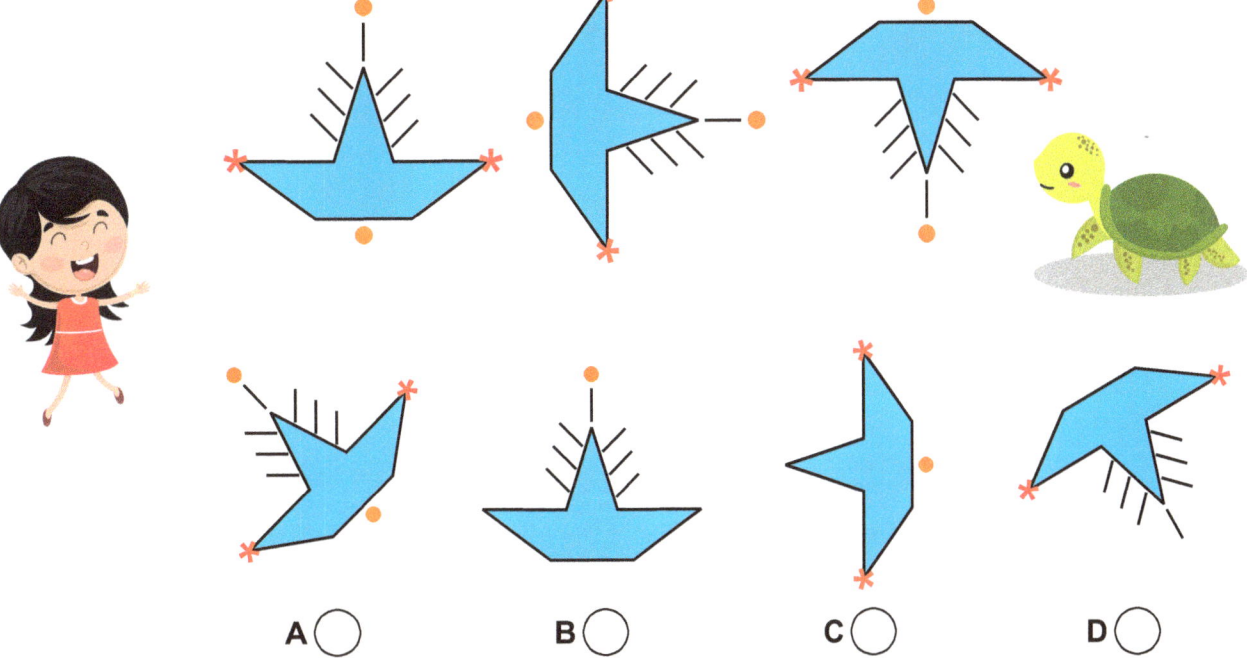

A◯ B◯ C◯ D◯

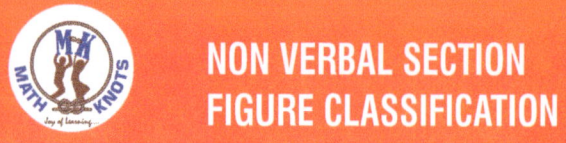

Q-7

Look at the question with the Monkey. The first three pictures belong to one group in a common way. Help Ethan to find out which of the below options belong to the same group. Identify the correct picture and help him to bubble the right choice.

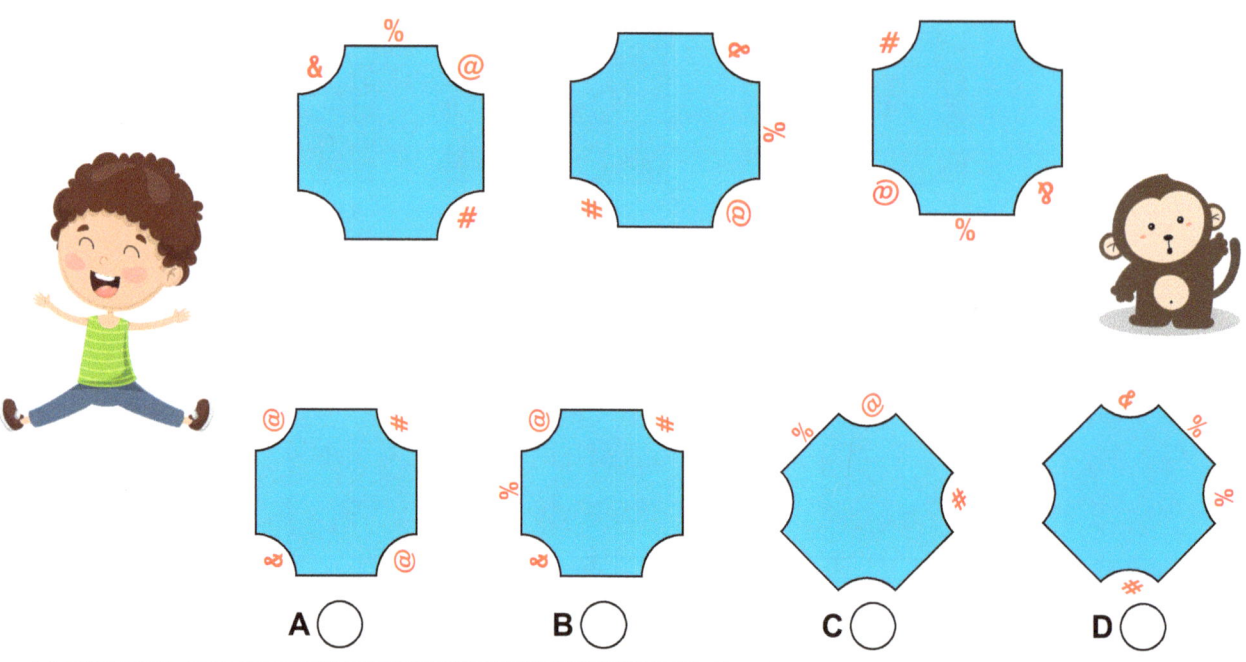

A◯   B◯   C◯   D◯

Q-8

Look at the question with the Narwhal Fish. The first three pictures belong to one group in a common way. Help Elizabeth to find out which of the below options belong to the same group. Identify the correct picture and help her to bubble the right choice.

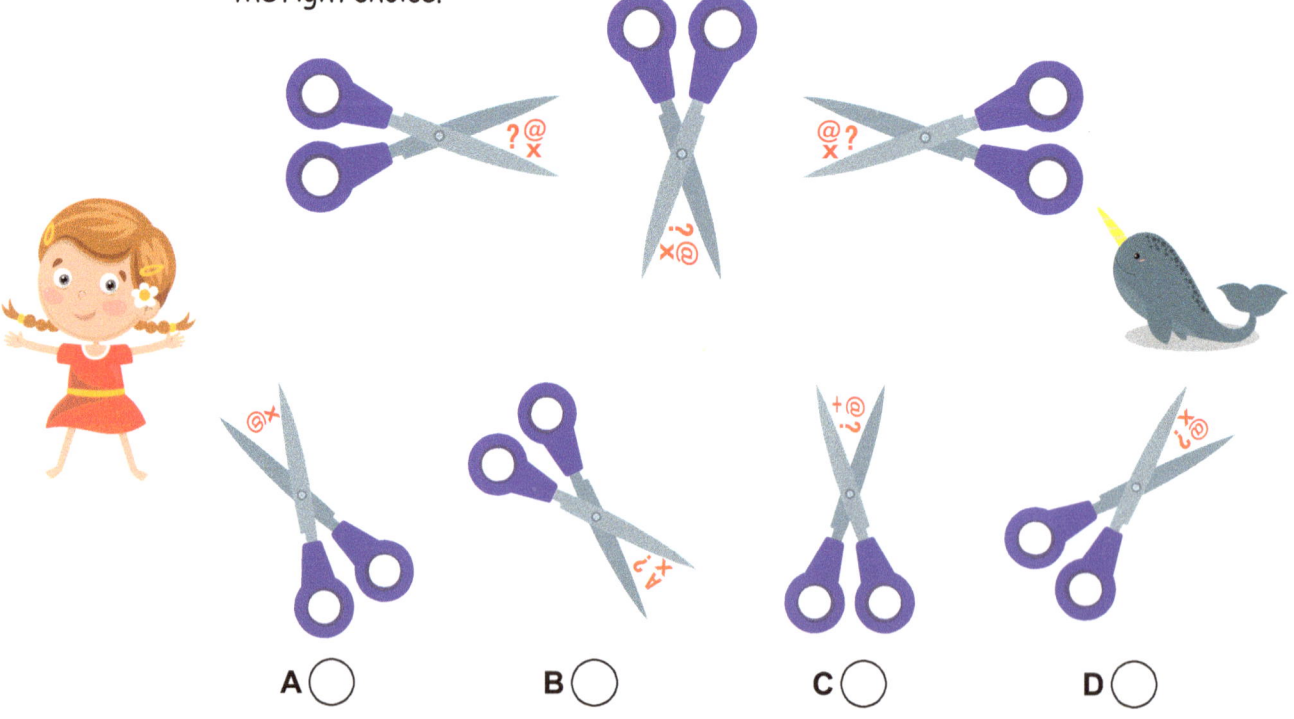

A◯   B◯   C◯   D◯

www.math-knots.com

Q-9 Look at the question with the Koala Bear. The first three pictures belong to one group in a common way. Help Andrew to find out which of the below options belong to the same group. Identify the correct picture and help him to bubble the right choice.

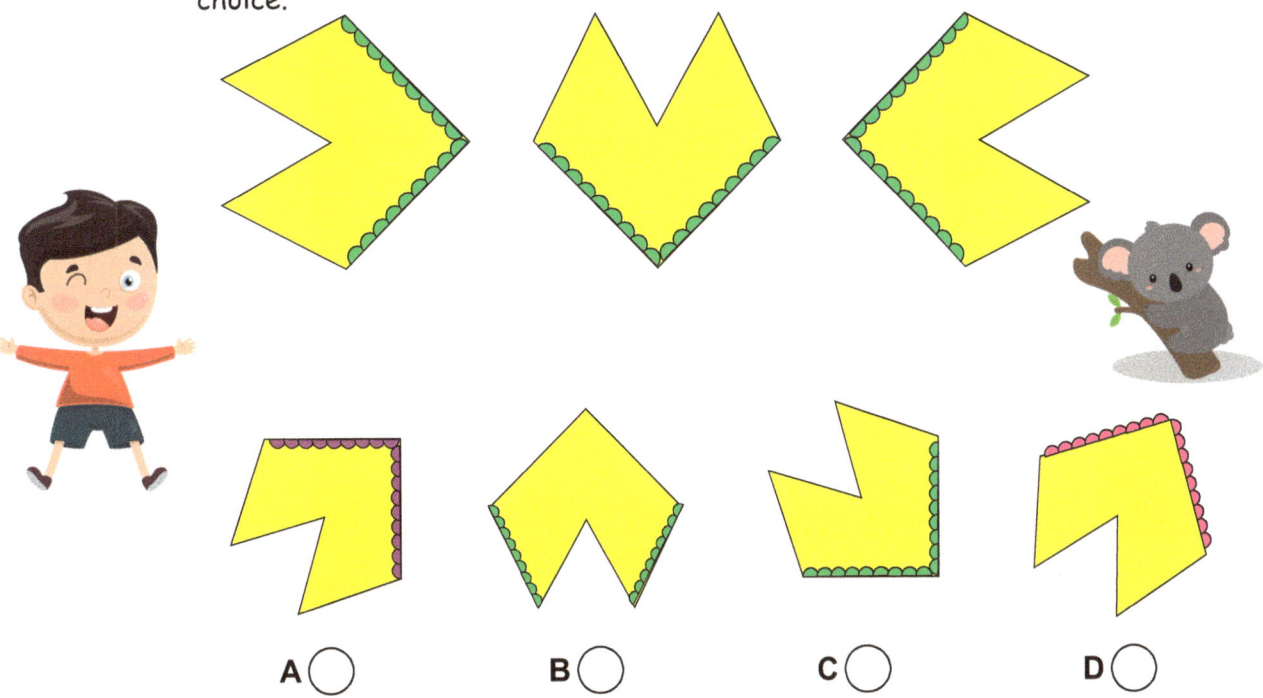

A ◯   B ◯   C ◯   D ◯

Q-10 Look at the question with the Lion. The first three pictures belong to one group in a common way. Help Jessica to find out which of the below options belong to the same group. Identify the correct picture and help her to bubble the right choice.

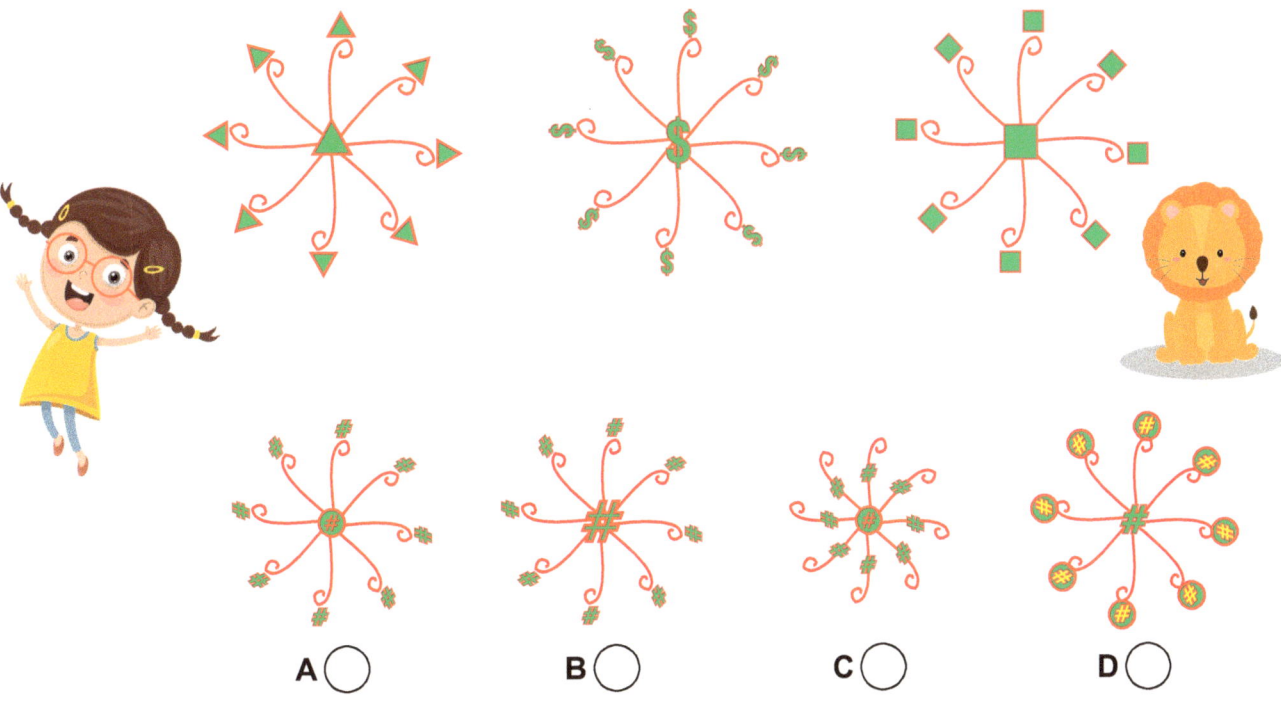

A ◯   B ◯   C ◯   D ◯

Q-11

Look at the question with the Iguana. The first three pictures belong to one group in a common way. Help Daniel to find out which of the below options belong to the same group. Identify the correct picture and help him to bubble the right choice.

A◯   B◯   C◯   D◯

Q-12

Look at the question with the Octopus. The first three pictures belong to one group in a common way. Help Julia to find out which of the below options belong to the same group. Identify the correct picture and help her to bubble the right choice.

A◯   B◯   C◯   D◯

www.math-knots.com

Q-13 Look at the question with the Dolphin. The first three pictures belong to one group in a common way. Help Anthony to find out which of the below options belong to the same group. Identify the correct picture and help him to bubble the right choice.

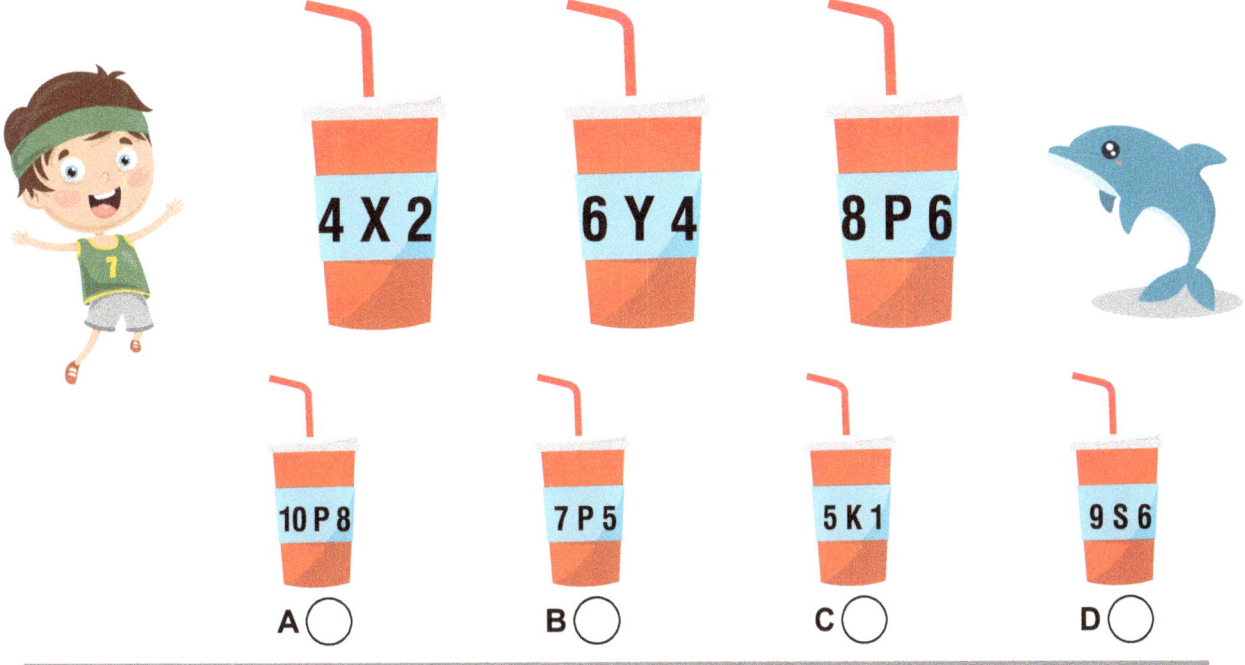

4 X 2   6 Y 4   8 P 6

10 P 8   7 P 5   5 K 1   9 S 6

A◯   B◯   C◯   D◯

Q-14 Look at the question with the Hedgehog. The first three pictures belong to one group in a common way. Help Jenna to find out which of the below options belong to the same group. Identify the correct picture and help her to bubble the right choice.

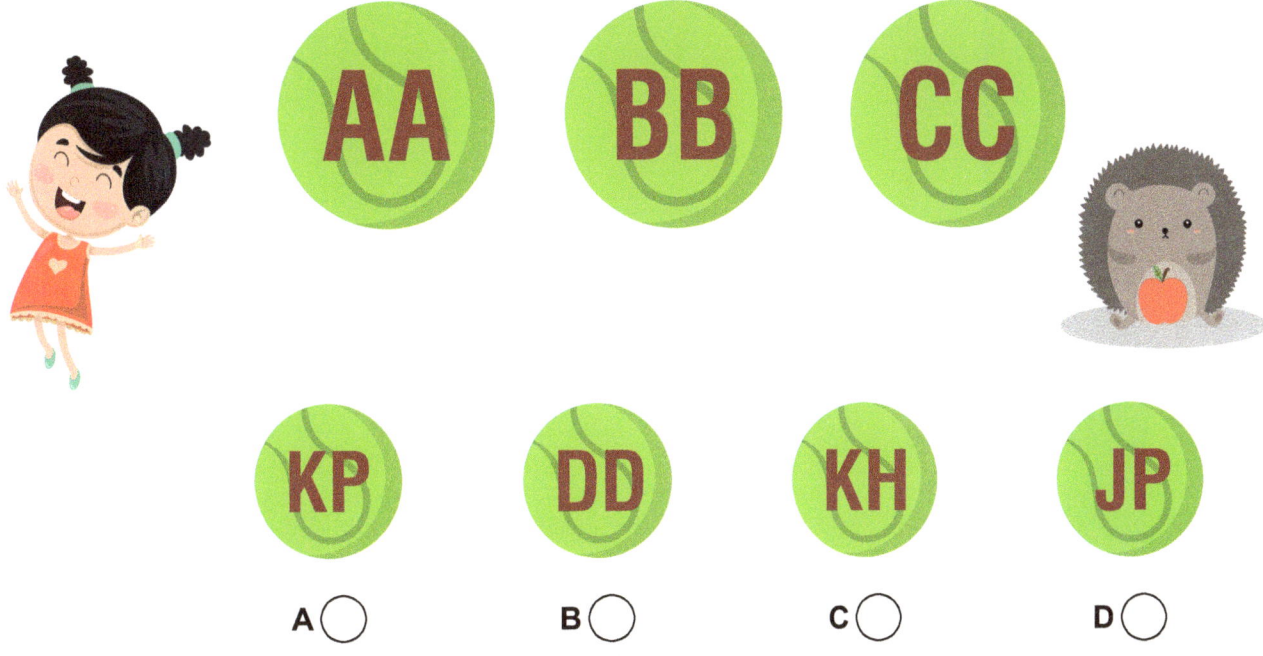

AA   BB   CC

KP   DD   KH   JP

A◯   B◯   C◯   D◯

www.math-knots.com

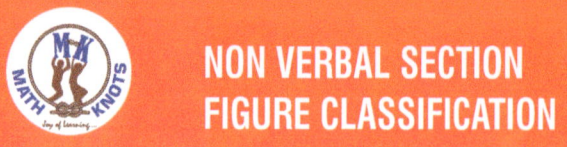
Q-15

Look at the question with the Fox. The first three pictures belong to one group in a common way. Help William to find out which of the below options belong to the same group. Identify the correct picture and help him to bubble the right choice.

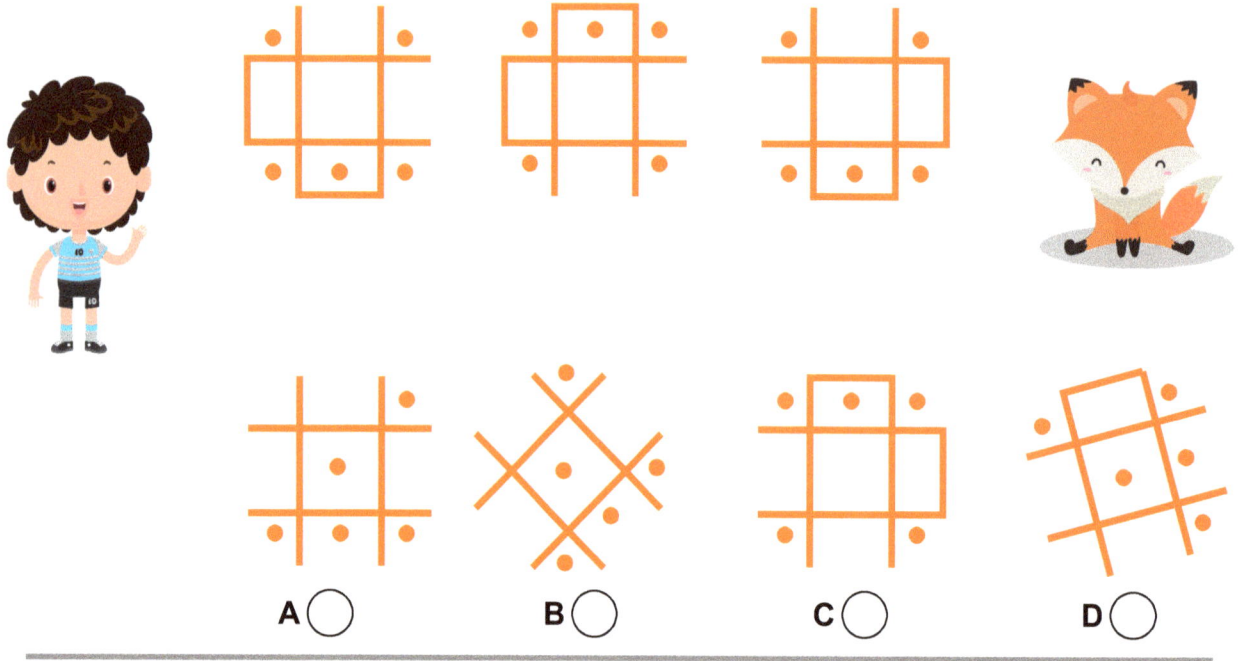

A◯   B◯   C◯   D◯

Q-16

Look at the question with the Giraffe. The first three pictures belong to one group in a common way. Help Mary to find out which of the below options belong to the same group. Identify the correct picture and help her to bubble the right choice.

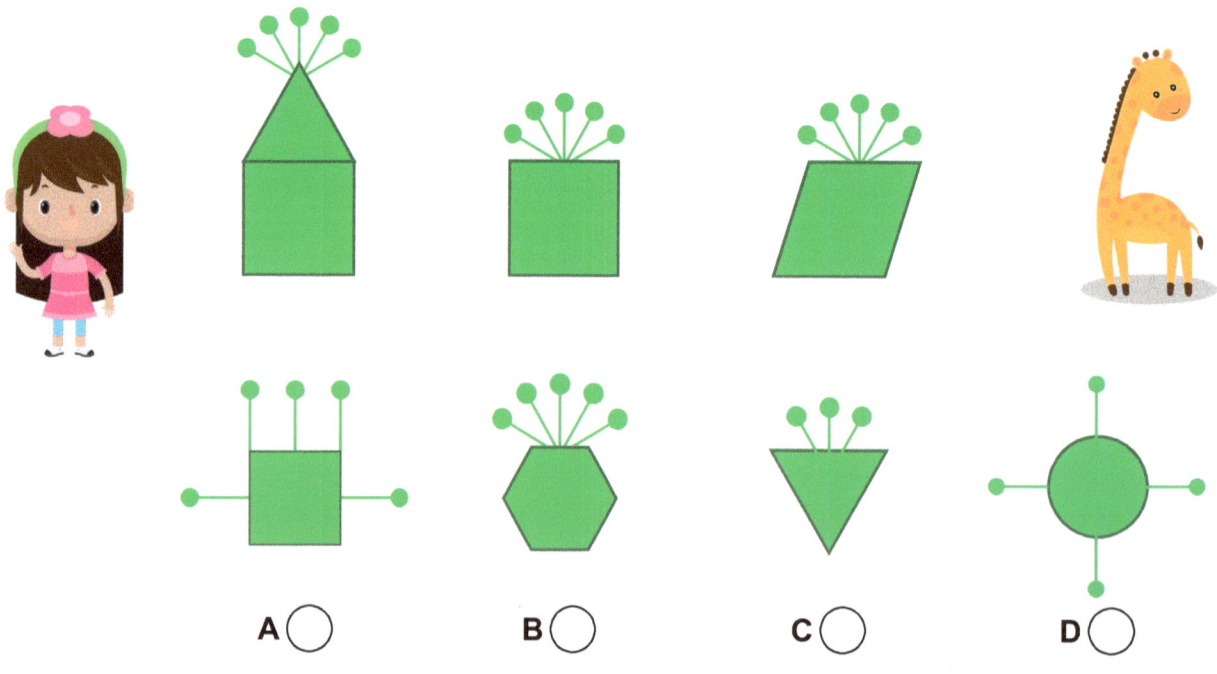

A◯   B◯   C◯   D◯

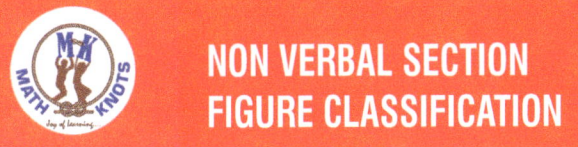
Q-17

Look at the question with the Alligator. The first three pictures belong to one group in a common way. Help David to find out which of the below options belong to the same group. Identify the correct picture and help him to bubble the right choice.

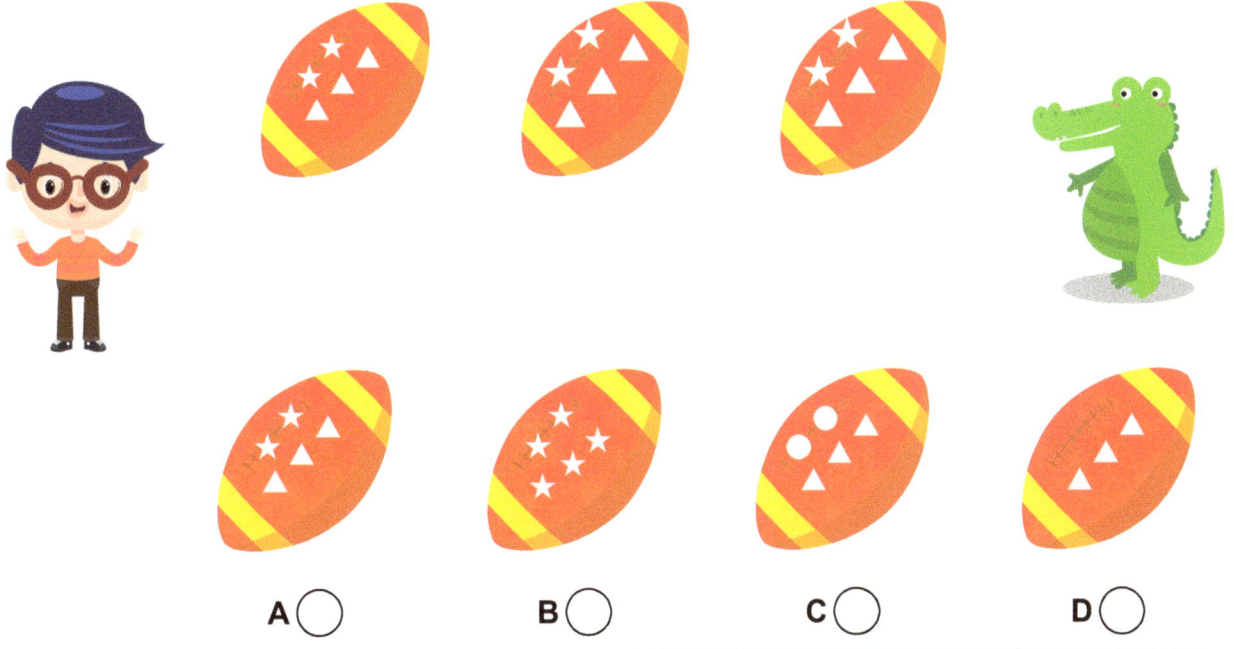

A ◯   B ◯   C ◯   D ◯

Q-18

Look at the question with the Bird. The first three pictures belong to one group in a common way. Help Amy to find out which of the below options belong to the same group. Identify the correct picture and help her to bubble the right choice.

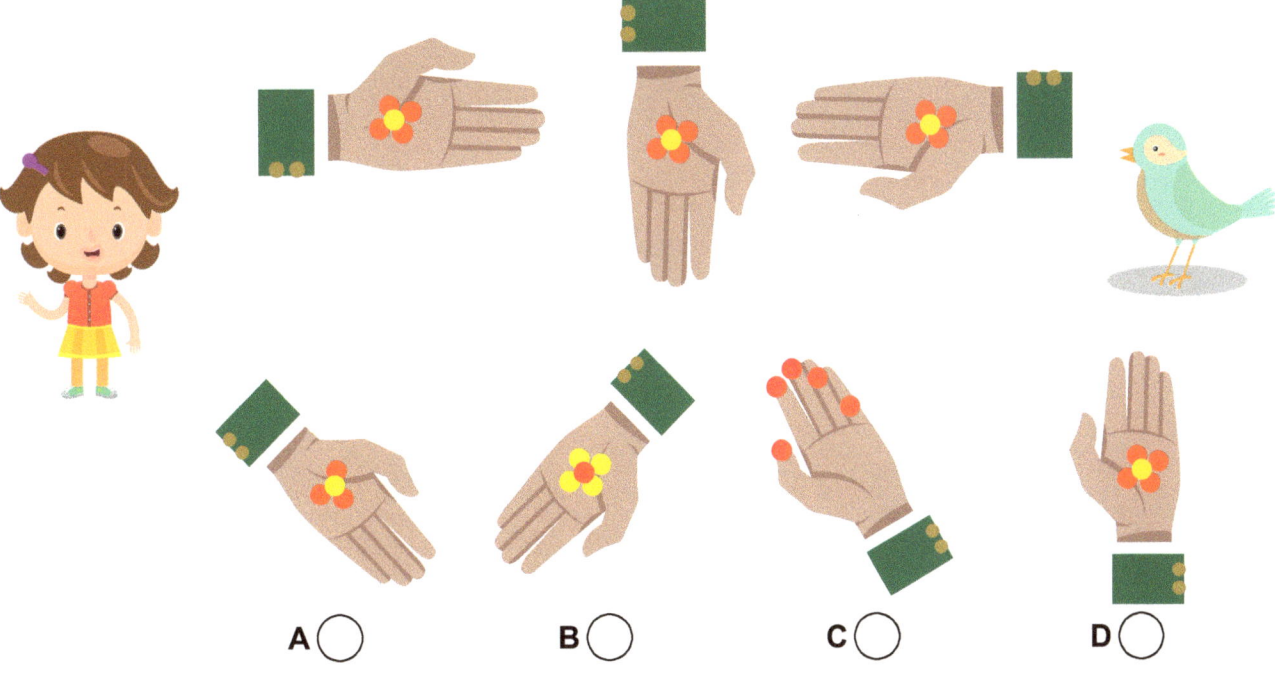

A ◯   B ◯   C ◯   D ◯

www.math-knots.com

TEST - 1

NON VERBAL SECTION

FIGURE MATRICES

Lets Start the Test...

www.math-knots.com

Sample Look at the question with the Grapes. The first row has some thing in common as the second row. Can you help Mary to identify what goes in the space of the question mark from the four given options A, B, C, and D. Choose the correct option.

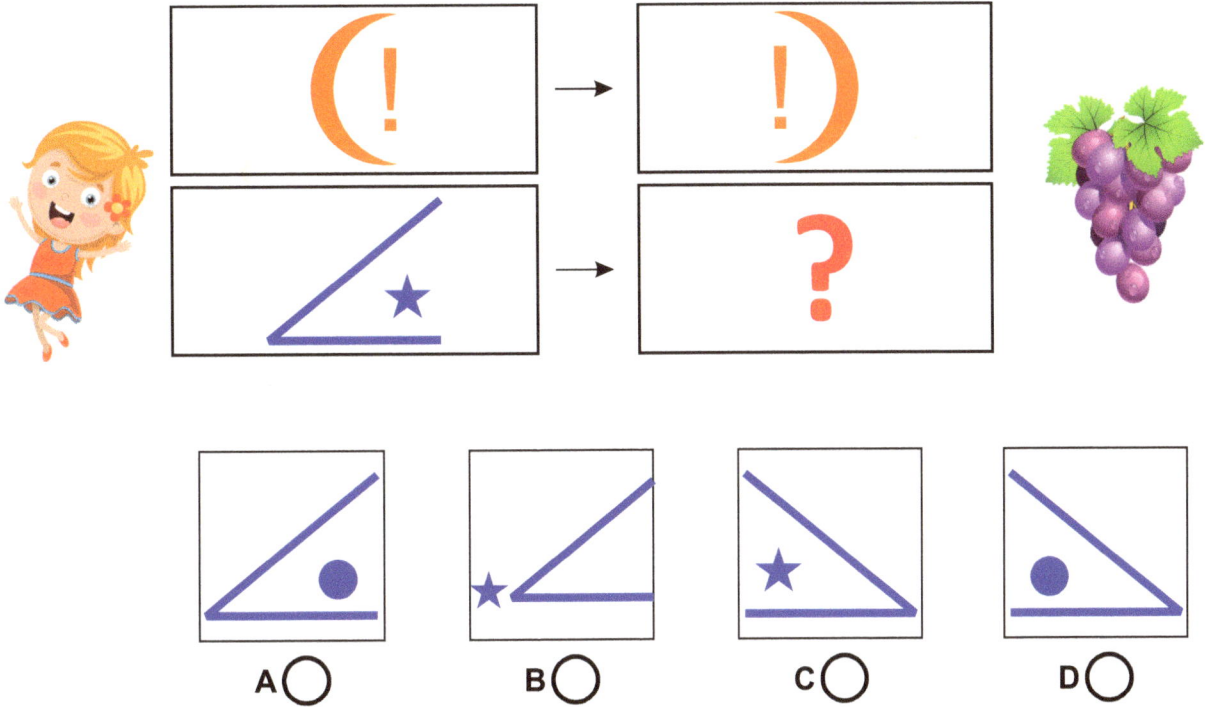

Solution : C

Option C is the right choice.

Two pictures in the first row are related in a certain way and the figures and flipped.

When the picture in the second row is flipped it will be match to option C.

Students need to pay attention. Figures can be turning clock wise into anti clock wise, and other possibilities.

www.math-knots.com

Q-1 Look at the question with the Truck. The first row has some thing in common as the second row. Can you help Diana to identify what goes in the space of the question mark from the four given options A, B, C, and D. Choose the correct option.

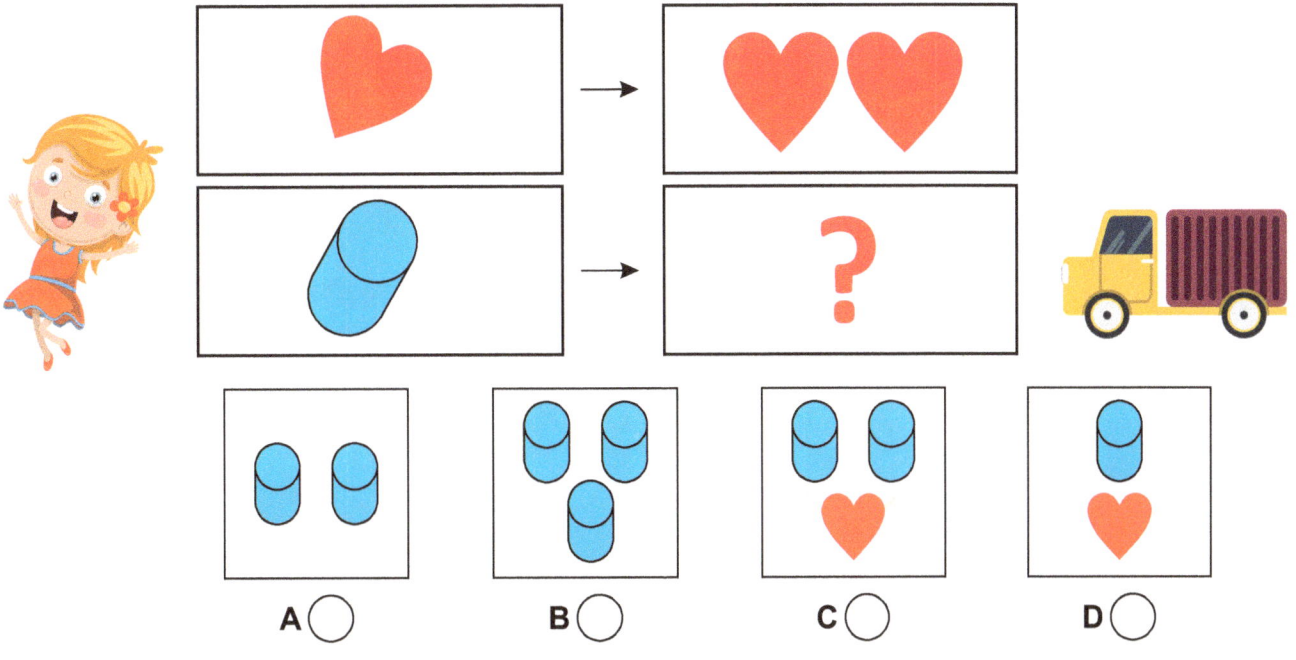

Q-2 Look at the question with the Mini Bus. The first row has some thing in common as the second row. Can you help Maria to identify what goes in the space of the question mark from the four given options A, B, C, and D. Choose the correct option.

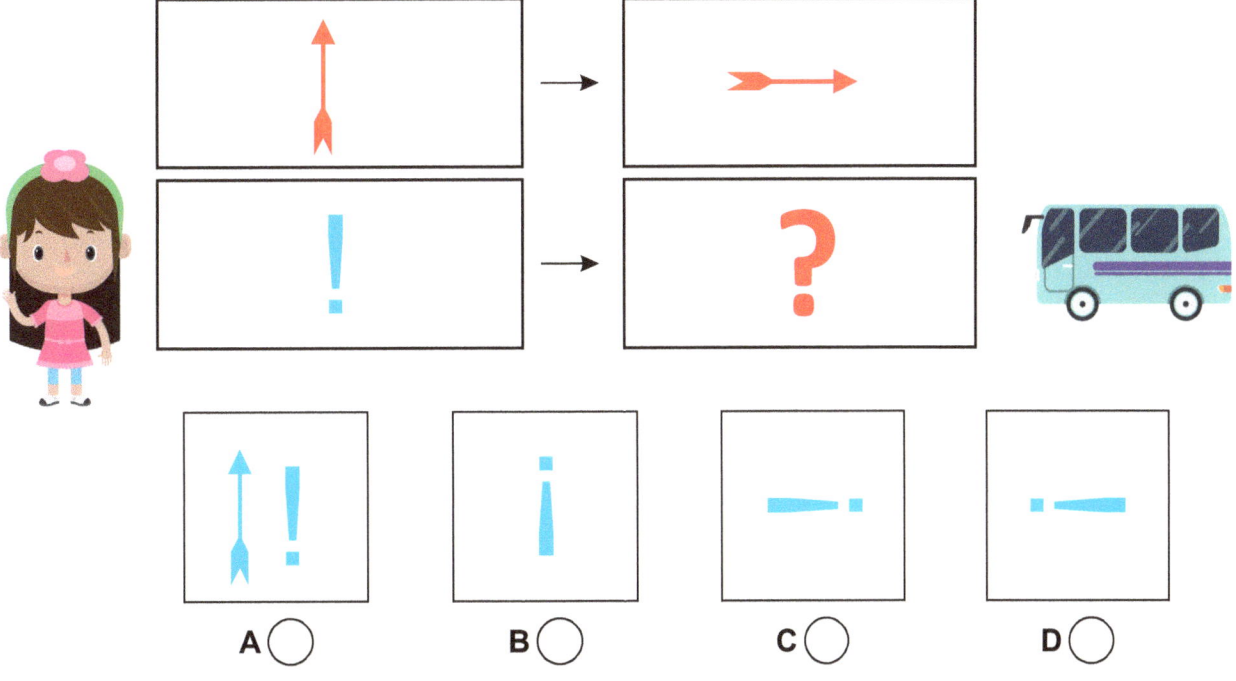

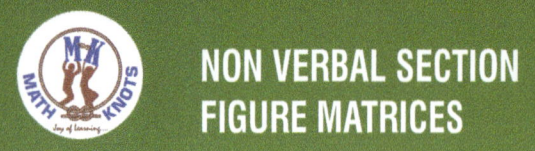

Q-3

Look at the question with the Jeep. The first row has some thing in common as the second row. Can you help George to identify what goes in the space of the question mark from the four given options A, B, C, and D. Choose the correct option.

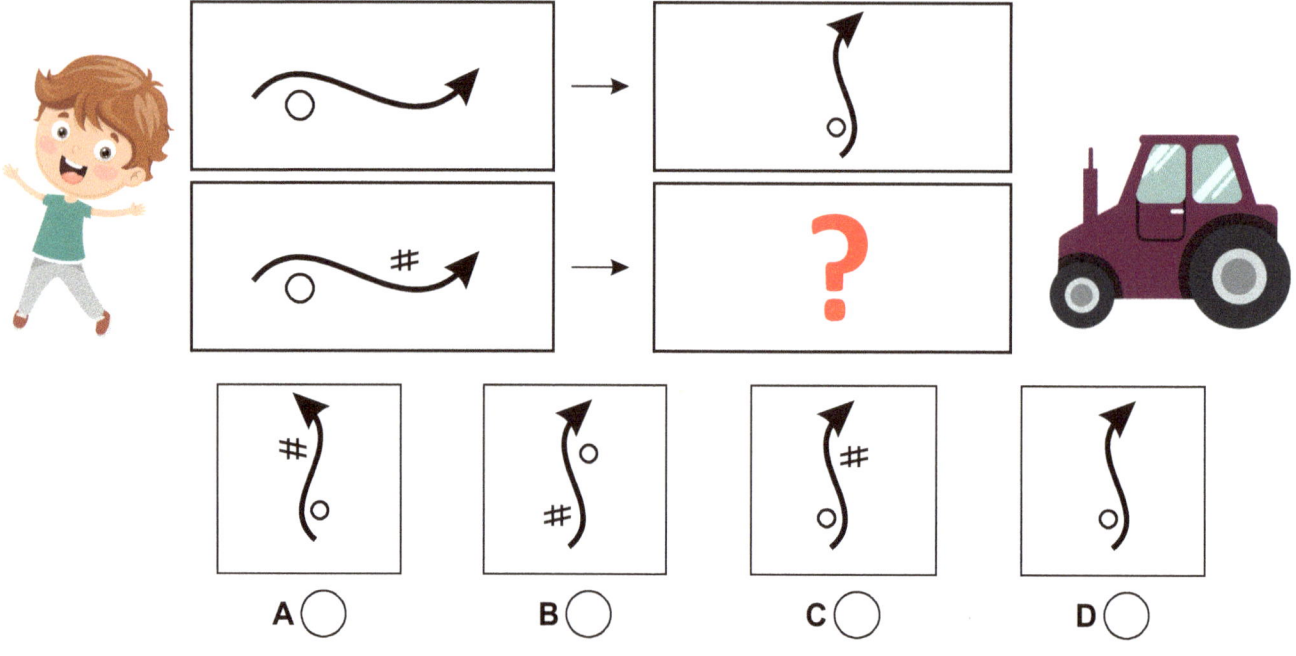

Q-4

Look at the question with the Train. The first row has some thing in common as the second row. Can you help Bryan to identify what goes in the space of the question mark from the four given options A, B, C, and D. Choose the correct option.

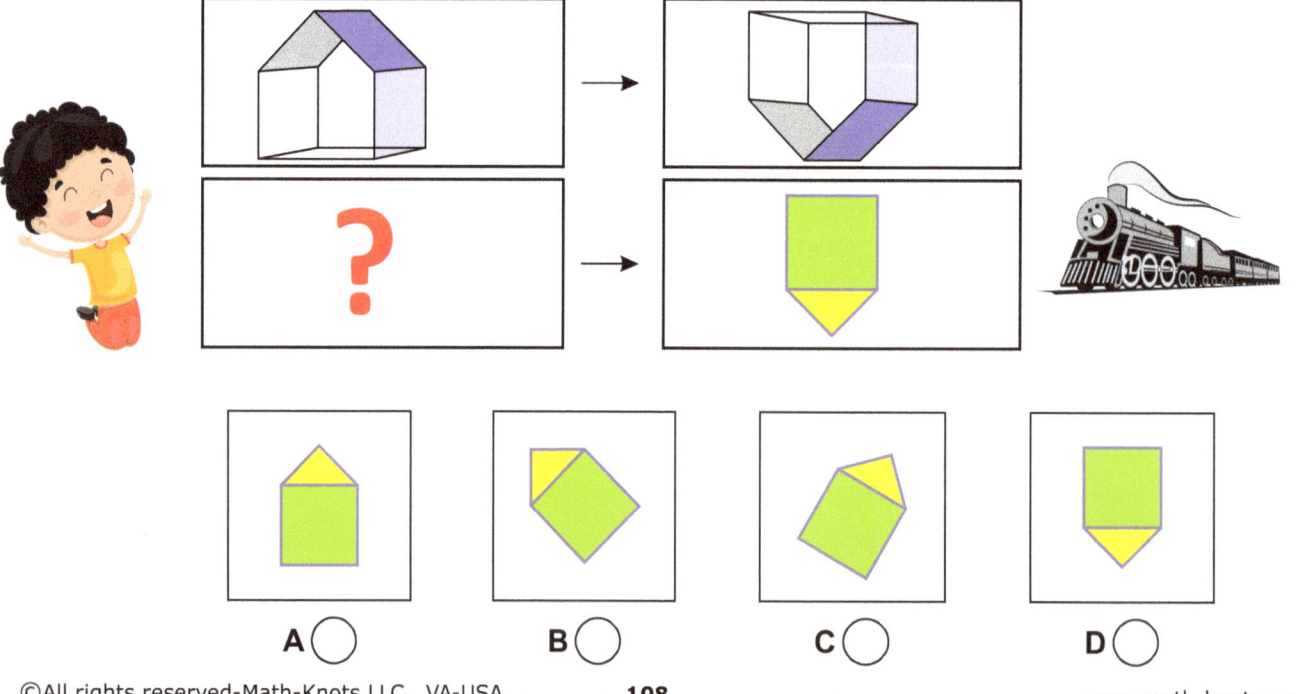

www.math-knots.com

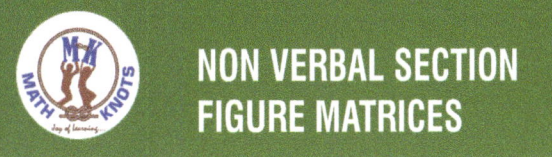
Q-5 Look at the question with the Oil Tanker . The first row has some thing in common as the second row. Can you help Ria to identify what goes in the space of the question mark from the four given options A, B, C, and D. Choose the correct option.

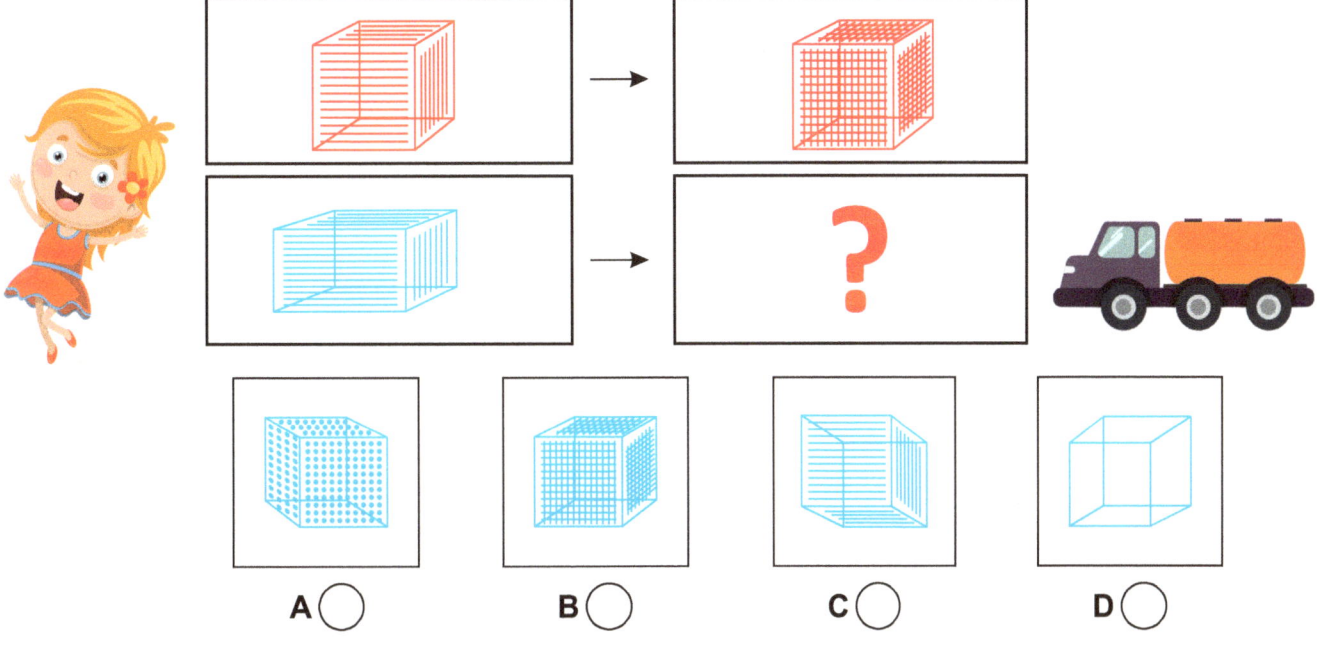

Q-6 Look at the question with the Ship. The first row has some thing in common as the second row. Can you help Julie to identify what goes in the space of the question mark from the four given options A, B, C, and D. Choose the correct option.

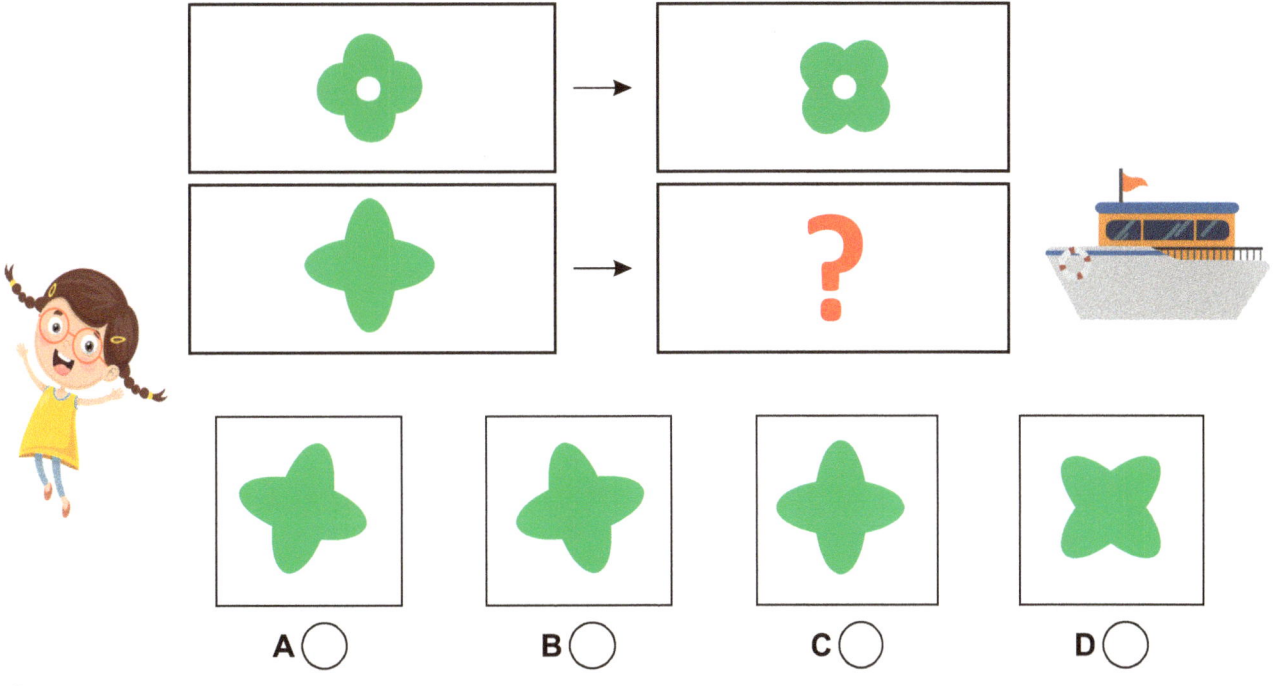

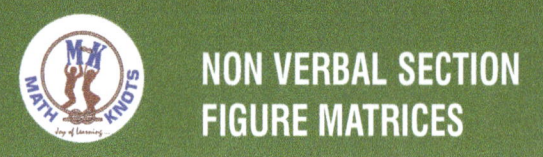
Q-7 Look at the question with the Fire Engine truck. The first row has some thing in common as the second row. Can you help Aryan to identify what goes in the space of the question mark from the four given options A, B, C, and D. Choose the correct option.

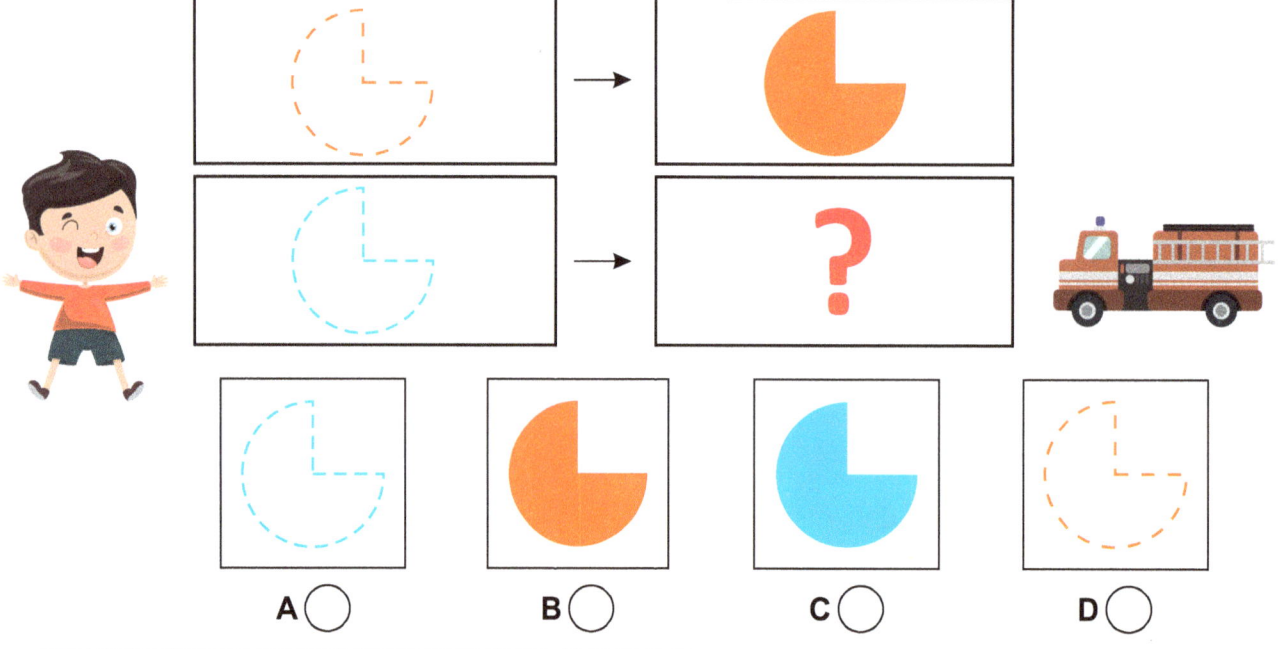

A ◯   B ◯   C ◯   D ◯

Q-8 Look at the question with the Crane. The first row has some thing in common as the second row. Can you help Mike to identify what goes in the space of the question mark from the four given options A, B, C, and D. Choose the correct option.

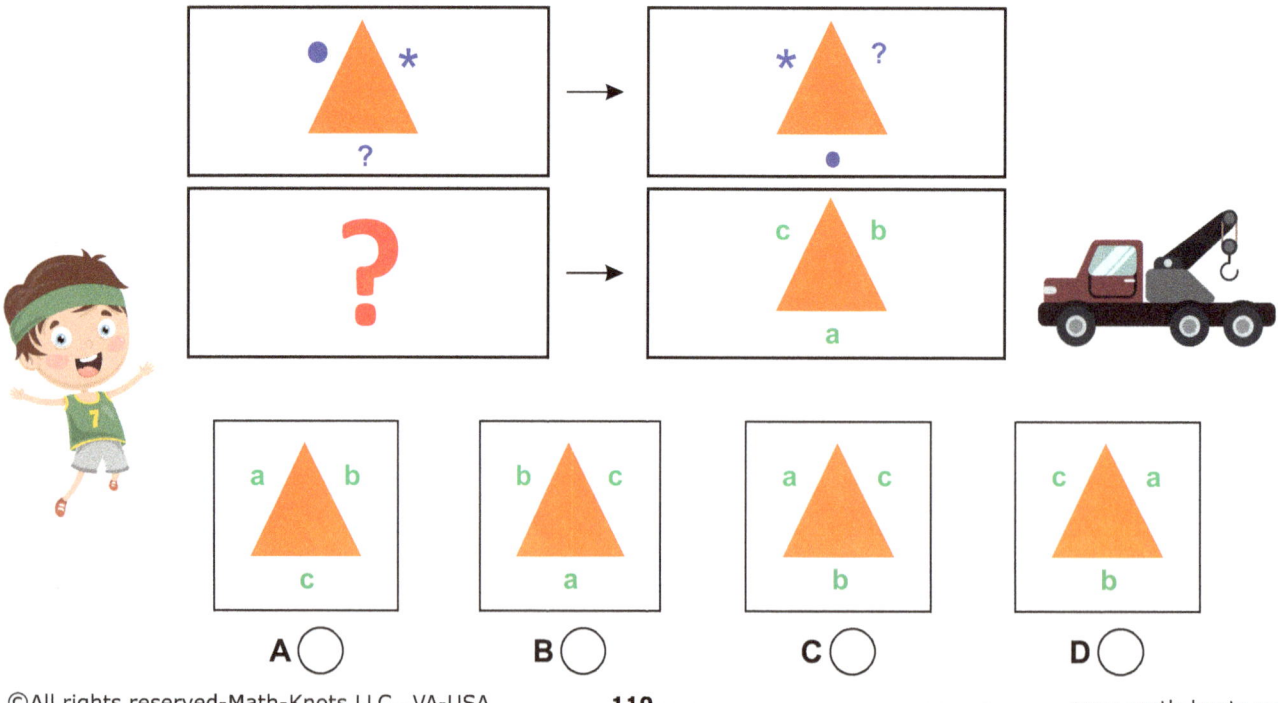

A ◯   B ◯   C ◯   D ◯

www.math-knots.com

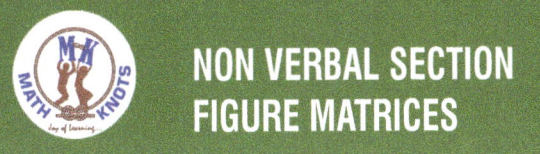

Q-9

Look at the question with the Bus. The first row has some thing in common as the second row. Can you help Cathy to identify what goes in the space of the question mark from the four given options A, B, C, and D. Choose the correct option.

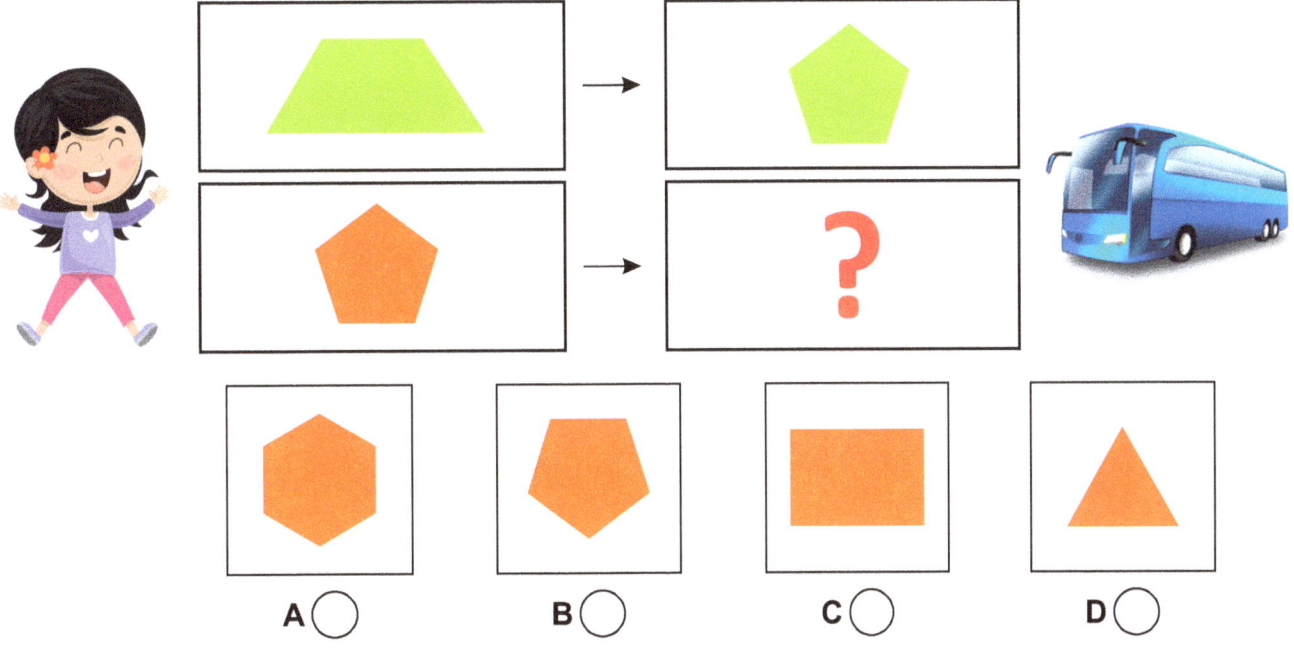

Q-10

Look at the question with the Scooter. The first row has some thing in common as the second row. Can you help Jason to identify what goes in the space of the question mark from the four given options A, B, C, and D. Choose the correct option.

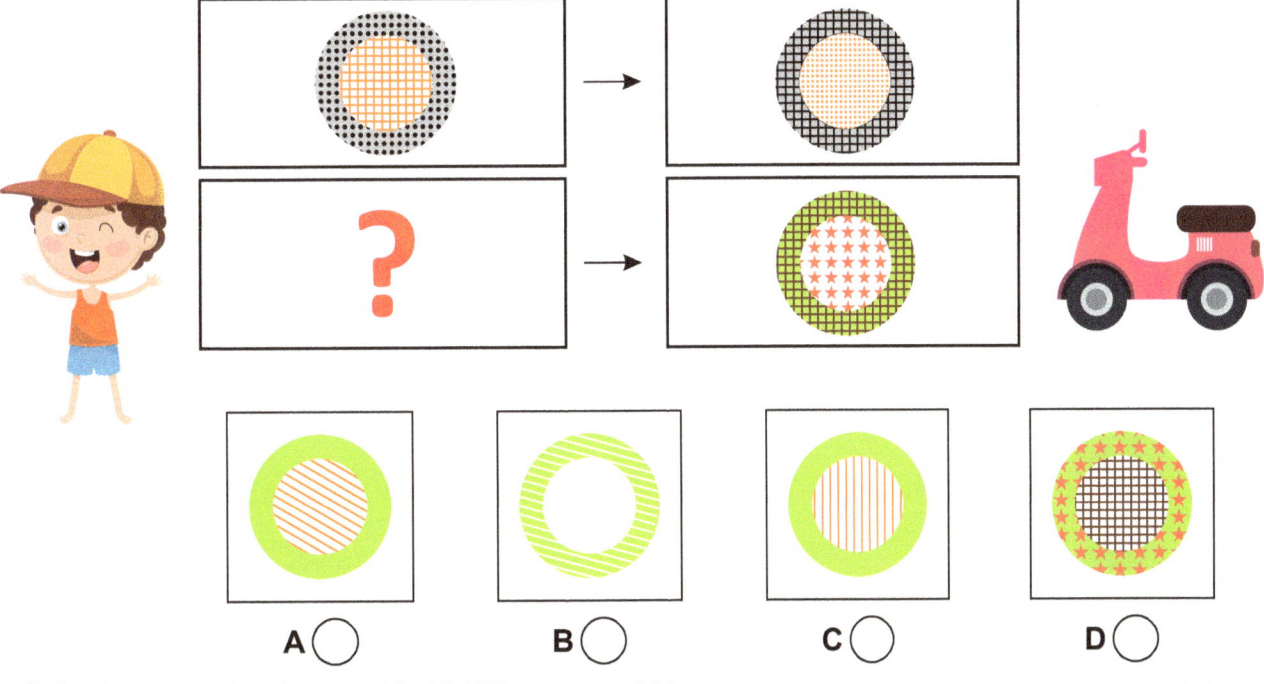

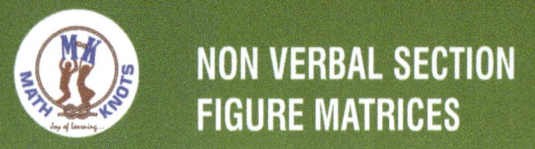

Q-11

Look at the question with the Bicycle. The first row has some thing in common as the second row. Can you help David to identify what goes in the space of the question mark from the four given options A, B, C, and D. Choose the correct option.

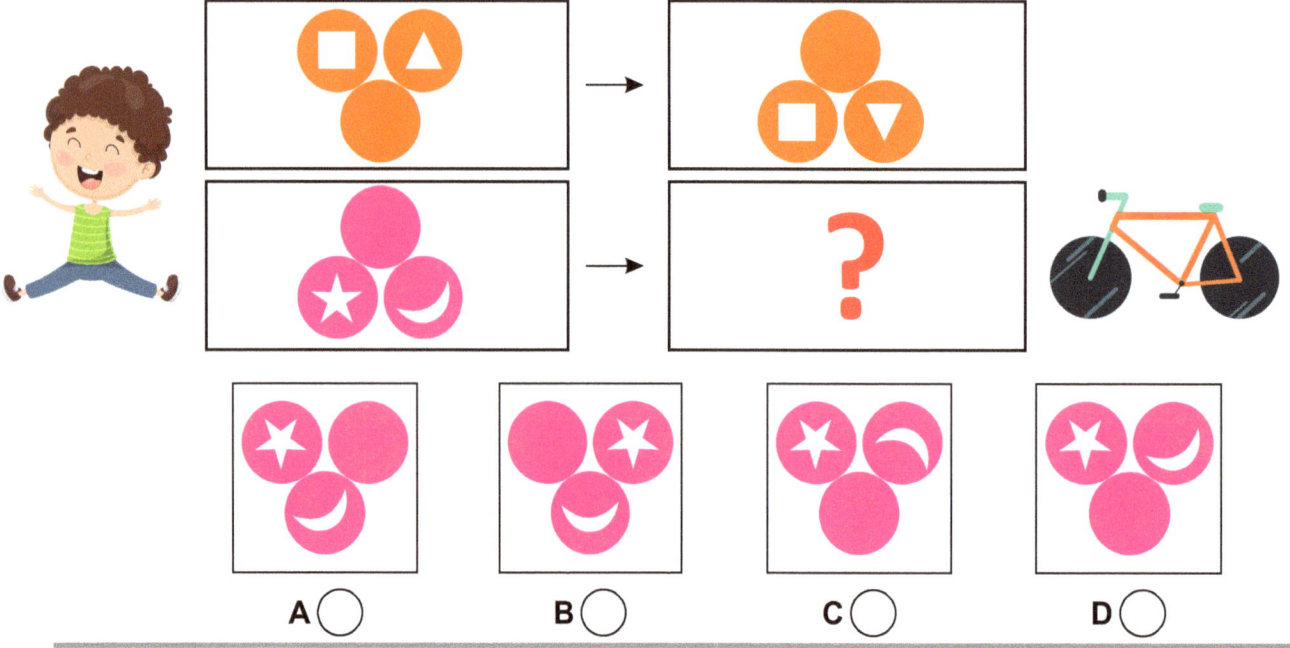

A ◯   B ◯   C ◯   D ◯

Q-12

Look at the question with the Hot Air Balloon. The first row has some thing in common as the second row. Can you help Mary to identify what goes in the space of the question mark from the four given options A, B, C, and D. Choose the correct option.

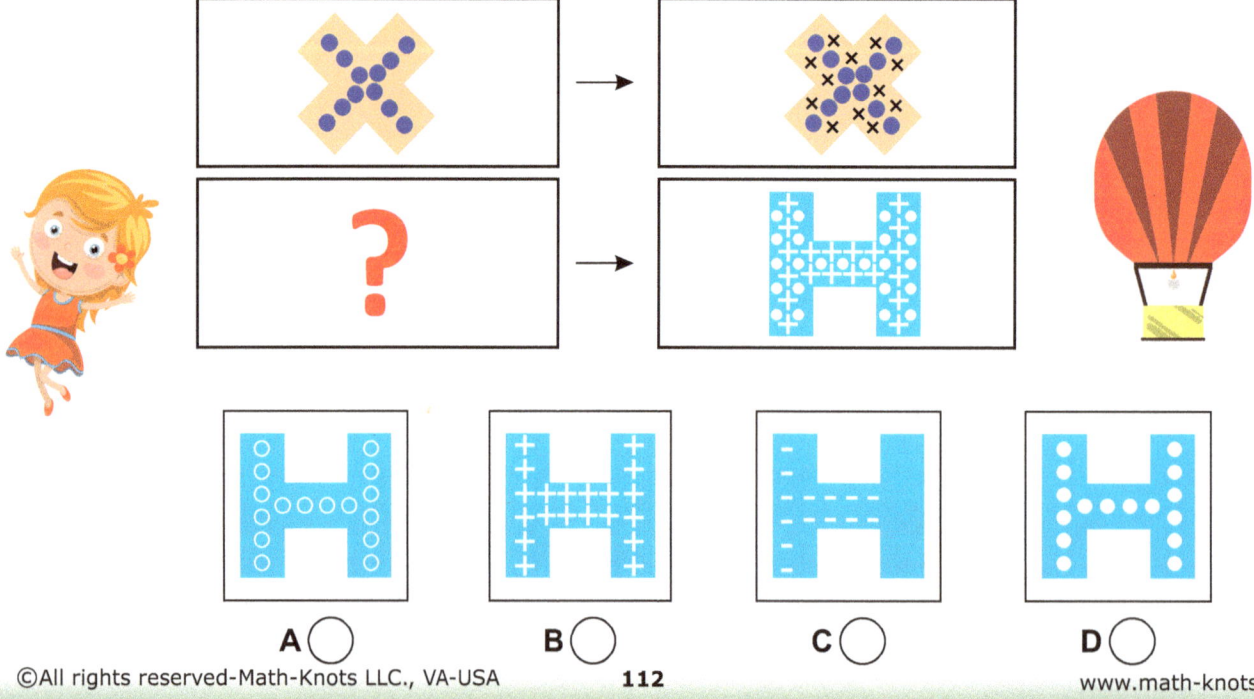

A ◯   B ◯   C ◯   D ◯

www.math-knots.com

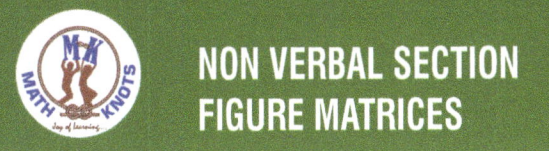

Q-13

Look at the question with the Car. The first row has some thing in common as the second row. Can you help Oscar to identify what goes in the space of the question mark from the four given options A, B, C, and D. Choose the correct option.

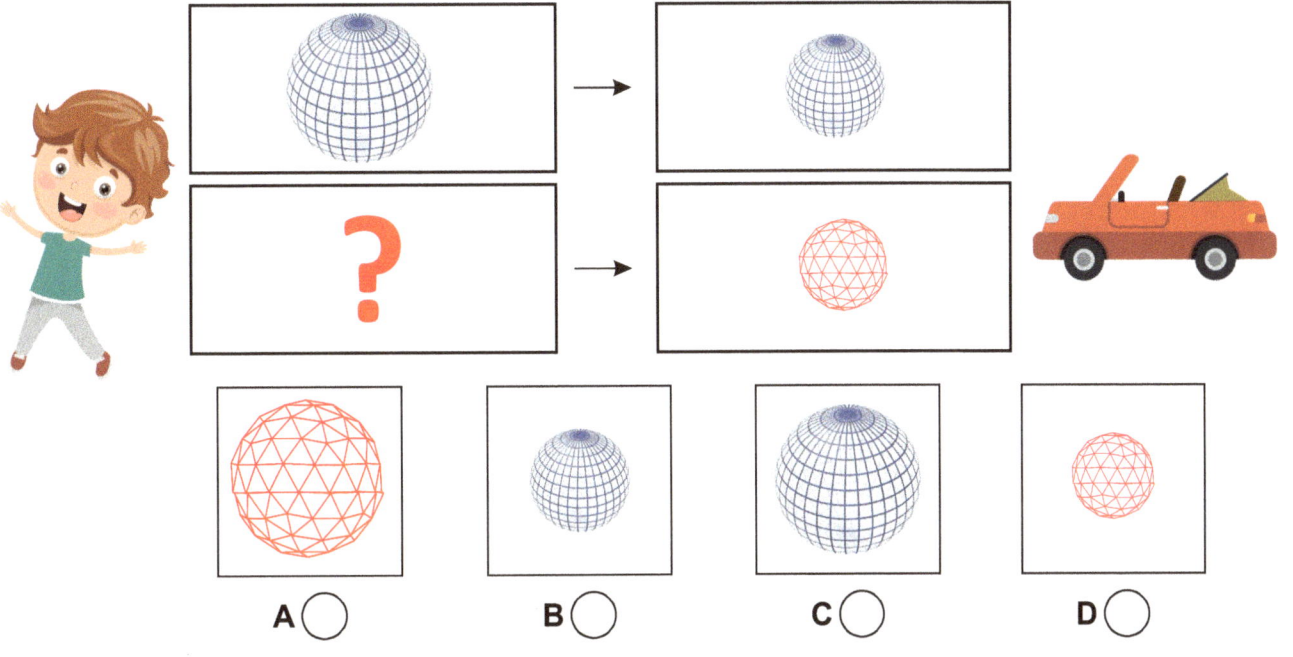

A ○   B ○   C ○   D ○

Q-14

Look at the question with the Cement Mixer. The first row has some thing in common as the second row. Can you help Grace to identify what goes in the space of the question mark from the four given options A, B, C, and D. Choose the correct option.

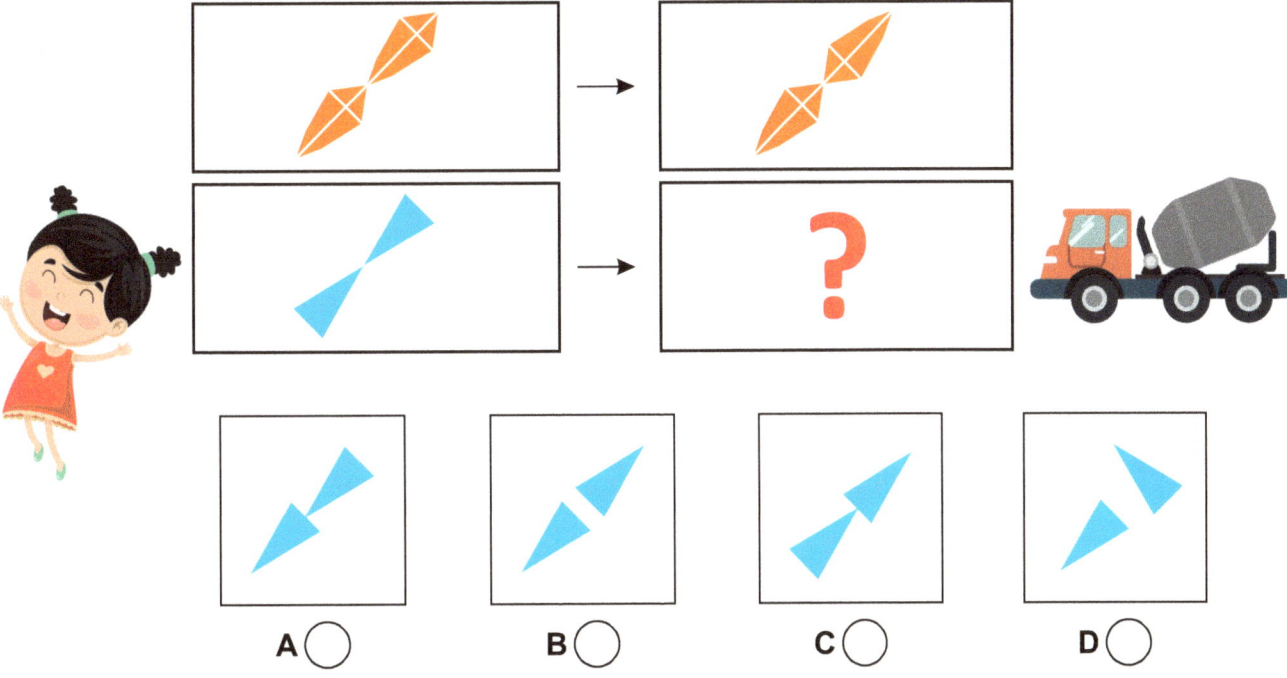

A ○   B ○   C ○   D ○

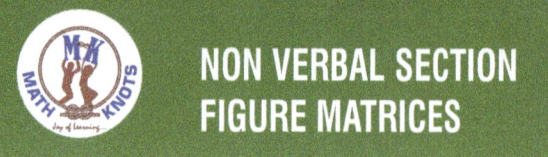

Q-15

Look at the question with the Mini Truck. The first row has some thing in common as the second row. Can you help Wesley to identify what goes in the space of the question mark from the four given options A, B, C, and D. Choose the correct option.

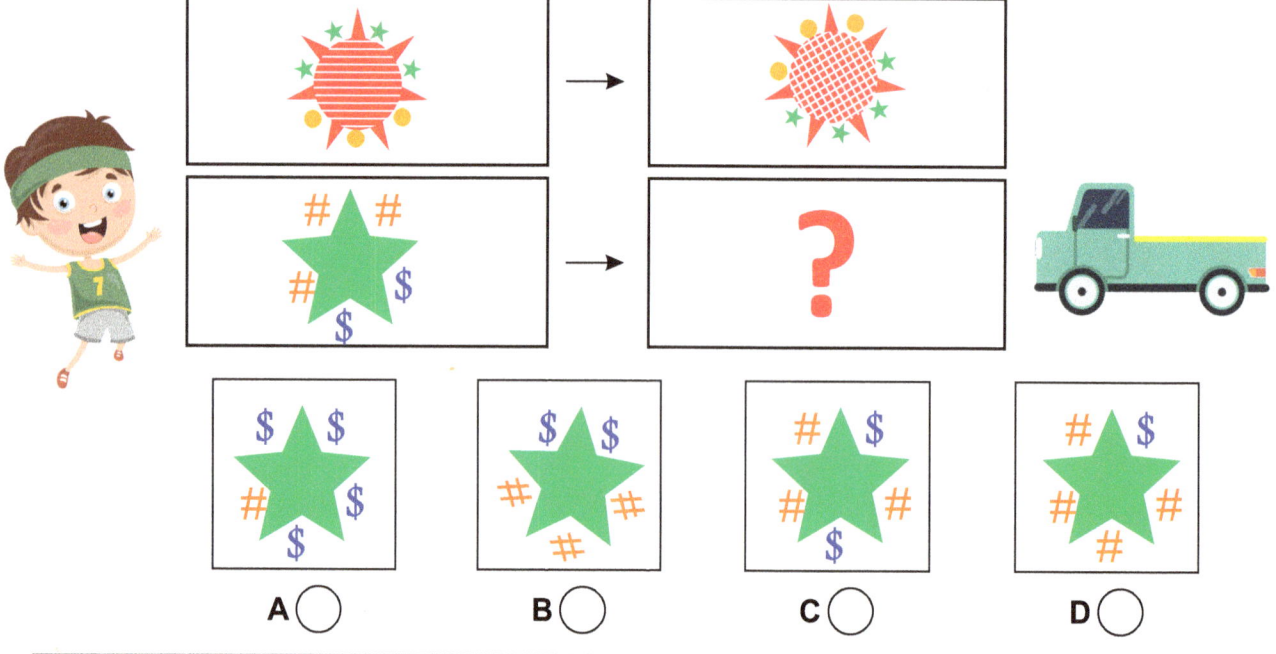

A ◯   B ◯   C ◯   D ◯

Q-16

Look at the question with the Helicopter. The first row has some thing in common as the second row. Can you help Jack to identify what goes in the space of the question mark from the four given options A, B, C, and D. Choose the correct option.

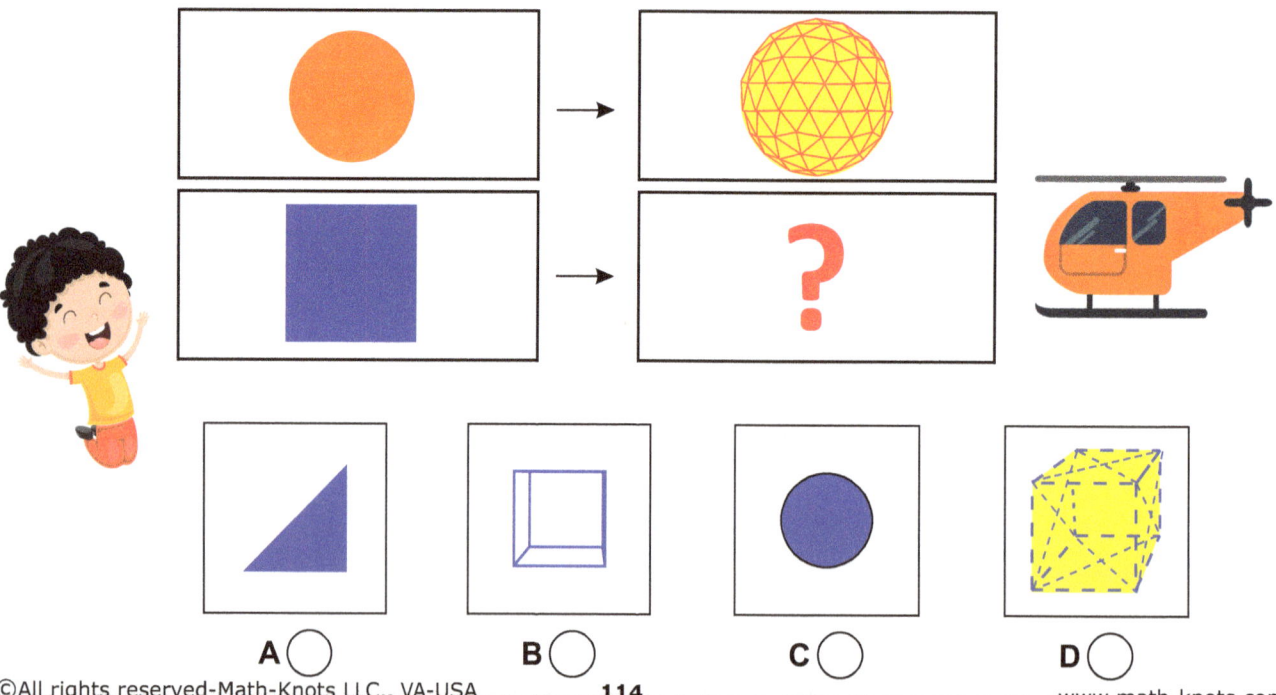

A ◯   B ◯   C ◯   D ◯

www.math-knots.com

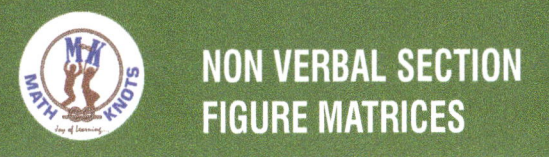

Q-17

Look at the question with the Aeroplane. The first row has some thing in common as the second row. Can you help Owen to identify what goes in the space of the question mark from the four given options A, B, C, and D. Choose the correct option.

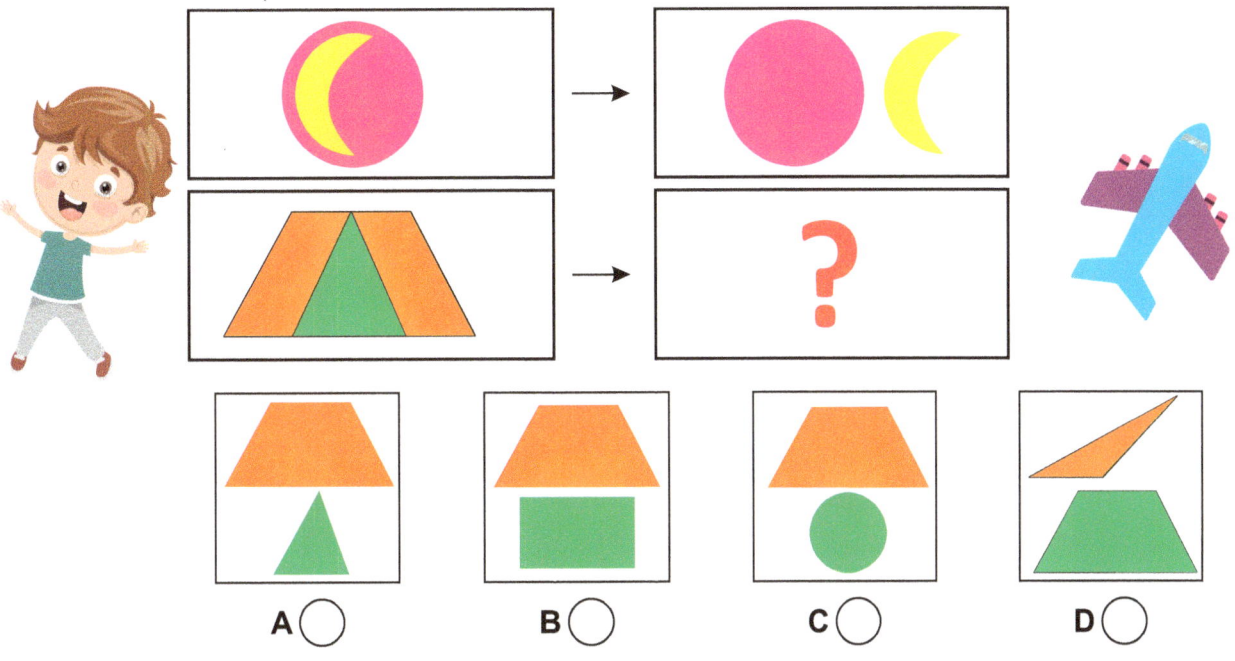

Q-18

Look at the question with the Ambulance. The first row has some thing in common as the second row. Can you help Rita to identify what goes in the space of the question mark from the four given options A, B, C, and D. Choose the correct option.

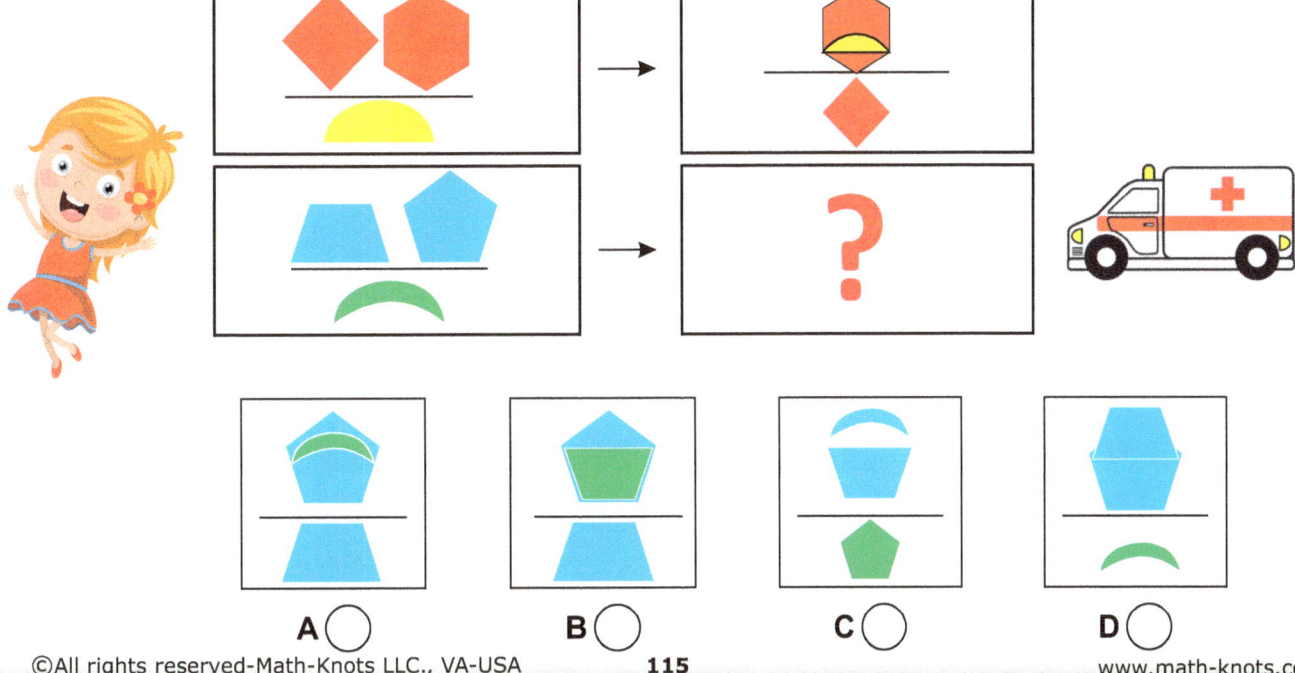

www.math-knots.com

www.math-knots.com

TEST - 1

NON VERBAL SECTION

PAPER FOLDING

Lets Start the Test...

www.math-knots.com

Sample

Look at the question and put your finger on Bee. Amy folded the paper and made holes to it as shown. When the paper is unfolded how does it look? Help her bubble the right option.

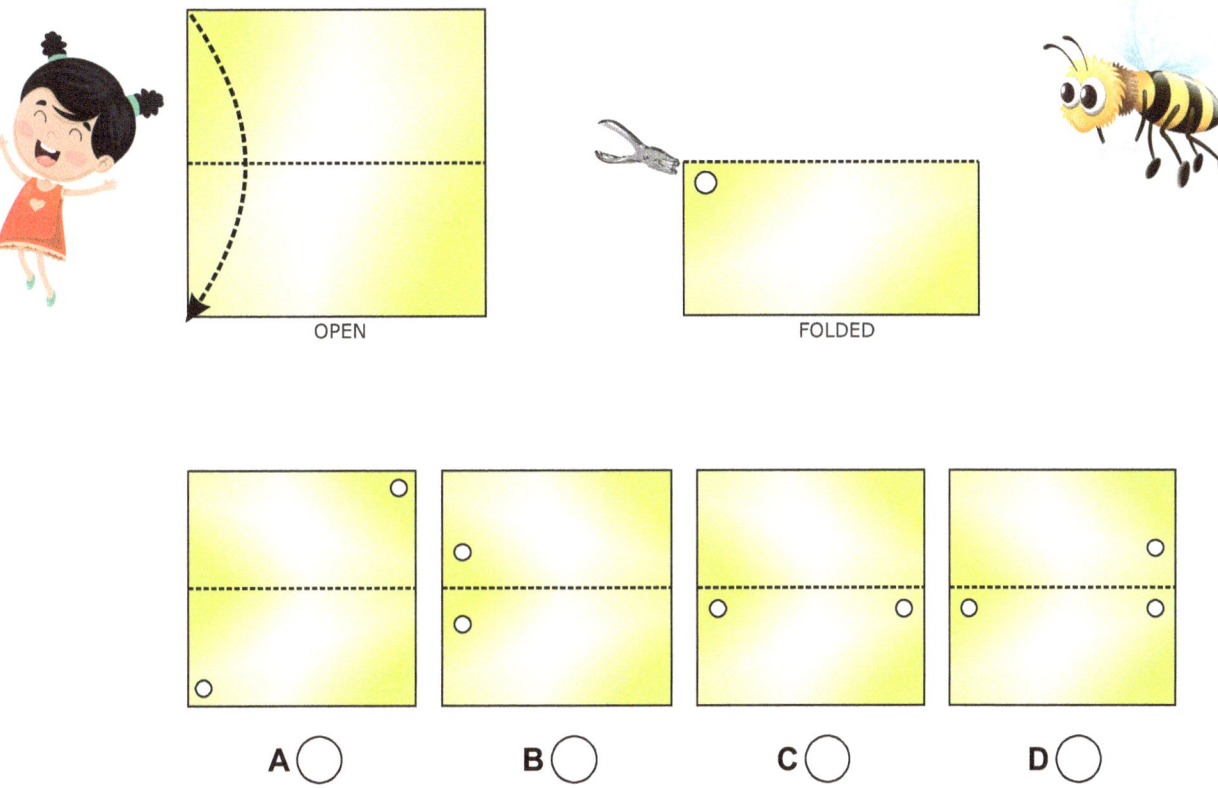

OPEN   FOLDED

A ◯   B ◯   C ◯   D ◯

Solution : B

A rectangle is folded once and hole is punched on top left corner. After punching the figure is unfolded the holes are shown in the middle left corner as shown in option B. Student choses the right option and fills the bubble completely.

www.math-knots.com

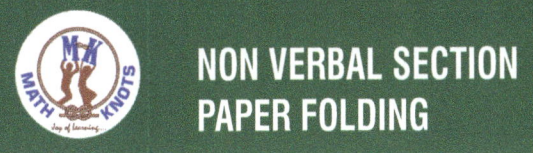

Q-1 Look at the question and put your finger on Star. Jack folded the paper and made holes to it as shown. When the paper is unfolded how does it look? Help him bubble the right option.

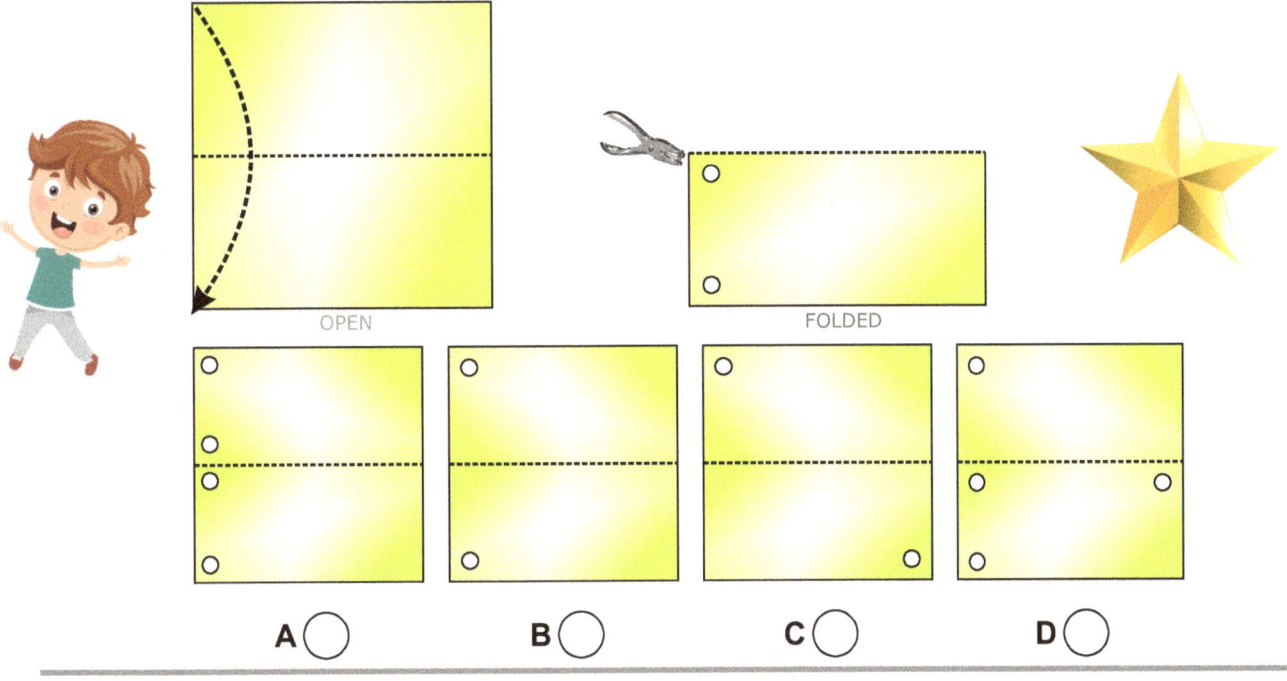

OPEN   FOLDED

A ◯   B ◯   C ◯   D ◯

Q-2 Look at the question and put your finger on Moon. Dora folded the paper and made holes to it as shown. When the paper is unfolded how does it look? Help her bubble the right option.

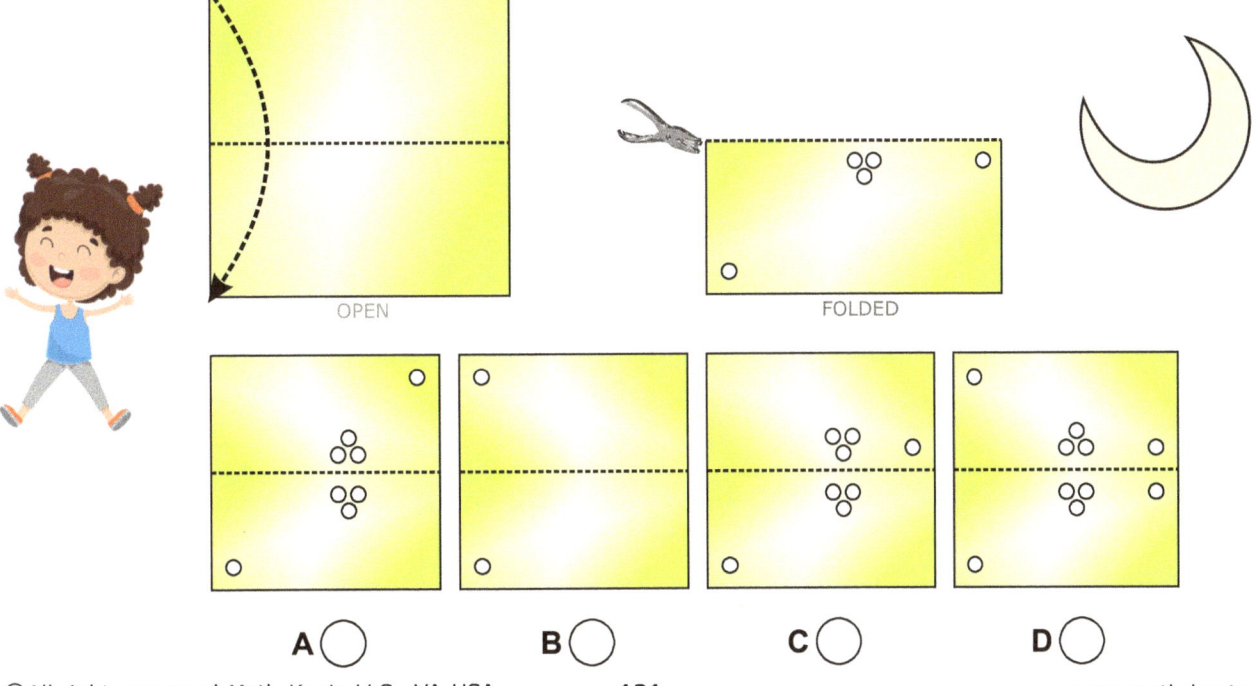

OPEN   FOLDED

A ◯   B ◯   C ◯   D ◯

www.math-knots.com

Q-3 Look at the question and put your finger on Sun. Johnson folded the paper and made holes to it as shown. When the paper is unfolded how does it look? Help him bubble the right option.

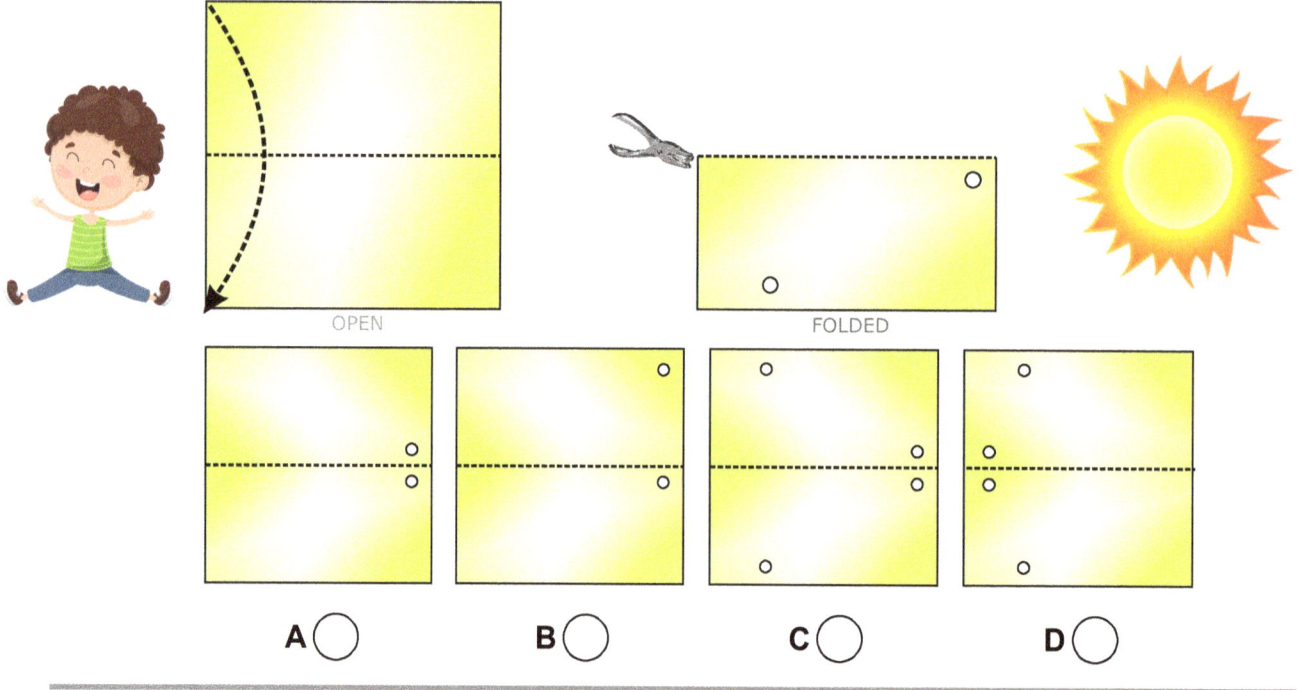

OPEN   FOLDED

A◯   B◯   C◯   D◯

Q-4 Look at the question and put your finger on Satellite. Emma folded the paper and made holes to it as shown. When the paper is unfolded how does it look? Help her bubble the right option.

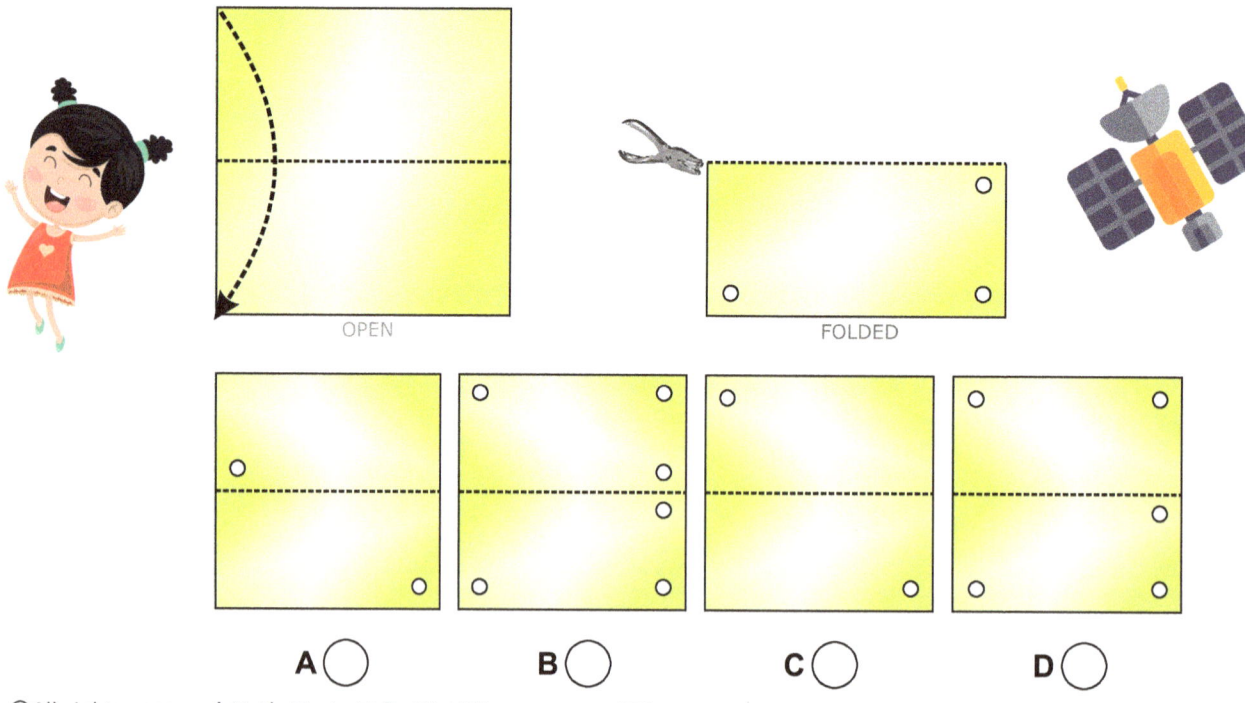

OPEN   FOLDED

A◯   B◯   C◯   D◯

www.math-knots.com

Q-5

Look at the question and put your finger on Rocket. Daniel folded the paper and made hole to it as shown. When the paper is unfolded how does it look? Help him bubble the right option.

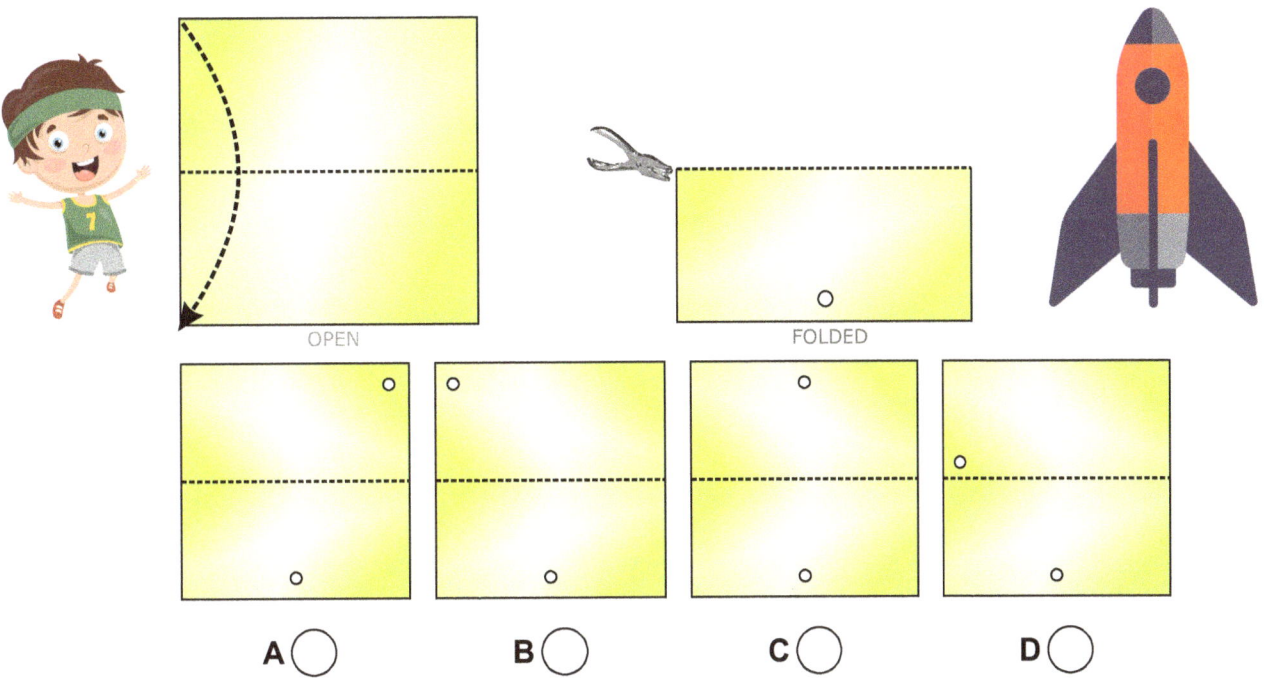

OPEN

FOLDED

A ◯   B ◯   C ◯   D ◯

Q-6

Look at the question and put your finger on Bulb. Emily folded the paper and made holes to it as shown. When the paper is unfolded how does it look? Help her bubble the right option.

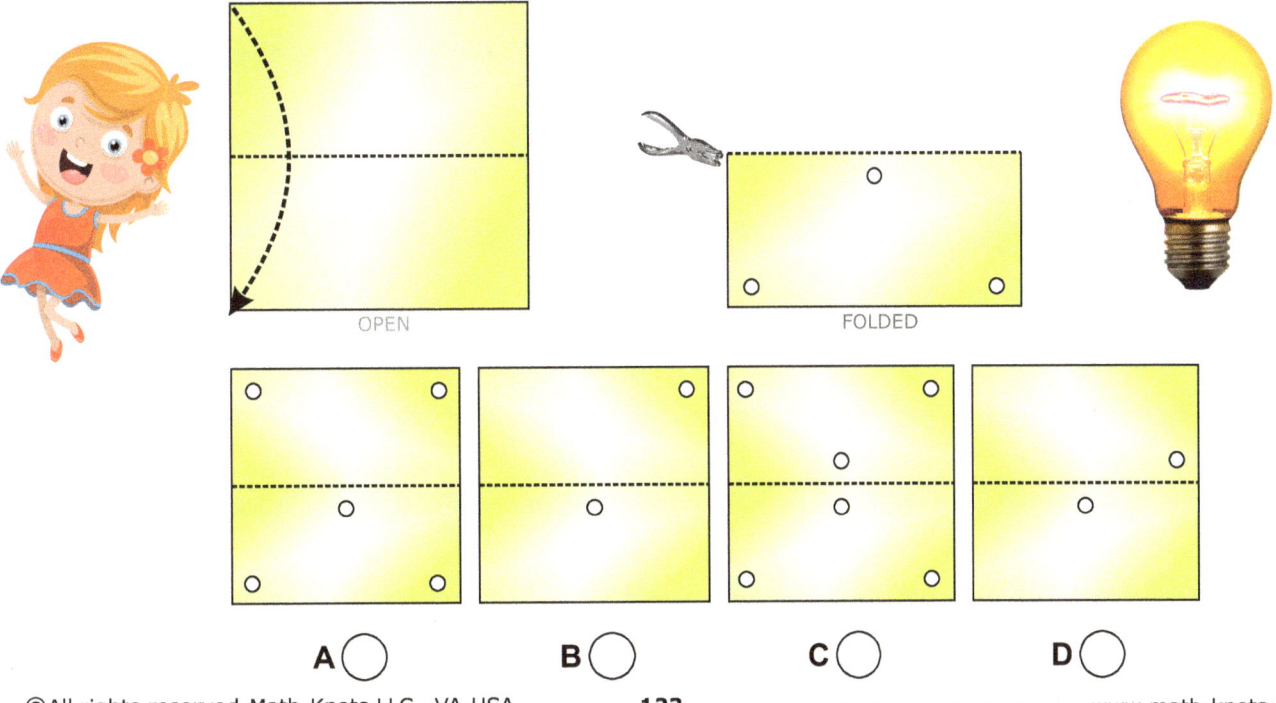

OPEN

FOLDED

A ◯   B ◯   C ◯   D ◯

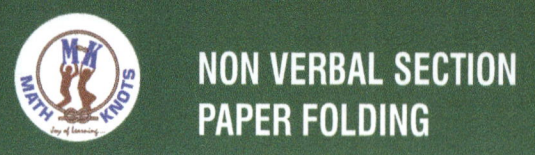

Q-7 Look at the question and put your finger on Satellite. Michael folded the paper and made holes to it as shown. When the paper is unfolded how does it look? Help him bubble the right option.

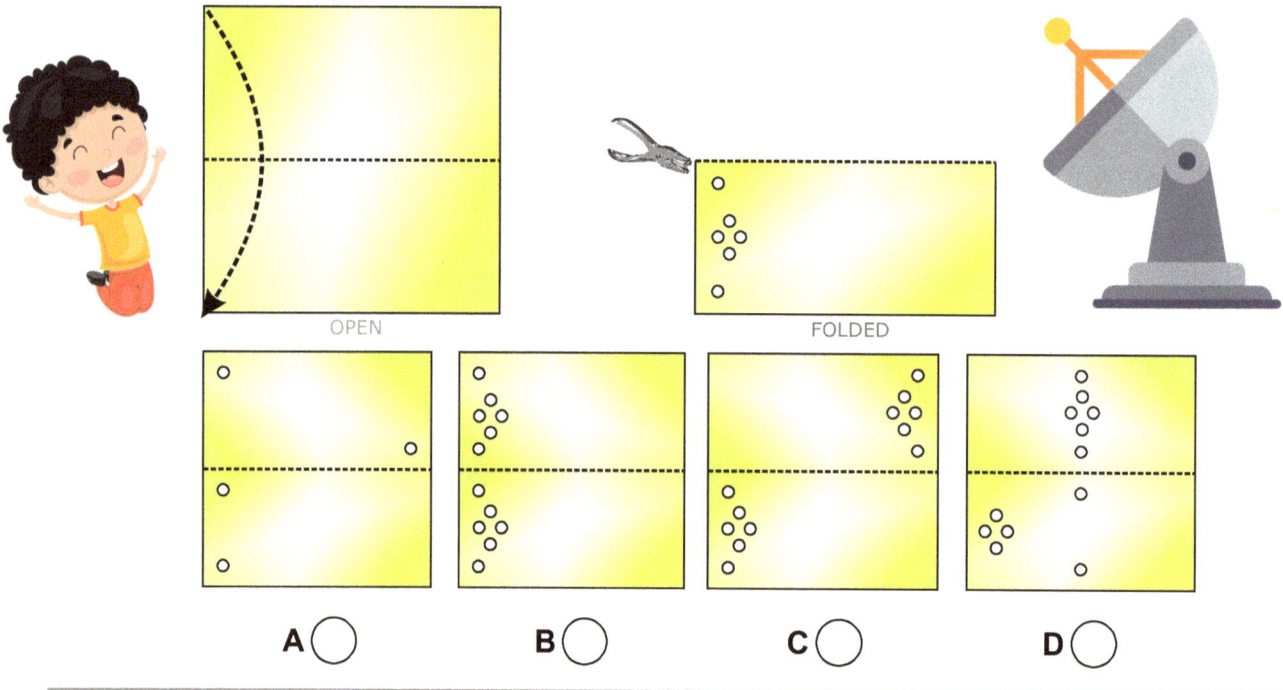

A ◯   B ◯   C ◯   D ◯

Q-8 Look at the question and put your finger on Telescope. Kathy folded the paper and made holes to it as shown. When the paper is unfolded how does it look? Help her bubble the right option.

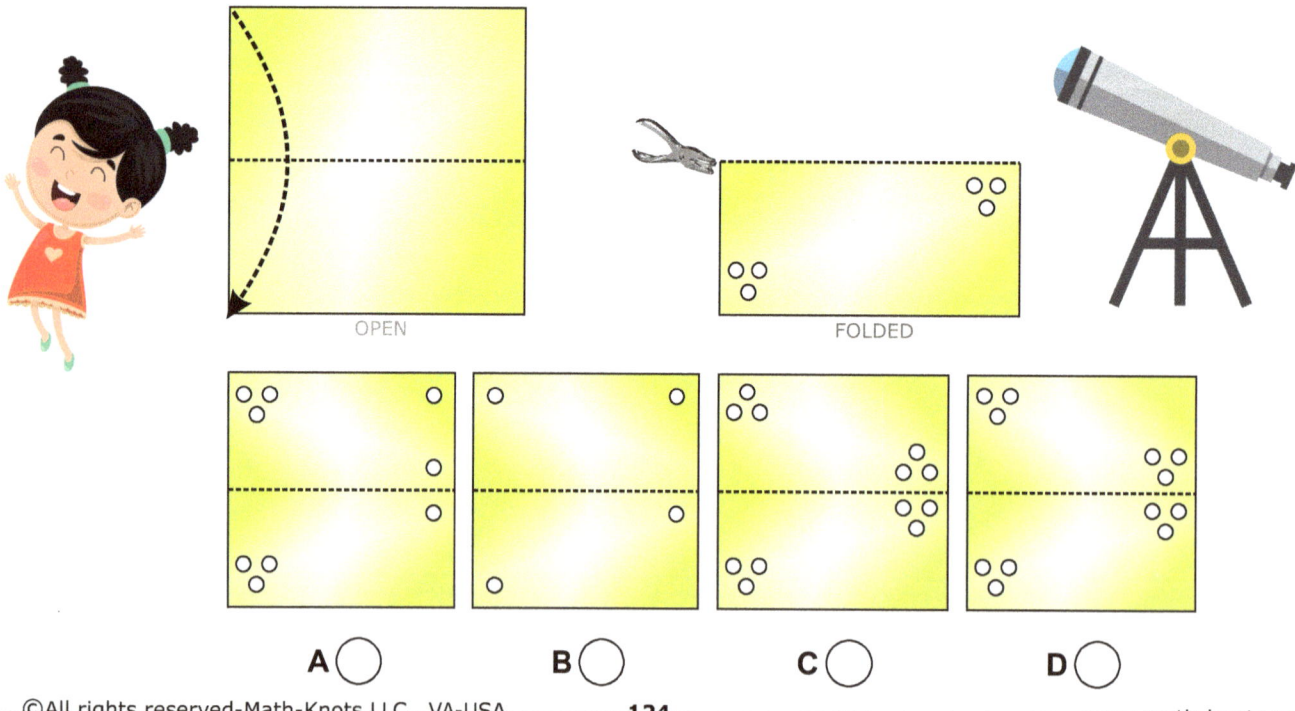

A ◯   B ◯   C ◯   D ◯

www.math-knots.com

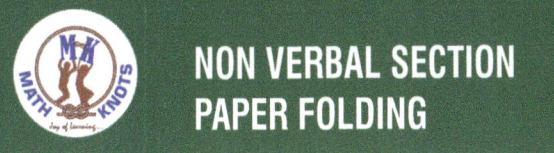

Q-9

Look at the question and put your finger on Globe. Madison folded the paper and made holes to it as shown. When the paper is unfolded how does it look? Help her bubble the right option.

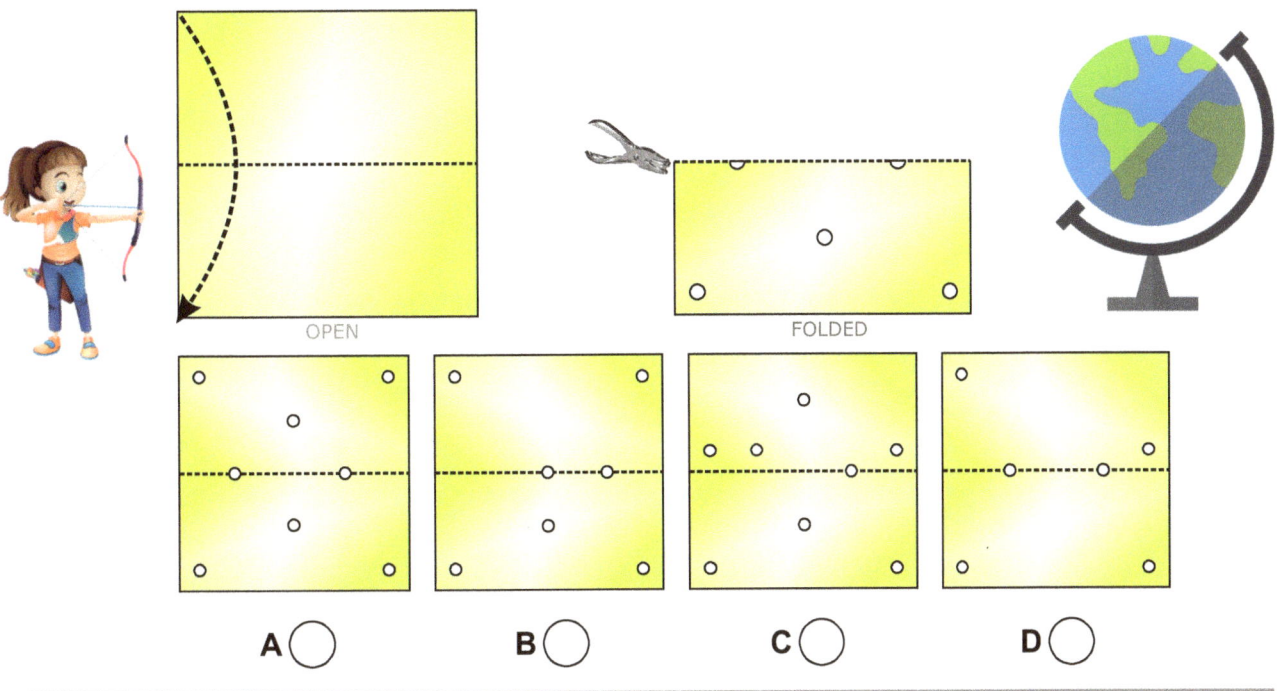

A ◯   B ◯   C ◯   D ◯

Q-10

Look at the question and put your finger on Saturn. Ryan folded the paper and made holes to it as shown. When the paper is unfolded how does it look? Help him bubble the right option.

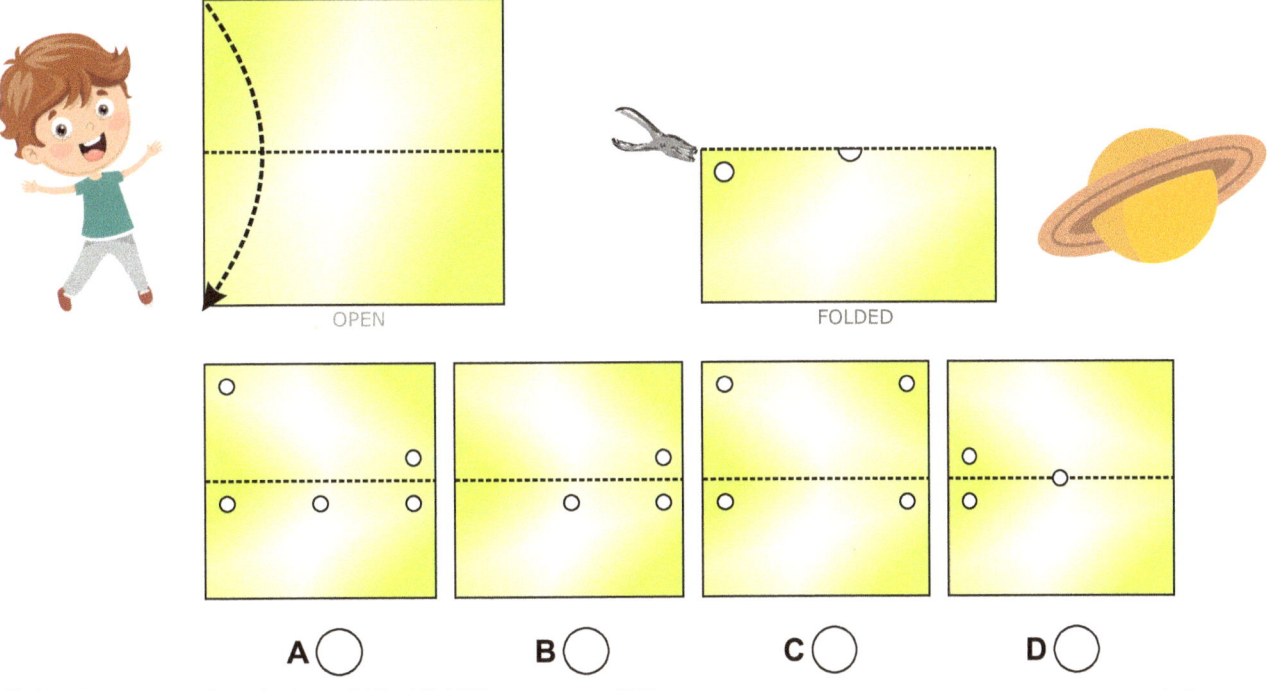

A ◯   B ◯   C ◯   D ◯

www.math-knots.com

Q-11

Look at the question and put your finger on Thermometer. James folded the paper and made holes to it as shown. When the paper is unfolded how does it look? Help him bubble the right option.

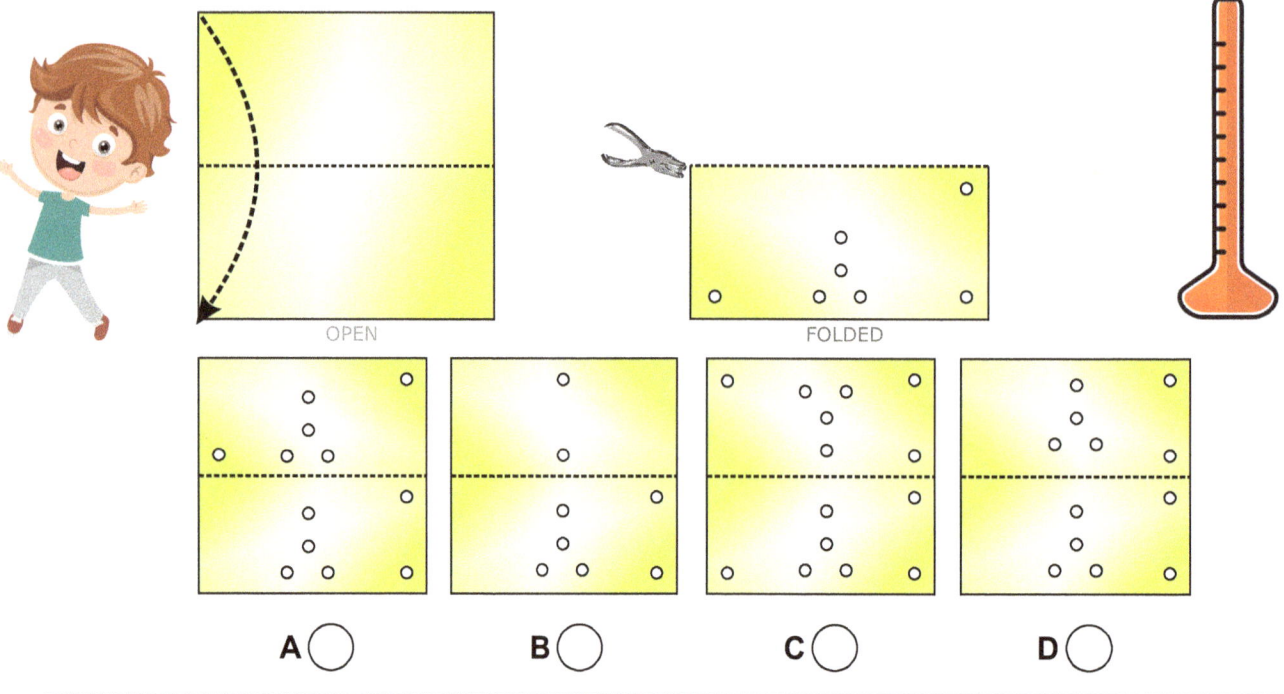

A ◯   B ◯   C ◯   D ◯

Q-12

Look at the question and put your finger on Microscope. Olivia folded the paper and made holes to it as shown. When the paper is unfolded how does it look? Help her bubble the right option.

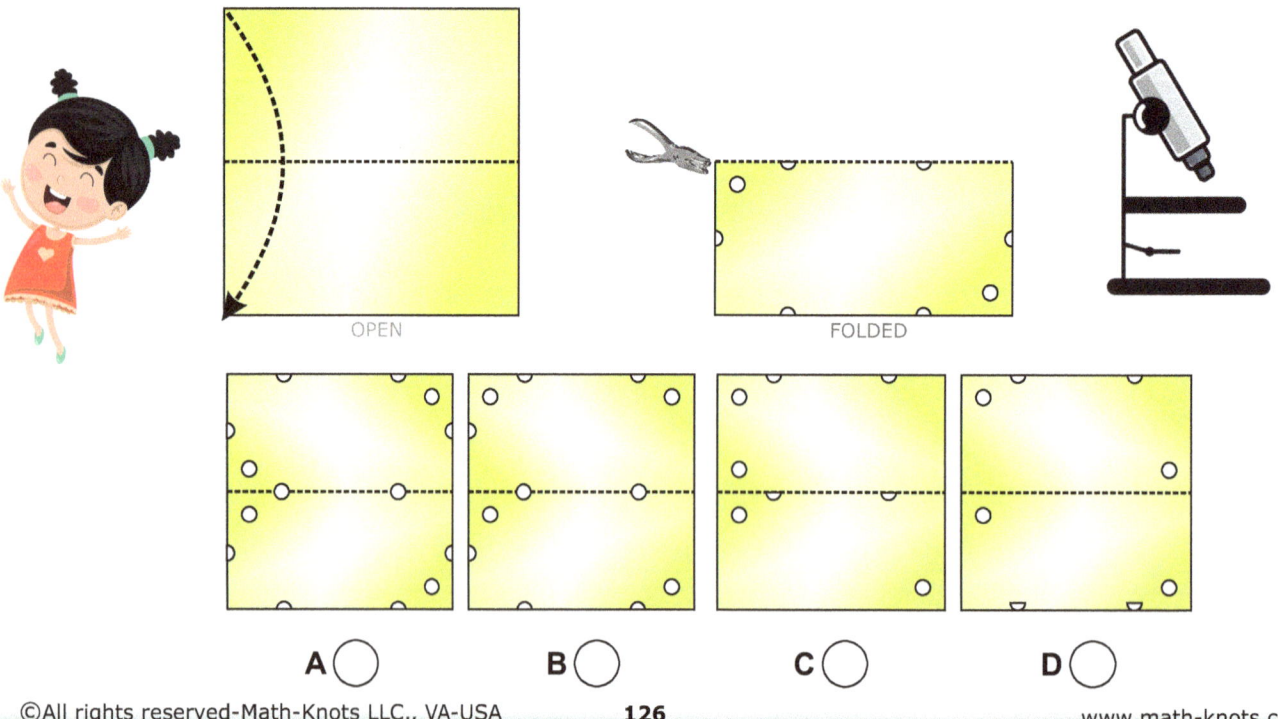

A ◯   B ◯   C ◯   D ◯

www.math-knots.com

Q-13 Look at the question and put your finger on Magnet. Christopher folded the paper and made hole to it as shown. When the paper is unfolded how does it look? Help him bubble the right option.

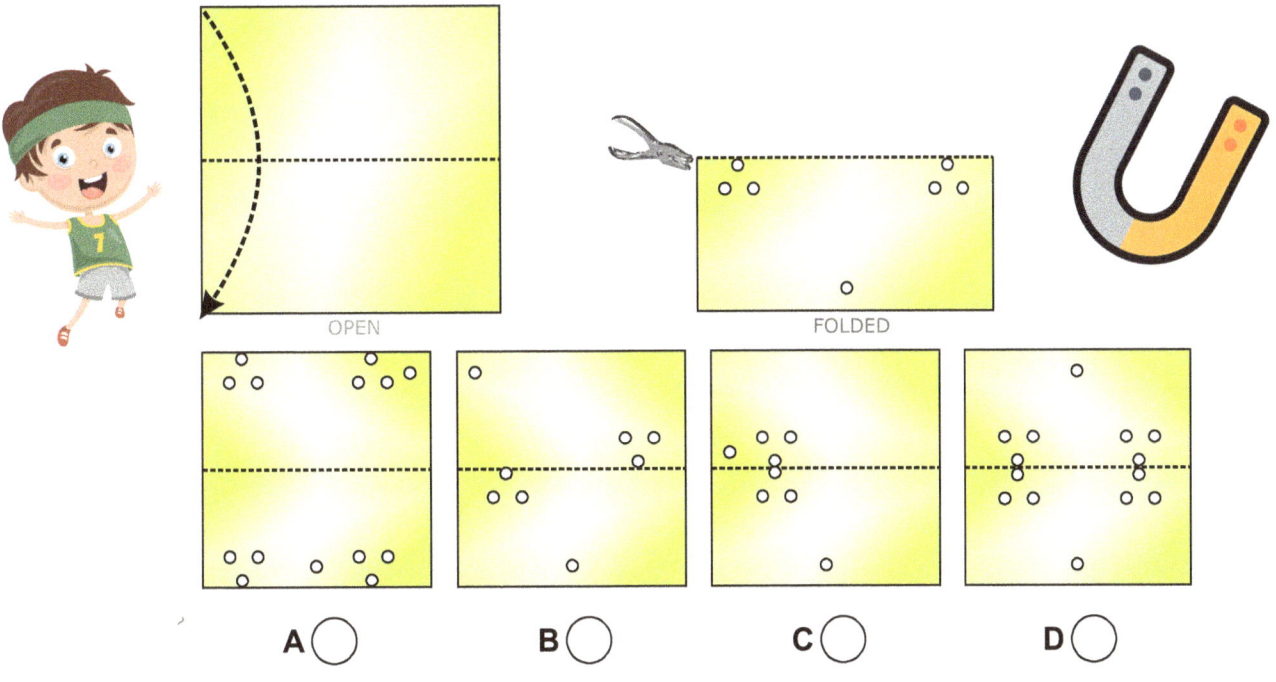

OPEN

FOLDED

A ◯   B ◯   C ◯   D ◯

Q-14 Look at the question and put your finger on Bearings. Emily folded the paper and made holes to it as shown. When the paper is unfolded how does it look? Help her bubble the right option.

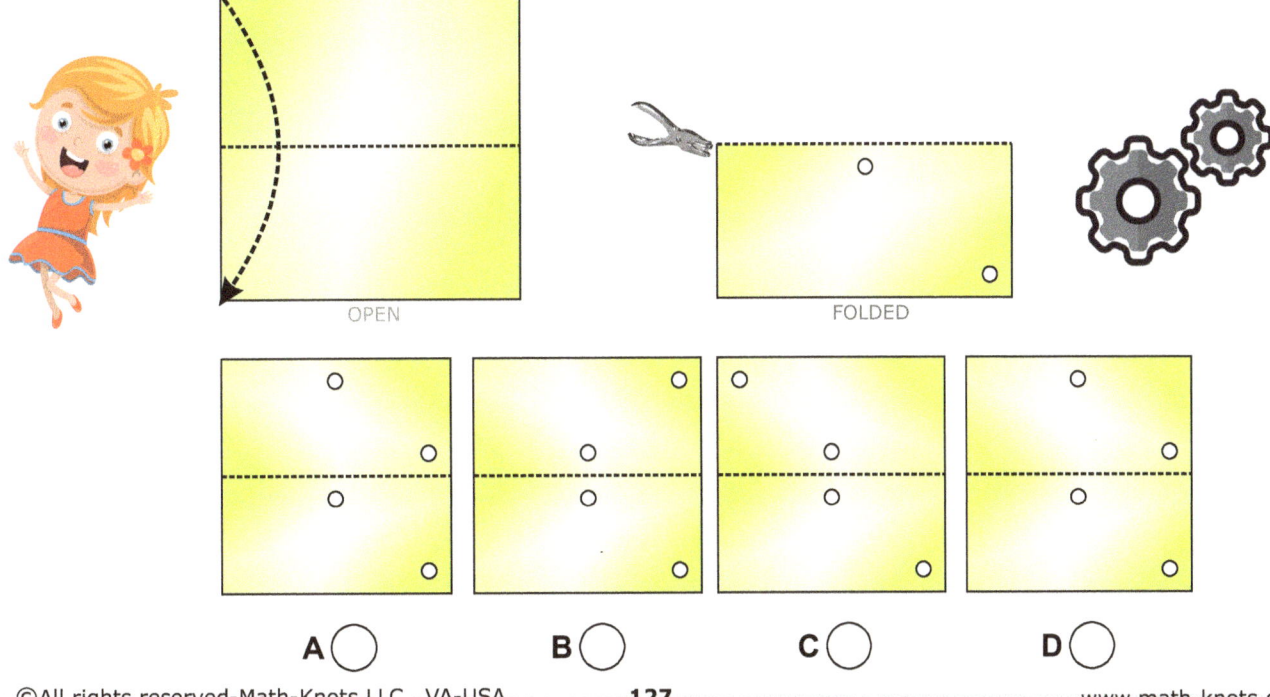

OPEN

FOLDED

A ◯   B ◯   C ◯   D ◯

Q-15 Look at the question and put your finger on Galaxy. Mathew folded the paper and made hole to it as shown. When the paper is unfolded how does it look? Help him bubble the right option.

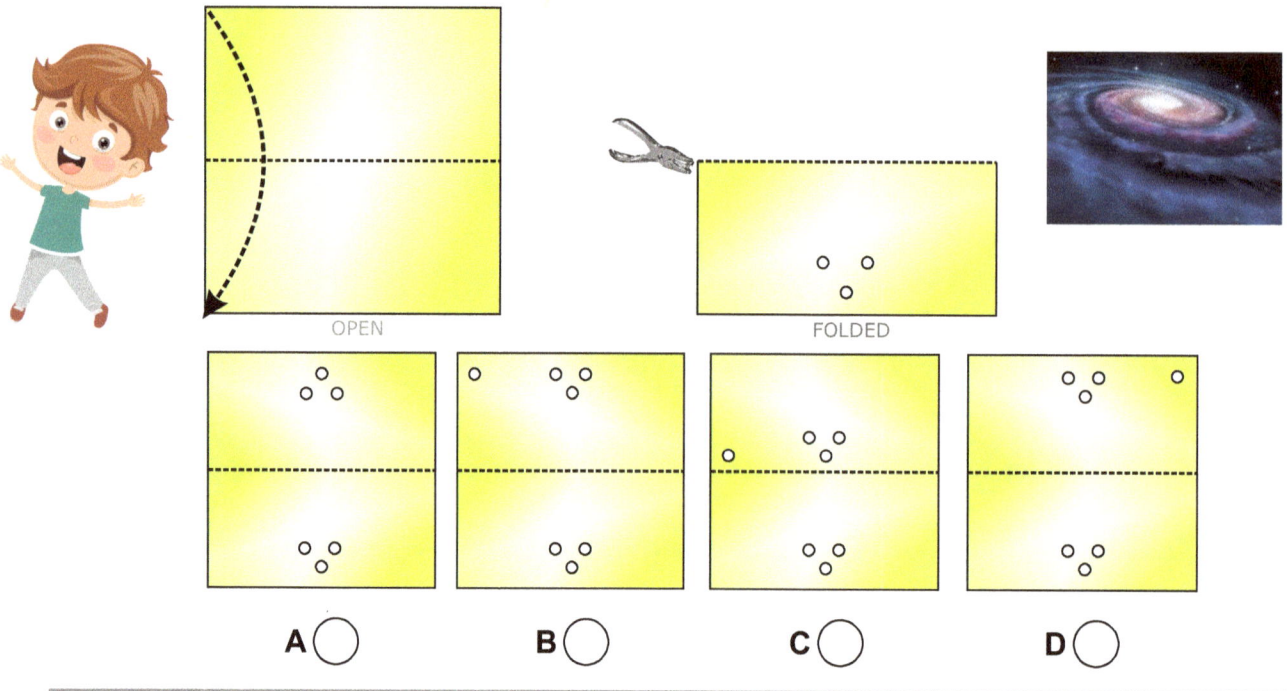

A ◯ B ◯ C ◯ D ◯

Q-16 Look at the question and put your finger on Clouds. Ashley folded the paper and made holes to it as shown. When the paper is unfolded how does it look? Help her bubble the right option.

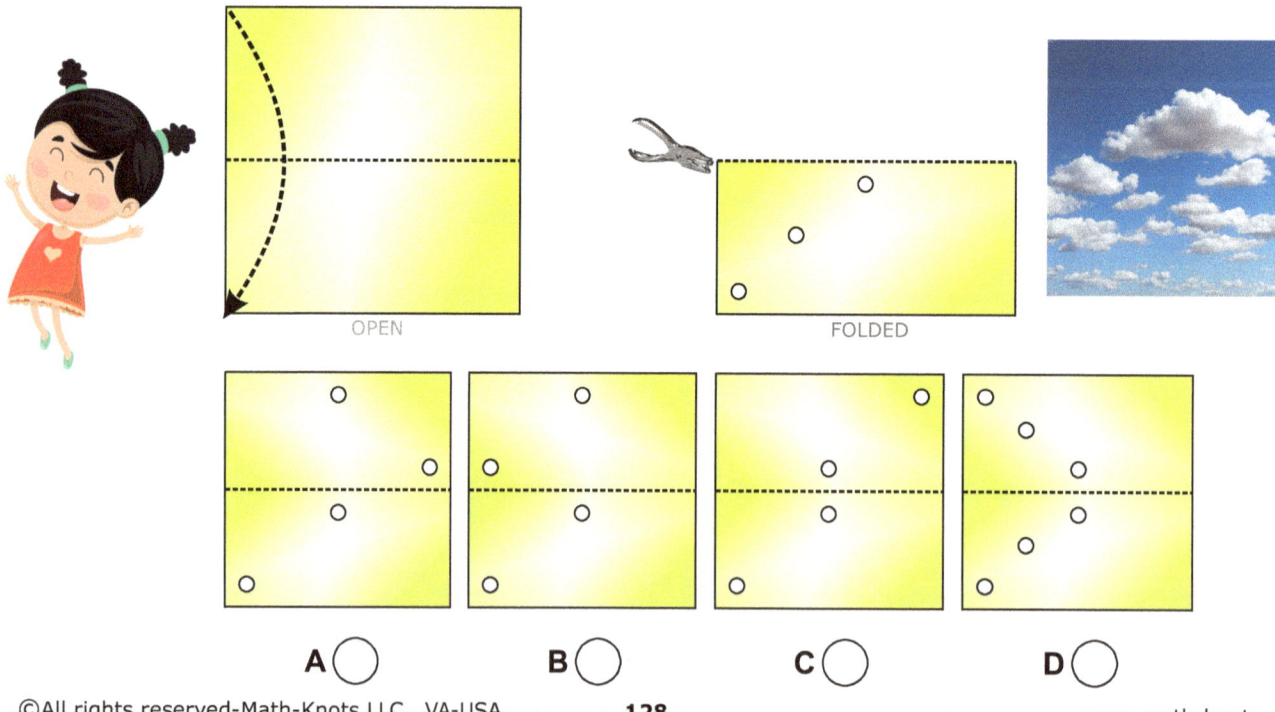

A ◯ B ◯ C ◯ D ◯

www.math-knots.com

NON VERBAL SECTION
PAPER FOLDING

TEST - 1

MATH KNOT CHALLENGE

Q-17

Look at the question and put your finger on DNA. Tyler folded the paper and made holes to it as shown. When the paper is unfolded how does it look? Help him bubble the right option.

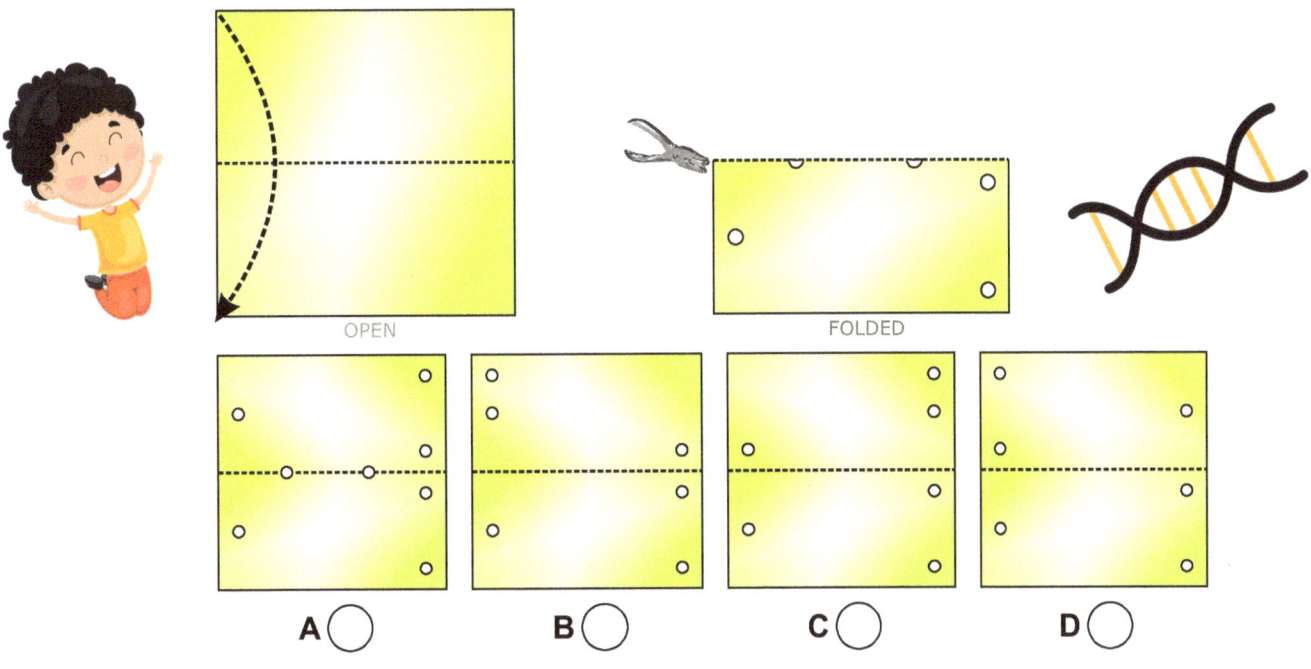

A ◯   B ◯   C ◯   D ◯

MATH KNOT CHALLENGE

Q-18

Look at the question and put your finger on Cone. Alexis folded the paper and made holes to it as shown. When the paper is unfolded how does it look? Help her bubble the right option.

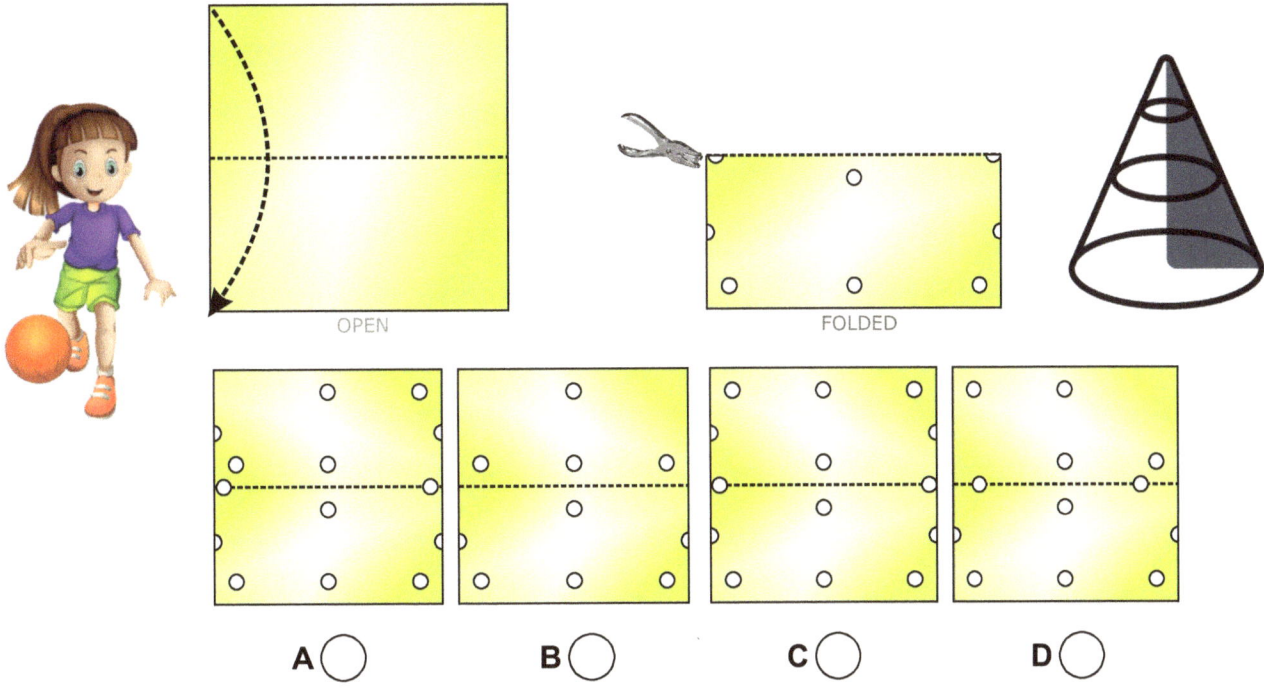

A ◯   B ◯   C ◯   D ◯

www.math-knots.com

MATH KNOT CHALLENGE

Q-19 Look at the question and put your finger on Beakers. Joseph folded the paper and made holes to it as shown. When the paper is unfolded how does it look? Help him bubble the right option.

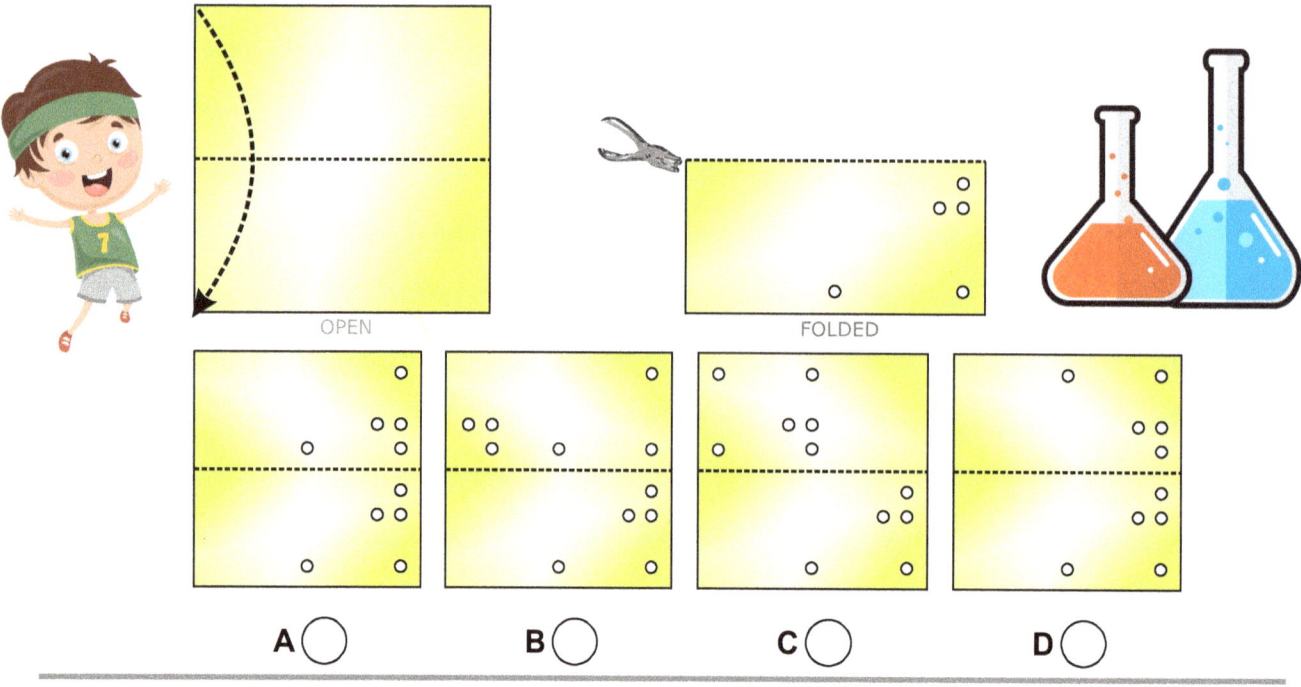

OPEN   FOLDED

A ◯   B ◯   C ◯   D ◯

MATH KNOT CHALLENGE

Q-20 Look at the question and put your finger on Safety Glasses. Sophia folded the paper and made holes to it as shown. When the paper is unfolded how does it look? Help her bubble the right option.

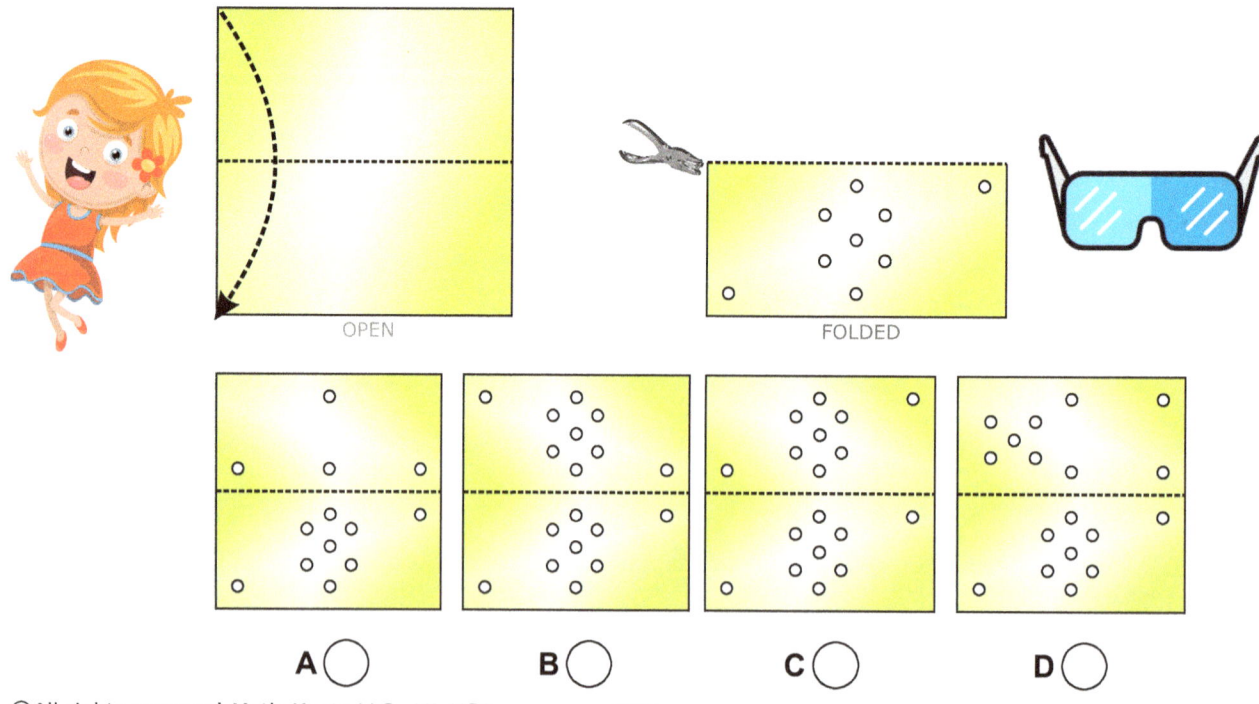

OPEN   FOLDED

A ◯   B ◯   C ◯   D ◯

www.math-knots.com

TEST - 2

VERBAL SECTION

VERBAL CLASSIFICATION

Lets Start the Test...

www.math-knots.com

Sample Three words are related in a certain way. Four options are given. Identify the choice that does not belong to the group?

One	Two	Three	
Six	Eight	Five	Gate
A◯	B◯	C◯	D◯

Solution : D

Three words in the question belong to one group. One of the four choices doesn't belong to the same group. Identify and bubble the correct choice.

In the given question all three in first row are words as well as numbers in words. Lets take a look at the answers. All choices are words but three are numbers in words and one other word gate, which is incorrect.

All the questions in verbal classification test 2 are to be answered following the below question (instruction).

Three words are related in a certain way. Four options are given. Identify the choice that <u>does not belong</u> to the group ?

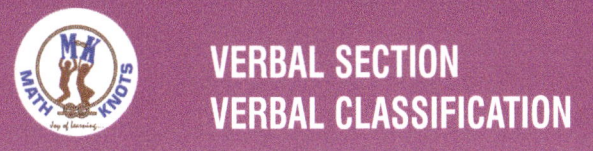

1. **Cave**   **Stable**   **Kennel**

   Burrow   Den   Canoe   Hive

   A ◯   B ◯   C ◯   D ◯

2. **Neptune**   **Pluto**   **Venus**

   Mars   Uranus   Earth   Moon

   A ◯   B ◯   C ◯   D ◯

3. **Rhombus**   **Triangle**   **Square**

   Cone   Circle   Rectangle   Trapezoid

   A ◯   B ◯   C ◯   D ◯

4. **Airplane** **Glider**   **Helicopter**

   Kite   Radar   Bird   Rocket

   A ◯   B ◯   C ◯   D ◯

5. **Calf**   **Kitten**   **Chick**

   Fawn   Pup   Cub   Pig

   A ◯   B ◯   C ◯   D ◯

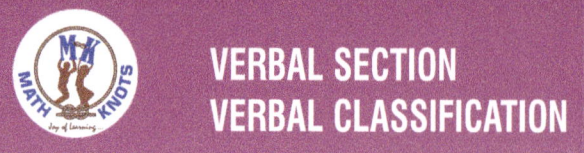
6.   **Mother**   **Daughter**   **Aunt**

Son   Grand Mother   Niece   Sister In Law

A◯   B◯   C◯   D◯

7.   **Tree**   **Bush**   **Shrub**

Vine   Plant   Leaf   Creeper

A◯   B◯   C◯   D◯

8.   **Monopoly**   **Ping-Pong**   **Cards**

Chess   Polo   Squash   Bowling

A◯   B◯   C◯   D◯

9.   **Tax**   **Dues**   **Levy**

Invoice   Quotation   Bill   Liability

A◯   B◯   C◯   D◯

10.   **Yam**   **Onion**   **Turnip**

Potato   Carrot   Ginger   Spinach

A◯   B◯   C◯   D◯

11. **Attorney**   **Lawyer**   **Judge**

Liquidator   Advocate   Barrister   Counselor

A ◯   B ◯   C ◯   D ◯

12. **Cutter**   **Sword**   **Rapier**

Knife   Dagger   Arrow   Spear

A ◯   B ◯   C ◯   D ◯

13. **July**   **January**   **August**

March   April   December   October

A ◯   B ◯   C ◯   D ◯

14. **Ice-Cream**   **Yogurt**   **Custard**

Milk   Cheese   Butter   Whip Cream

A ◯   B ◯   C ◯   D ◯

15. **Support**   **Footing**   **Base**

Foundation   Bottom   Underlying   Exterior

A ◯   B ◯   C ◯   D ◯

16.   Eye   Thumb   Kidney

Lung   Knee   Nose   Shoulder

A◯   B◯   C◯   D◯

17.   Basket Ball   Hockey   Soccer

Soccer   Billiard   Tennis   Lacrosse

A◯   B◯   C◯   D◯

18.   Namib   Black Rock   Sahara

Europe   Atacama   Thar   Antarctic

A◯   B◯   C◯   D◯

TEST - 2

VERBAL SECTION

SENTENCE COMPLETION

Lets Start the Test...

www.math-knots.com

www.math-knots.com

Sample Look at the question with the Tennis Ball. Maya is trying to solve the below brain teaser. "Rik has more stamps then Ryan. Ryan has more stamps than Luke. Who has more stamps?" Bubble the correct option.

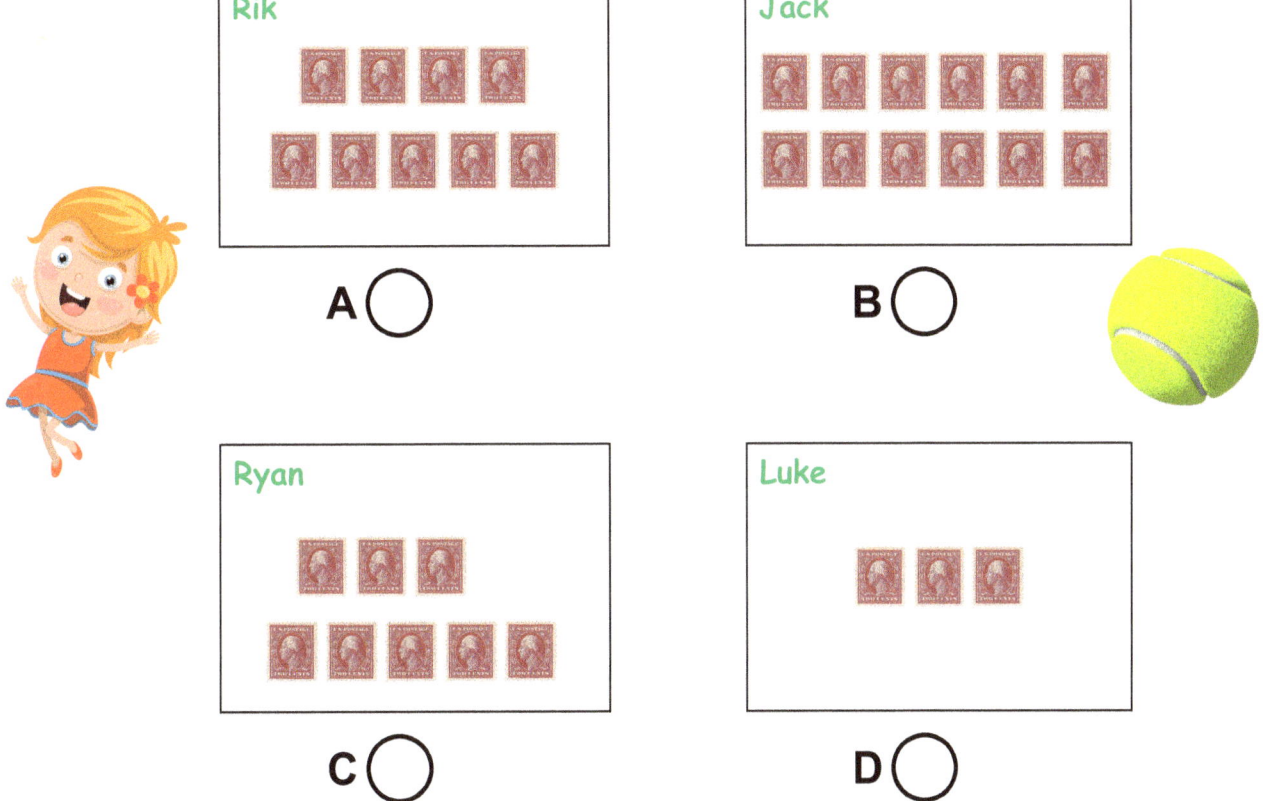

Solution : A

The Correct choice is A. The question doesn't compare with what Jack has.

Rik has the most stamps.

Rik >   Ryan >   Luke

www.math-knots.com

Q-1 Look at the question with the Garden. Grace is trying to find which of the below can swim in water? What do you think she shall choose from the below choices? Bubble the correct option.

Q-2 Look at the question with the Hot Dog. Mary is trying to find an object and two pair of objects? What do you think she shall choose from the below choices? Bubble the correct option.

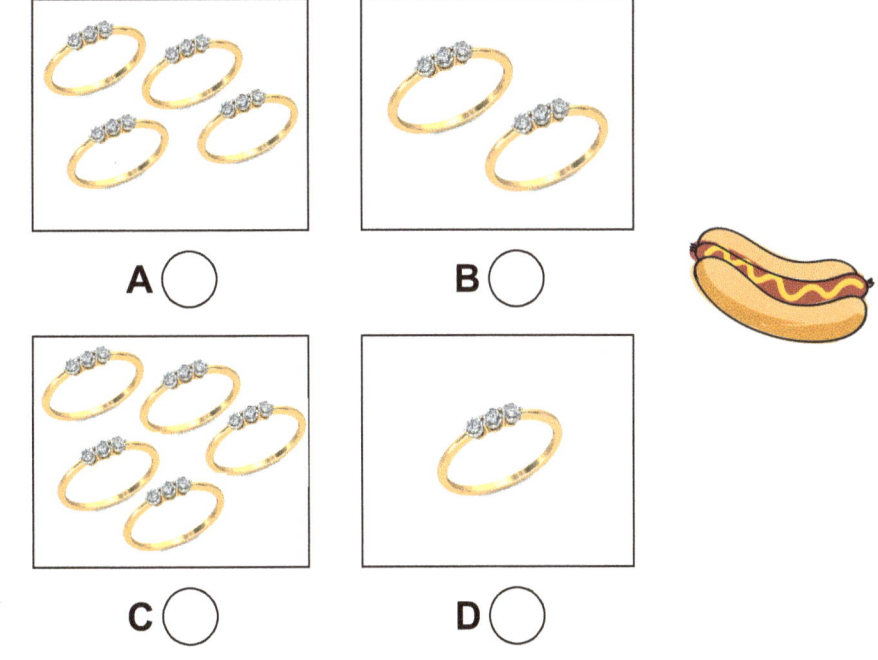

www.math-knots.com

Q-3 Look at the question with the TV. Carter is trying to find which of the below objects uses electricity? What do you think he shall choose from the below choices? Bubble the correct option.

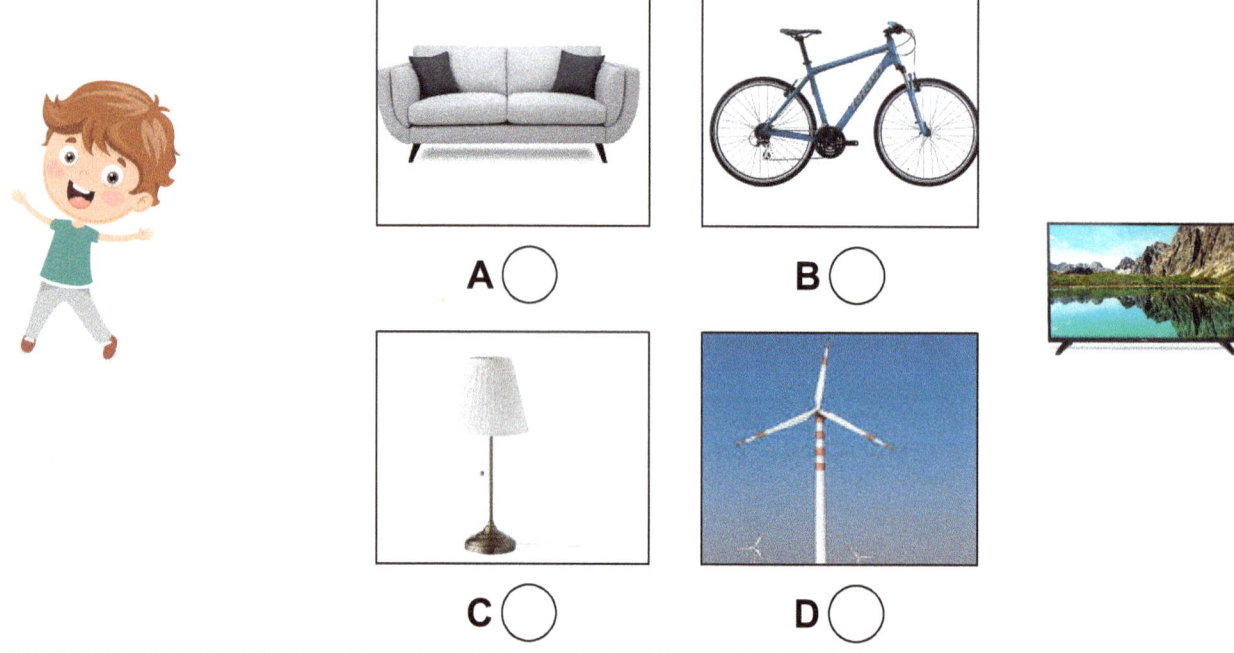

Q-4 Look at the question with the Flag. Dylan is trying to find the ball which is used in a sport that uses post? What do you think he shall choose from the below choices? Bubble the correct option.

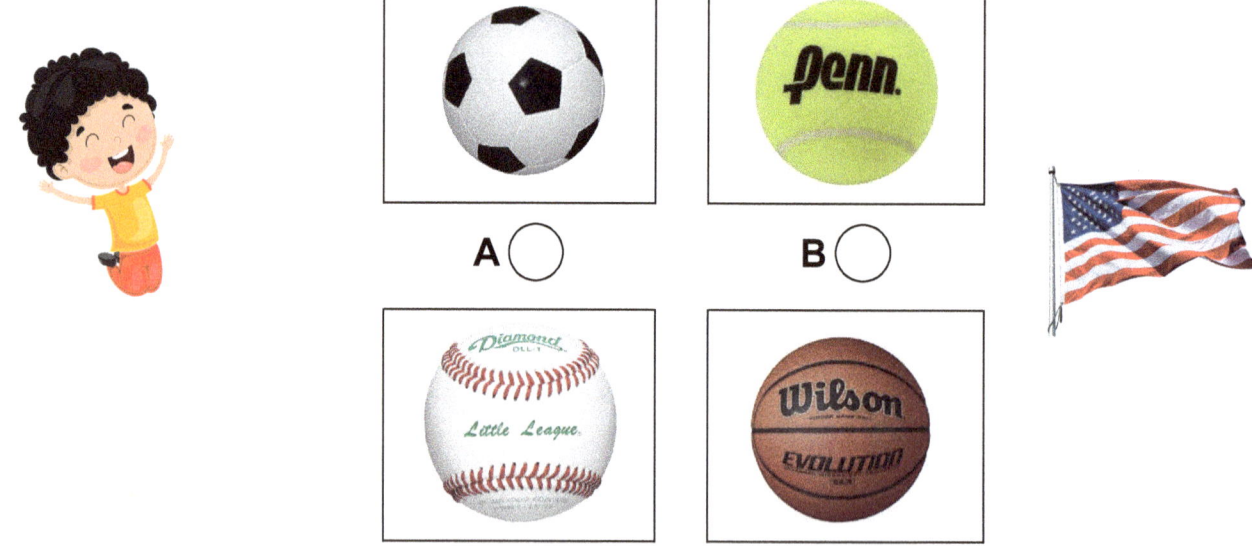

www.math-knots.com

Q-5 Look at the question with the Speedometer. Zoey went to the store to get her school supplies. What do you think she shall choose from the below choices? Bubble the correct option.

A ◯   B ◯

C ◯   D ◯

Q-6 Look at the question with the Wheel. Ella wants to paint her study room. Which of the below objects does she needs to measure the room dimensions. Bubble the correct option.

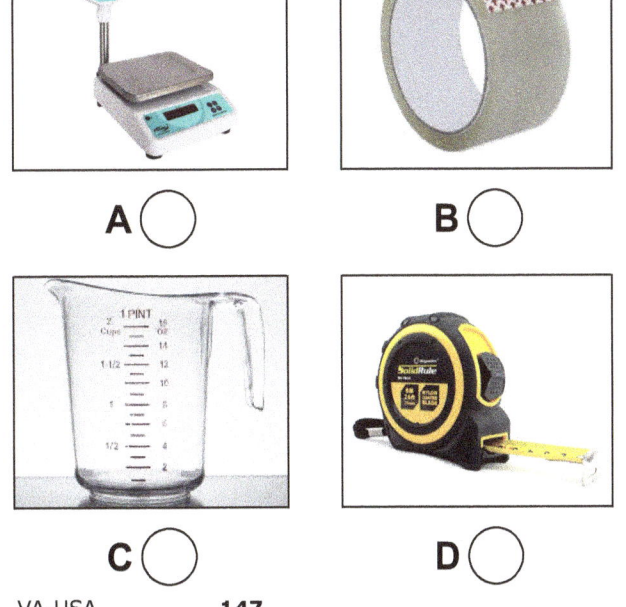

A ◯   B ◯

C ◯   D ◯

www.math-knots.com

Q-7

Look at the question with the Desk top. Luke is finding an object that is made of wood for his science project. Which of the below objects does he need to choose? Bubble the correct option.

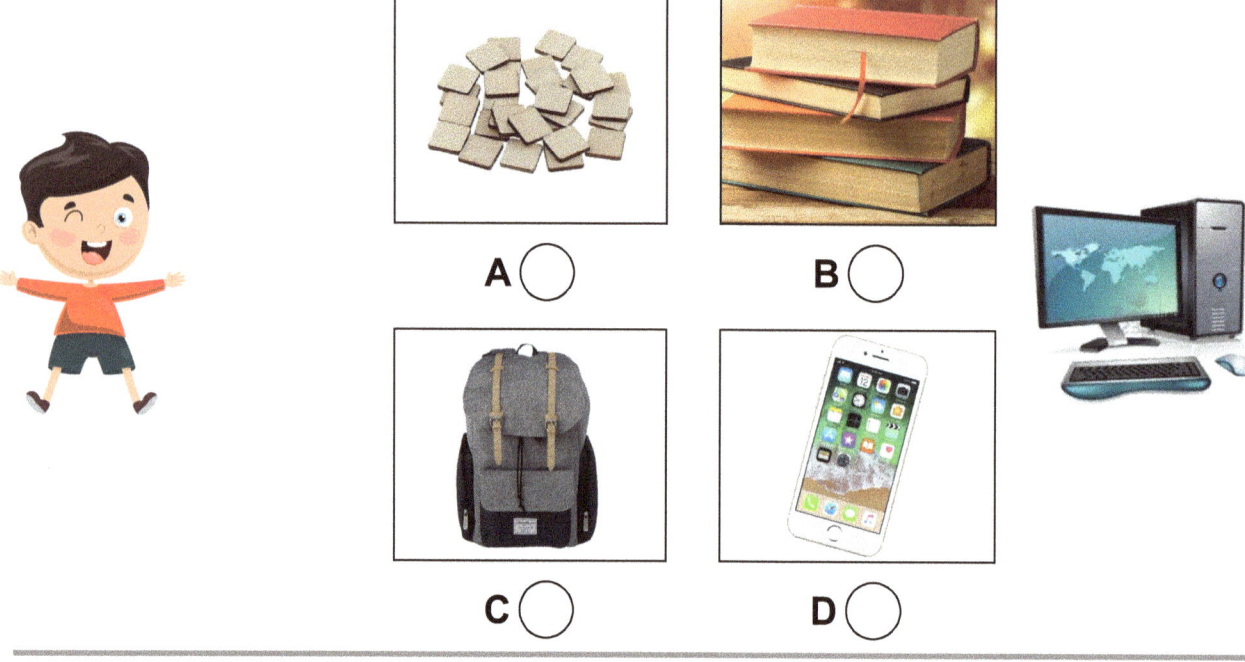

A◯   B◯

C◯   D◯

Q-8

Look at the question with the Car Tag. Owen and Stella together drew a nice picture in the beach sand. A gigantic wave comes and washes off the picture partially. Which of the below picture shows their drawing now ? Bubble the correct option.

A◯   B◯

C◯   D◯

www.math-knots.com

Q-9

Look at the question with the Laptop. Leyla wants to go on a cruise to Alaska. Can you help her to choose right transportation from the given choices below? Bubble the correct option.

A ◯

B ◯

C ◯

D ◯

Q-10

Look at the question with the Twitter symbol. Dylan wants to go on a walk to his friend's house which is fifteen minutes away. Today's Weather forecast says thunderstorms and Rain. What do you think he shall carry with him while walking to friend's home? Bubble the correct option.

A ◯

B ◯

C ◯

D ◯

www.math-knots.com

Q-11 Look at the question with the Mic. Isaac is going to his friend Ryan's birthday party. What do you think he shall choose from the below to keep the present bought for his friend? Bubble the correct option.

A ◯   B ◯

C ◯   D ◯

Q-12 Look at the question with the Head Phones. Stella is trying to choose a double object from the below choices. Help her bubble the correct option.

A ◯   B ◯

C ◯   D ◯

www.math-knots.com

Q-13 Look at the question with the Globe. Julian is trying to choose a half a pair of objects from the below choices. Help him bubble the correct option.

A ◯   B ◯

C ◯   D ◯

Q-14 Look at the question with the Spectacles. Zoe is fixing a book shelf and her electric screw driver runs out of charge. She is trying to find a connector to charge. Help her to choose from the below choices. Bubble the correct option.

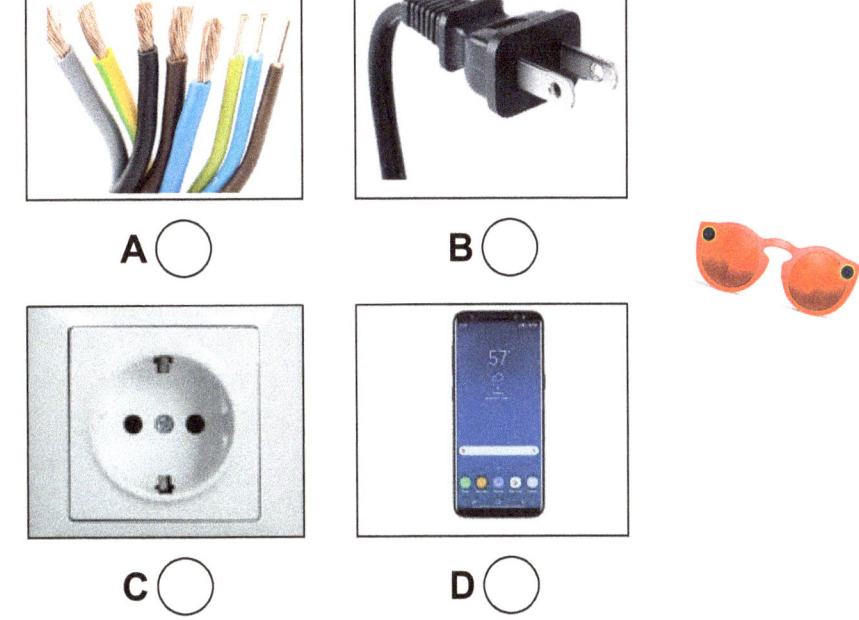

A ◯   B ◯

C ◯   D ◯

Q-15 Look at the question with the Speakers. Julia is looking for her hair clips. Help her to choose from the below choices. Bubble the correct option.

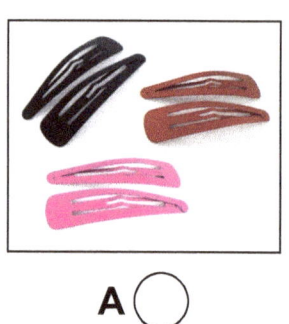

A ◯

B ◯

C ◯

D ◯

Q-16 Look at the question with the Face Book icon. Jaxon is reading his vocabulary list of the week. He wonders what does flock means? Help him to choose from the below choices representing the meaning of flock. Bubble the correct option.

A ◯

B ◯

C ◯

D ◯

www.math-knots.com

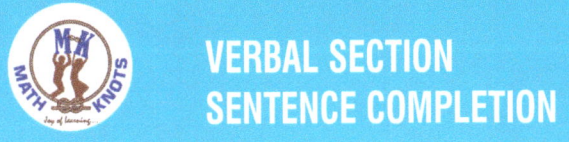

Q-17

Look at the question with the Wi-Fi icon. Aaron fixes his new basketball hoop. After fixing he realizes the missing parts. Which of the below choices shows Aaron's hoop after the fix is made. Bubble the correct option.

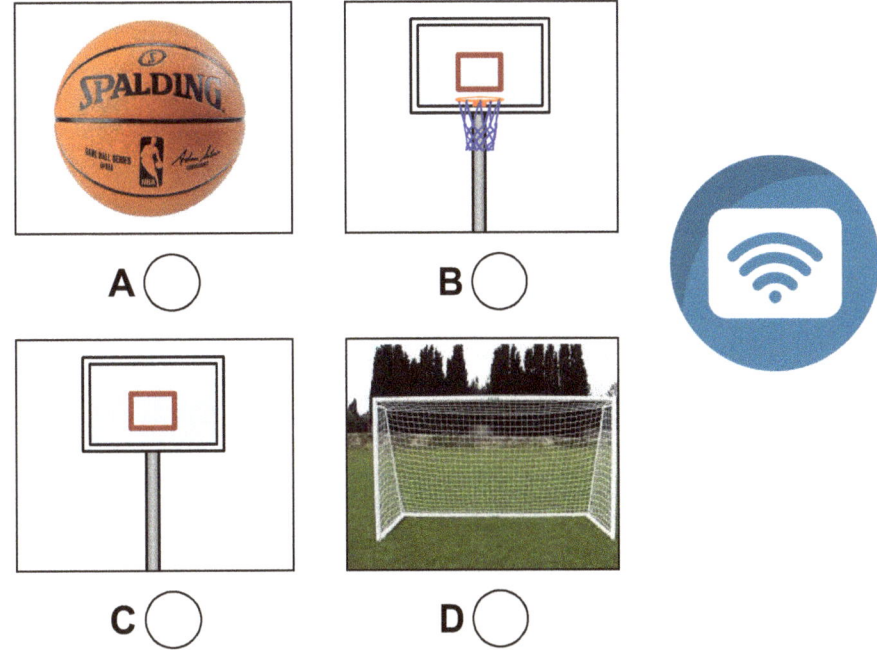

A ◯   B ◯

C ◯   D ◯

Q-18

Look at the question with the Key Board. Leah is part of her middle school music club where she plays a percussion instrument. Which of the below choices shows the instrument she must me playing. Bubble the correct option.

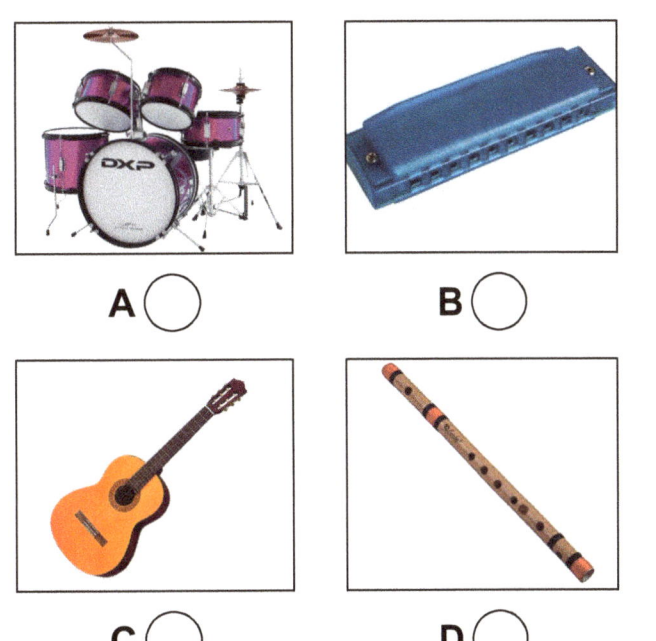

A ◯   B ◯

C ◯   D ◯

www.math-knots.com

TEST - 2

VERBAL SECTION

VERBAL ANALOGIES

Lets Start the Test...

www.math-knots.com

www.math-knots.com

Sample The first two words are related in a certain way as the next two words. Identify the missing word.

Clouds : White :: Sky : ?

Yellow | Bold | Blue | Silver
○ | ○ | ○ | ○

Solution : B

First analogy is color of the clouds which is white. Color of sky is blue.

Right choice is B.

Student needs to think through how the first two are related and then relate it

to next analogy in the same way. Bubble the correct option.

All the questions in verbal analogies test 2 are to be answered following the below question (instruction).

The first two words are related in a certain way as the next two words. Identify the missing word.

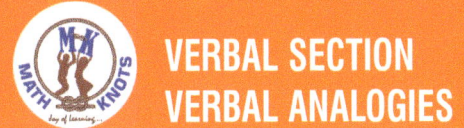
1.   Father : Dad :: Grand father : ?

Grand Ma   Grand   Dads Dad   Grand Pa

A◯   B◯   C◯   D◯

2.   Circle : Zero :: Septagon : ?

Seven   Three   Four   Five

A◯   B◯   C◯   D◯

3.   Bark : Brown   :: Leaves :   ?

Yellow   Orange   Green   Pale

A◯   B◯   C◯   D◯

4.   Goose : Water :: Rabbit :   ?

Burrow   Sty   Trees   Cage

A◯   B◯   C◯   D◯

5.   Bus : Road :: Sub marine :   ?

Road   Water   Sail   Sky

A◯   B◯   C◯   D◯

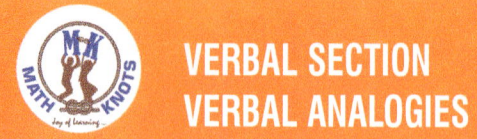
6.   **Basket Ball : Baskets :: Soccer ball :   ?**

Goals	Fouls	Runs	Hits
A ◯	B ◯	C ◯	D ◯

7.   **Green : Go :: Red : ?**

Orange	Slow	Stop	Detour
A ◯	B ◯	C ◯	D ◯

8.   **Winter : December :: Fall :   ?**

May	October	April	August
A ◯	B ◯	C ◯	D ◯

9.   **Pear : Trees :: Pumpkin : ?**

Vine	Shrubs	Under Ground	Plants
A ◯	B ◯	C ◯	D ◯

10.   **Hen : Chick :: Giraffe : ?**

Lamb	Kid	Calf	Pup
A ◯	B ◯	C ◯	D ◯

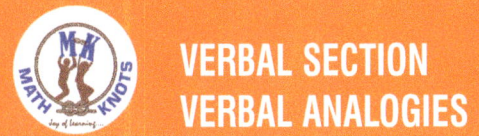
11.   Rabbit : Kit :: Fish : ?

Colt   Fry   Infant   Cub

A◯   B◯   C◯   D◯

12.   Reptiles : 4 legs :: Amphibian : ?

8 legs   2 legs   6 legs   4 legs

A◯   B◯   C◯   D◯

13.   Manometer : Air pressure :: Magentograph : ?

Voltage   Magnetic Field   Length   Current

A◯   B◯   C◯   D◯

14.   Legs : Walk :: Wings : ?

Fly   Move   Flap   Run

A◯   B◯   C◯   D◯

15.   Note : Music :: Letters : ?

Alphabets   Print   Read   Words

A◯   B◯   C◯   D◯

16.   Mammals : Four Legs :: Insects :   ?

Eight Legs   Four legs   Six Legs   Two legs

A◯   B◯   C◯   D◯

17.   Map : Fold :: Globe :   ?

Spin   Bounce   Toss   Hold

A◯   B◯   C◯   D◯

18.   Trash : Garbage :: Recycle :   ?

Trash   Pollute   Energy   Reuse

A◯   B◯   C◯   D◯

TEST - 2

QUANTITATIVE APTITUDE

NUMBER ANALOGIES

Lets Start the Test...

Sample

Look at the question with the Parrot. Two boxes in the first row are related in a certain way which is similar to two boxes in the second row. Ken is trying to fill the bubble under the correct option. Help him to select from options A, B, C, and D.

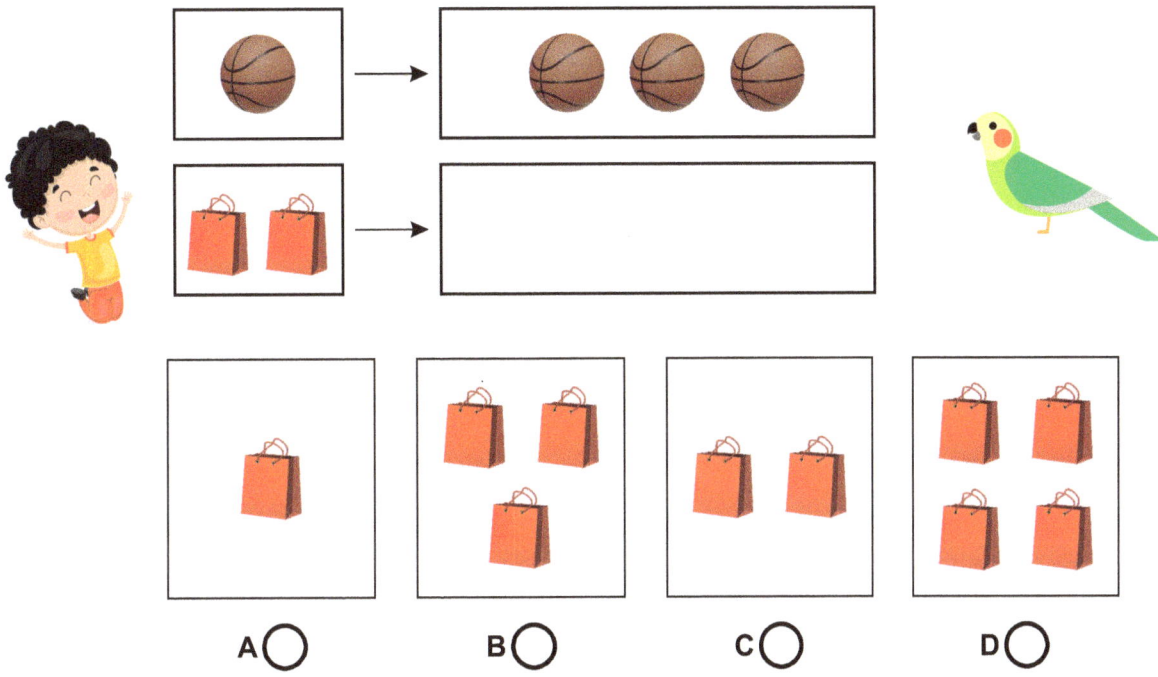

Solution : D

In first row, one ball to three balls [(1+2) adding two more]

In second row, two bags by adding two more will become four bags.

The analogies can be formed by adding or subtracting a certain number meaning increasing or decreasing by a certain quantity. Students needs to understand the right analogy and bubble the correct option.

www.math-knots.com

Q-1 Look at the question with the Wood Pecker. Count the stars in the first picture. Help Sam to bubble the option which shows two more stars than the first picture.

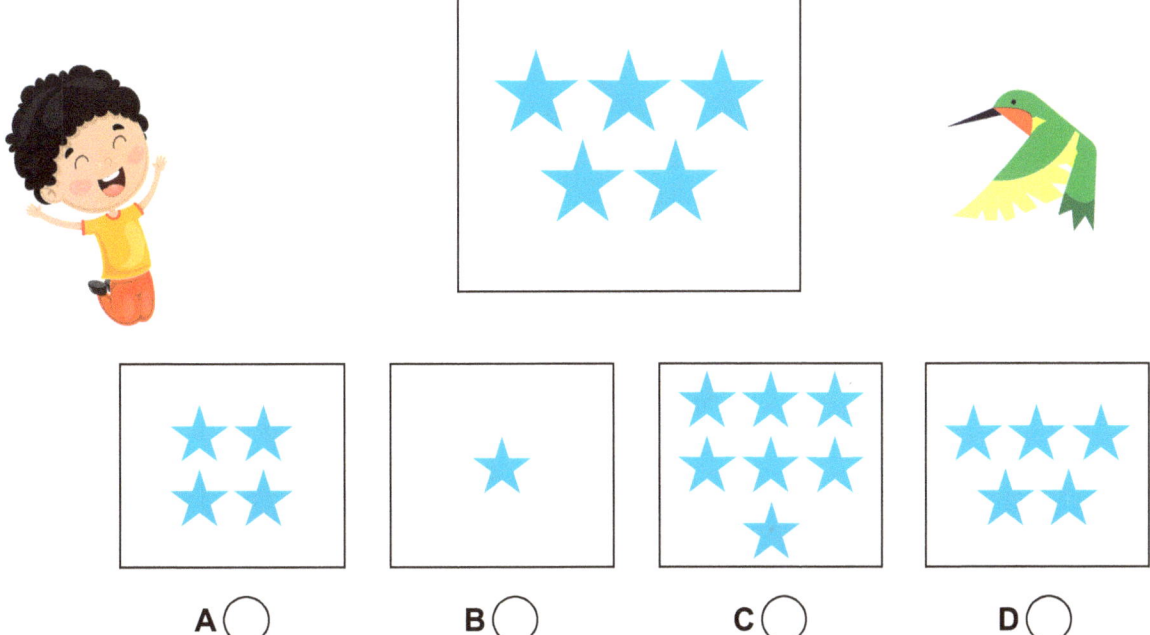

A ◯   B ◯   C ◯   D ◯

Q-2 Look at the question with the Crow. Count the marbles in the first picture. Help Mary to bubble the option which shows same number of marbles.

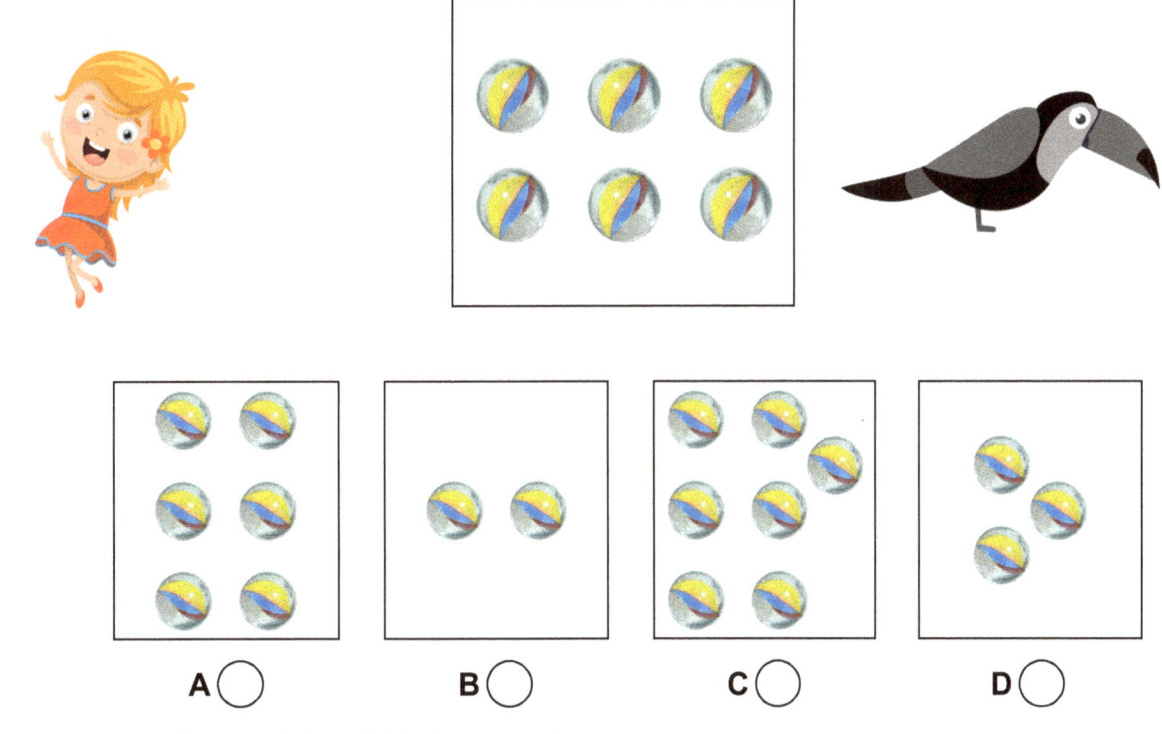

A ◯   B ◯   C ◯   D ◯

www.math-knots.com

Q-3 Look at the question with the Sparrow. Count the heart in the first picture. Help Fred to bubble the option which shows two fewer heart than the first picture.

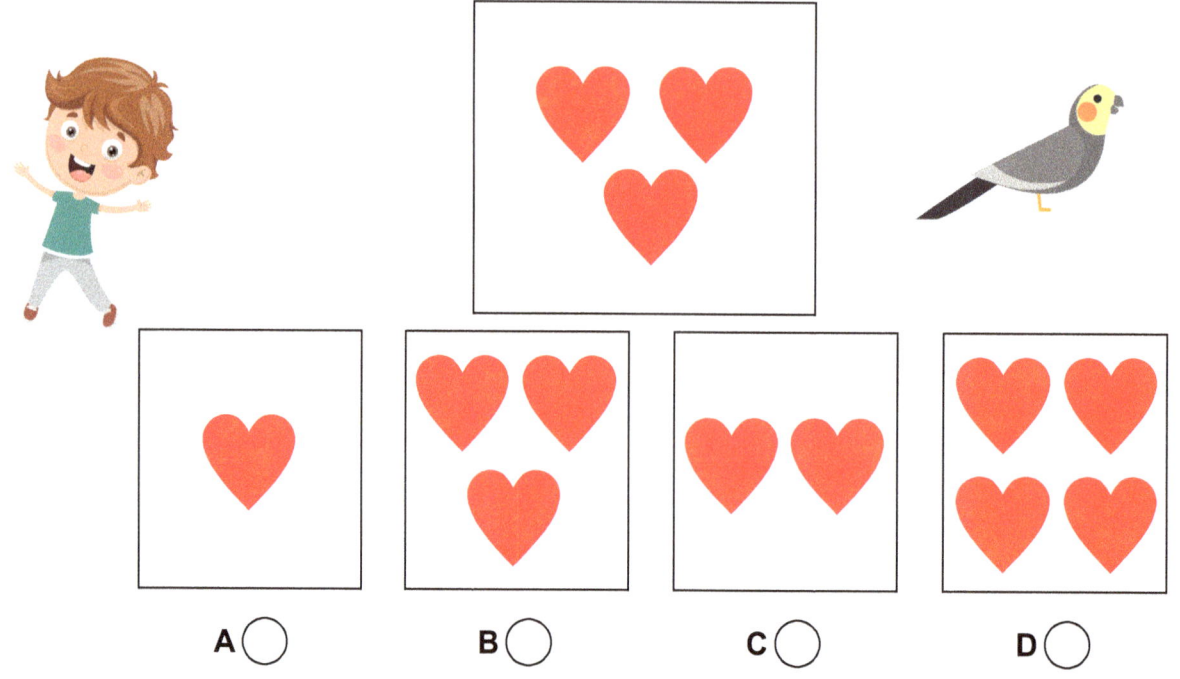

A ⃝   B ⃝   C ⃝   D ⃝

Q-4 Look at the question with the Pelican. Count the stickers in the first picture. Help Robert to bubble the option which shows one more sticker than the first picture.

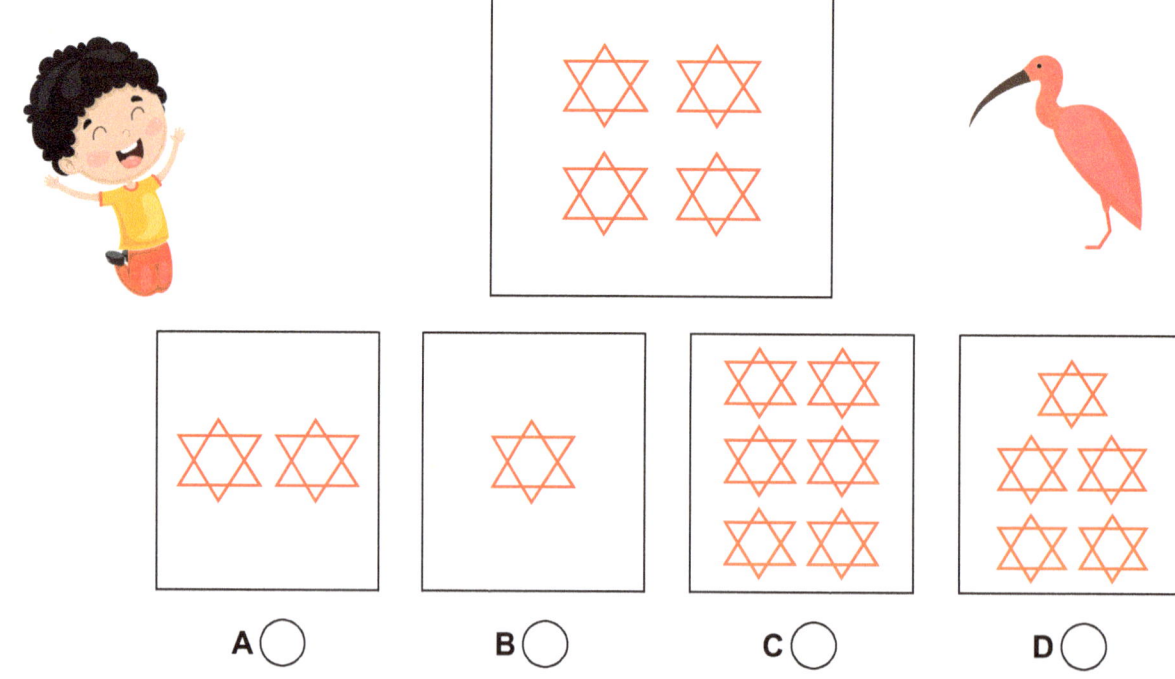

A ⃝   B ⃝   C ⃝   D ⃝

www.math-knots.com

Q-5 Look at the question with the Swan. Count the Triangles in the first picture. Help David to bubble the option which shows three fewer triangles than the first picture.

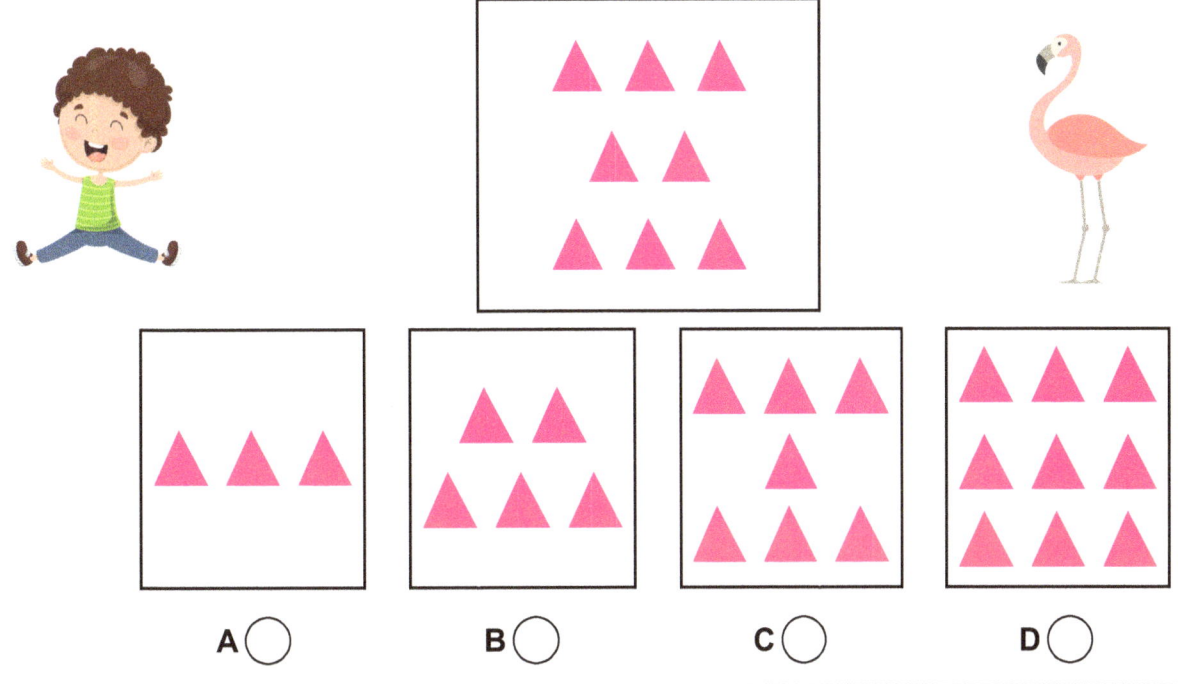

A ◯   B ◯   C ◯   D ◯

Q-6 Look at the question with the Parrot. Count the flowers in the first picture. Help Sofia to bubble the option which shows one more flower than the first picture.

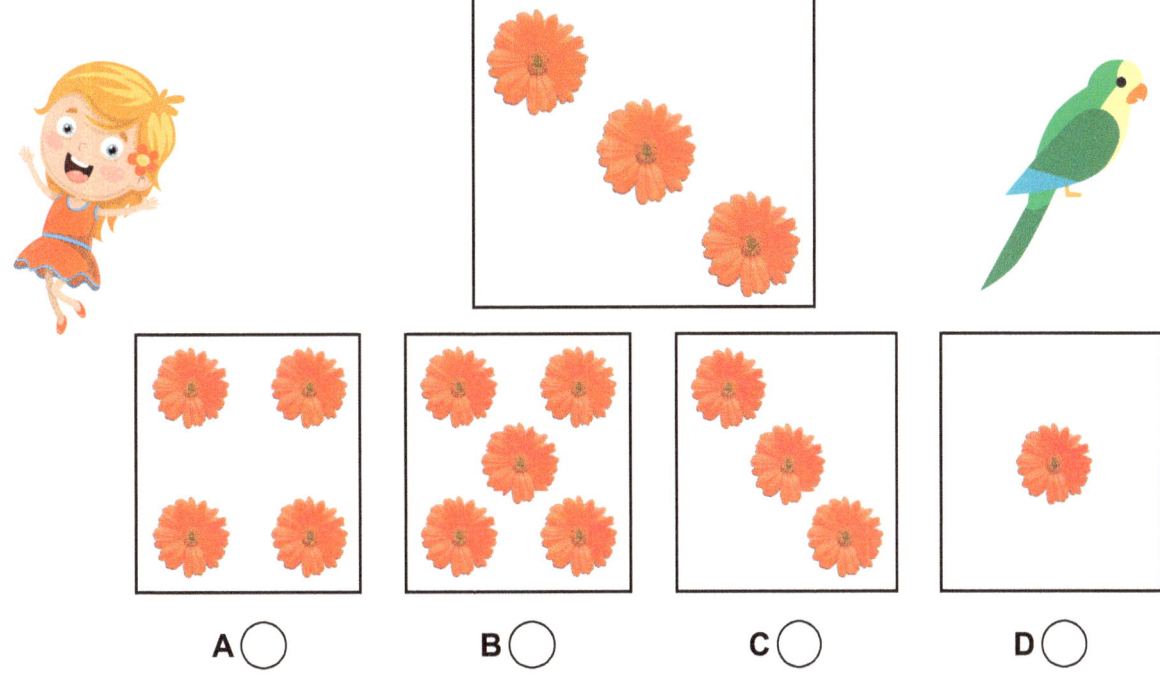

A ◯   B ◯   C ◯   D ◯

www.math-knots.com

Q-7 Look at the question with the Sand Piper. Count the squares in the first picture. Help Ava to bubble the option which shows two more squares than the first picture.

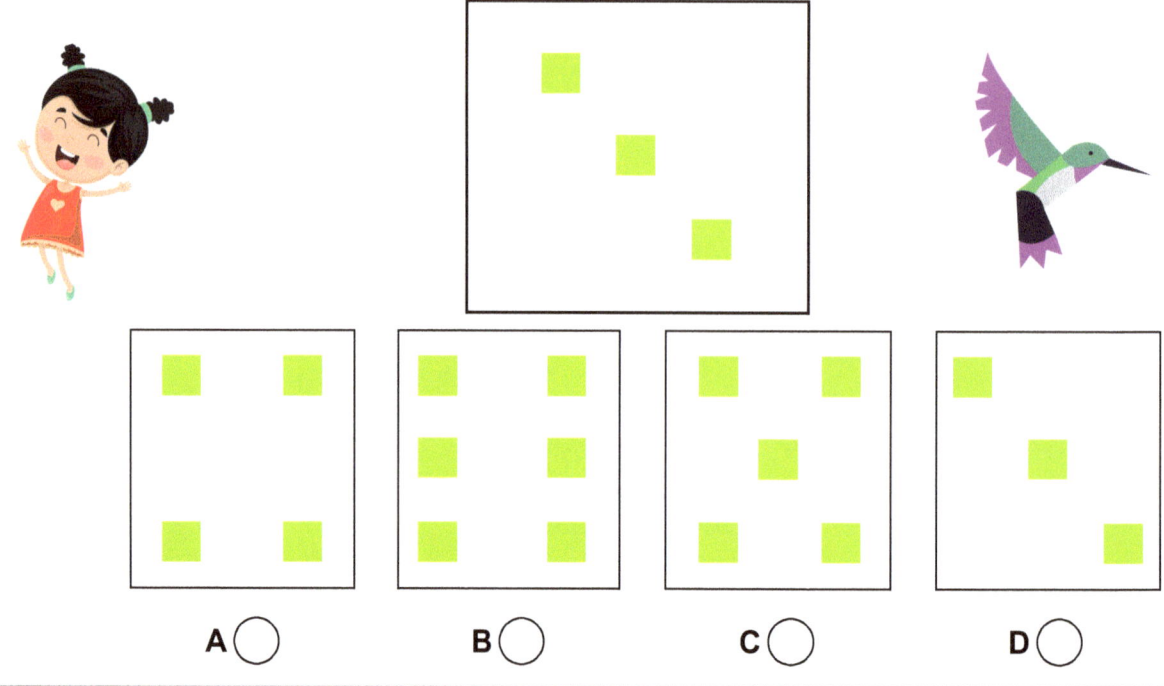

A ◯   B ◯   C ◯   D ◯

Q-8 Look at the question with the Butterfly. Count the leaves in the first picture. Help Johnson to bubble the option which shows half the number of leaves in the first picture.

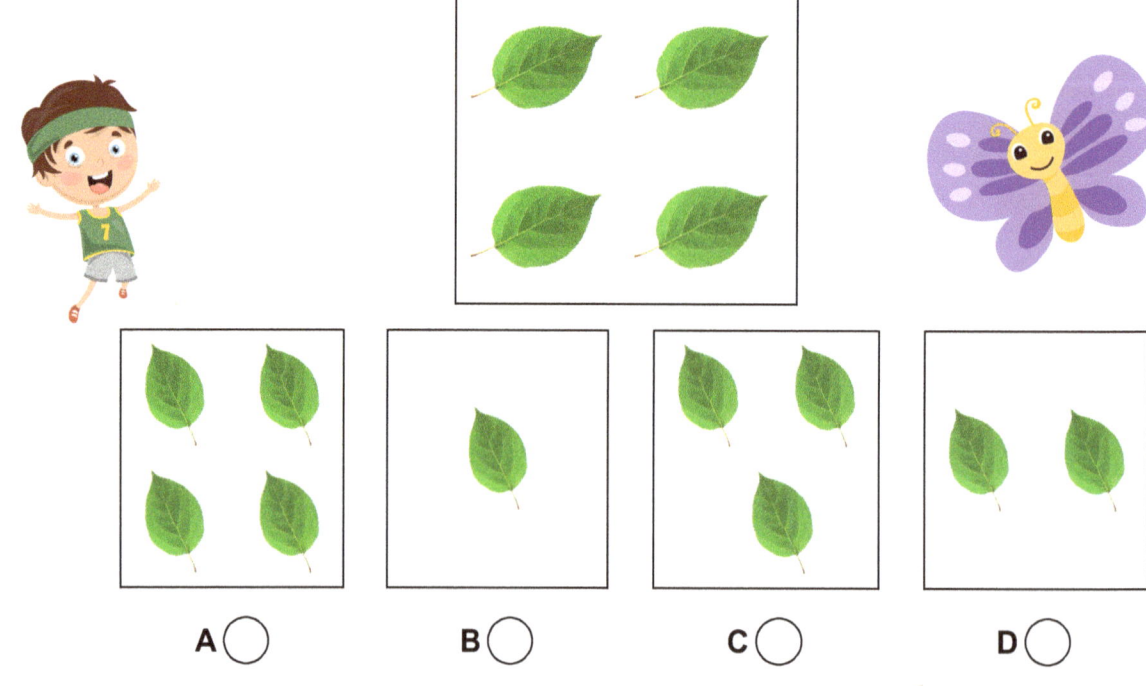

A ◯   B ◯   C ◯   D ◯

Q-9 Look at the question with the Lady Bug. Count the stickers in the first picture. Help Alexander to bubble the option which shows three more stickers than the first picture.

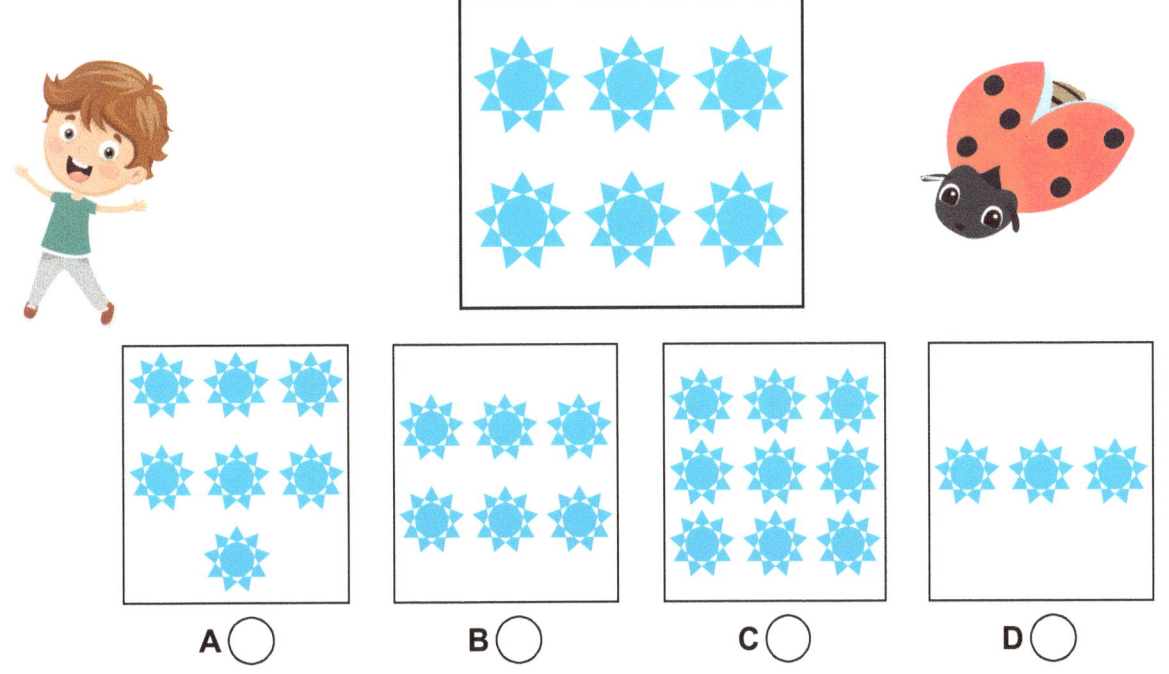

A ◯   B ◯   C ◯   D ◯

Q-10 Look at the question with the Bee. Count the Parrots in the first picture. Help Fred to bubble the option which shows two fewer parrots than the first picture.

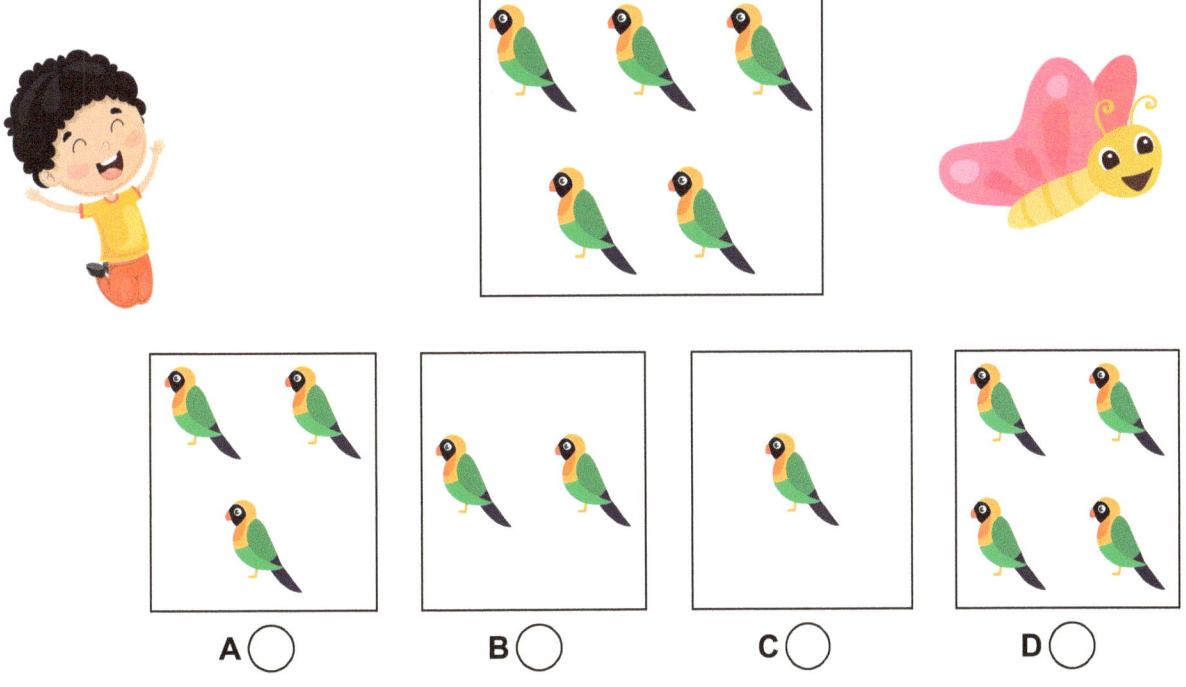

A ◯   B ◯   C ◯   D ◯

www.math-knots.com

Q-11 Look at the question with the Duck. Count the birds in the first picture. Help Ella to bubble the option which shows twice the number of birds than the first picture.

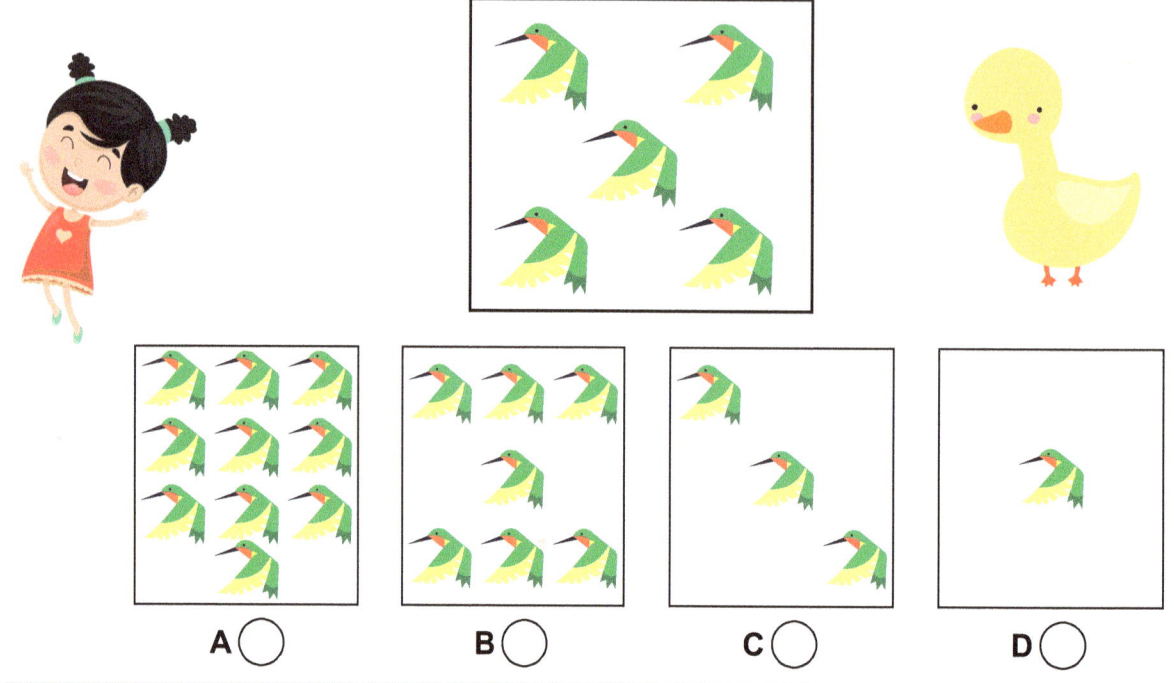

A ◯   B ◯   C ◯   D ◯

Q-12 Look at the question with the Owl. Count the birds in the first picture. Help Samuel to bubble the option which shows half the number of birds than the first picture.

A ◯   B ◯   C ◯   D ◯

174

Q-13 Look at the question with the Cat. Count the hats in the first picture. Help Anthony to bubble the option which shows three times the number of hats than the first picture.

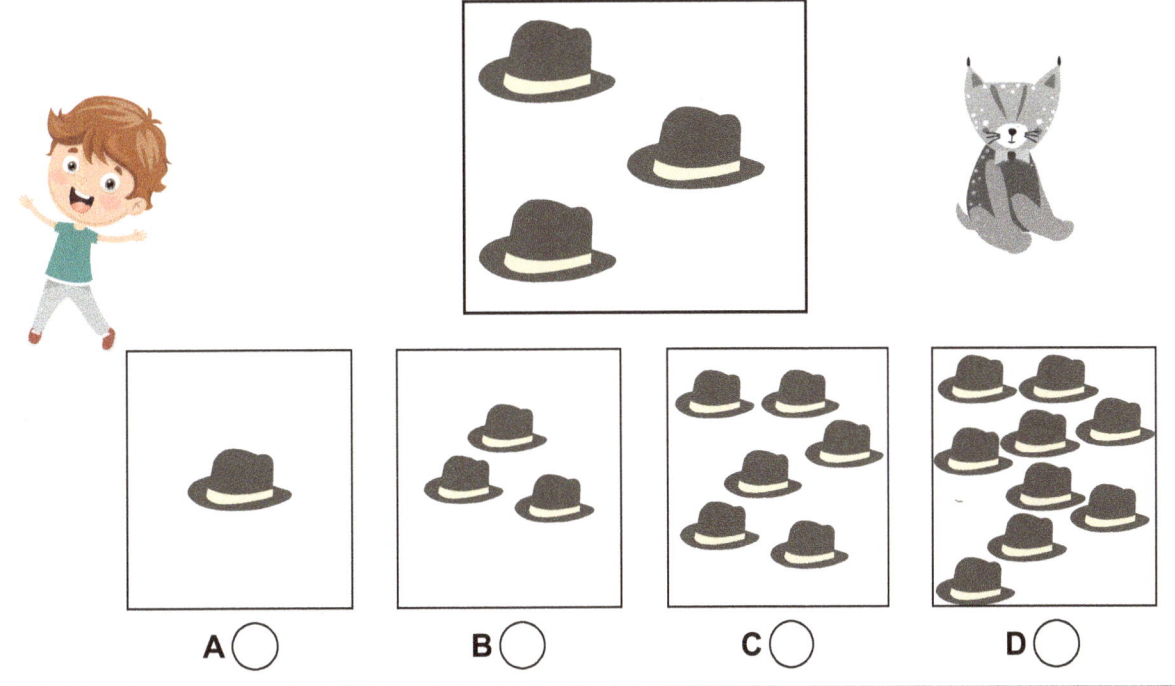

A◯   B◯   C◯   D◯

Q-14 Look at the question with the Sheep. Count the watches in the first picture. Help Skylar to bubble the option which shows one less watch than the first picture.

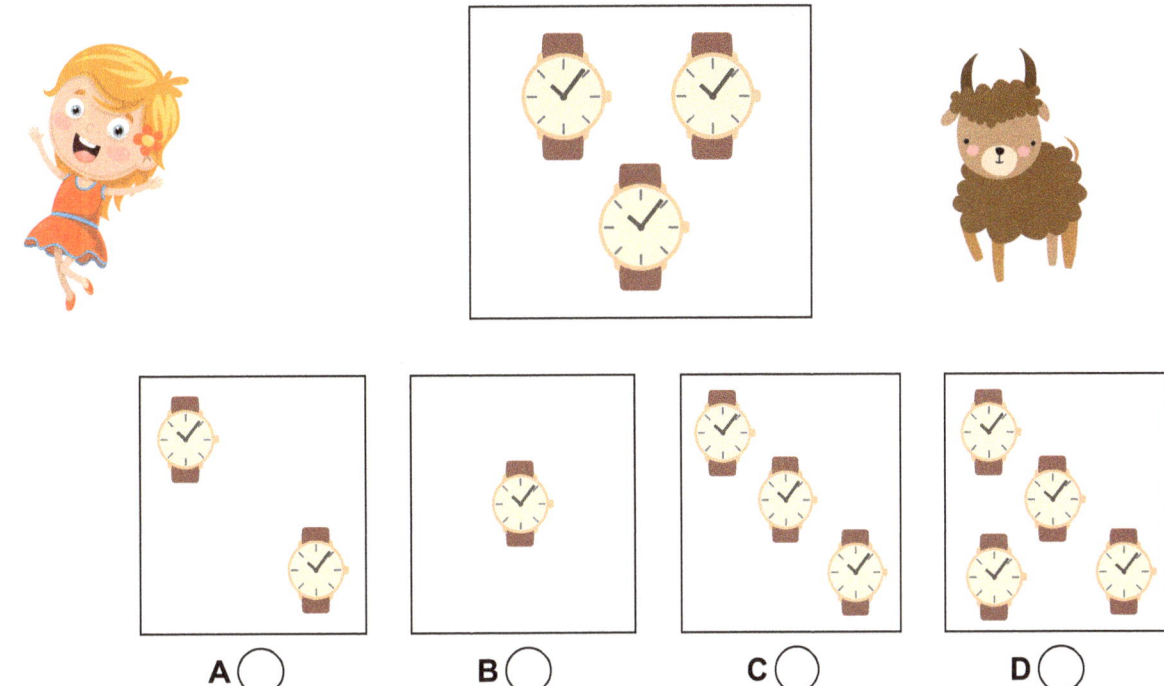

A◯   B◯   C◯   D◯

www.math-knots.com

Q-15 Look at the question with the Monkey. Count the bags in the first picture. Help Maria to bubble the option which shows two more bags than the first picture.

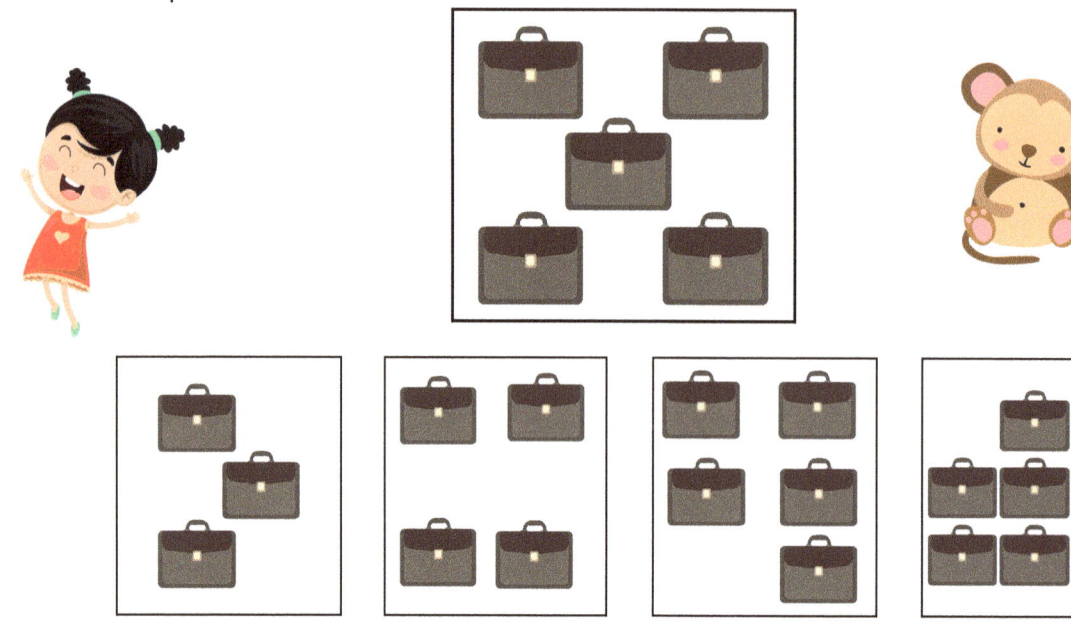

A ◯ B ◯ C ◯ D ◯

Q-16 Look at the question with the Rain Deer. Count the ties in the first picture. Help Mathew to bubble the option which shows three fewer ties than the first picture.

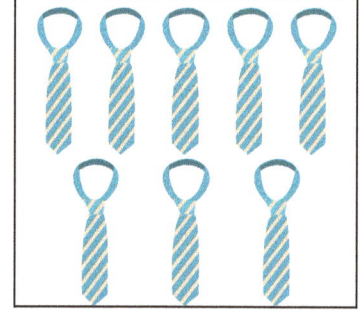

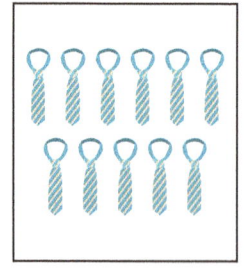
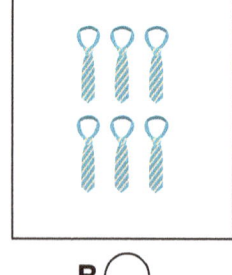
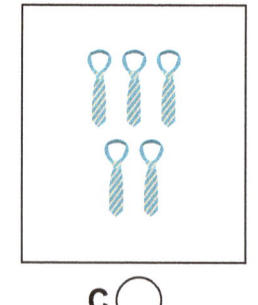

A ◯ B ◯ C ◯ D ◯

www.math-knots.com

Q-17 Look at the question with the Elephant. Count the dresses in the first picture. Help Sri to bubble the option which shows one more dress than the first picture.

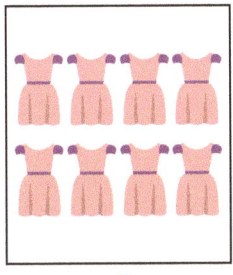

A◯ B◯ C◯ D◯

Q-18 Look at the question with the Lion. Count the shirts in the first picture. Help Chloe to bubble the option which shows three fewer shirts than the first picture.

A◯ B◯ C◯ D◯

www.math-knots.com

TEST - 2

QUANTITATIVE APTITUDE

NUMBER SERIES

Lets Start the Test...

www.math-knots.com

Sample

Look at the question with the Triangle. Cathy is making a pattern with her hexagon shaped beads. Can you help her to identify what goes in the empty string from the given four options A,B,C, and D.

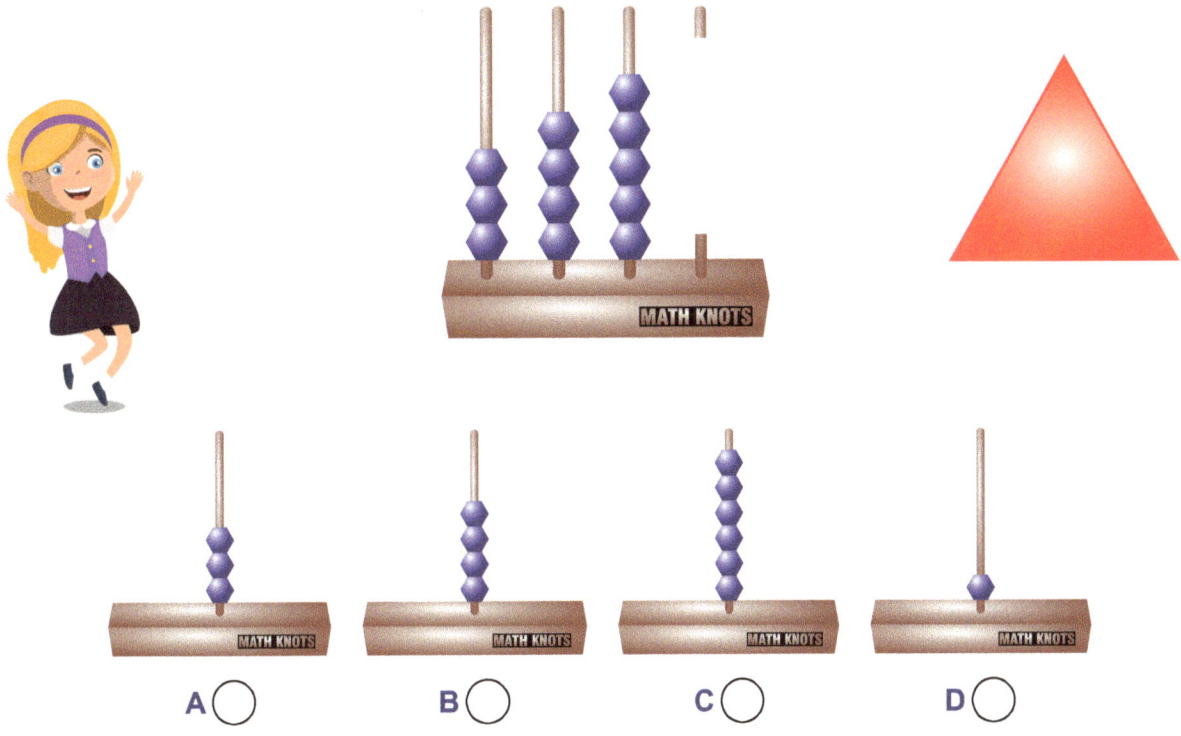

A◯   B◯   C◯   D◯

Solution : C

3,4,5.....

The beads are increasing by 1. So next string should have six beads. Option C is the correct choice. The patterns can increase or decrease by a certain number of beads students are supposed to identify the correct pattern and answer the correct choice.

www.math-knots.com

Q-1 Look at the question with the Flying Saucer. Mary is making a pattern with her hexagon shaped beads. Can you help her to identify what goes in the empty string from the given four options A,B,C, and D.

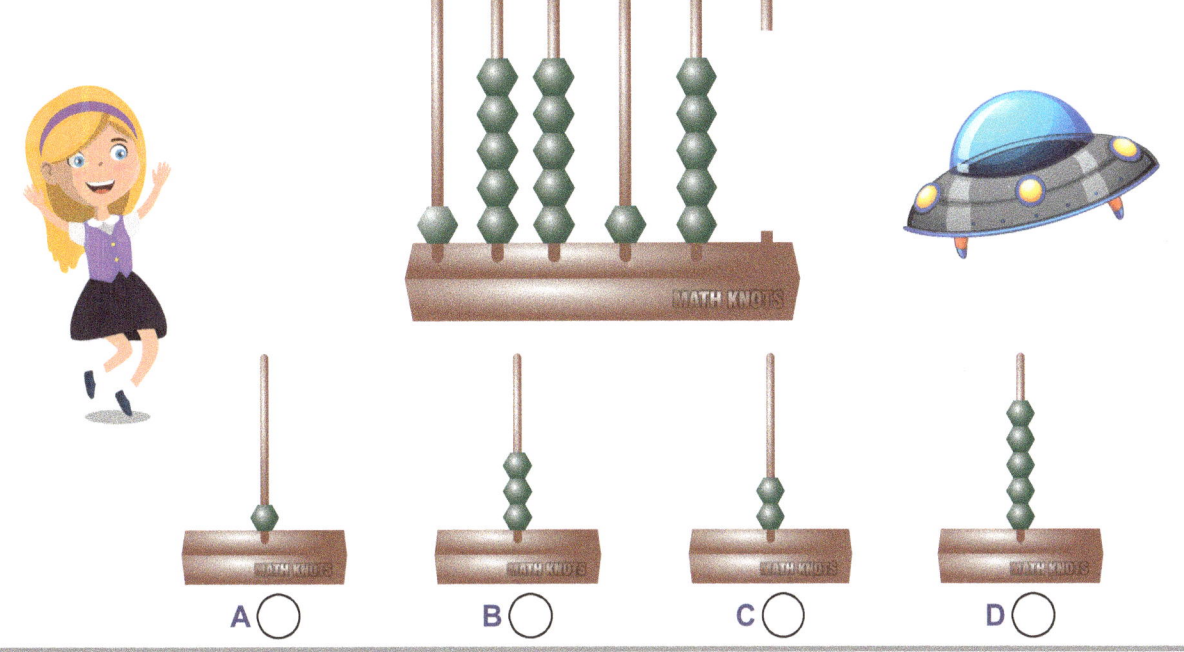

A ◯ B ◯ C ◯ D ◯

Q-2 Look at the question with the Earth. James is making a pattern with his hexagon shaped beads. Can you help him to identify what goes in the empty string from the given four options A,B,C, and D.

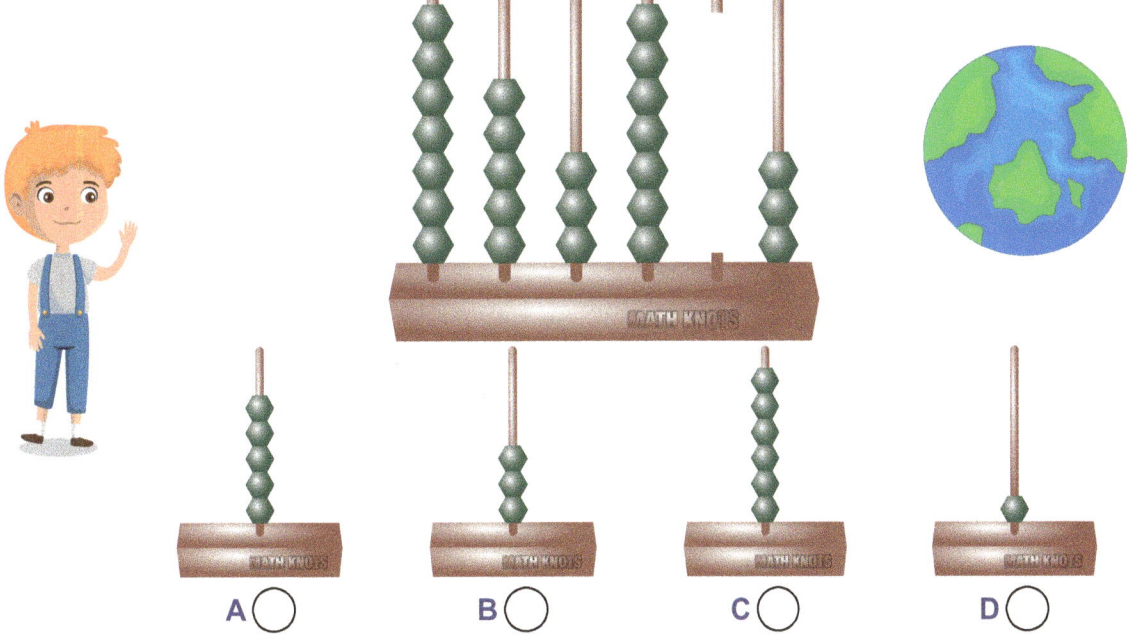

A ◯ B ◯ C ◯ D ◯

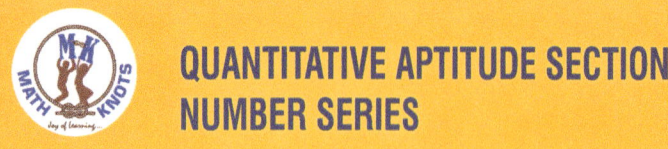
Q-3

Look at the question with the Sun. John is making a pattern with his hexagon shaped beads. Can you help him to identify what goes in the empty string from the given four options A,B,C, and D.

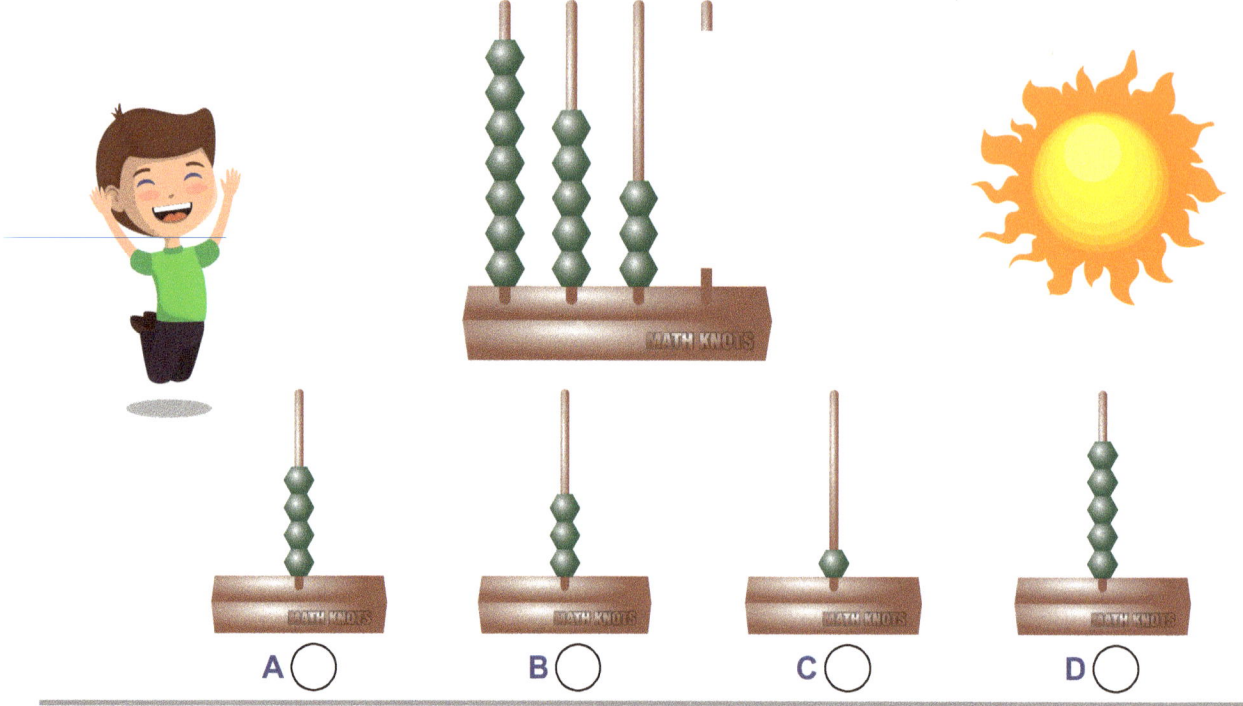

A ◯   B ◯   C ◯   D ◯

Q-4

Look at the question with the Rocket. Mason is making a pattern with his hexagon shaped beads. Can you help him to identify what goes in the empty string from the given four options A,B,C, and D.

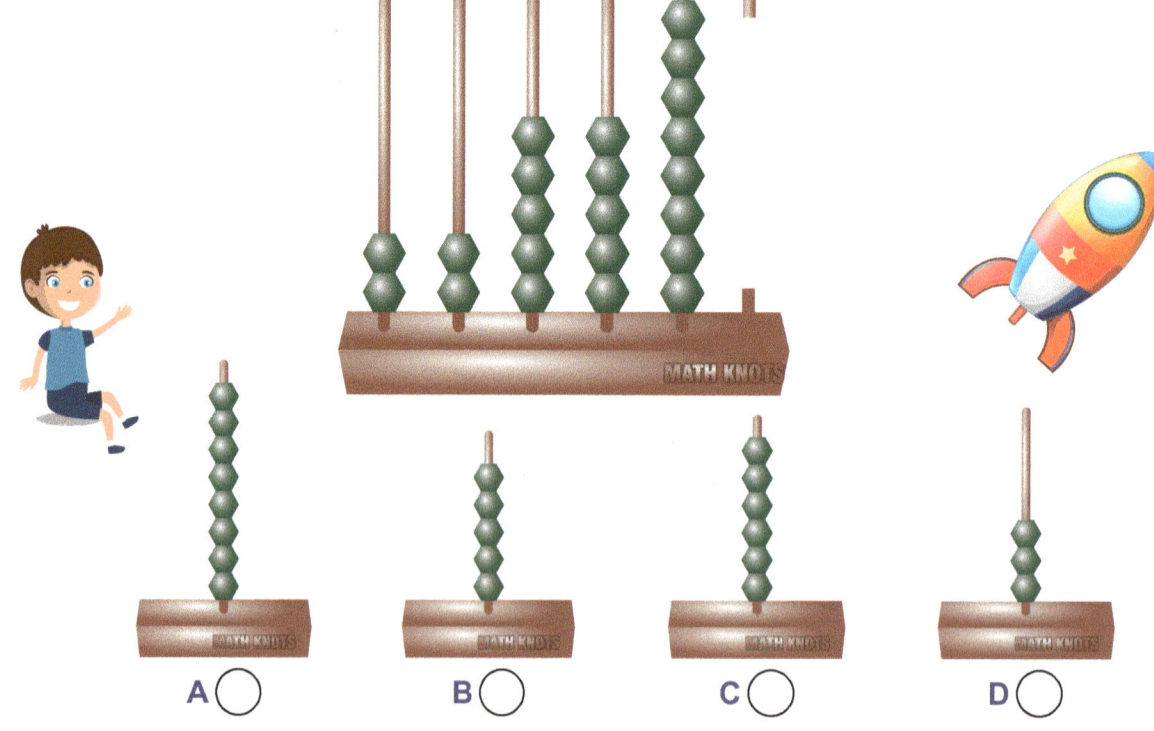

A ◯   B ◯   C ◯   D ◯

www.math-knots.com

Q-5

Look at the question with the Space Shuttle. Elijah is making a pattern with her hexagon shaped beads. Can you help her to identify what goes in the empty string from the given four options A,B,C, and D.

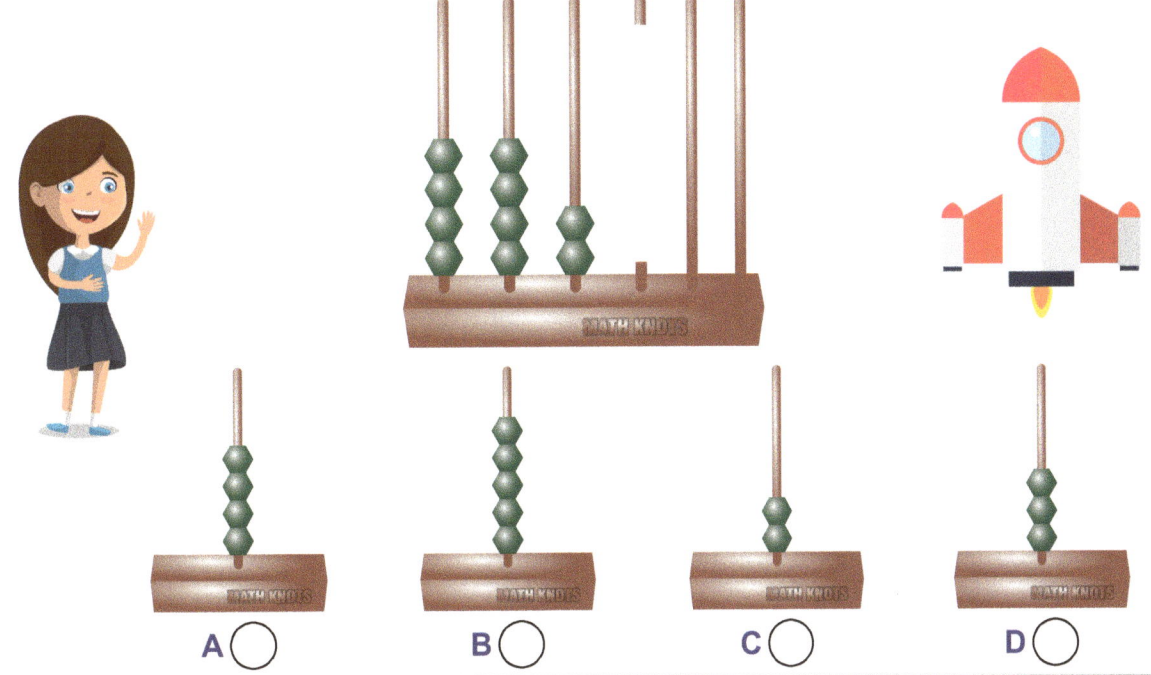

A ◯   B ◯   C ◯   D ◯

Q-6

Look at the question with the Astronaut. Noah is making a pattern with her hexagon shaped beads. Can you help her to identify what goes in the empty string from the given four options A,B,C, and D.

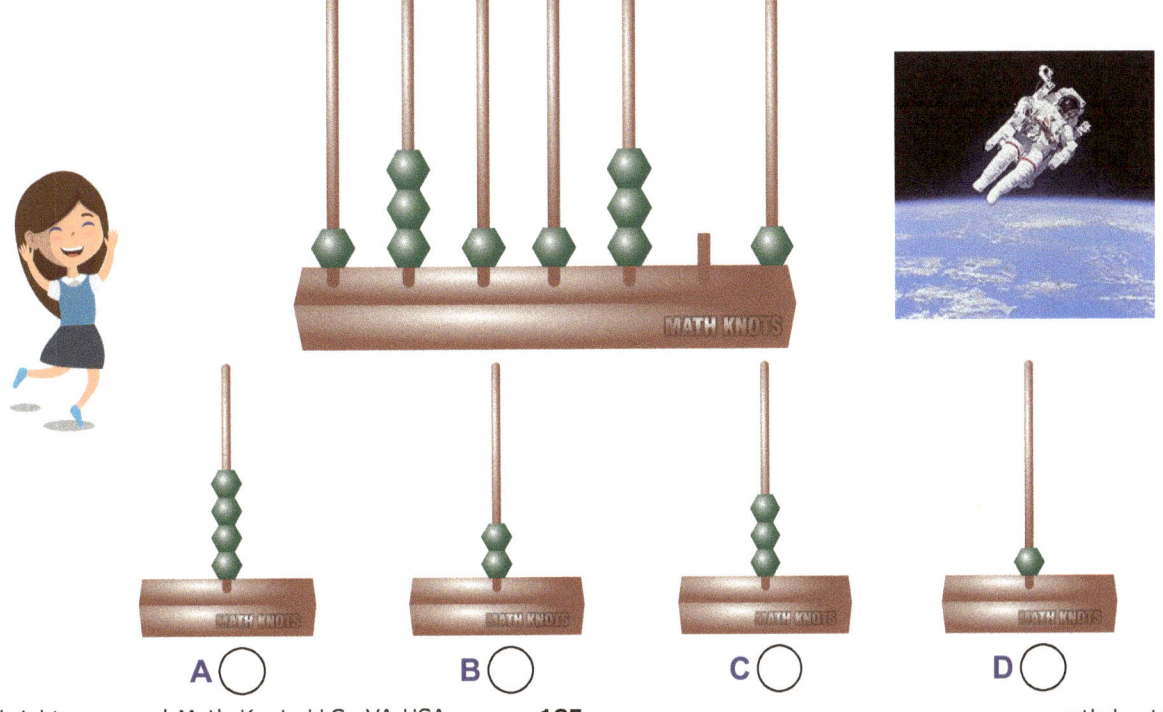

A ◯   B ◯   C ◯   D ◯

www.math-knots.com

Q-7

Look at the question with the Rocket. Emily is making a pattern with her hexagon shaped beads. Can you help her to identify what goes in the empty string from the given four options A,B,C, and D.

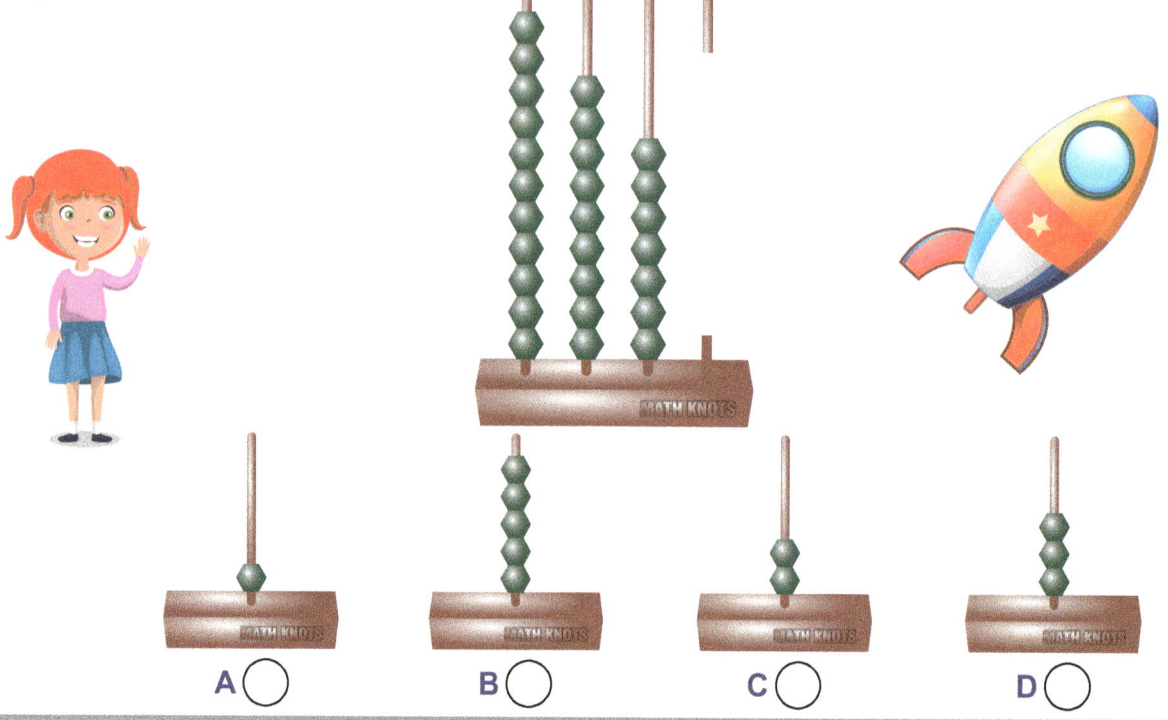

A ○   B ○   C ○   D ○

Q-8

Look at the question with the Saturn. Samuel is making a pattern with his hexagon shaped beads. Can you help him to identify what goes in the empty string from the given four options A,B,C, and D.

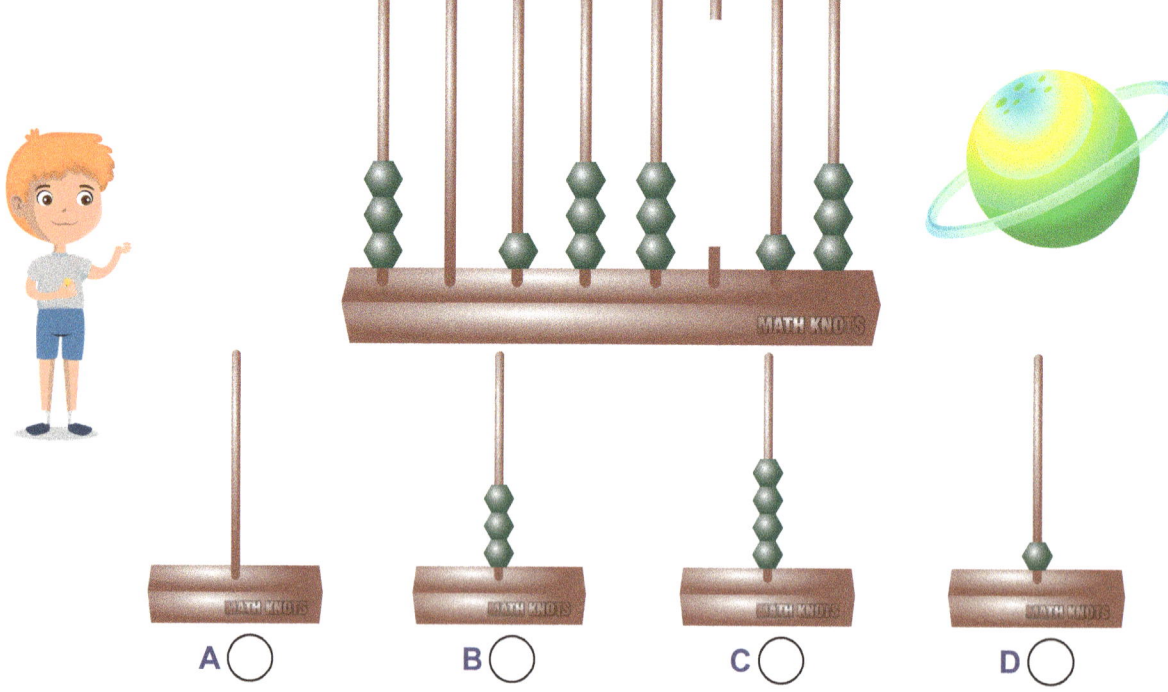

A ○   B ○   C ○   D ○

www.math-knots.com

Q-9 Look at the question with the Astronaut. Jacob is making a pattern with his hexagon shaped beads. Can you help him to identify what goes in the empty string from the given four options A, B, C, and D.

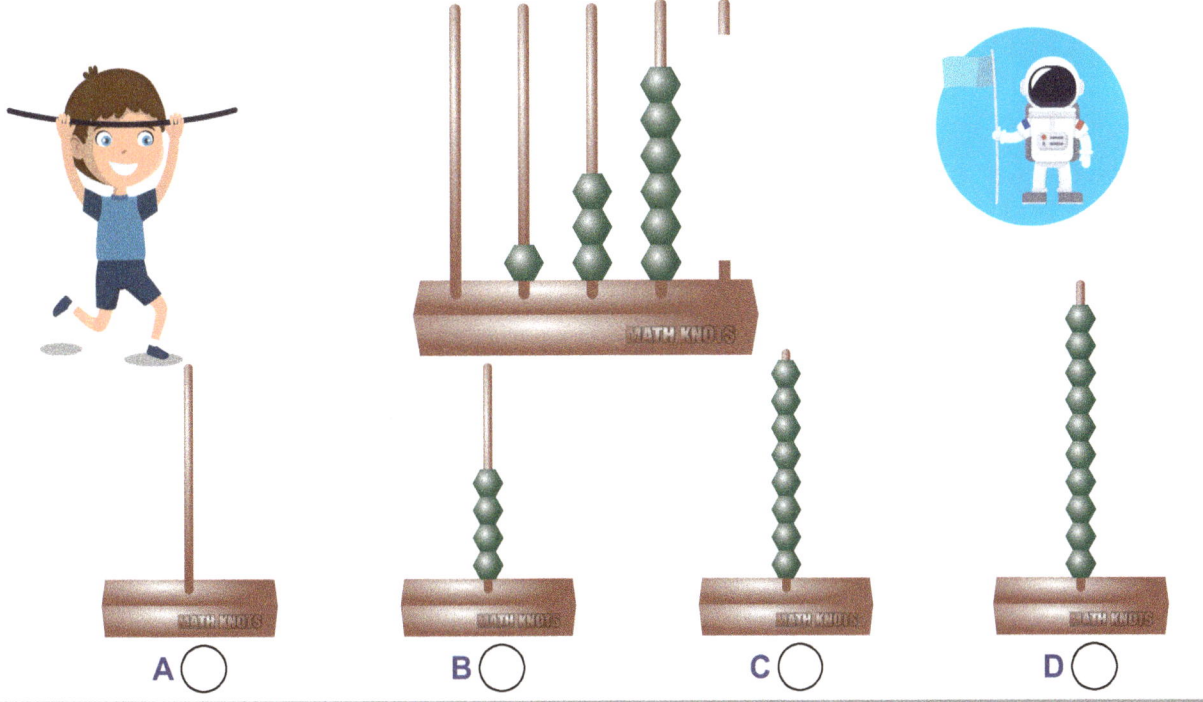

A ◯   B ◯   C ◯   D ◯

Q-10 Look at the question with the Meteor. Jaxon is making a pattern with her hexagon shaped beads. Can you help her to identify what goes in the empty string from the given four options A, B, C, and D.

A ◯   B ◯   C ◯   D ◯

www.math-knots.com

Q-11 Look at the question with the Rocket. Grayson is making a pattern with his hexagon shaped beads. Can you help him to identify what goes in the empty string from the given four options A, B, C, and D.

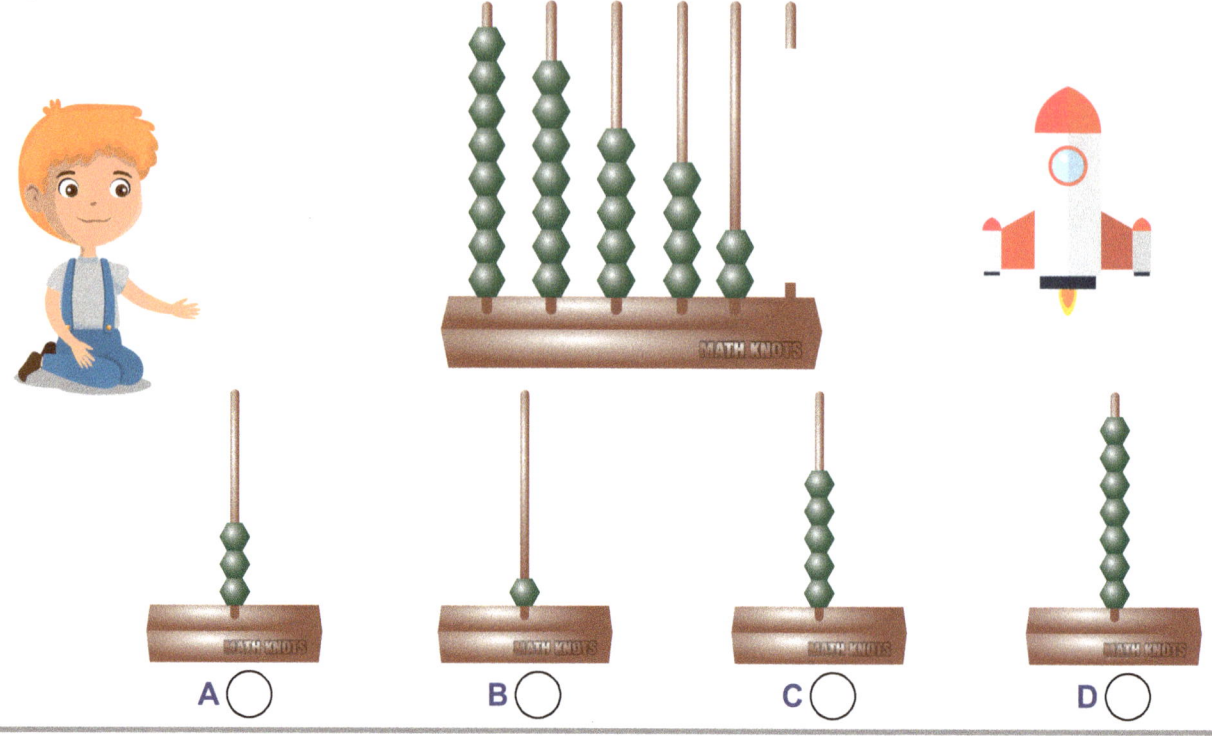

A ◯   B ◯   C ◯   D ◯

Q-12 Look at the question with the Star. Jayden is making a pattern with his hexagon shaped beads. Can you help him to identify what goes in the empty string from the given four options A, B, C, and D.

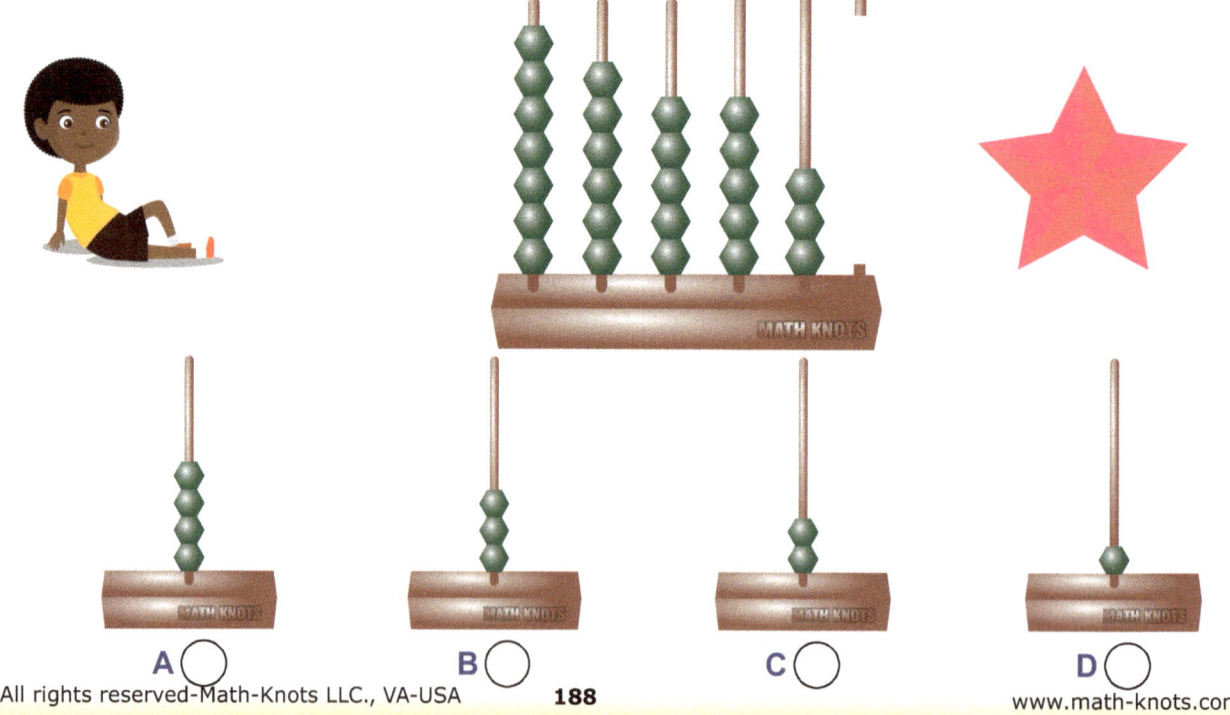

A ◯   B ◯   C ◯   D ◯

www.math-knots.com

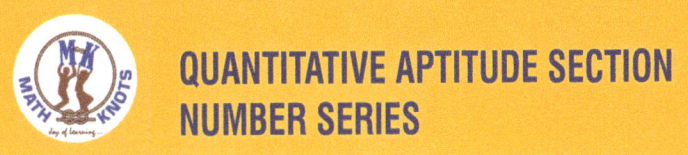
Q-13 Look at the question with the Galaxy. Isabella is making a pattern with her hexagon shaped beads. Can you help her to identify what goes in the empty string from the given four options A, B, C, and D.

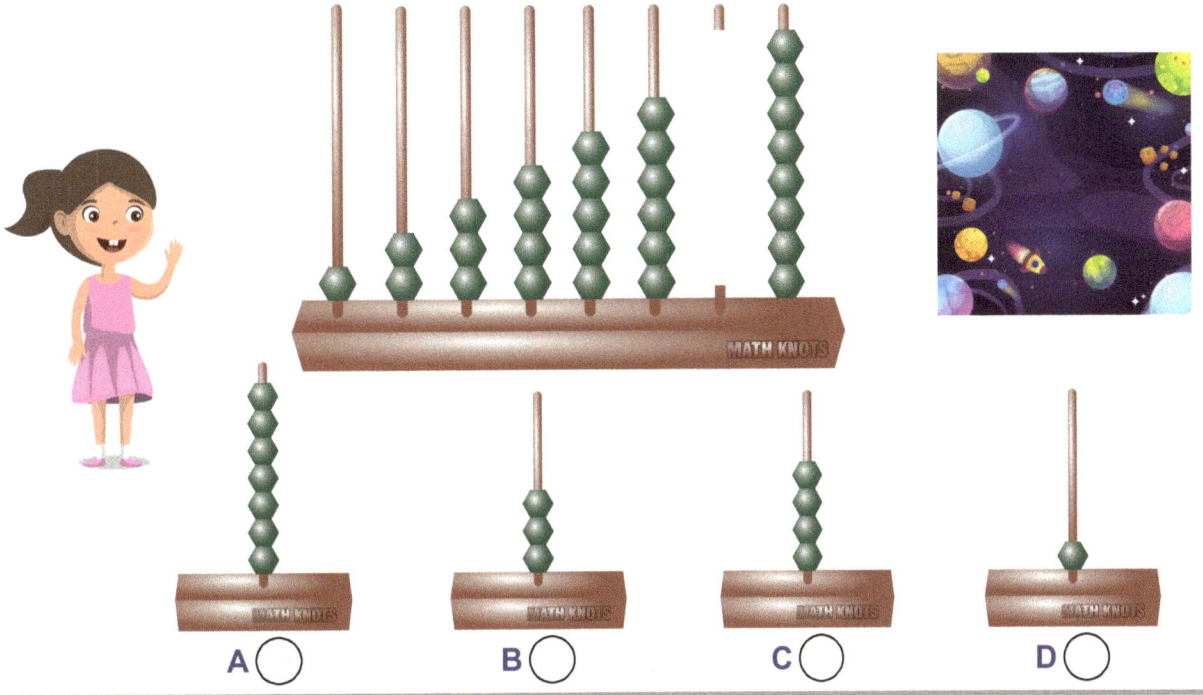

A ⃝   B ⃝   C ⃝   D ⃝

Q-14 Look at the question with the Telescope. Emma is making a pattern with her hexagon shaped beads. Can you help her to identify what goes in the empty string from the given four options A, B, C, and D.

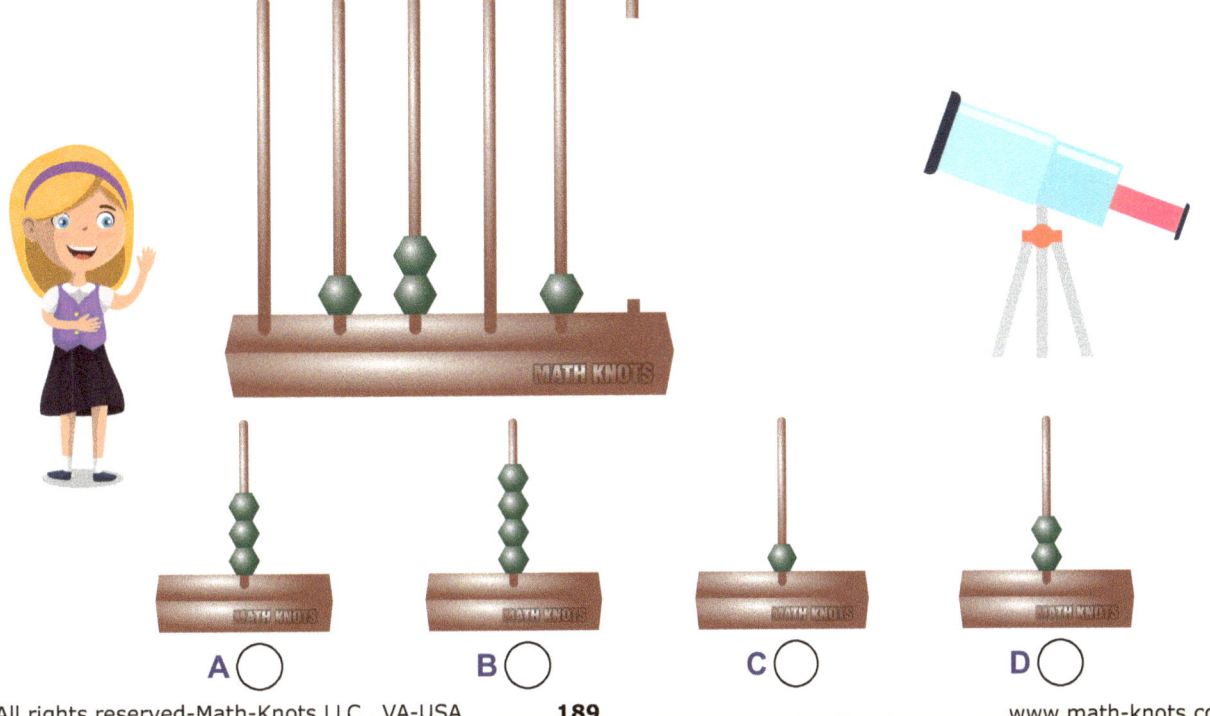

A ⃝   B ⃝   C ⃝   D ⃝

Q-15 Look at the question with the Orbit. Ava is making a pattern with her hexagon shaped beads. Can you help her to identify what goes in the empty string from the given four options A,B,C, and D.

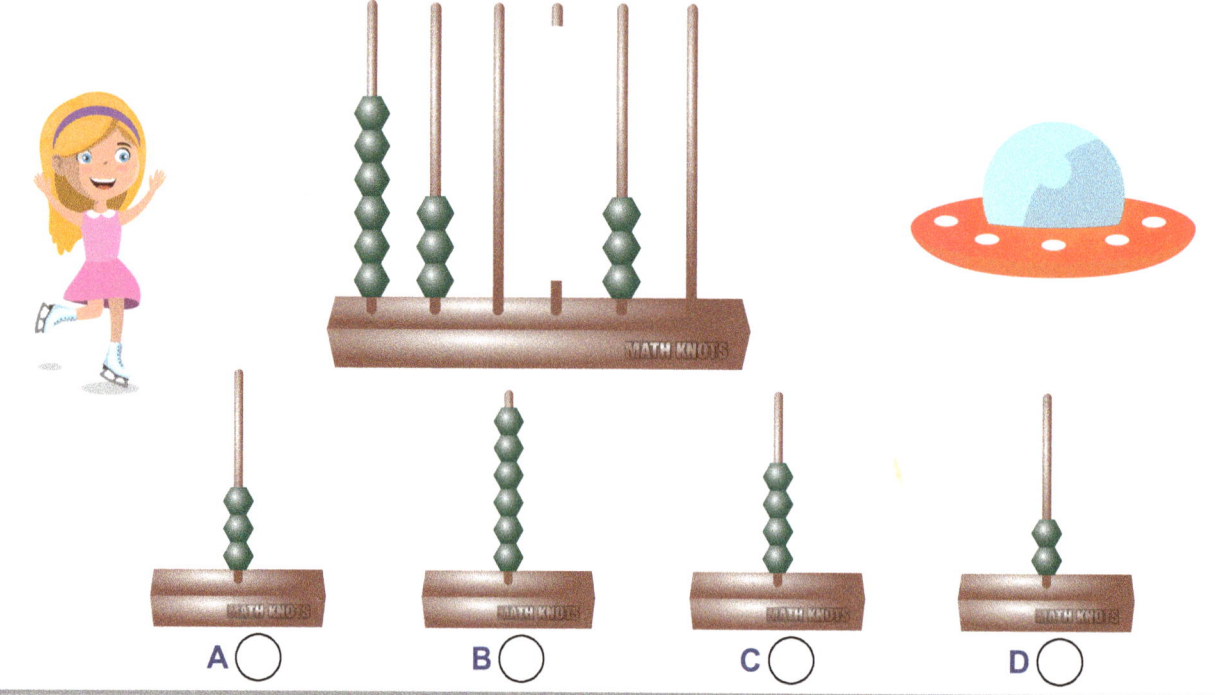

A ◯   B ◯   C ◯   D ◯

Q-16 Look at the question with the Satellite. Olivia is making a pattern with her hexagon shaped beads. Can you help her to identify what goes in the empty string from the given four options A,B,C, and D.

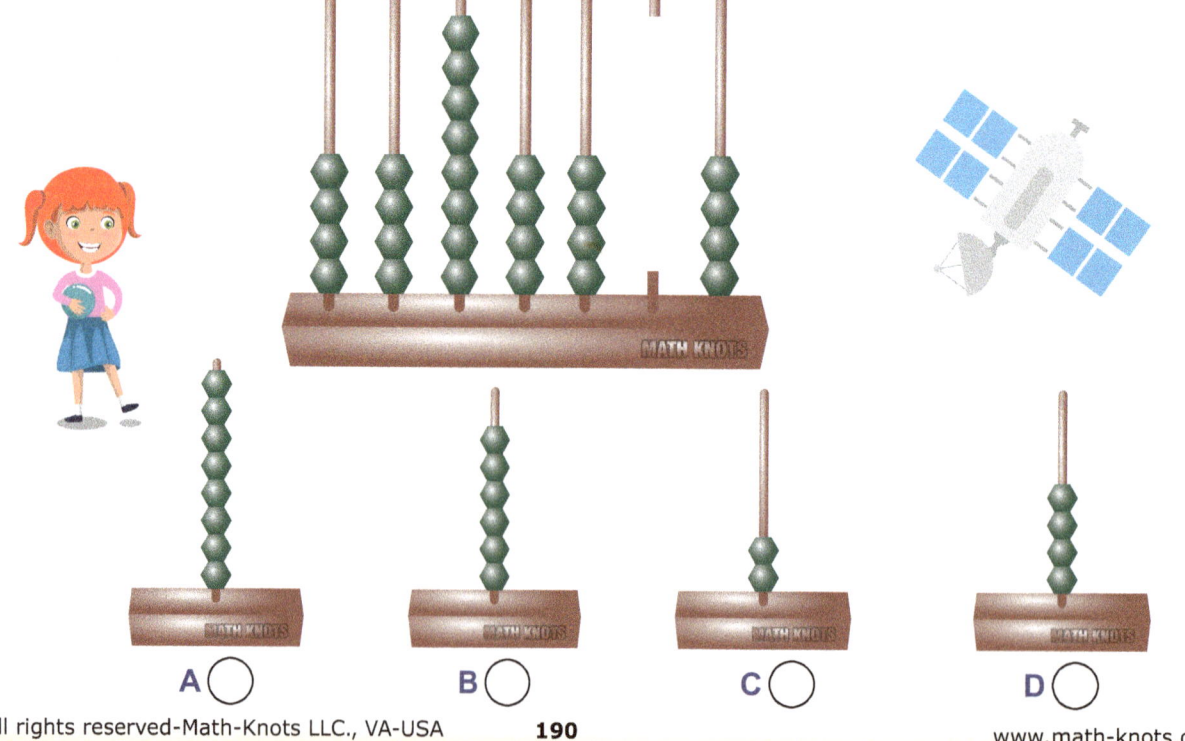

A ◯   B ◯   C ◯   D ◯

www.math-knots.com

Q-17 Look at the question with the Lab Equipment. Charlotte is making a pattern with her hexagon shaped beads. Can you help her to identify what goes in the empty string from the given four options A ,B ,C, and D.

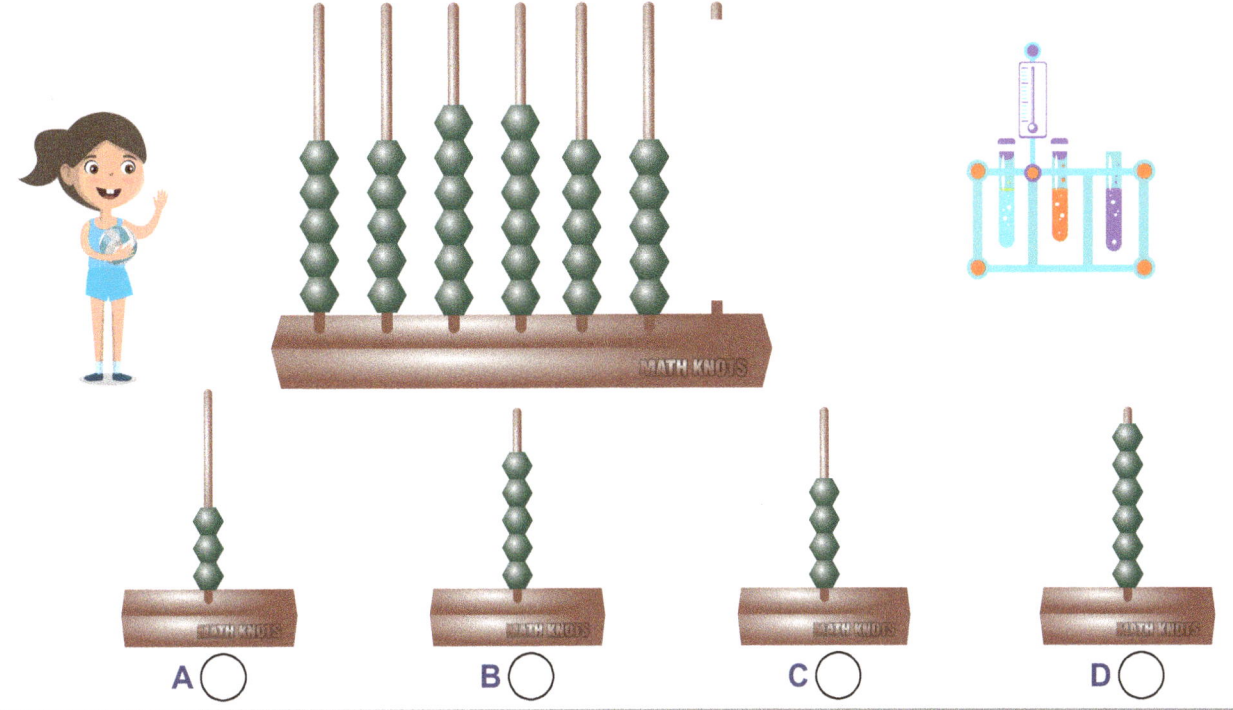

A ⃝   B ⃝   C ⃝   D ⃝

Q-18 Look at the question with the Lab Equipment. Claud is making a pattern with his hexagon shaped beads. Can you help him to identify what goes in the empty string from the given four options A ,B ,C, and D.

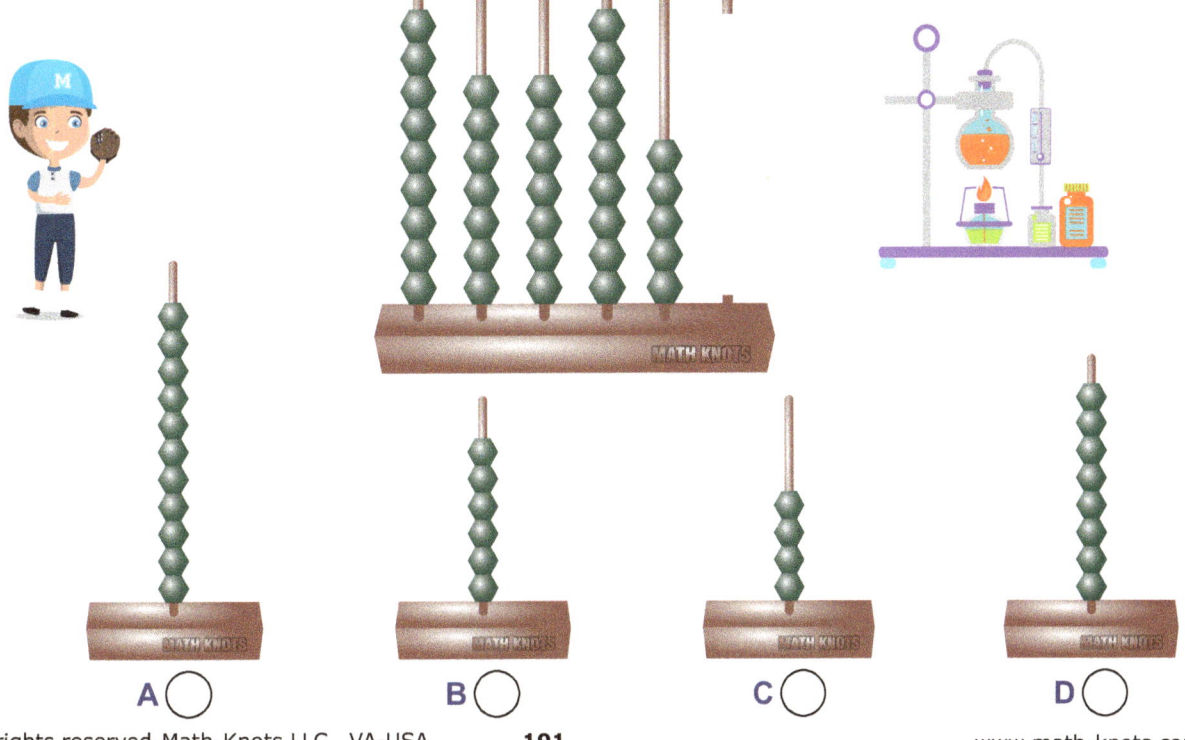

A ⃝   B ⃝   C ⃝   D ⃝

www.math-knots.com

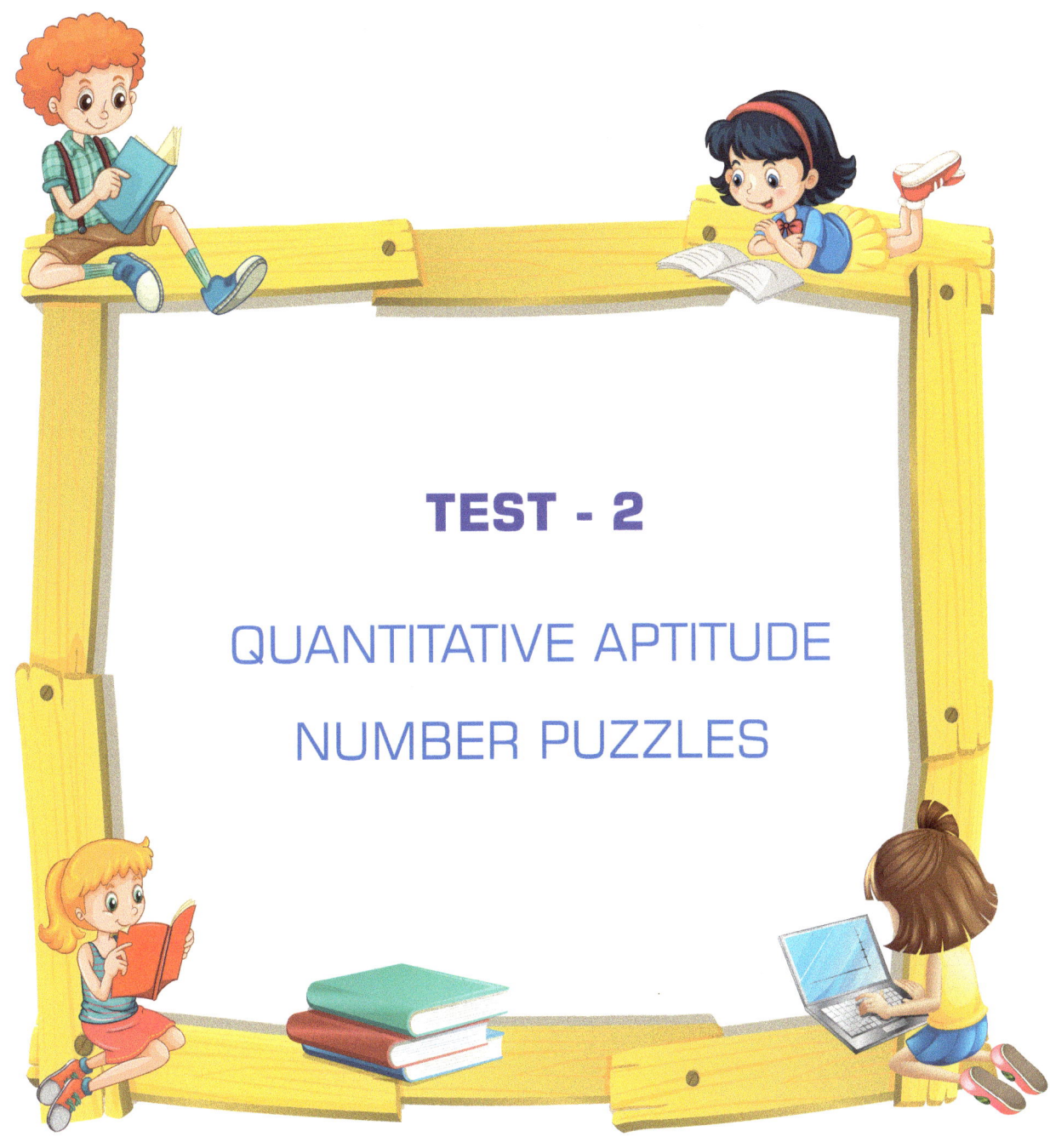

TEST - 2

QUANTITATIVE APTITUDE

NUMBER PUZZLES

Lets Start the Test...

www.math-knots.com

Sample

Look at the question and put your finger on the Guitar. Ryan is wondering what is the missing number under the question mark ? Help him to find the missing number under the question mark and fill in the bubble.

A ○	B ○	C ○	D ○
1	**0**	**5**	**2**

Solution : A

How much should be added to 2 to make it 3

3 - 2 = 1

Meaning if we add 1 to 2 we get a total of three.

Q-1 Look at the question with the Dolphin. Chen is wondering what is the missing number under the question mark ? Help him to find the missing number under the question mark and fill in the bubble.

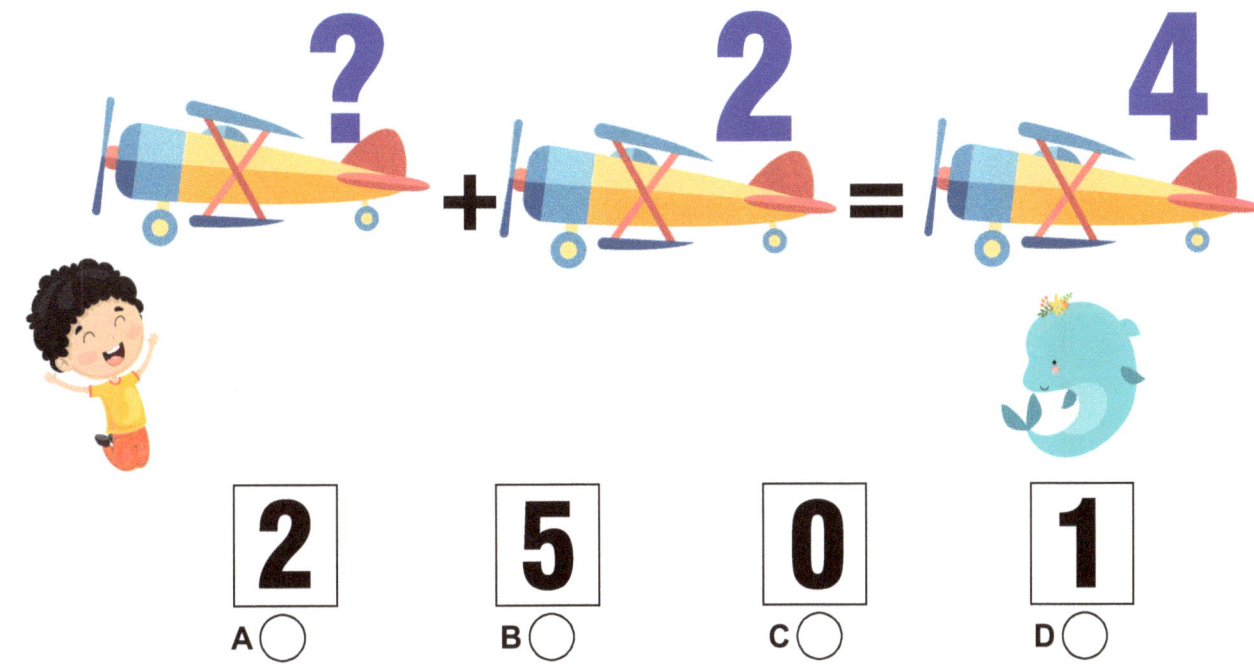

2	**5**	**0**	**1**
A ⚪	B ⚪	C ⚪	D ⚪

Q-2 Look at the question with the Cat. Ria is wondering what is the missing number is under the question mark ? Help her to find the missing number under the question mark and fill in the bubble.

2	**4**	**1**	**8**
A ⚪	B ⚪	C ⚪	D ⚪

www.math-knots.com

Q-3

Look at the question with the Alligator. Ryan is wondering what is the missing number under the question mark ? Help him to find the missing number under the question mark and fill in the bubble.

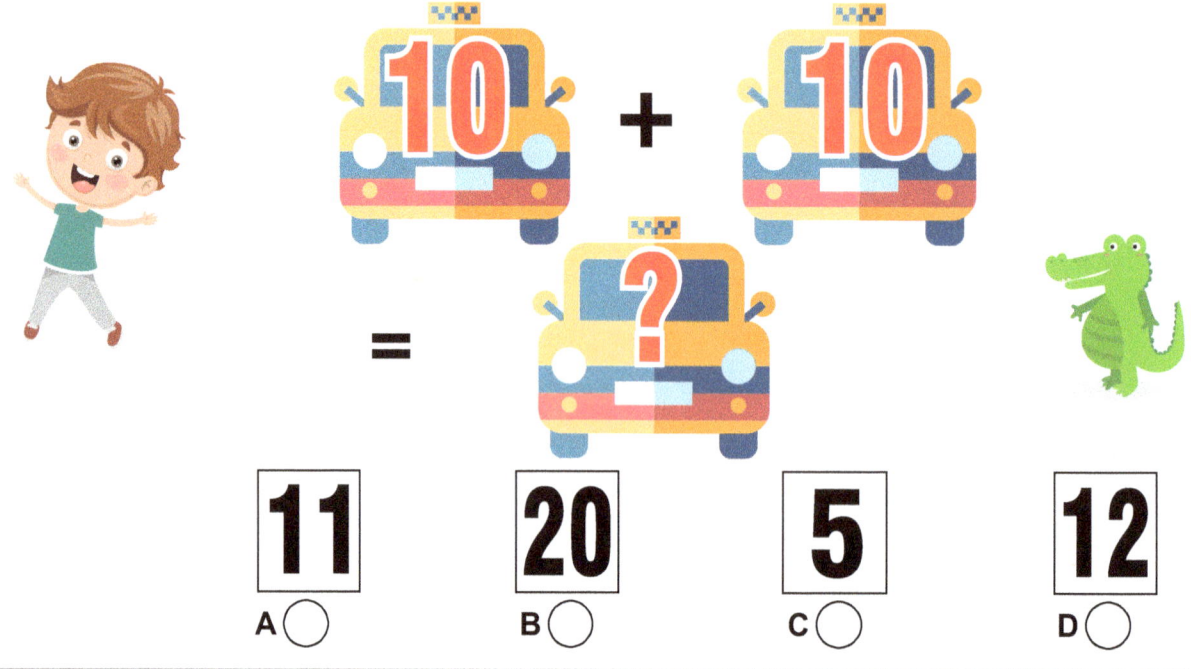

11	20	5	12
A ◯	B ◯	C ◯	D ◯

Q-4

Look at the question with the Bird. Ali is wondering what is the missing number under the question mark ? Help him to find the missing number under the question mark and fill in the bubble.

5	4	7	2
A ◯	B ◯	C ◯	D ◯

www.math-knots.com

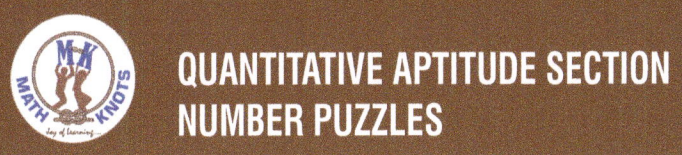
Q-5 Look at the question with the Cow. Jia is wondering what is the missing number under the question mark ? Help her to find the missing number under the question mark and fill in the bubble.

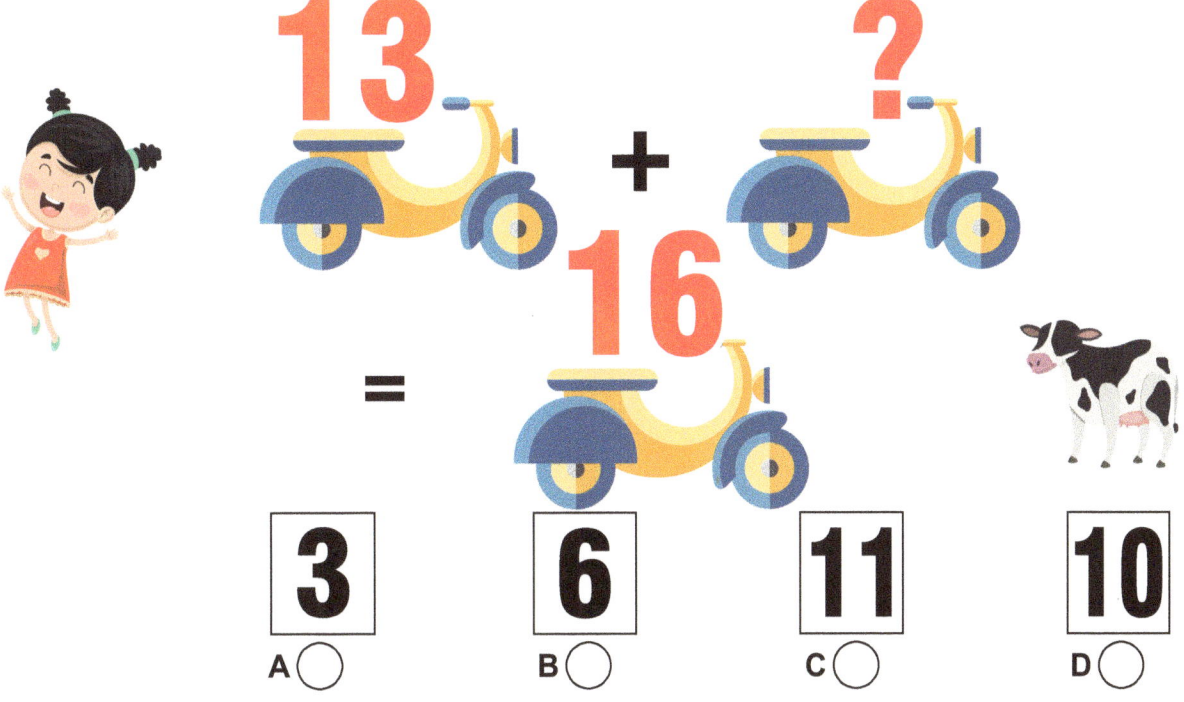

3	6	11	10
A◯	B◯	C◯	D◯

Q-6 Look at the question with the Whale. Sam is wondering what is the missing number under the question mark ? Help her to find the missing number under the question mark and fill in the bubble.

5	6	1	0
A◯	B◯	C◯	D◯

www.math-knots.com

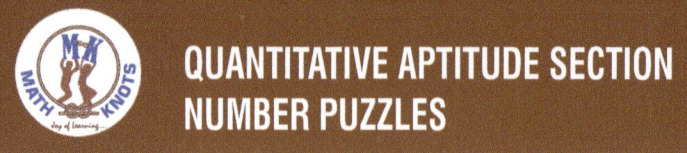
Q-7 Look at the question with the Elephant. Siya is wondering what is the missing number under the question mark? Help her to find the missing number under the question mark and fill in the bubble.

15	2	5	0
A ○	B ○	C ○	D ○

Q-8 Look at the question with the Fox. Mike is wondering what is the missing number under the question mark? Help him to find the missing number under the question mark and fill in the bubble.

0	6	1	8
A ○	B ○	C ○	D ○

www.math-knots.com

Q-9

Look at the question with the Giraffe. Reva is wondering what is the missing number under the question mark ? Help her to find the missing number under the question mark and fill in the bubble.

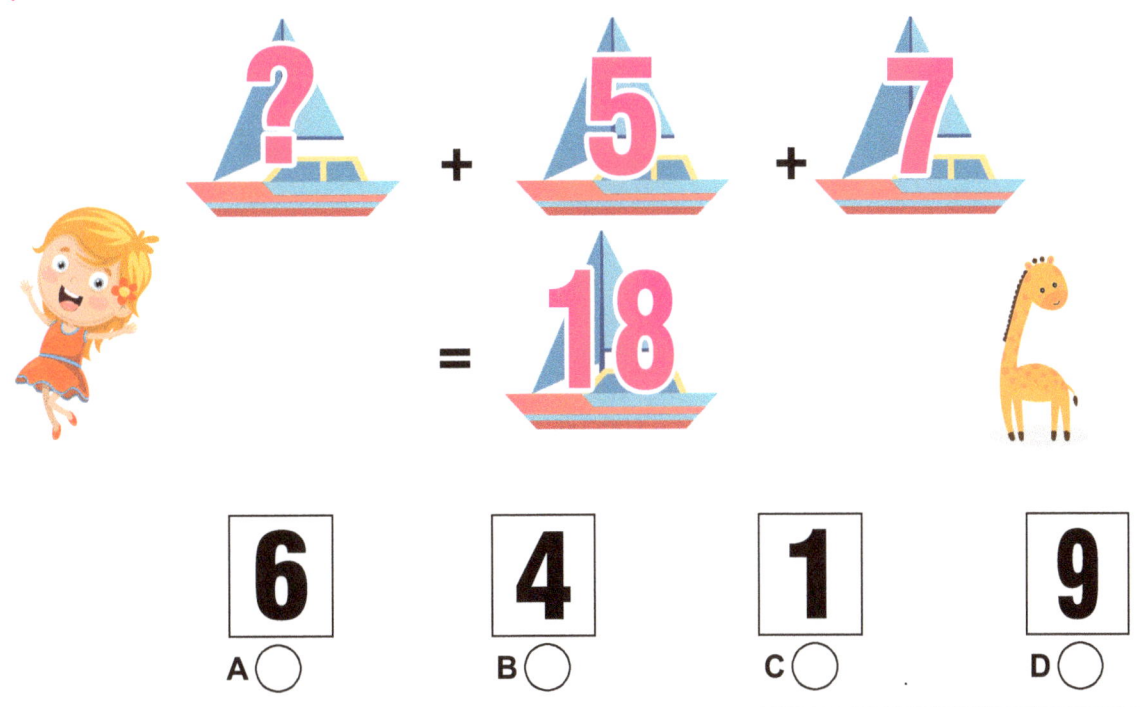

6	4	1	9
A ○	B ○	C ○	D ○

Q-10

Look at the question with the Hegehog. Bob is wondering what is the missing number under the question mark ? Help him to find the missing number under the question mark and fill in the bubble.

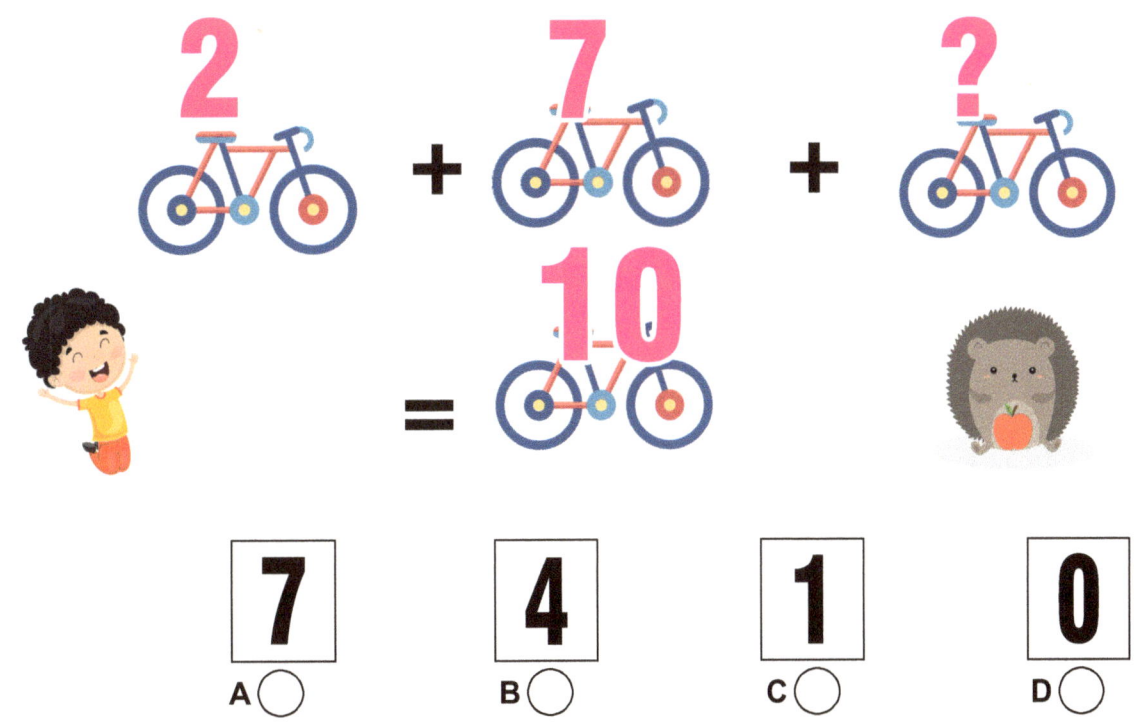

7	4	1	0
A ○	B ○	C ○	D ○

www.math-knots.com

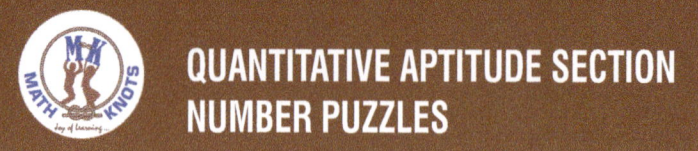
Q-11 Look at the question with the Iguana. Rima is wondering what is the missing number under the question mark ? Help her to find the missing number under the question mark and fill in the bubble.

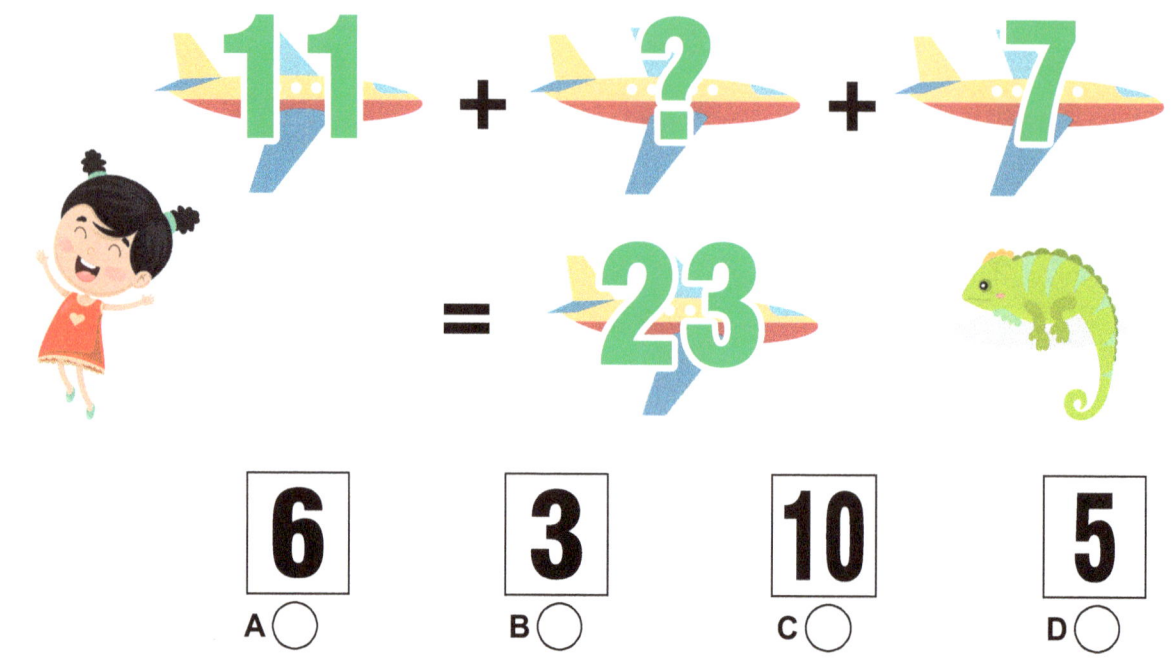

6	3	10	5
A◯	B◯	C◯	D◯

Q-12 Look at the question with the Jelly Fish. Dan is wondering what is the missing number under the question mark ? Help him to find the missing number under the question mark and fill in the bubble.

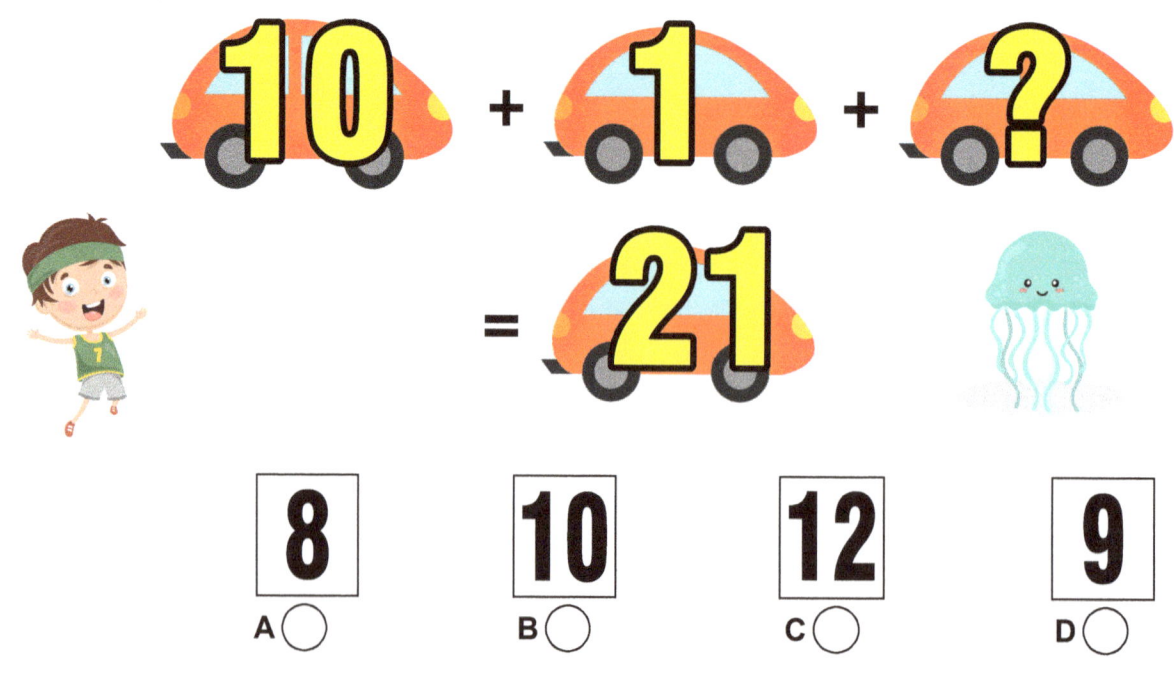

8	10	12	9
A◯	B◯	C◯	D◯

www.math-knots.com

Q-13 Look at the question with the Koala Bear. Rita is wondering what is the missing number under the question mark ? Help her to find the missing number under the question mark and fill in the bubble.

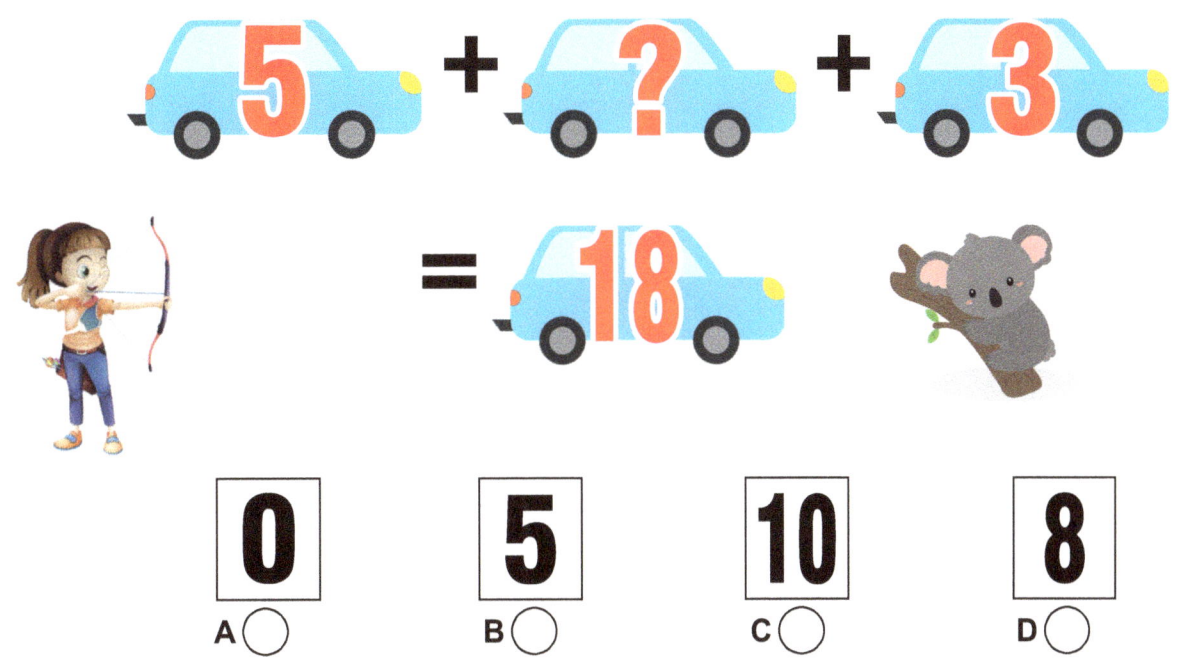

A ⃝ 0   B ⃝ 5   C ⃝ 10   D ⃝ 8

Q-14 Look at the question with the Lion. Kate is wondering what is the missing number under the question mark ? Help her to find the missing number under the question mark and fill in the bubble.

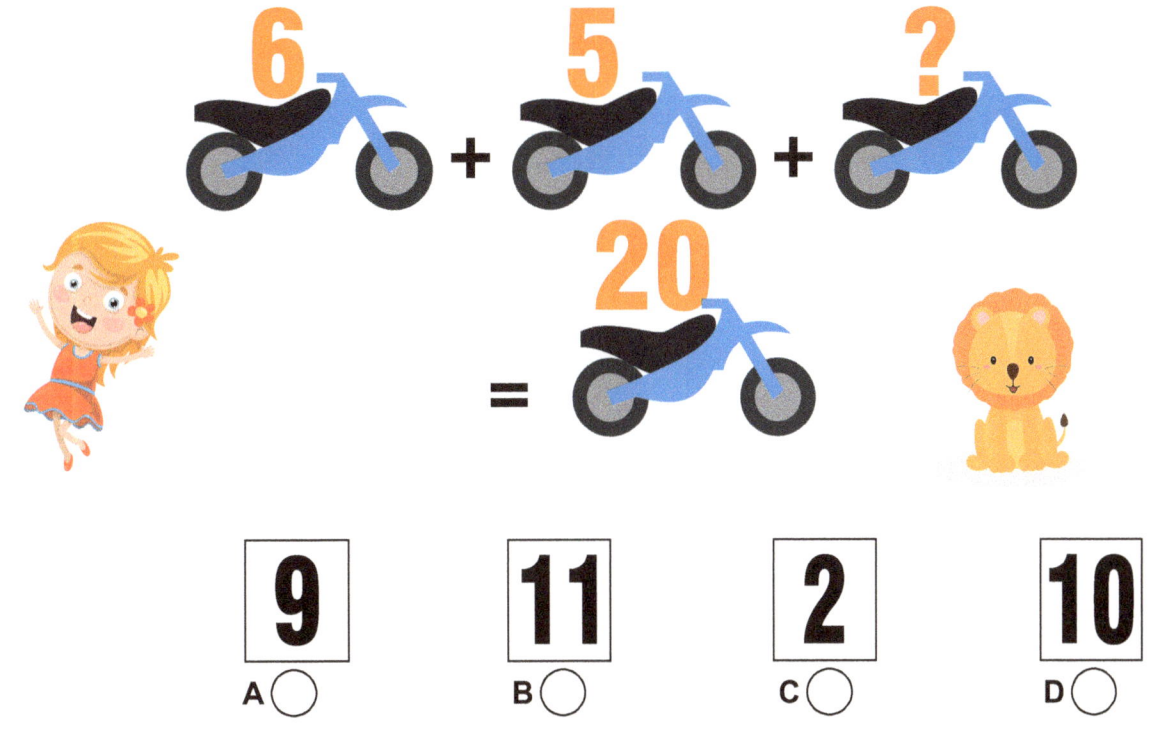

A ⃝ 9   B ⃝ 11   C ⃝ 2   D ⃝ 10

www.math-knots.com

Q-15 Look at the question with the Monkey. Ana is wondering what is the missing number under the question mark ? Help her to find the missing number under the question mark and fill in the bubble.

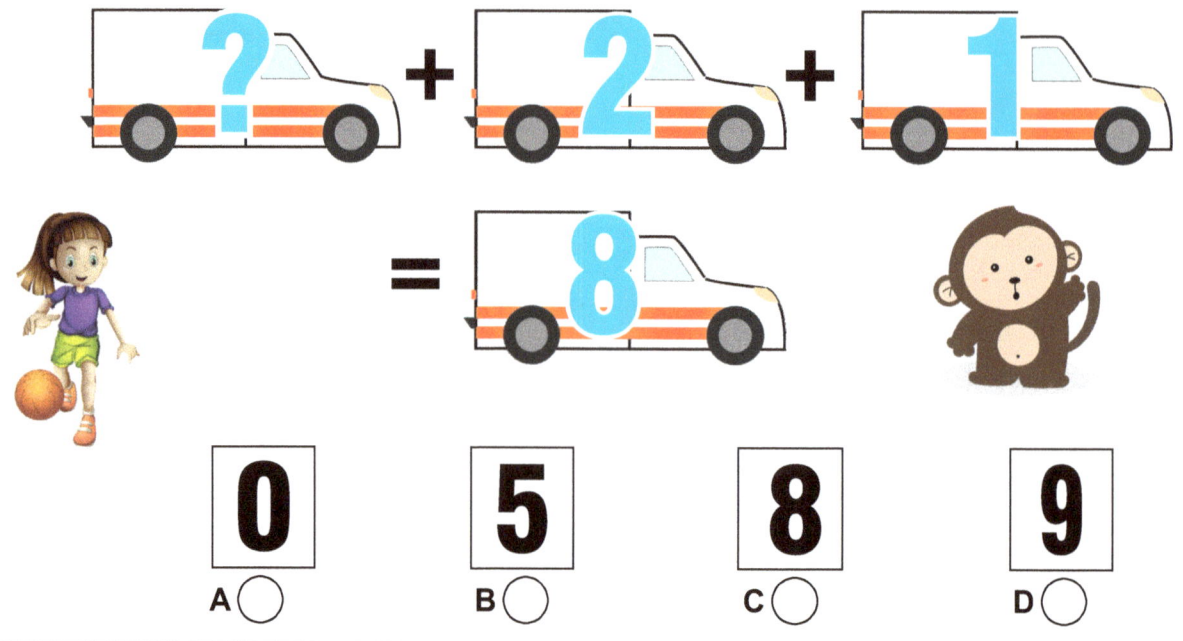

0	**5**	**8**	**9**
A⭕	B⭕	C⭕	D⭕

Q-16 Look at the question with the Whale. Carol is wondering what is the missing number under the question mark ? Help her to find the missing number under the question mark and fill in the bubble.

1	**10**	**3**	**0**
A⭕	B⭕	C⭕	D⭕

www.math-knots.com

Q-17 Look at the question with the Octopus. Mathew is wondering what is the missing number under the question mark ? Help him to find the missing number under the question mark and fill in the bubble.

A ◯ 3

B ◯ 15

C ◯ 4

D ◯ 0

Q-18 Look at the question with the Pig. Rose is wondering what is the missing number under the question mark ? Help her to find the missing number under the question mark and fill in the bubble.

A ◯ 5

B ◯ 6

C ◯ 7

D ◯ 10

www.math-knots.com

Q-19

Look at the question with the Quail. Benjamin is wondering what is the missing number under the question mark ? Help him to find the missing number under the question mark and fill in the bubble.

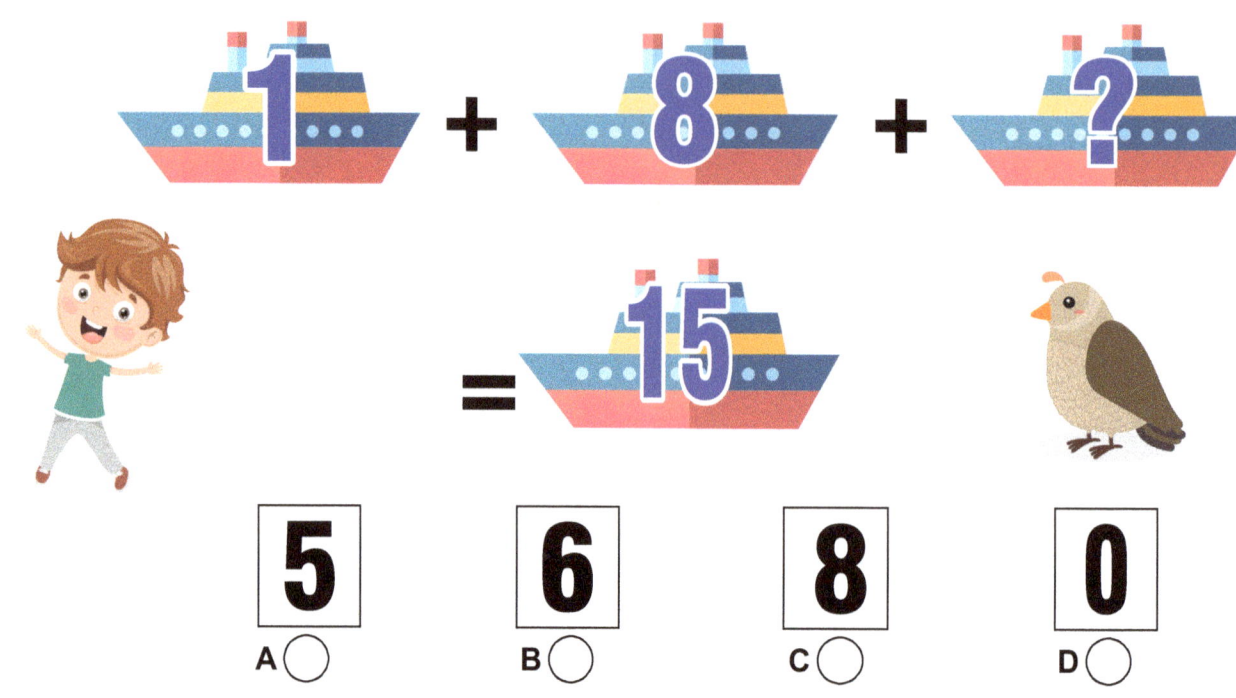

A ◯	B ◯	C ◯	D ◯
5	6	8	0

Q-20

Look at the question with the Raccoon. Caralin is wondering what is the missing number under the question mark ? Help her to find the missing number under the question mark and fill in the bubble.

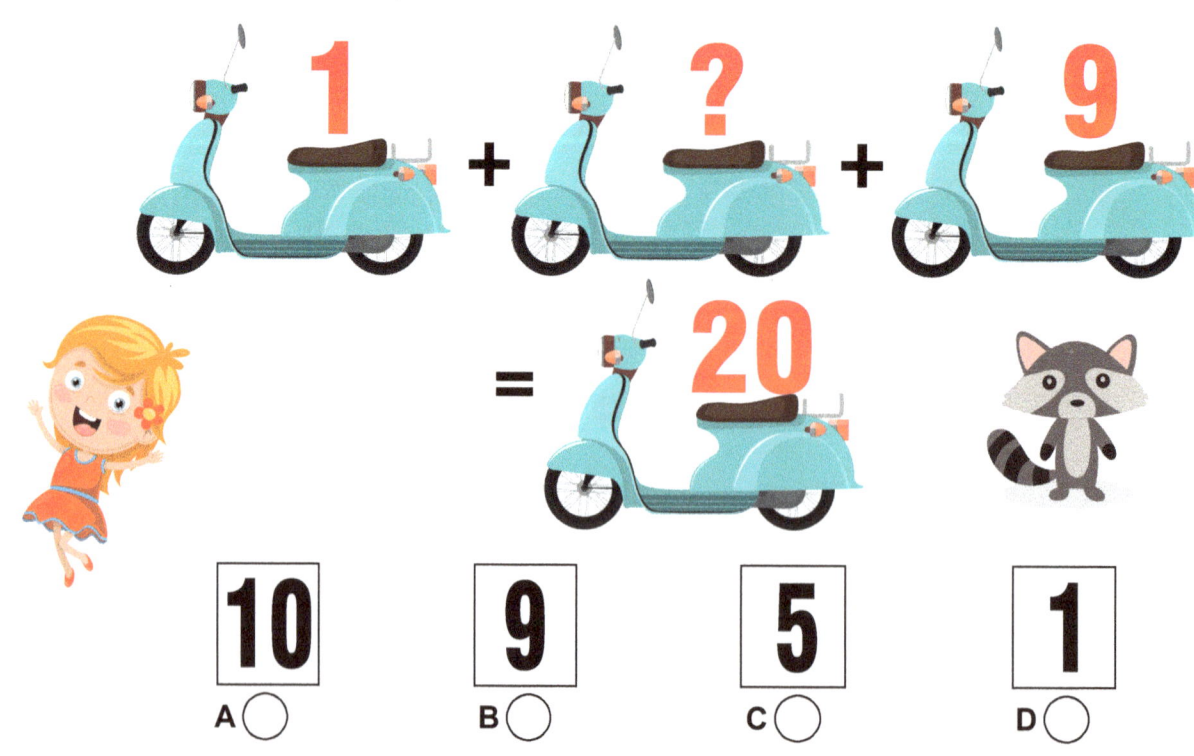

A ◯	B ◯	C ◯	D ◯
10	9	5	1

www.math-knots.com

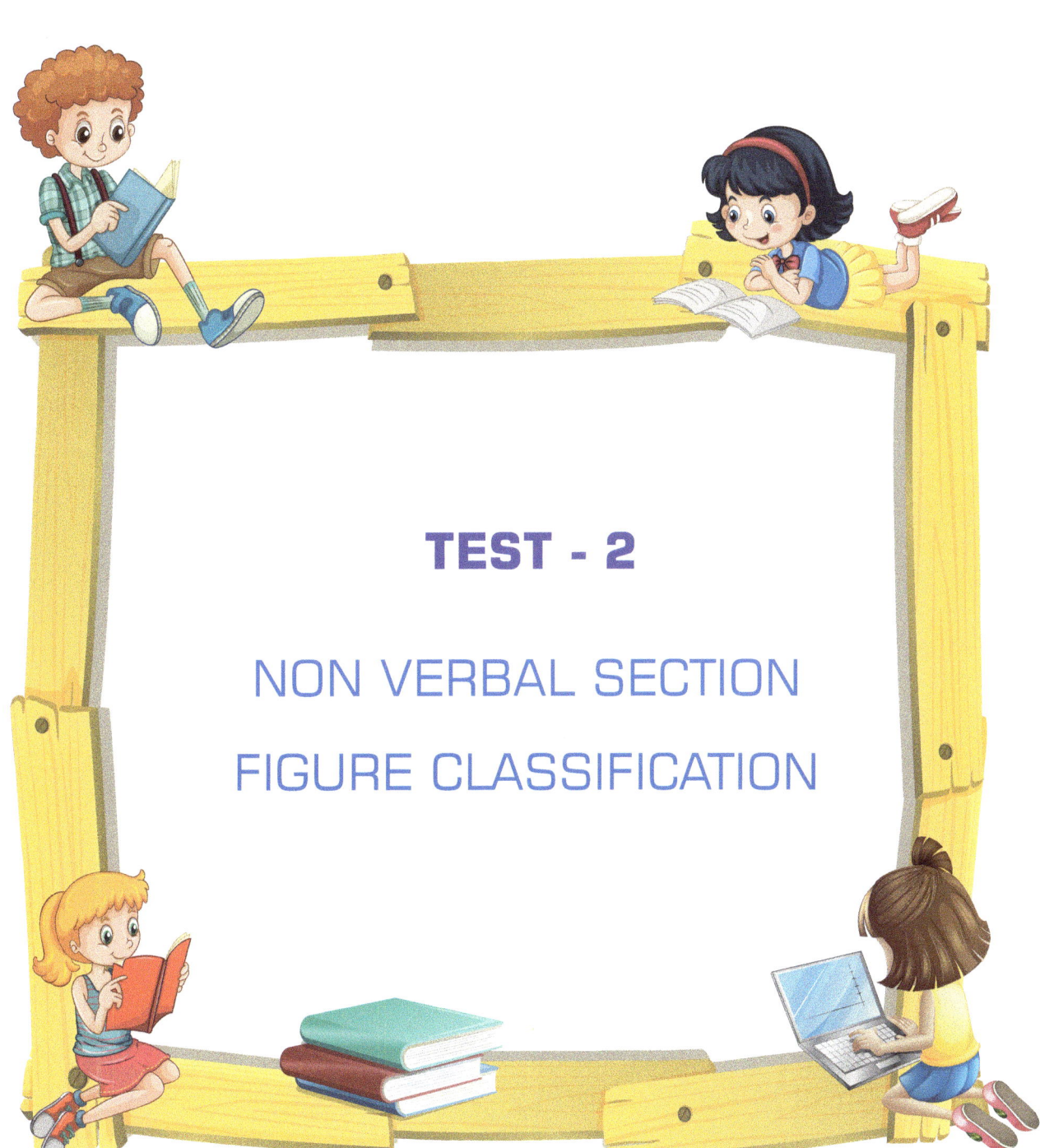

TEST - 2

NON VERBAL SECTION

FIGURE CLASSIFICATION

Lets Start the Test...

www.math-knots.com

Sample Look at the question with the Tree. The first three pictures belong to one group in a common way. Help Bob to find out which of the below options belong to the same group. Identify the correct picture and help him to bubble the right choice.

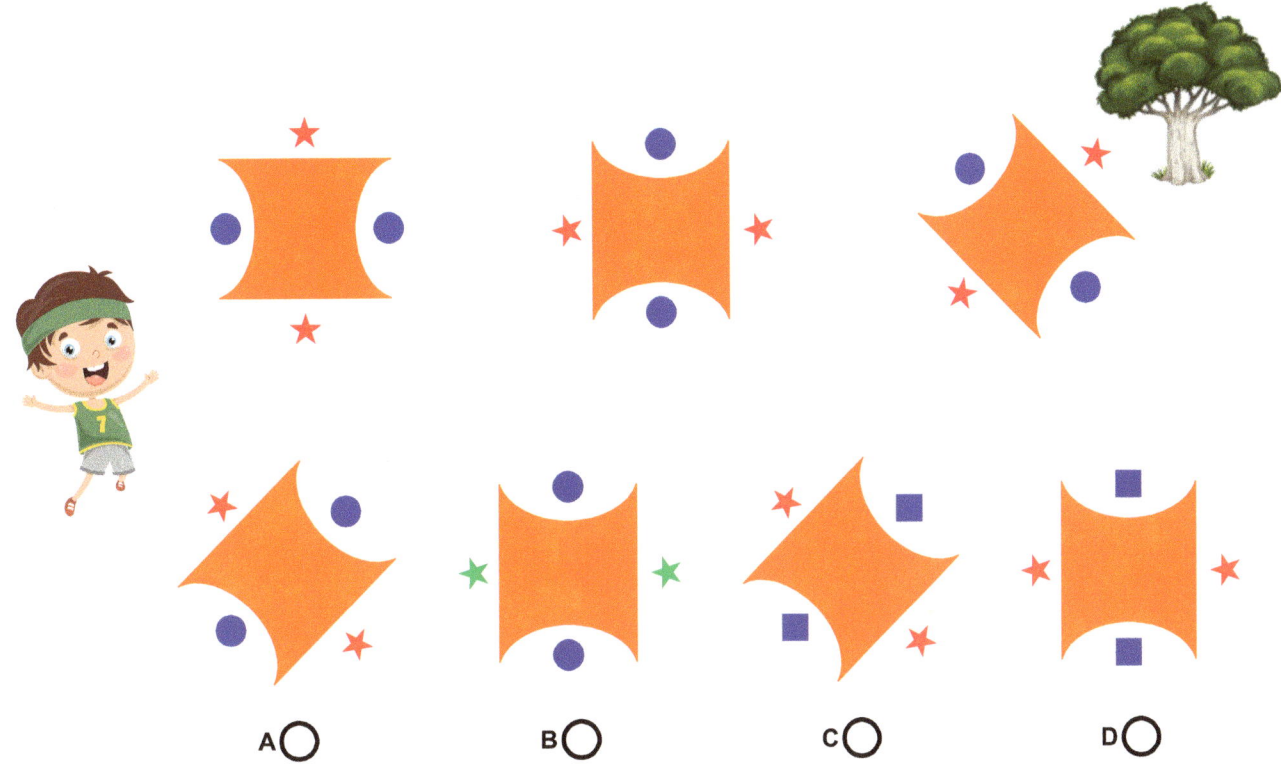

A◯   B◯   C◯   D◯

Solution : A

Option A is the only right choice. Option A matches the rest of the figure group in the same way. The other option vary in some way. Pay attention to all options before answering the right choice.

210   www.math-knots.com

Q-1

Look at the question with the Dolphin. The first three pictures belong to one group in a common way. Help Anthony to find out which of the below options belong to the same group. Identify the correct picture and help him to bubble the right choice.

A ◯   B ◯   C ◯   D ◯

Q-2

Look at the question with the Hedgehog. The first three pictures belong to one group in a common way. Help Jenna to find out which of the below options belong to the same group. Identify the correct picture and help her to bubble the right choice.

A ◯   B ◯   C ◯   D ◯

Q-3

Look at the question with the Fox. The first three pictures belong to one group in a common way. Help William to find out which of the below options belong to the same group. Identify the correct picture and help him to bubble the right choice.

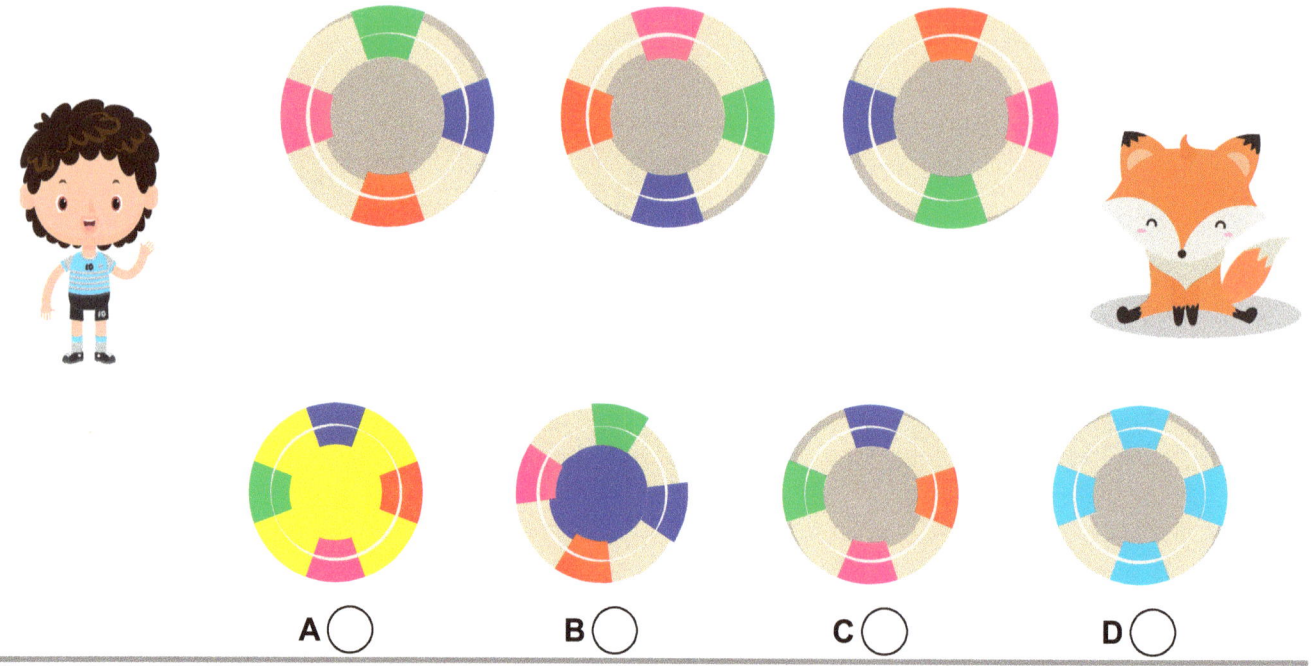

A ⃝   B ⃝   C ⃝   D ⃝

Q-4

Look at the question with the Giraffe. The first three pictures belong to one group in a common way. Help Mary to find out which of the below options belong to the same group. Identify the correct picture and help her to bubble the right choice.

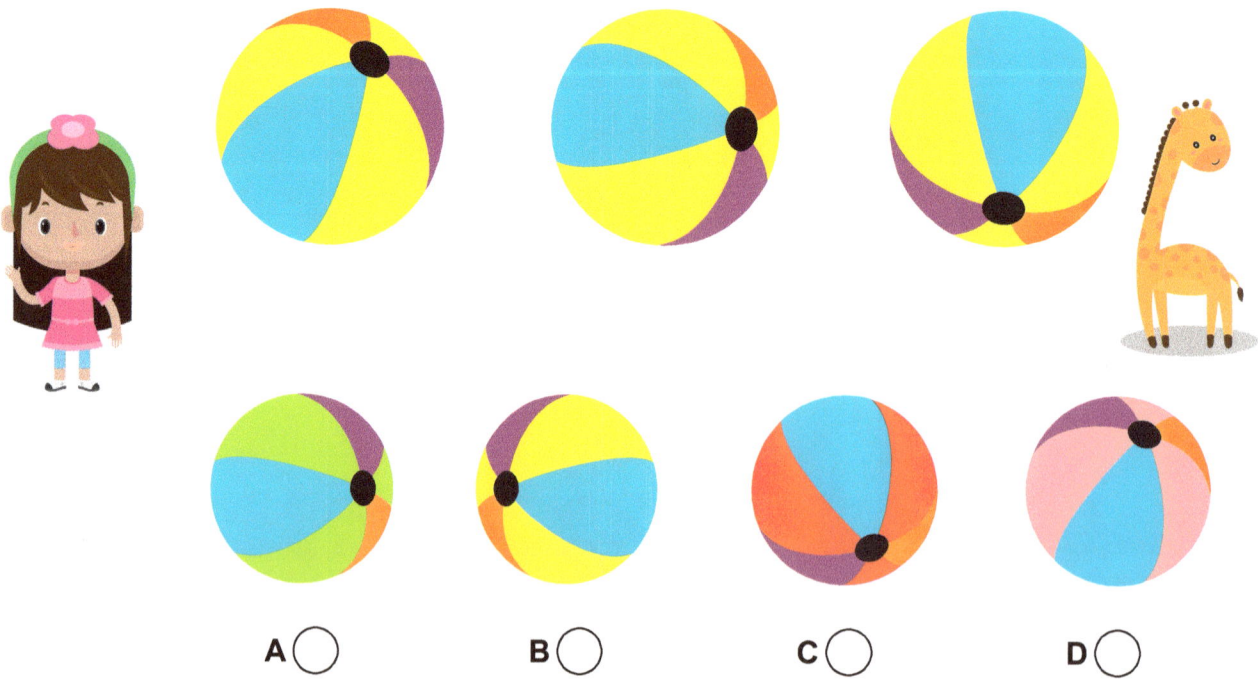

A ⃝   B ⃝   C ⃝   D ⃝

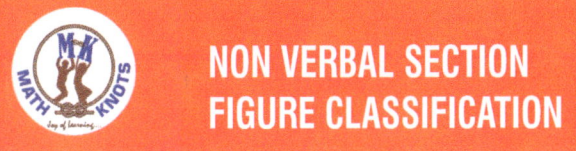

Q-5 Look at the question with the Alligator. The first three pictures belong to one group in a common way. Help David to find out which of the below options belong to the same group. Identify the correct picture and help him to bubble the right choice.

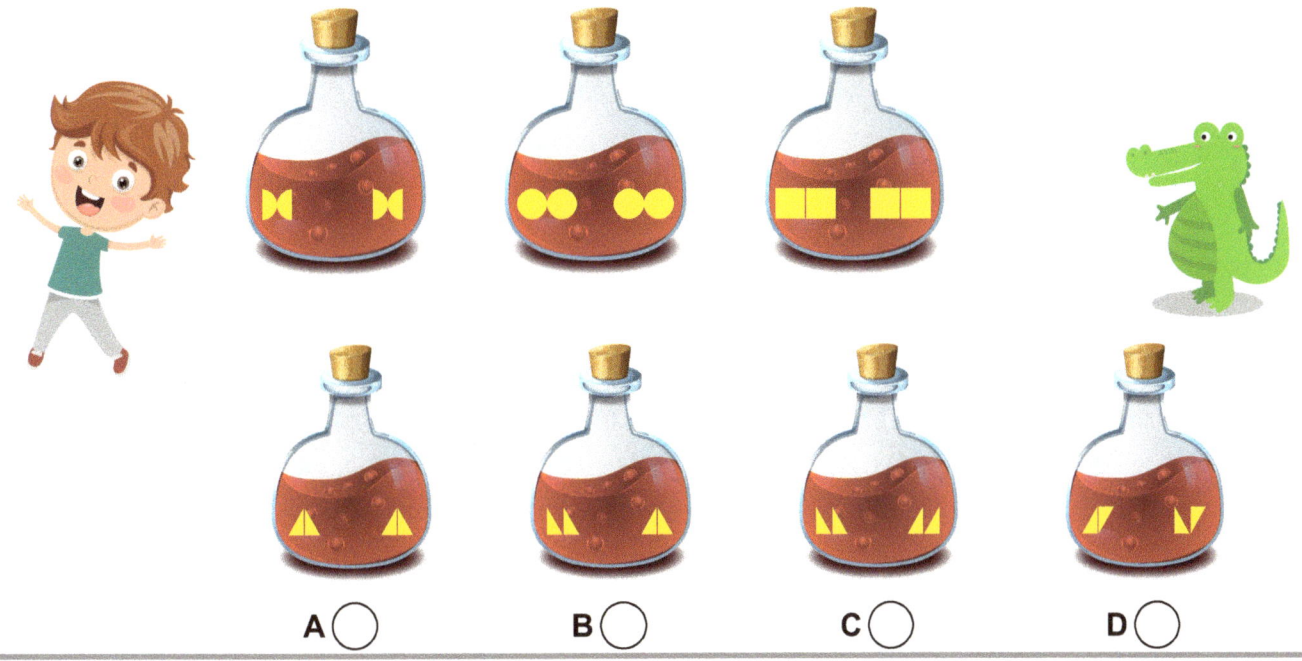

A ○   B ○   C ○   D ○

Q-6 Look at the question with the Bird. The first three pictures belong to one group in a common way. Help Amy to find out which of the below options belong to the same group. Identify the correct picture and help her to bubble the right choice.

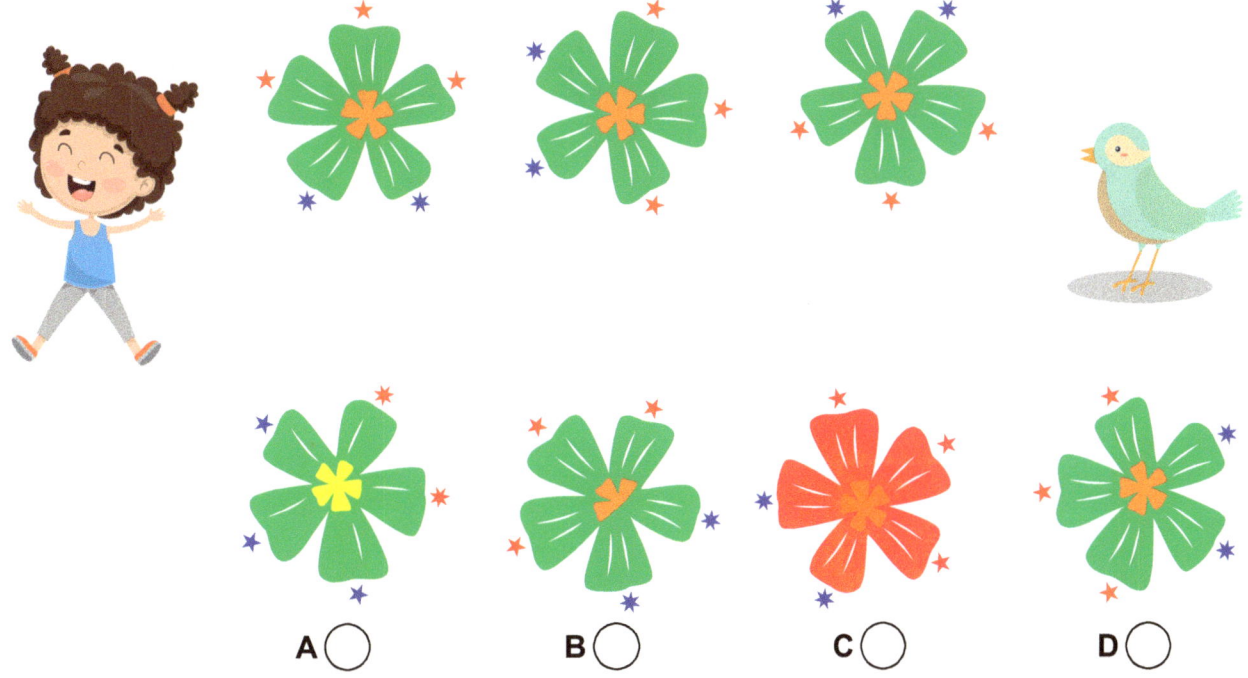

A ○   B ○   C ○   D ○

www.math-knots.com

Q-7

Look at the question with the Cow. The first three pictures belong to one group in a common way. Help Jack to find out which of the below options belong to the same group. Identify the correct picture and help him to bubble the right choice.

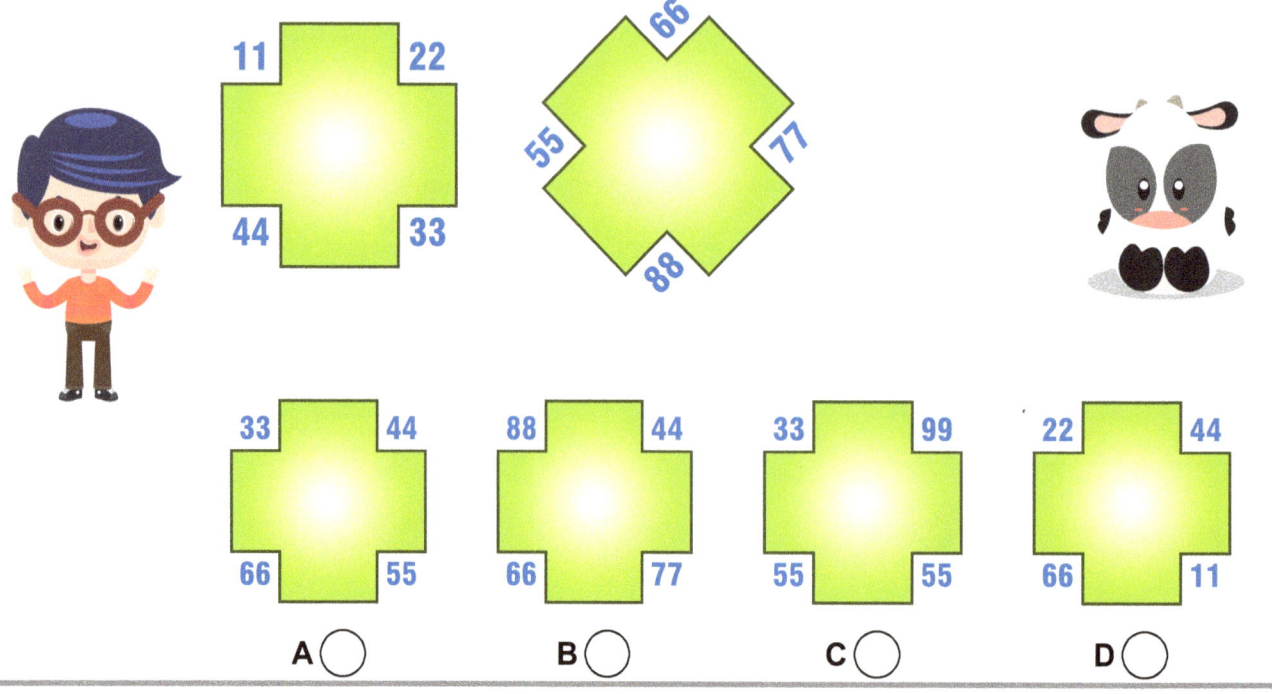

Q-8

Look at the question with the Pig. The first three pictures belong to one group in a common way. Help Mia to find out which of the below options belong to the same group. Identify the correct picture and help her to bubble the right choice.

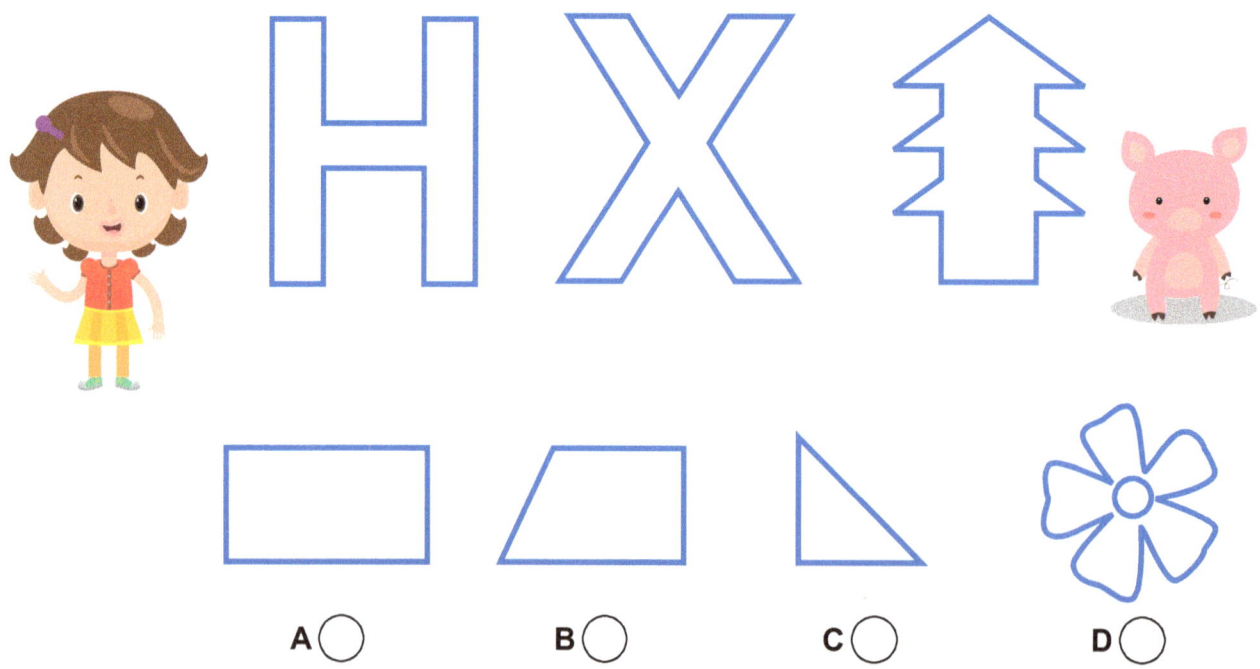

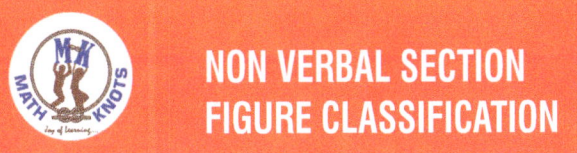

Q-9

Look at the question with the Sheep. The first three pictures belong to one group in a common way. Help Lucus to find out which of the below options belong to the same group. Identify the correct picture and help him to bubble the right choice.

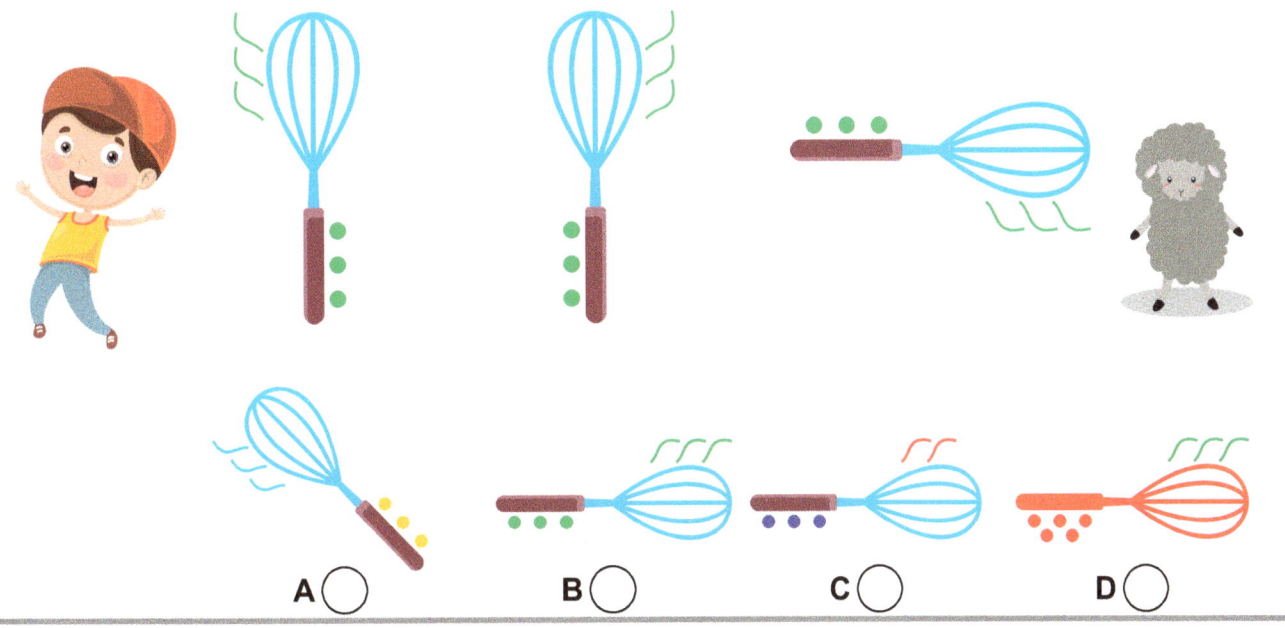

A ◯   B ◯   C ◯   D ◯

Q-10

Look at the question with the Yak. The first three pictures belong to one group in a common way. Help Esha to find out which of the below options belong to the same group. Identify the correct picture and help her to bubble the right choice.

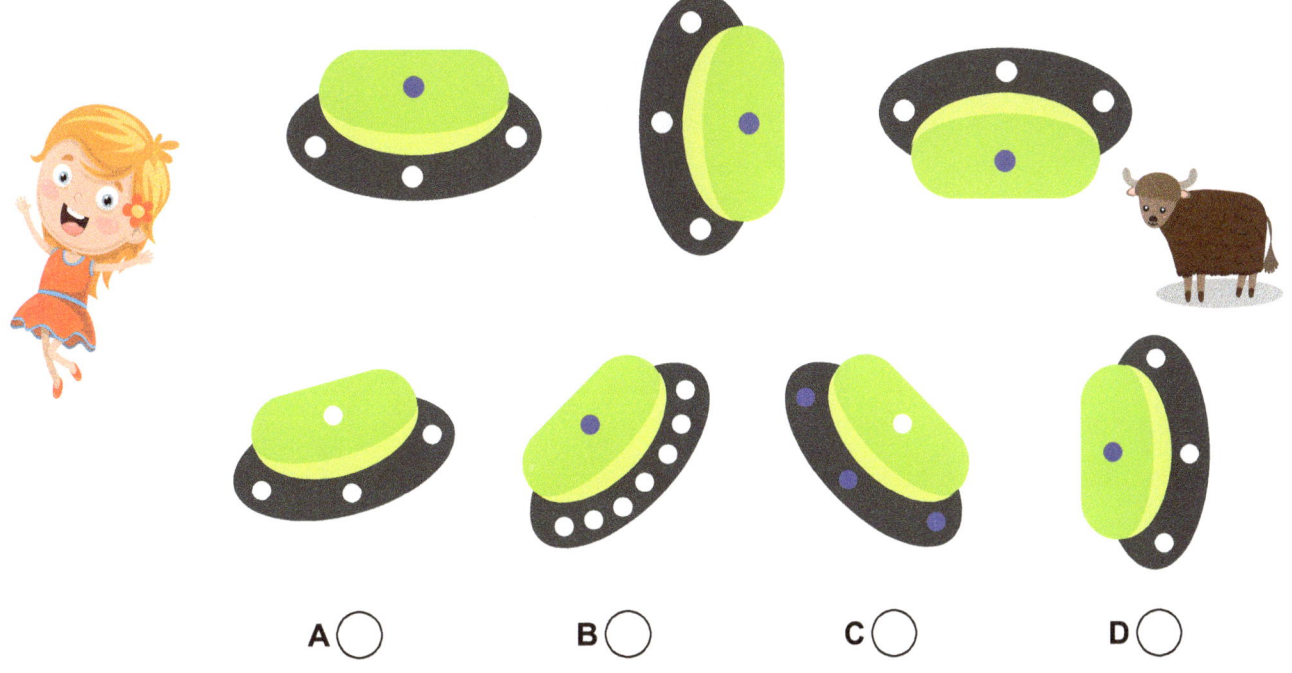

A ◯   B ◯   C ◯   D ◯

Q-11

Look at the question with the Zebra. The first three pictures belong to one group in a common way. Help Jaxon to find out which of the below options belong to the same group. Identify the correct picture and help him to bubble the right choice.

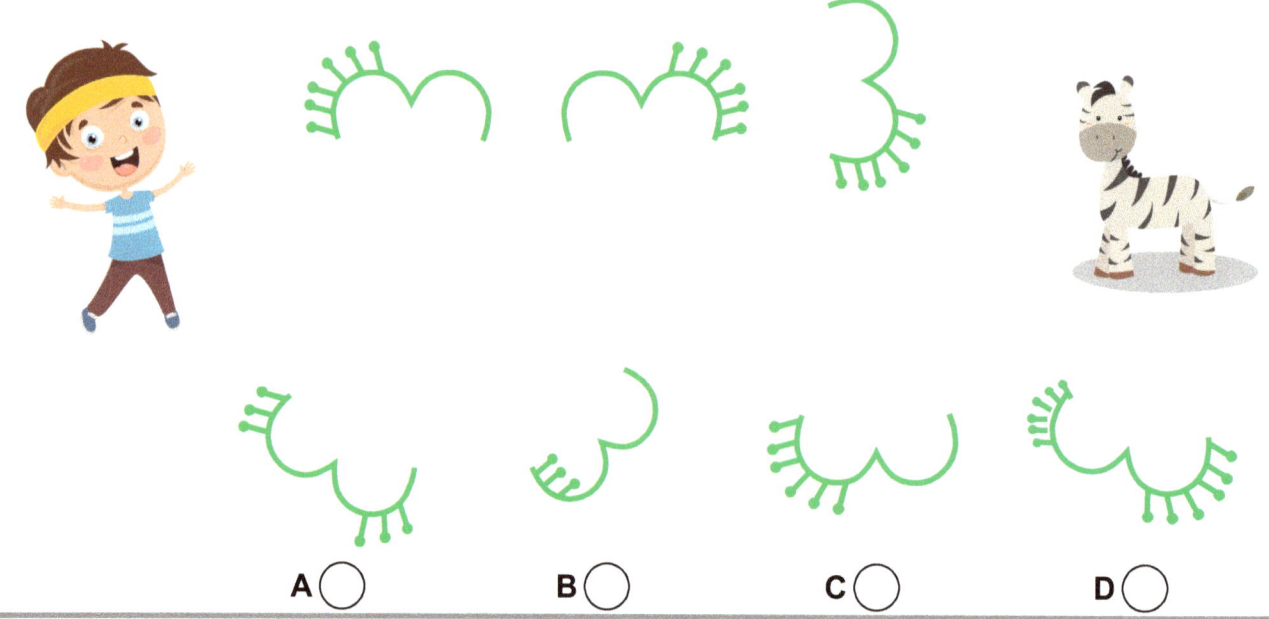

A ◯   B ◯   C ◯   D ◯

Q-12

Look at the question with the X-ray fish. The first three pictures belong to one group in a common way. Help Ella to find out which of the below options belong to the same group. Identify the correct picture and help her to bubble the right choice.

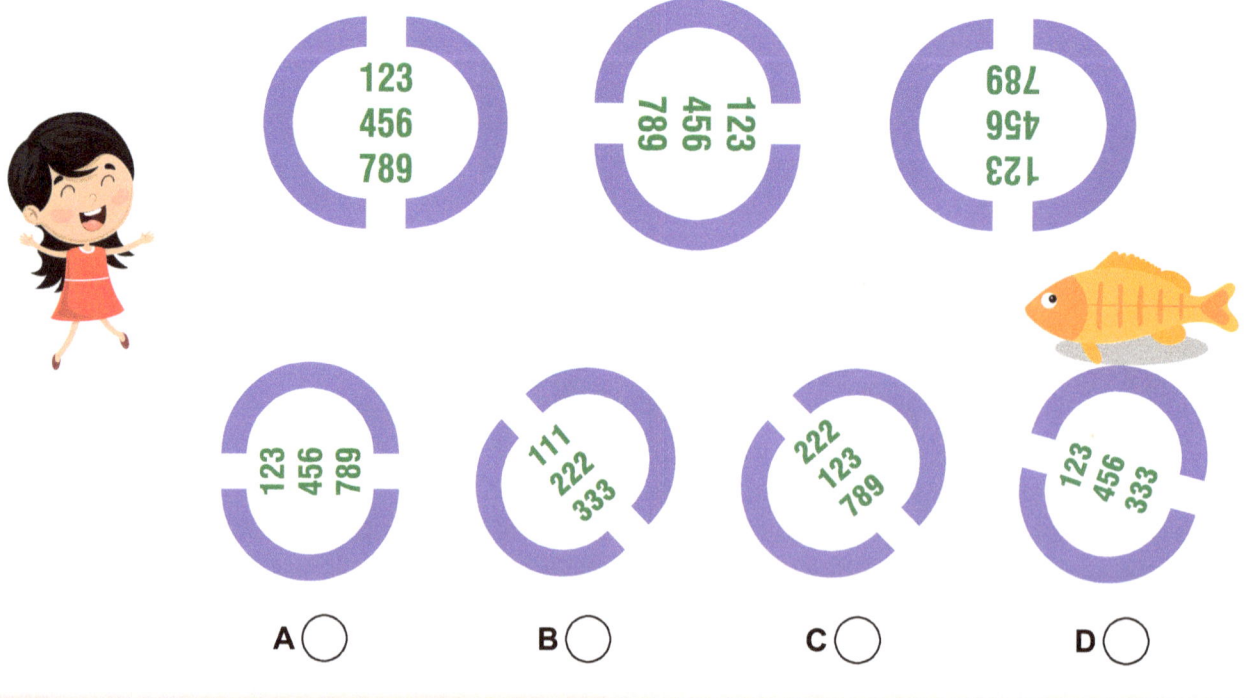

A ◯   B ◯   C ◯   D ◯

www.math-knots.com

Q-13 Look at the question with the Bear. The first three pictures belong to one group in a common way. Help Carter to find out which of the below options belong to the same group. Identify the correct picture and help him to bubble the right choice.

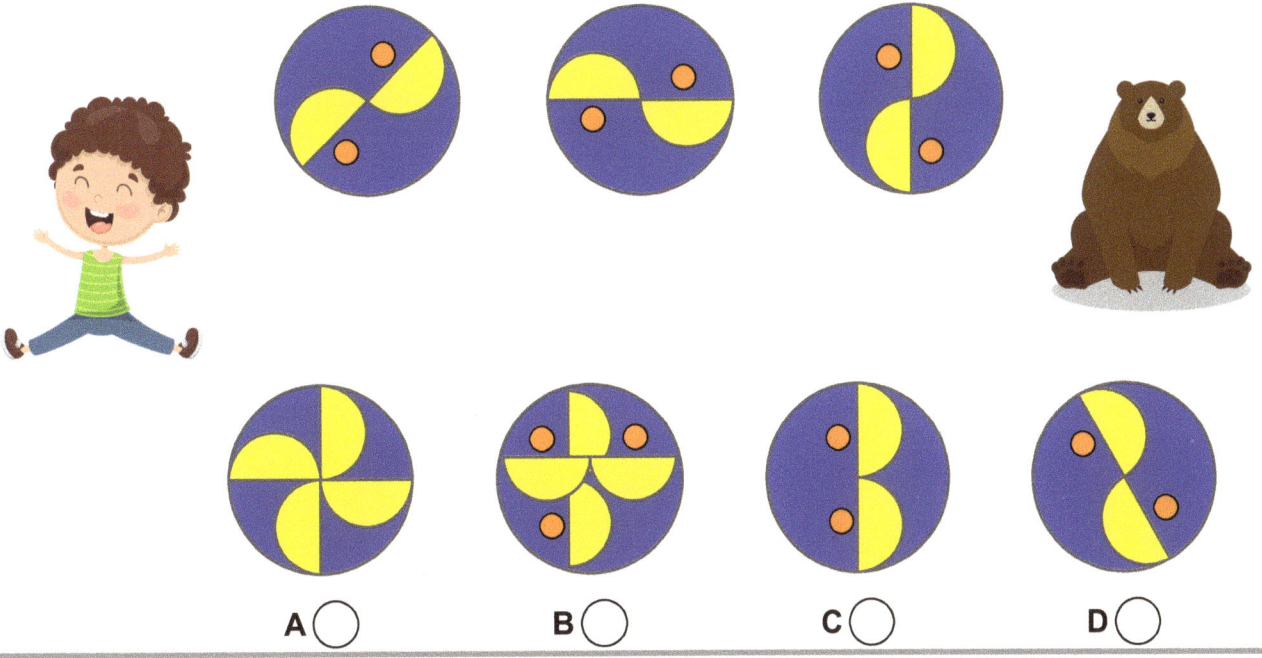

A ◯   B ◯   C ◯   D ◯

Q-14 Look at the question with the Peacock. The first three pictures belong to one group in a common way. Help Bella to find out which of the below options belong to the same group. Identify the correct picture and help her to bubble the right choice.

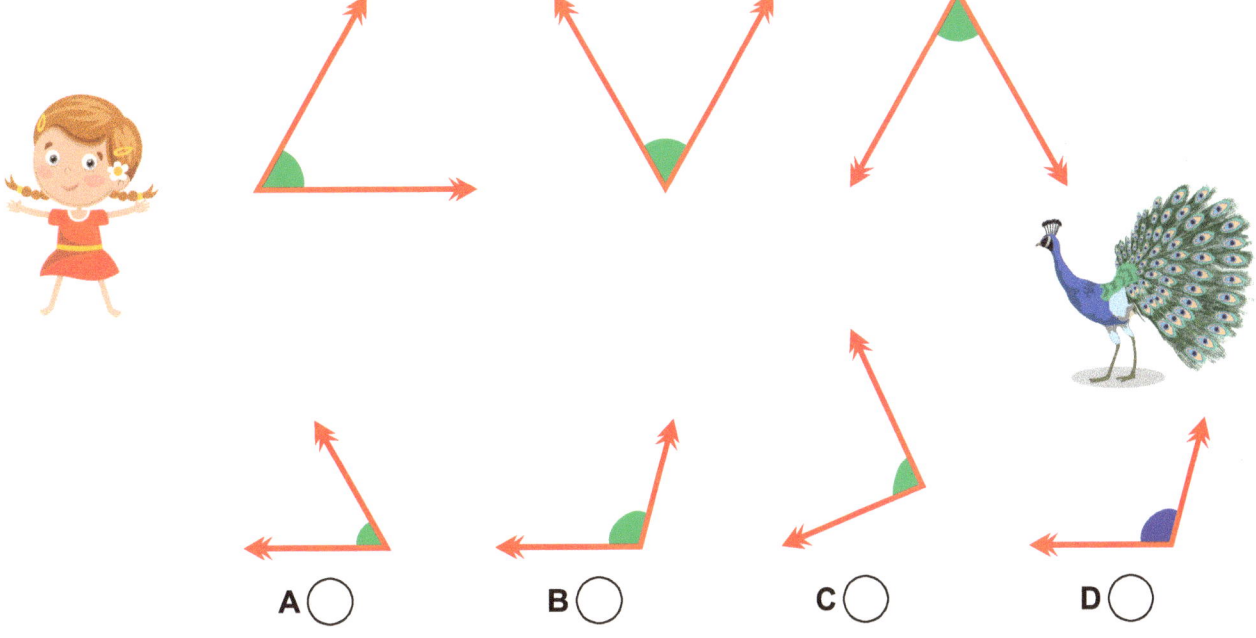

A ◯   B ◯   C ◯   D ◯

www.math-knots.com

Q-15

Look at the question with the Parrot. The first three pictures belong to one group in a common way. Help Samuel to find out which of the below options belong to the same group. Identify the correct picture and help him to bubble the right choice.

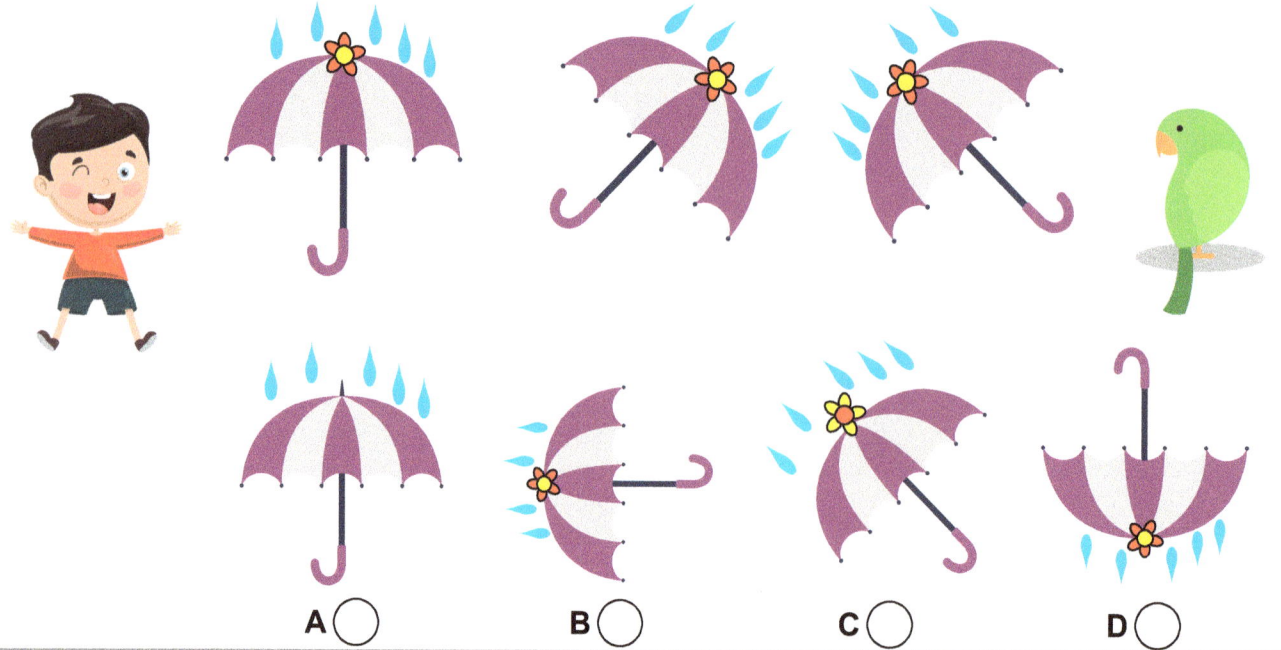

A ◯   B ◯   C ◯   D ◯

Q-16

Look at the question with the Ladybug. The first three pictures belong to one group in a common way. Help Rachel to find out which of the below options belong to the same group. Identify the correct picture and help her to bubble the right choice.

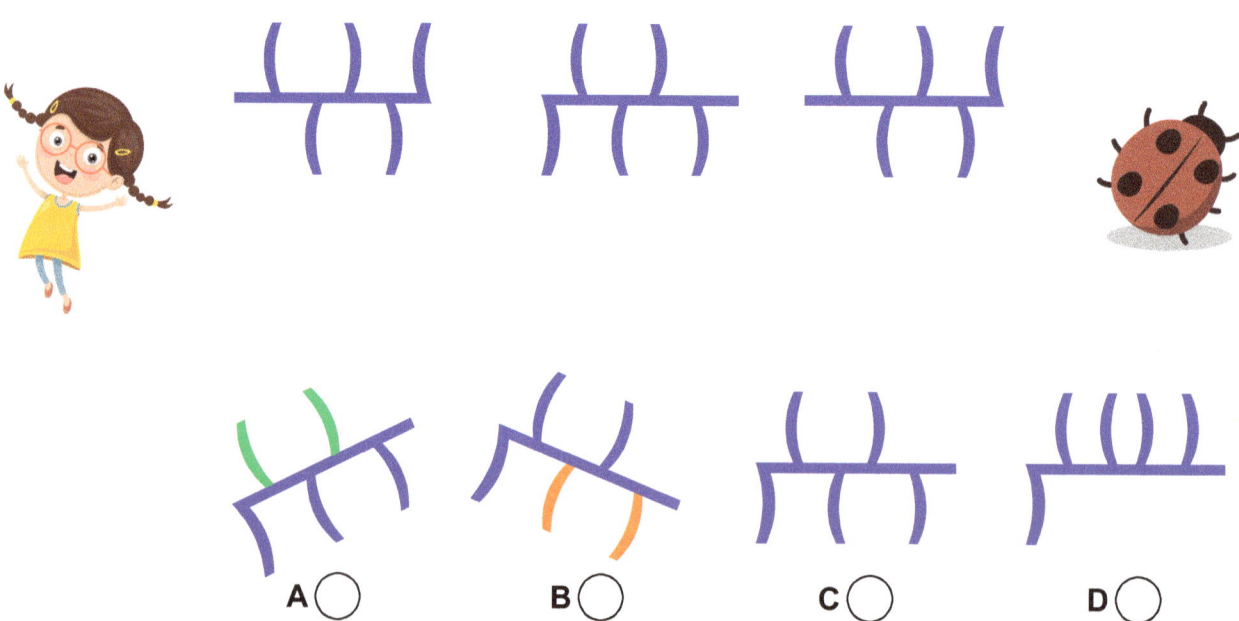

A ◯   B ◯   C ◯   D ◯

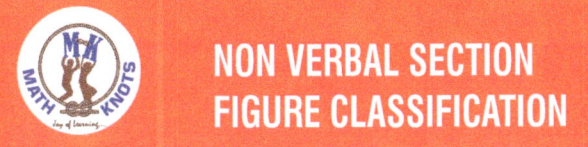
Q-17 Look at the question with the Butterfly. The first three pictures belong to one group in a common way. Help Henry to find out which of the below options belong to the same group. Identify the correct picture and help him to bubble the right choice.

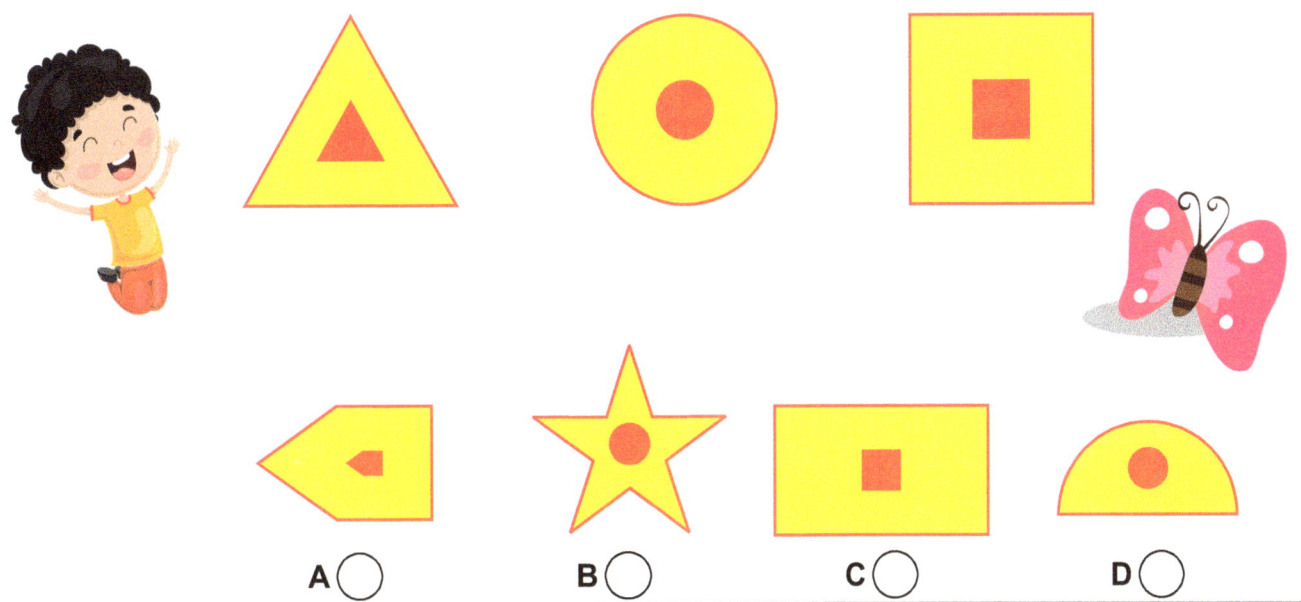

A◯   B◯   C◯   D◯

Q-18 Look at the question with the Grasshopper. The first three pictures belong to one group in a common way. Help Linda to find out which of the below options belong to the same group. Identify the correct picture and help her to bubble the right choice.

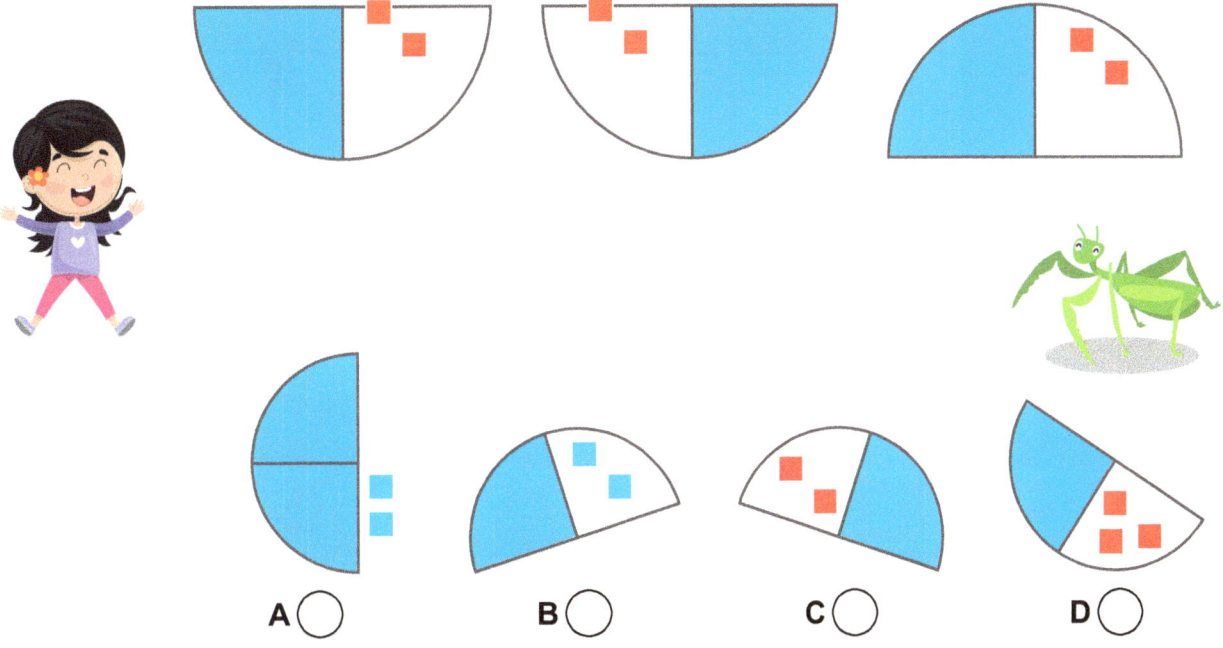

A◯   B◯   C◯   D◯

www.math-knots.com

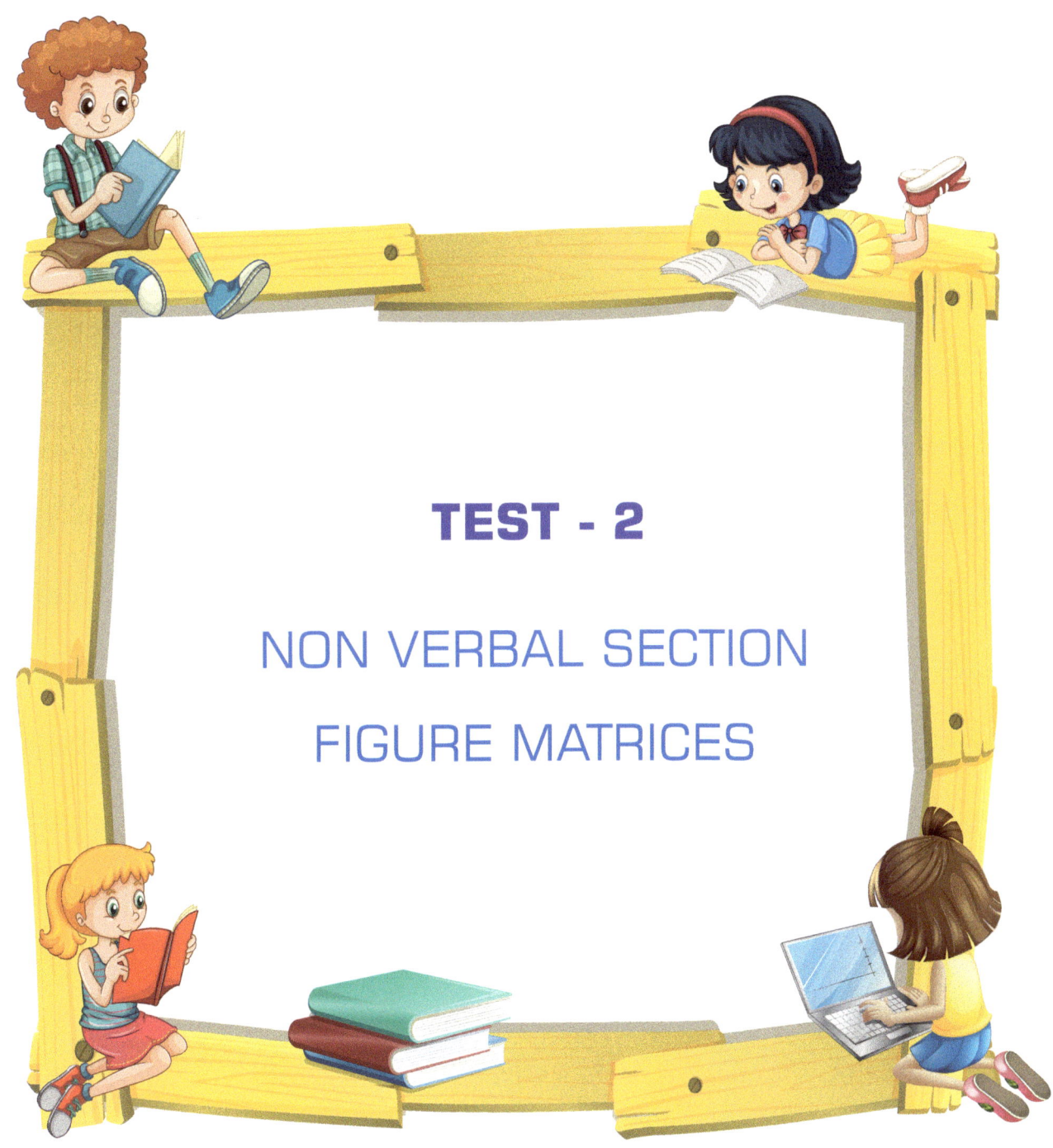

TEST - 2

NON VERBAL SECTION

FIGURE MATRICES

Lets Start the Test...

Sample

Look at the question with the Grapes. The first row has some thing in common as the second row. Can you help Mary to identify what goes in the space of the question mark from the four given options A, B, C, and D. Choose the correct option.

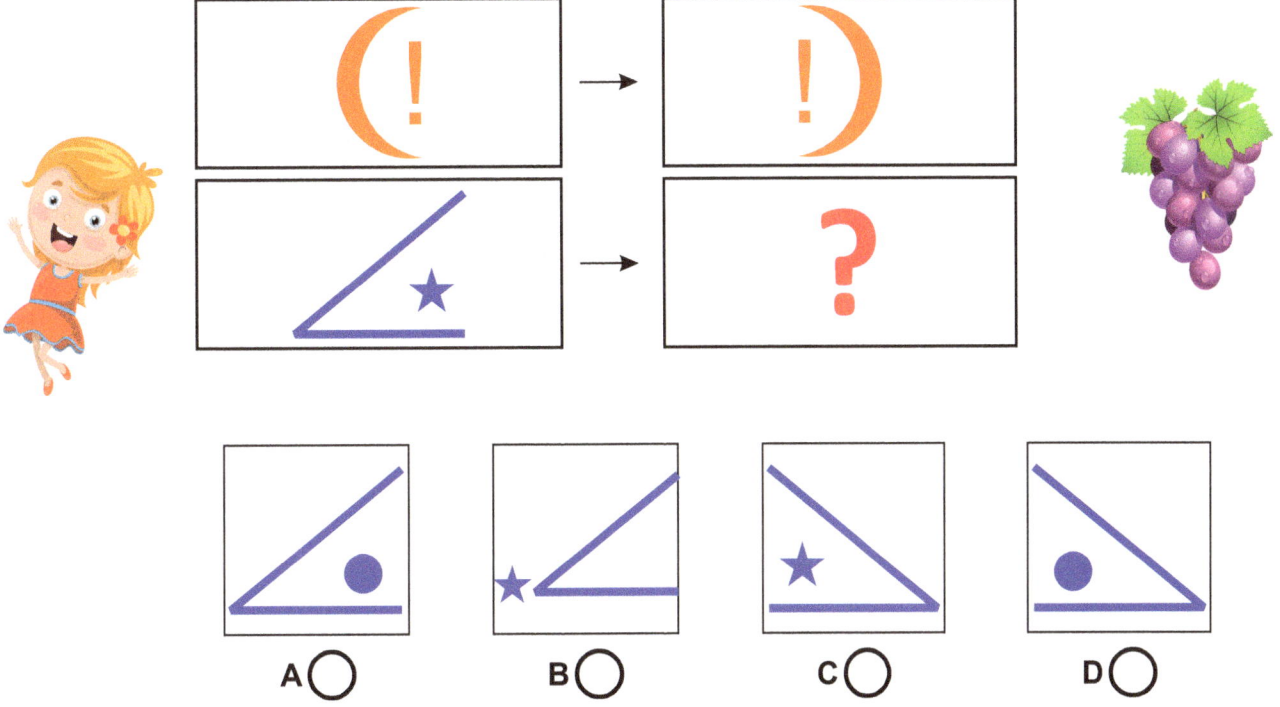

Solution : C

Option C is the right choice.

Two pictures in the first row are related in a certain way and the figures and flipped.

When the picture in the second row is flipped it will be match to option C.

Students need to pay attention. Figures can be turning clock wise into anti clock wise and other possibilities.

Q-1 Look at the question with the Zebra. The first row has some thing in common as the second row. Can you help William to identify what goes in the space of the question mark from the four given options A, B, C, and D. Choose the correct option.

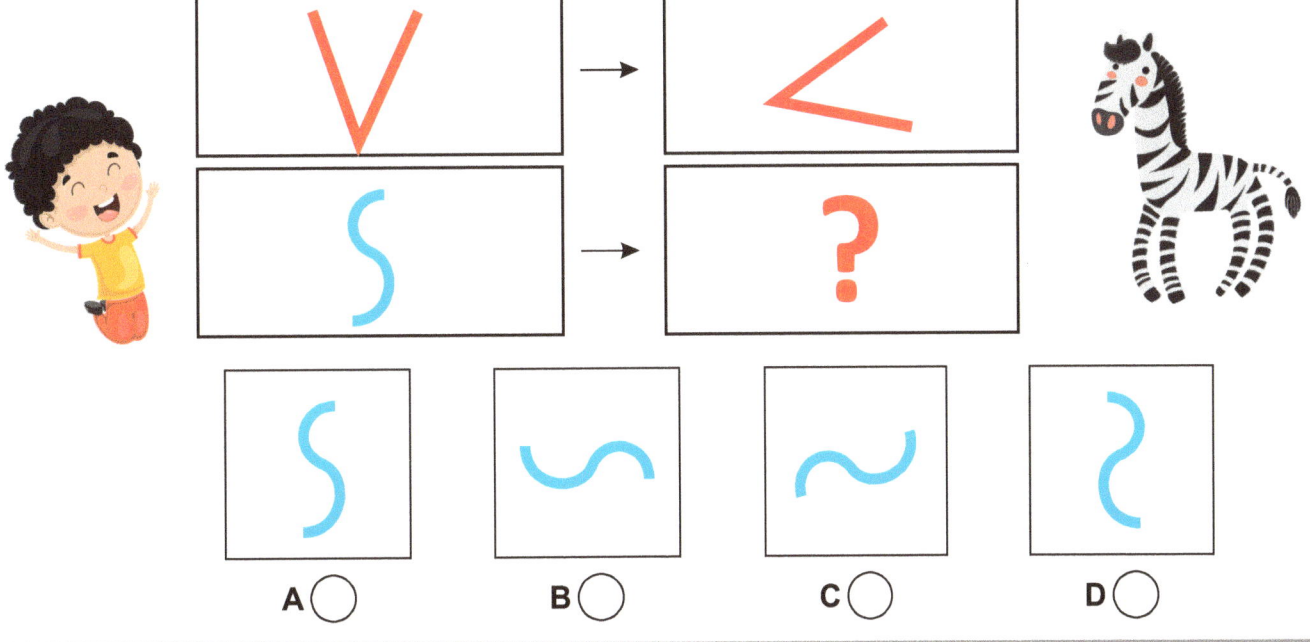

A◯   B◯   C◯   D◯

Q-2 Look at the question with the Yak. The first row has some thing in common as the second row. Can you help Emma to identify what goes in the space of the question mark from the four given options A, B, C, and D. Choose the correct option.

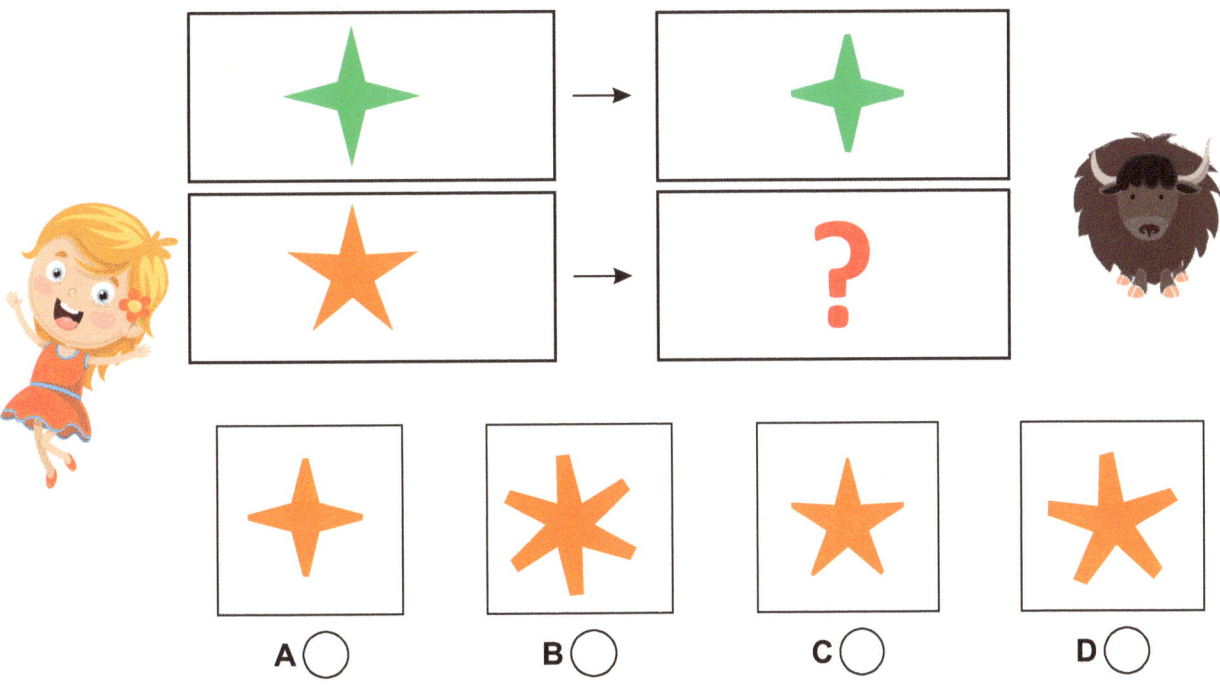

A◯   B◯   C◯   D◯

www.math-knots.com

Q-3

Look at the question with the Fish. The first row has some thing in common as the second row. Can you help Neel to identify what goes in the space of the question mark from the four given options A, B, C, and D. Choose the correct option.

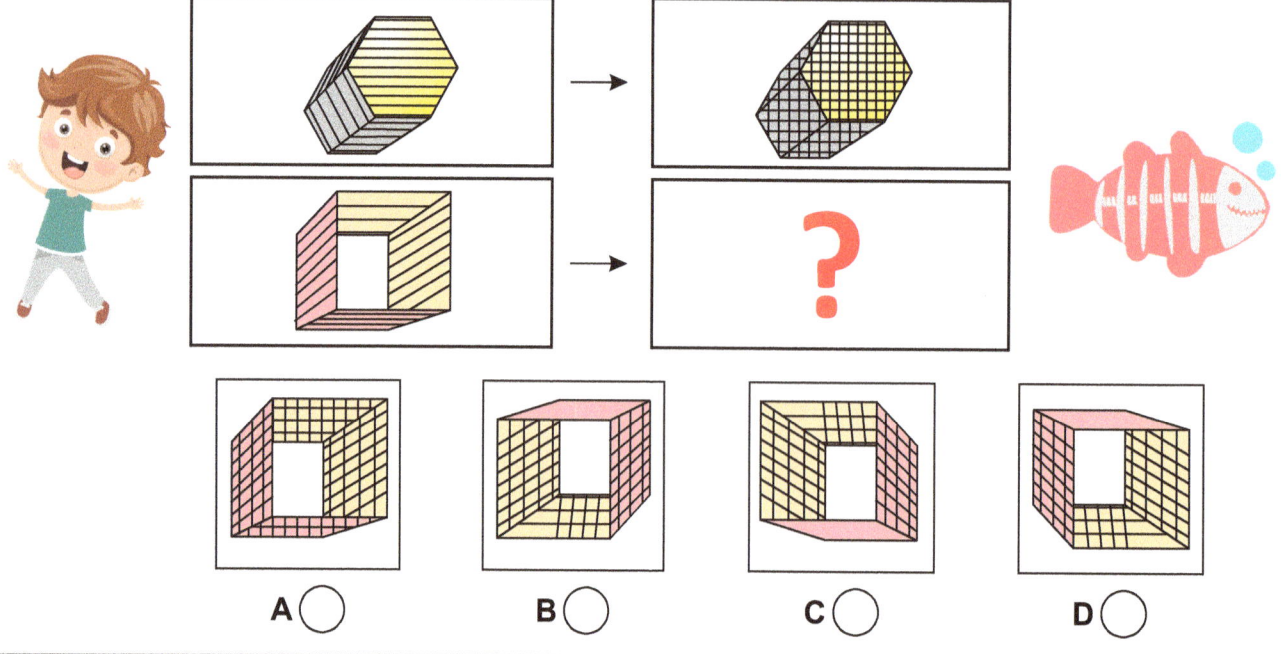

Q-4

Look at the question with the Whale. The first row has some thing in common as the second row. Can you help Liam to identify what goes in the space of the question mark from the four given options A, B, C, and D. Choose the correct option.

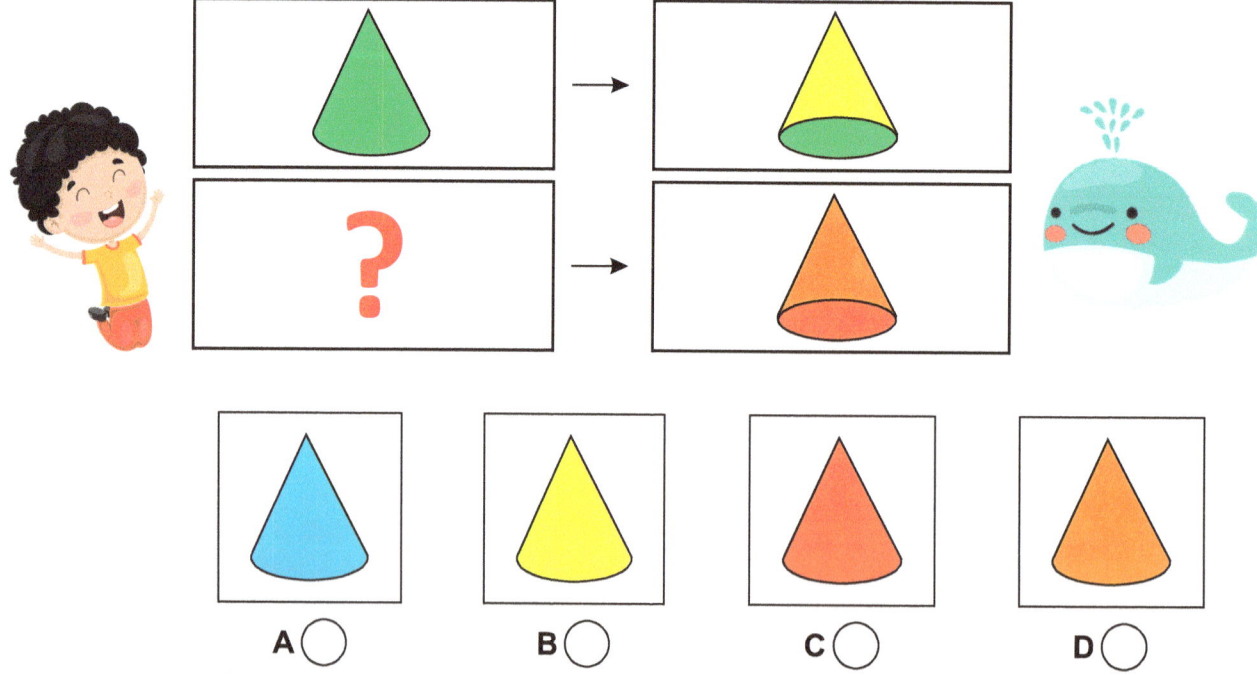

Q-5 Look at the question with the Bird. The first row has some thing in common as the second row. Can you help James to identify what goes in the space of the question mark from the four given options A, B, C, and D. Choose the correct option.

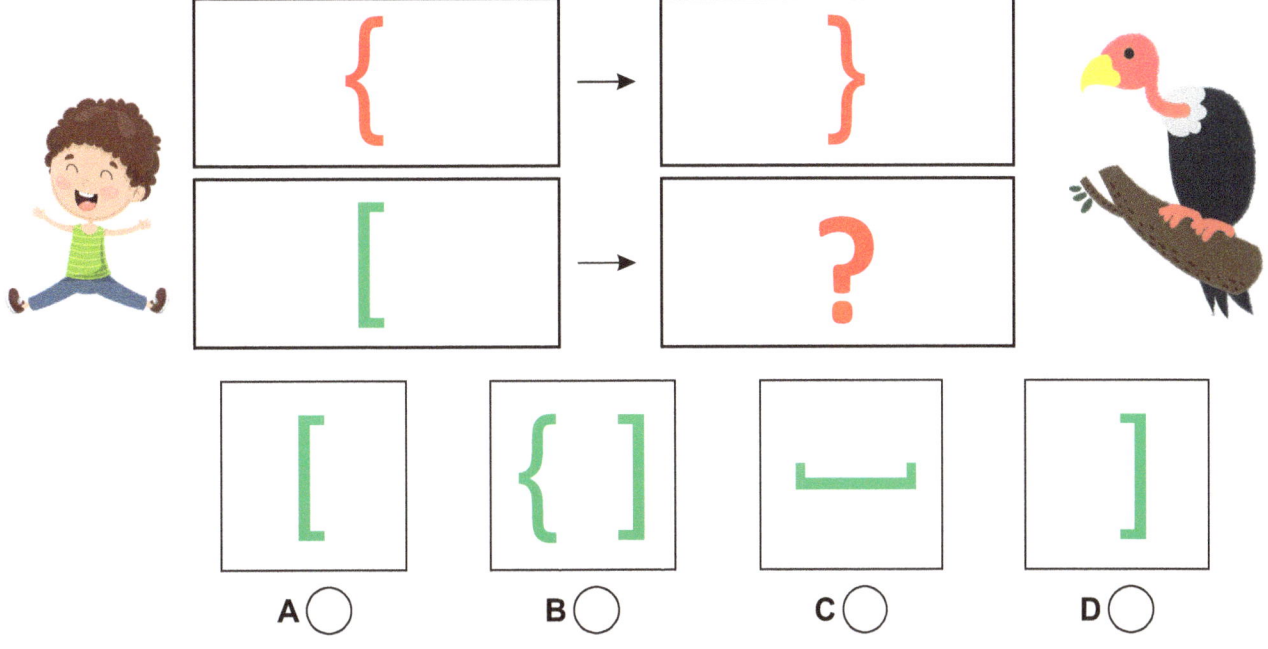

A ◯   B ◯   C ◯   D ◯

Q-6 Look at the question with the Whore. The first row has some thing in common as the second row. Can you help Olivia to identify what goes in the space of the question mark from the four given options A, B, C, and D. Choose the correct option.

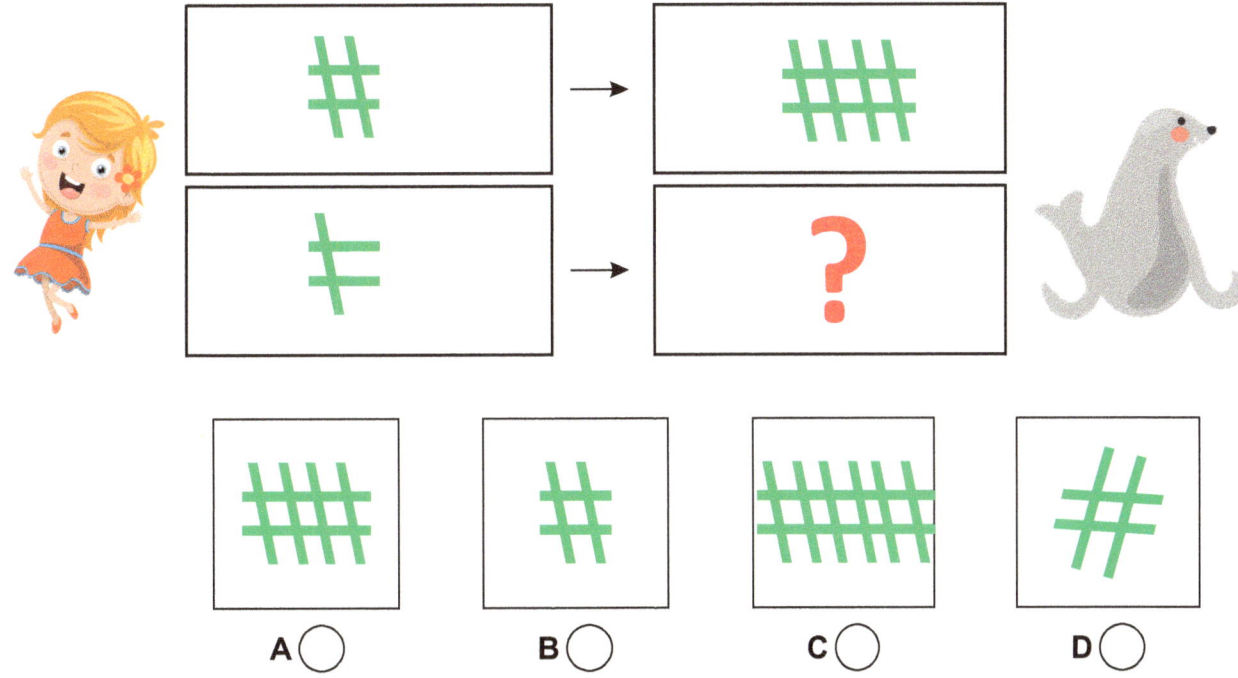

A ◯   B ◯   C ◯   D ◯

www.math-knots.com

Q-7

Look at the question with the Monkey. The first row has some thing in common as the second row. Can you help Diana to identify what goes in the space of the question mark from the four given options A, B, C, and D. Choose the correct option.

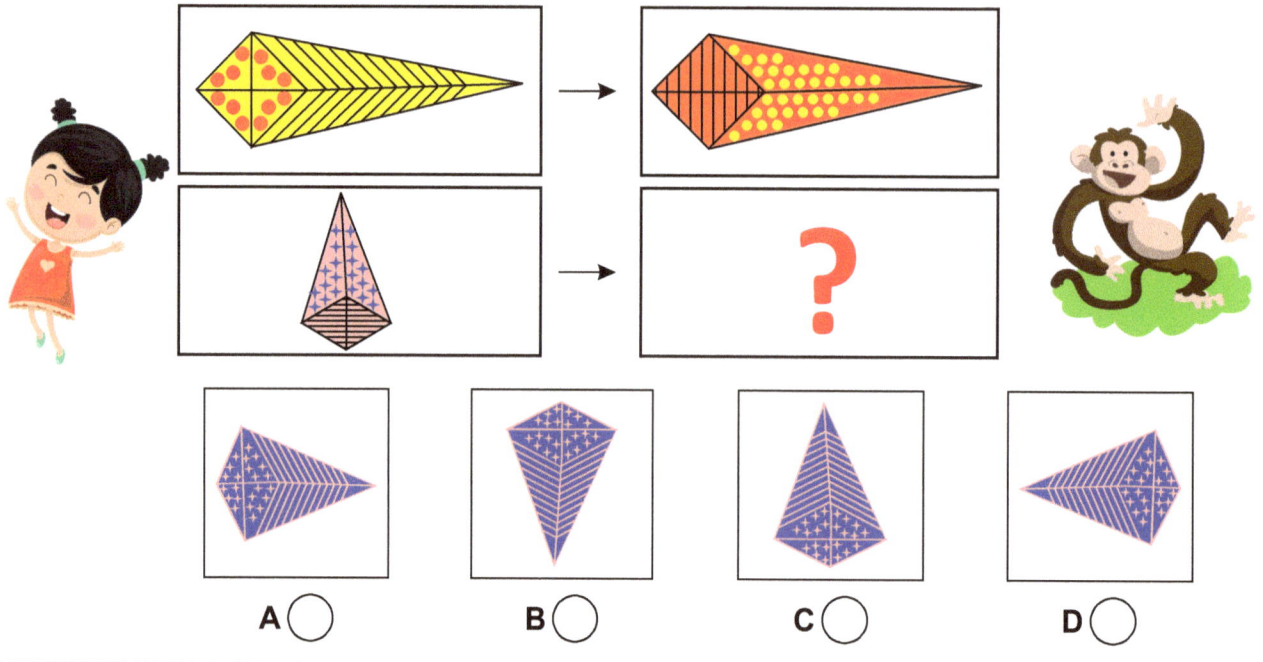

A ◯   B ◯   C ◯   D ◯

Q-8

Look at the question with the Camel. The first row has some thing in common as the second row. Can you help Jack to identify what goes in the space of the question mark from the four given options A, B, C, and D. Choose the correct option.

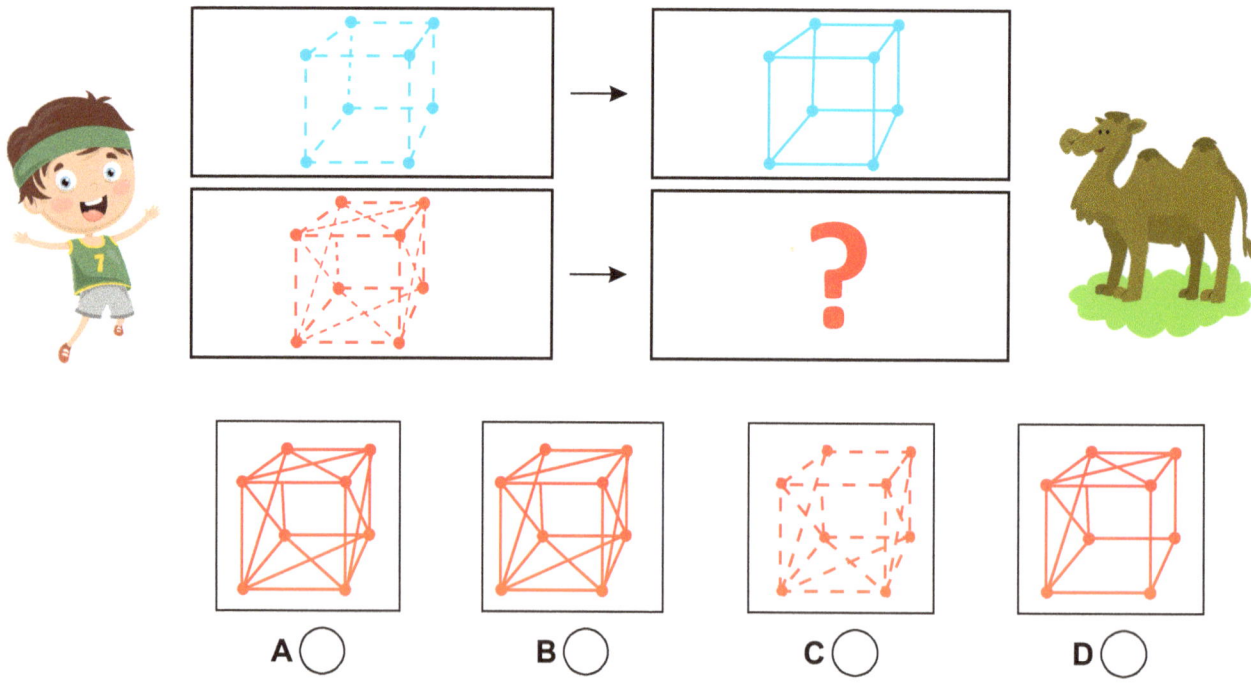

A ◯   B ◯   C ◯   D ◯

Q-9

Look at the question with the Lion. The first row has some thing in common as the second row. Can you help Rik to identify what goes in the space of the question mark from the four given options A, B, C, and D. Choose the correct option.

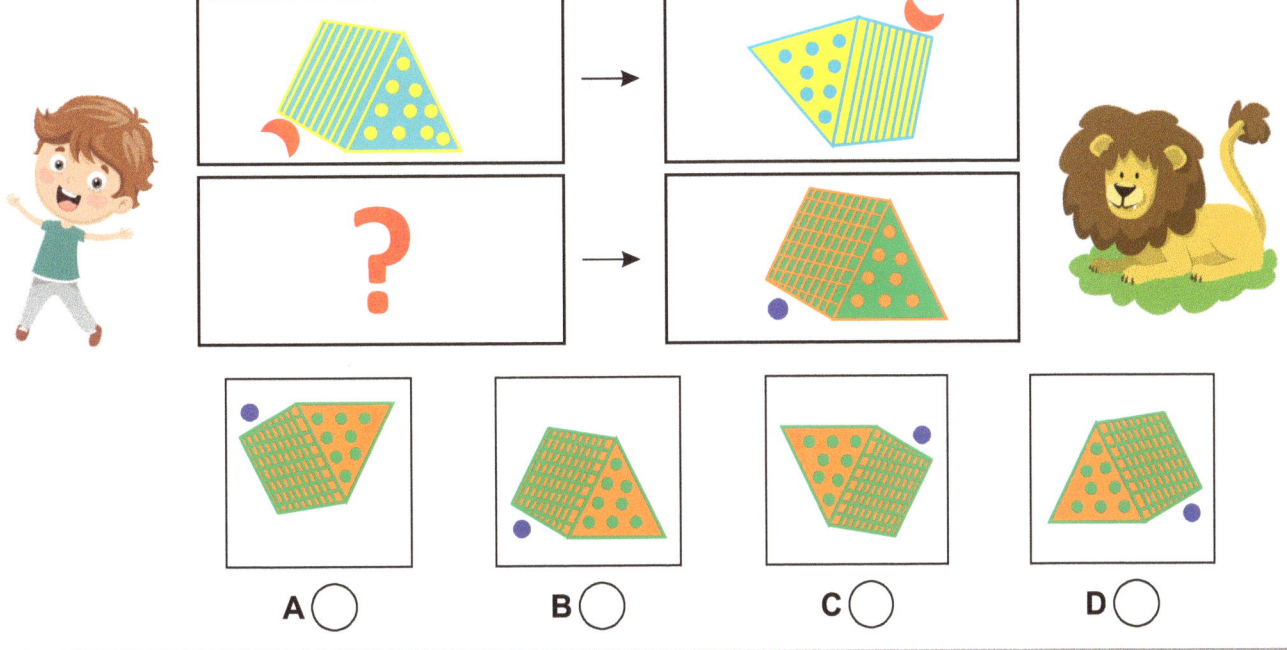

Q-10

Look at the question with the Aligator. The first row has some thing in common as the second row. Can you help Elli to identify what goes in the space of the question mark from the four given options A, B, C, and D. Choose the correct option.

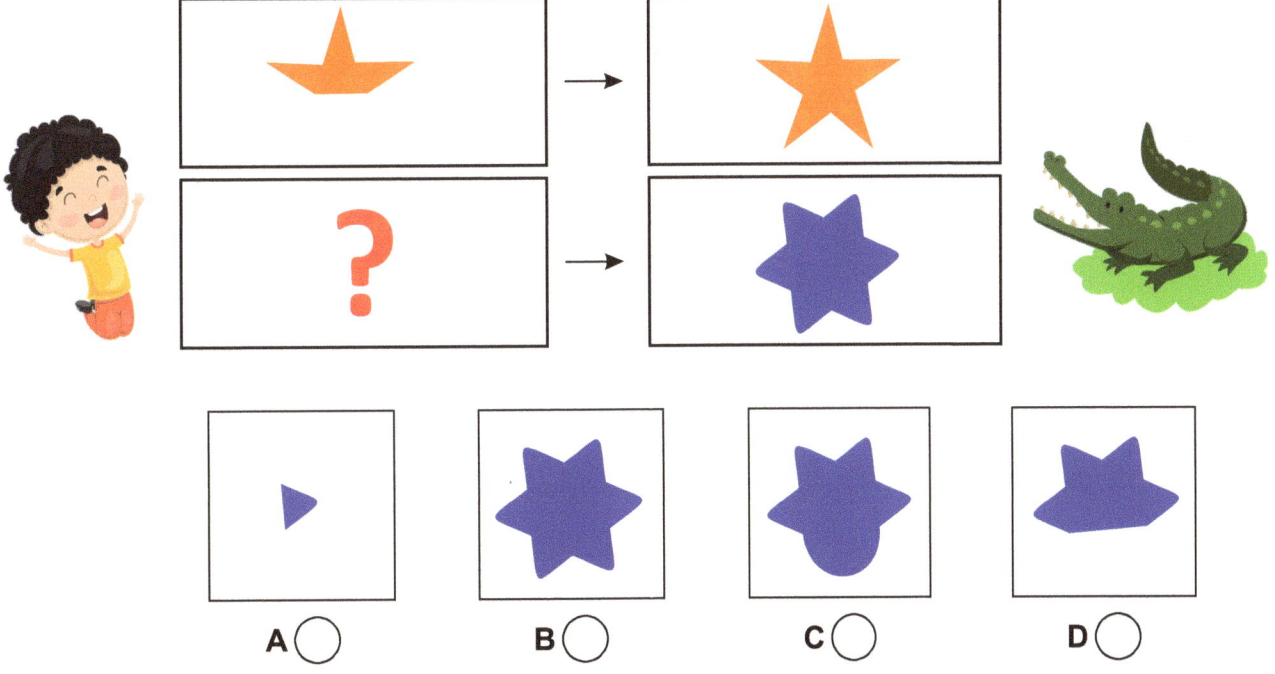

www.math-knots.com

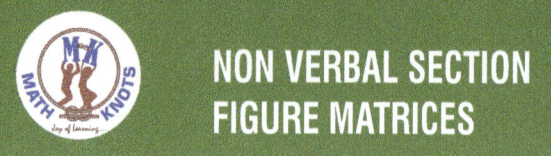

Q-11

Look at the question with the Sheep. The first row has some thing in common as the second row. Can you help Beth to identify what goes in the space of the question mark from the four given options A, B, C, and D. Choose the correct option.

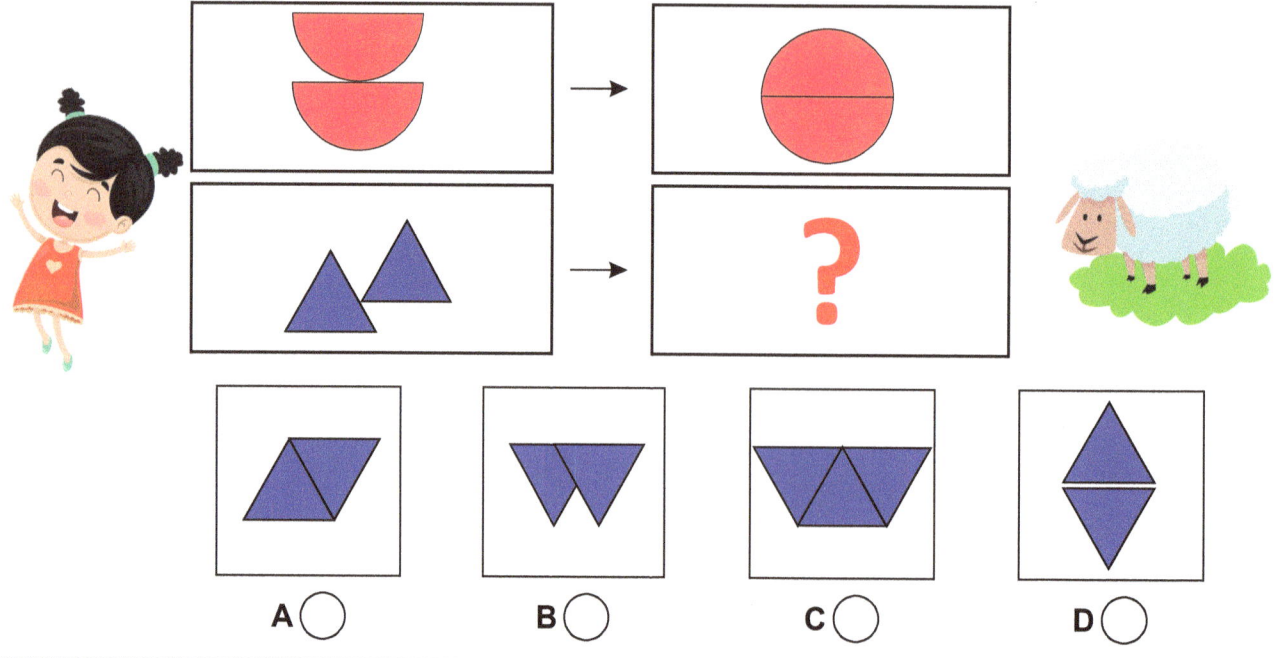

A ◯   B ◯   C ◯   D ◯

Q-12

Look at the question with the Dog. The first row has some thing in common as the second row. Can you help Mike to identify what goes in the space of the question mark from the four given options A, B, C, and D. Choose the correct option.

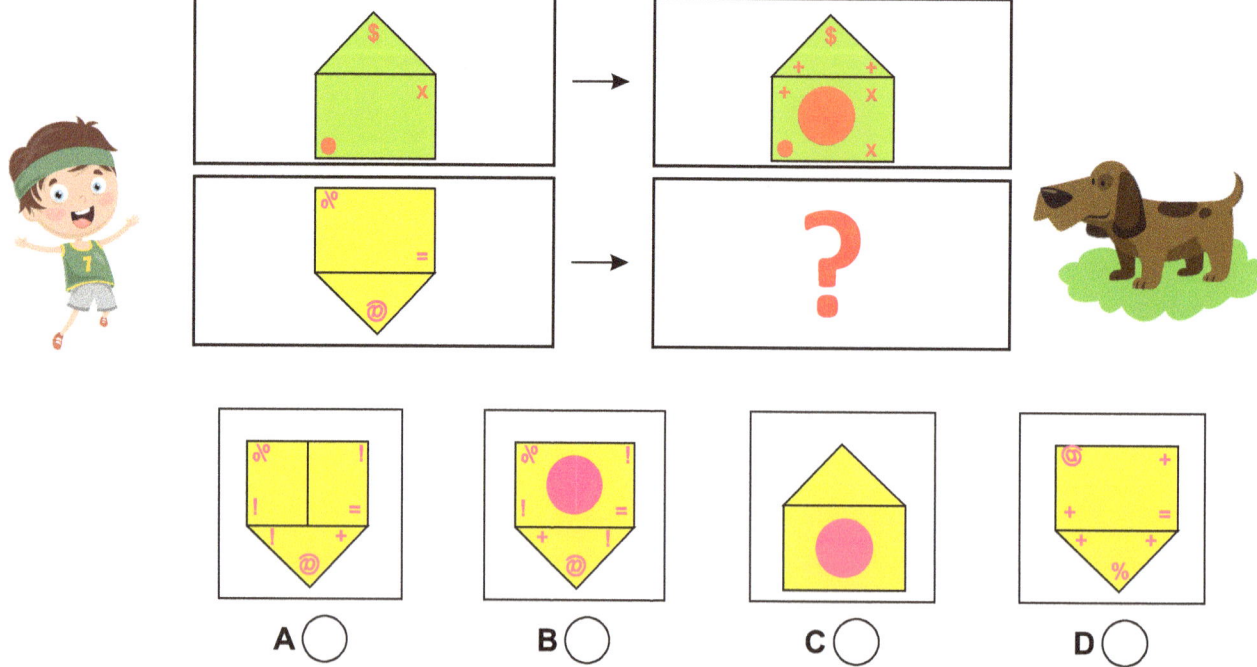

A ◯   B ◯   C ◯   D ◯

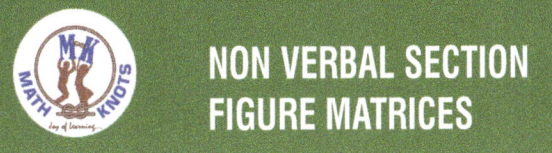

Q-13 Look at the question with the Cat. The first row has some thing in common as the second row. Can you help Samantha to identify what goes in the space of the question mark from the four given options A, B, C, and D. Choose the correct option.

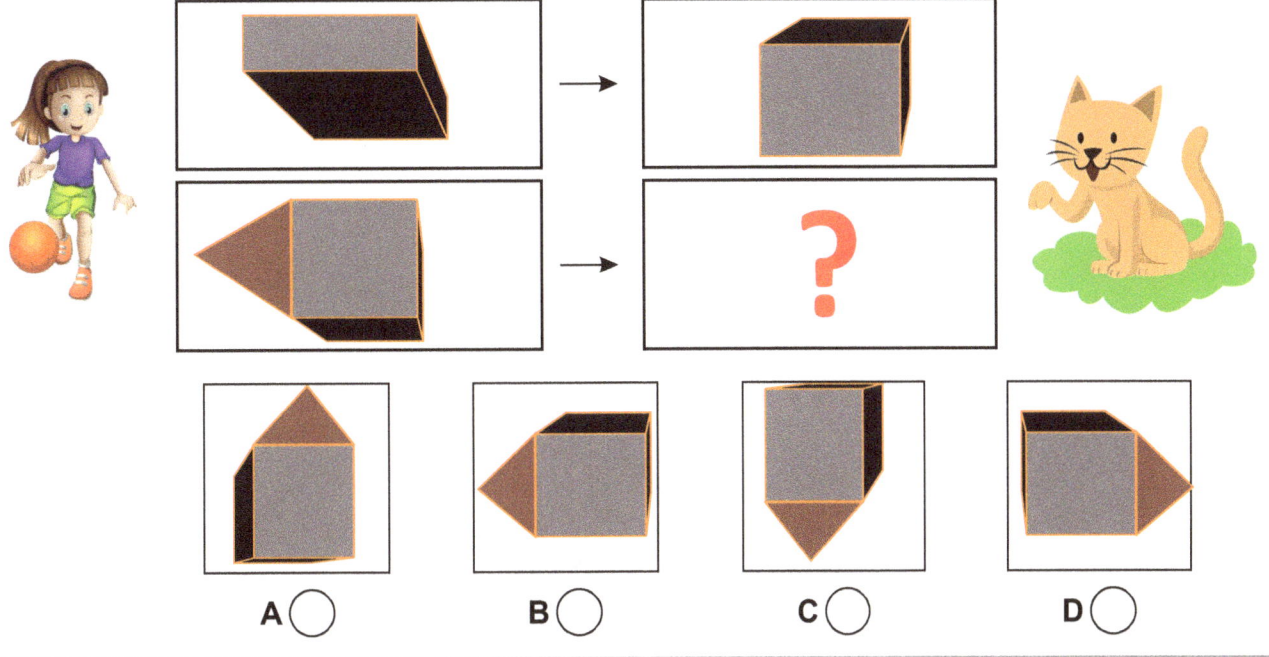

Q-14 Look at the question with the Cow. The first row has some thing in common as the second row. Can you help Lucy to identify what goes in the space of the question mark from the four given options A, B, C, and D. Choose the correct option.

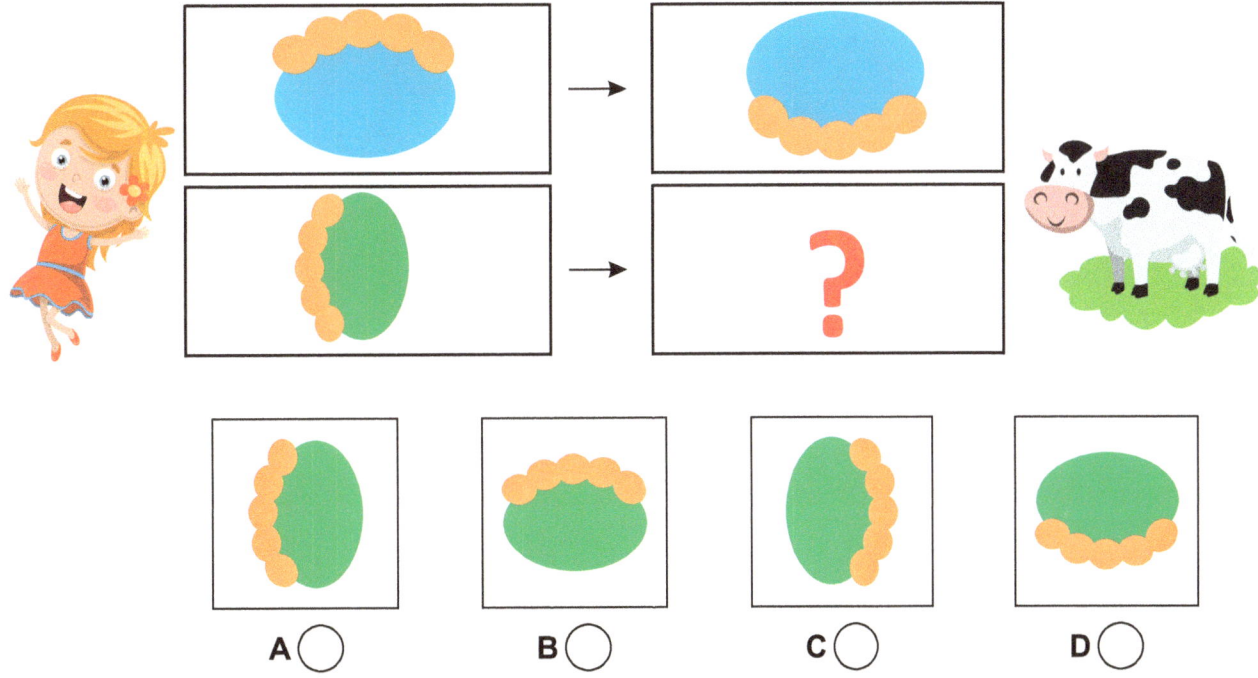

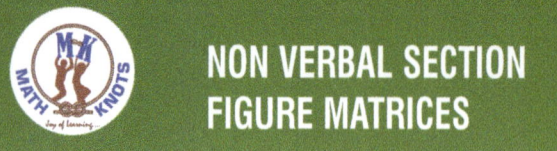

Q-15

Look at the question with the Pig. The first row has some thing in common as the second row. Can you help Amy to identify what goes in the space of the question mark from the four given options A, B, C, and D. Choose the correct option.

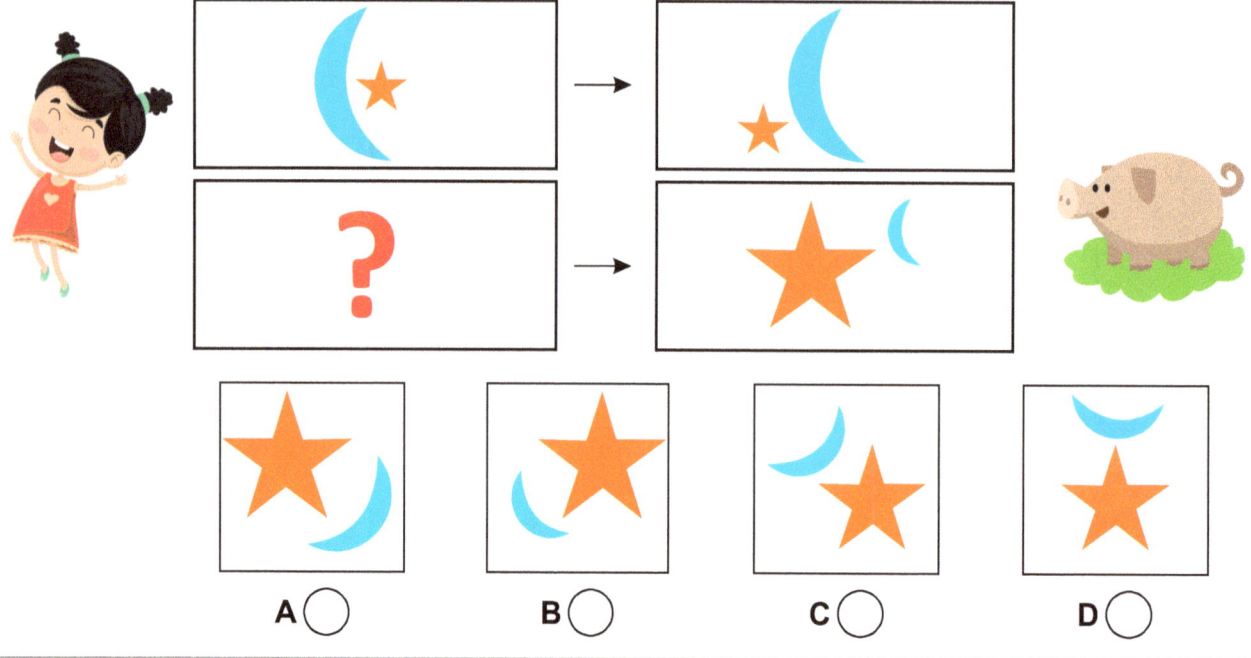

Q-16

Look at the question with the Rhinosorous. The first row has some thing in common as the second row. Can you help Logan to identify what goes in the space of the question mark from the four given options A, B, C, and D. Choose the correct option.

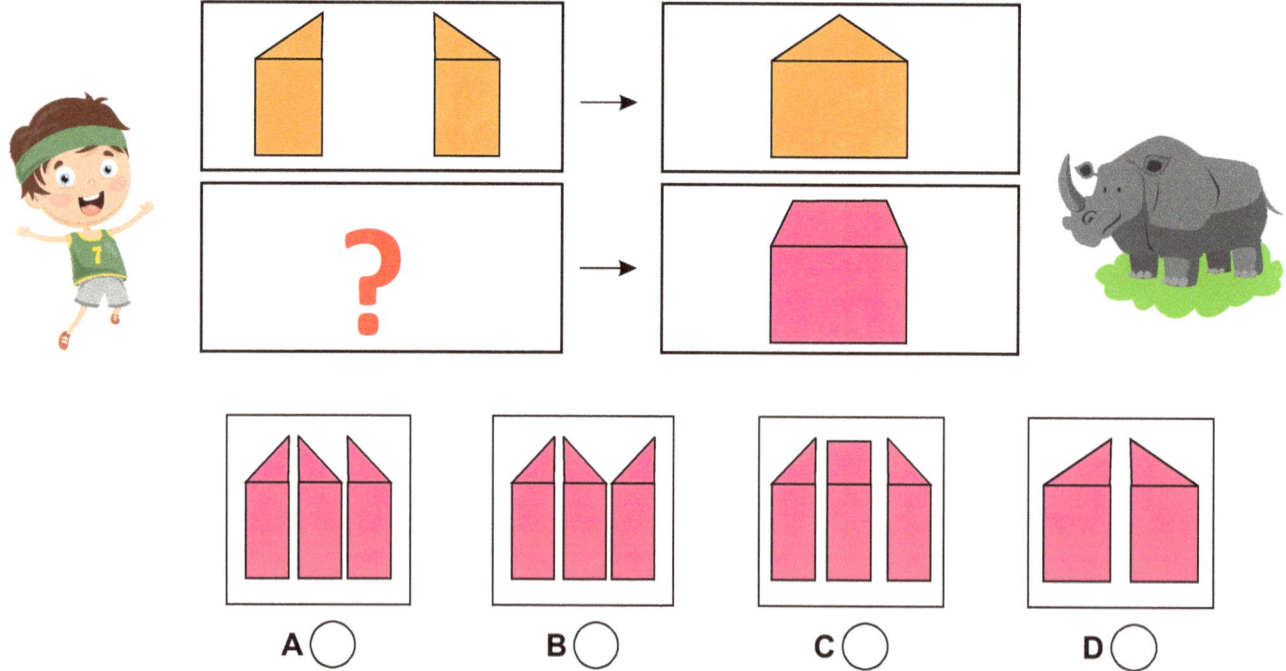

Q-17 Look at the question with the Giraffe. The first row has some thing in common as the second row. Can you help John to identify what goes in the space of the question mark from the four given options A, B, C, and D. Choose the correct option.

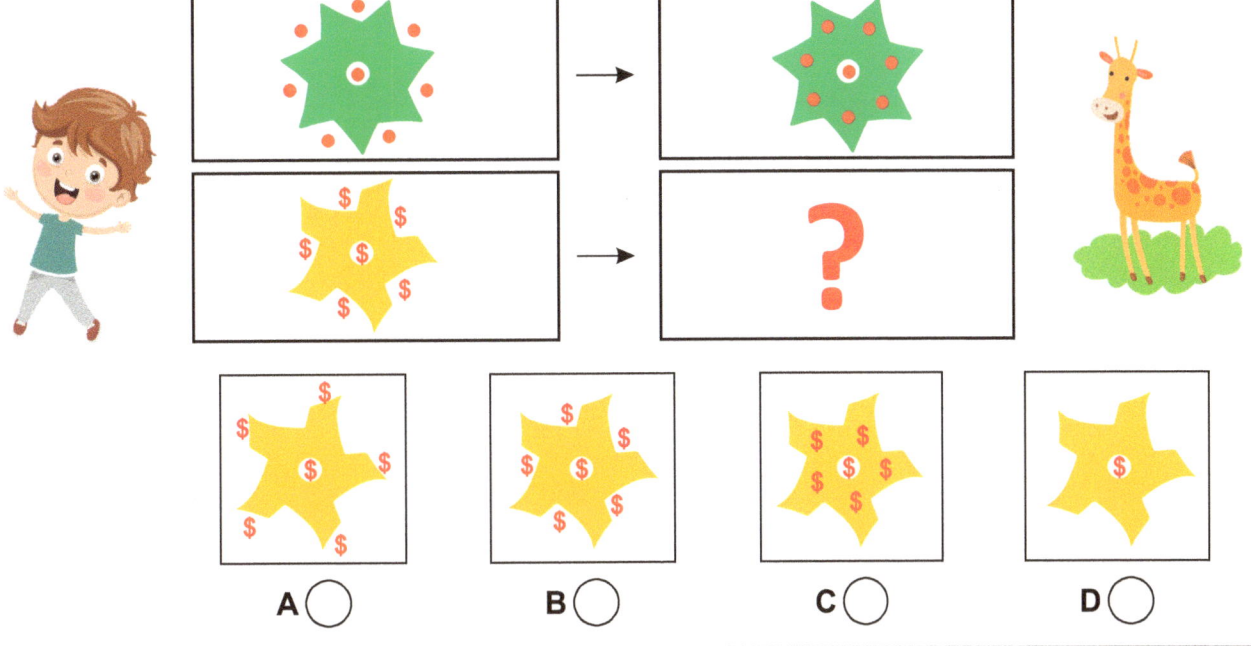

Q-18 Look at the question with the Donkey. The first row has some thing in common as the second row. Can you help Rachel to identify what goes in the space of the question mark from the four given options A, B, C, and D. Choose the correct option.

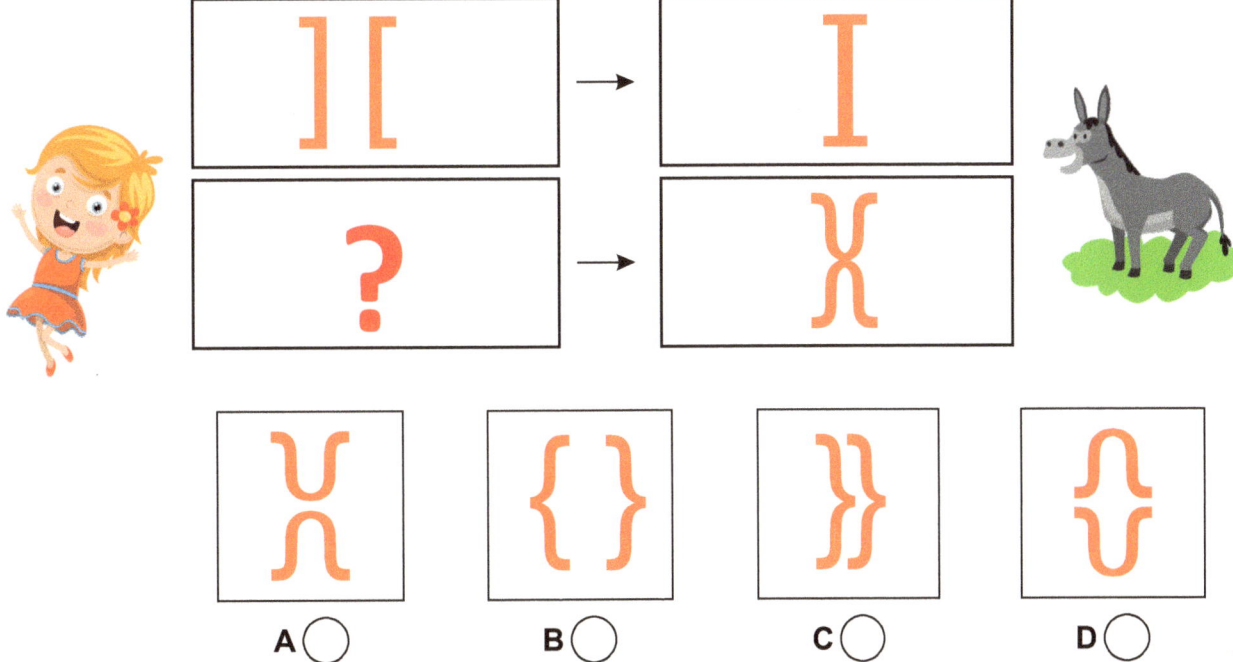

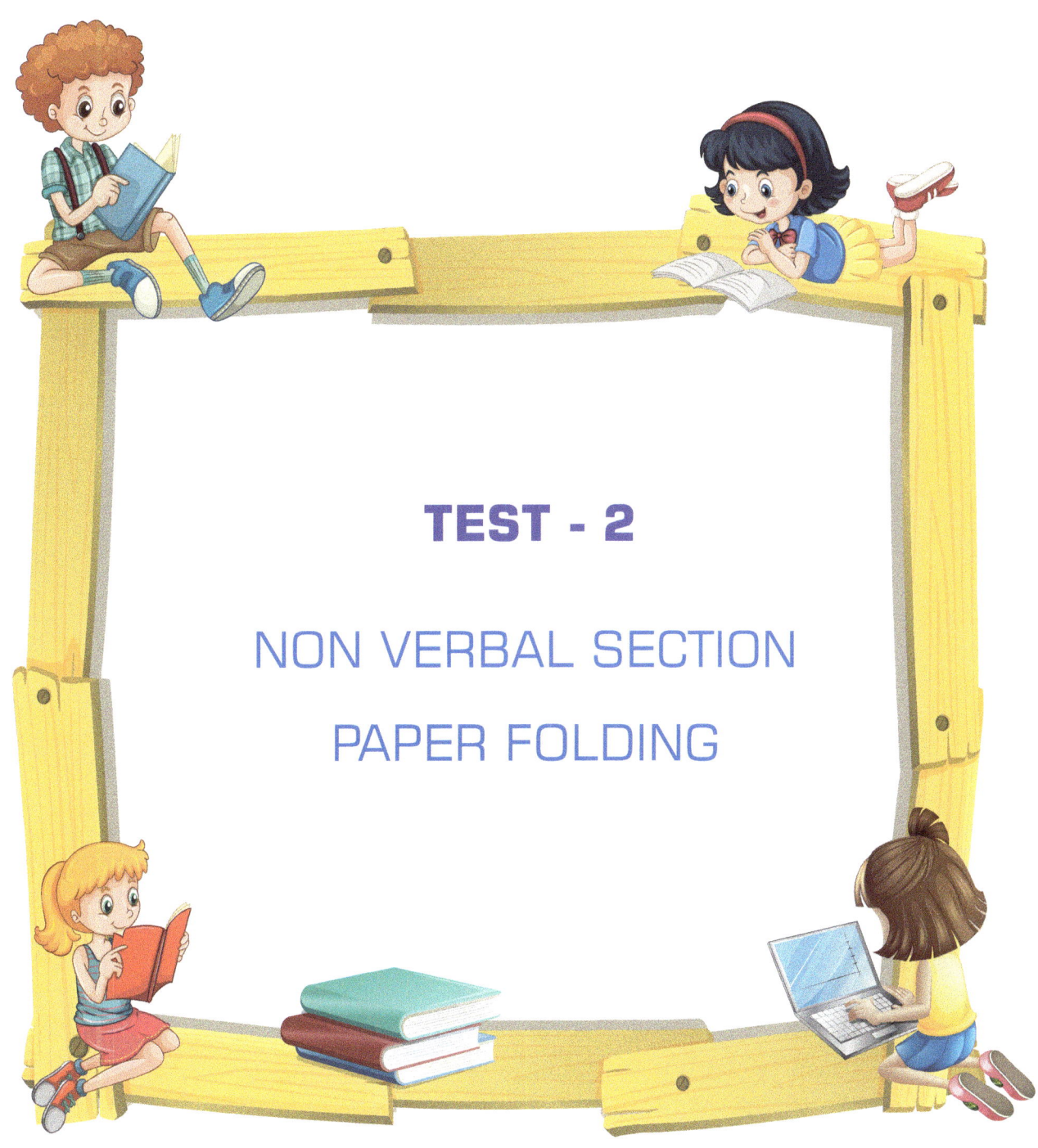

TEST - 2

NON VERBAL SECTION

PAPER FOLDING

Lets Start the Test...

www.math-knots.com

Sample Look at the question and put your finger on Bee. Amy folded the paper and made holes to it as shown. When the paper is unfolded how does it look? Help her bubble the right option.

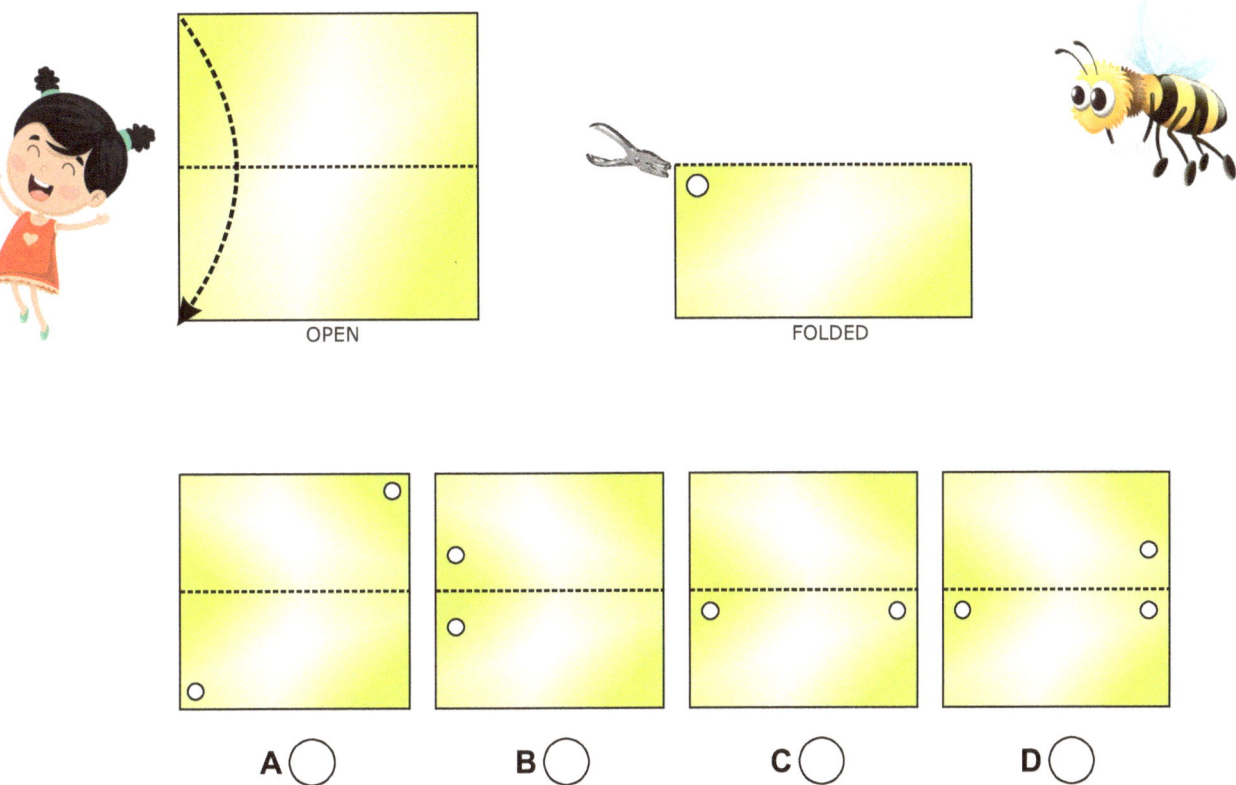

OPEN

FOLDED

A◯ B◯ C◯ D◯

Solution : B

A rectangle is folded once and hole is punched on top left corner. After punching the figure is unfolded the holes are shown in the middle left corner as shown in option B. Student choses the right option and fills the bubble completely.

www.math-knots.com

Q-1

Look at the question and put your finger on Hot Air Baloon. Jack folded the paper and made hole to it as shown. When the paper is unfolded how does it look? Help him bubble the right option.

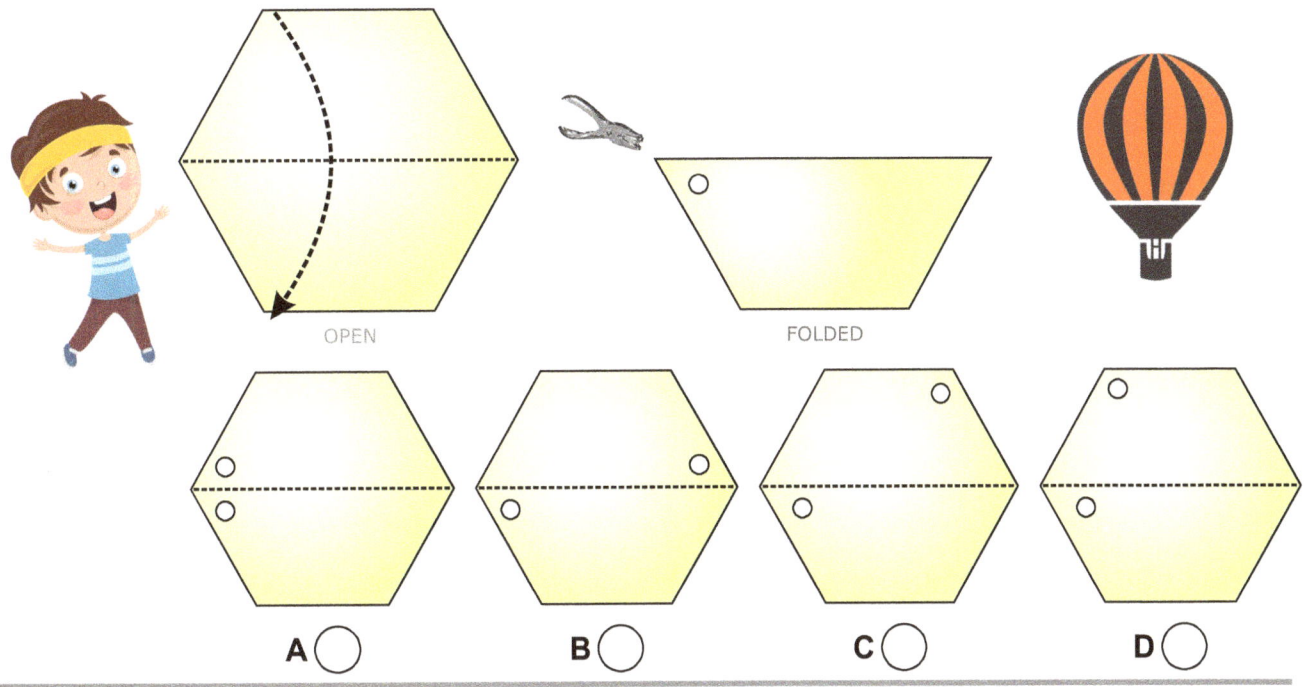

Q-2

Look at the question and put your finger on Helicopter. Emily folded the paper and made holes to it as shown. When the paper is unfolded how does it look? Help her bubble the right option.

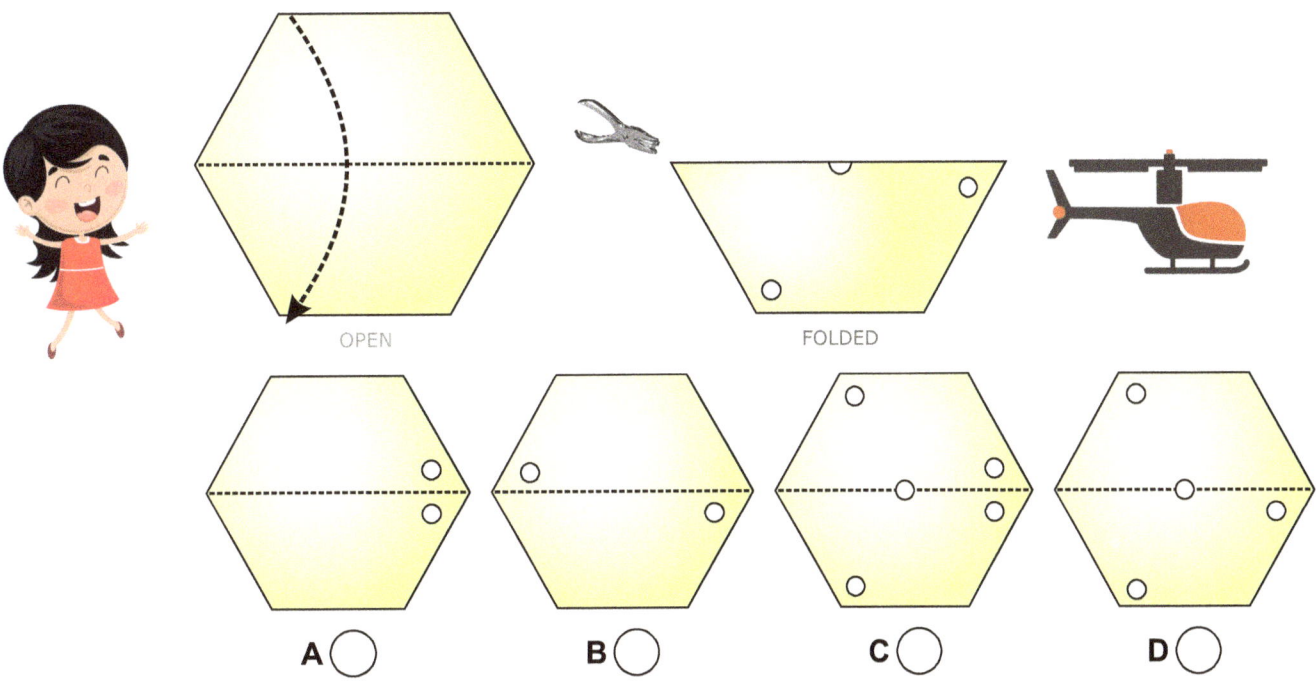

Q-3

Look at the question and put your finger on Ship. William folded the paper and made hole to it as shown. When the paper is unfolded how does it look? Help him bubble the right option.

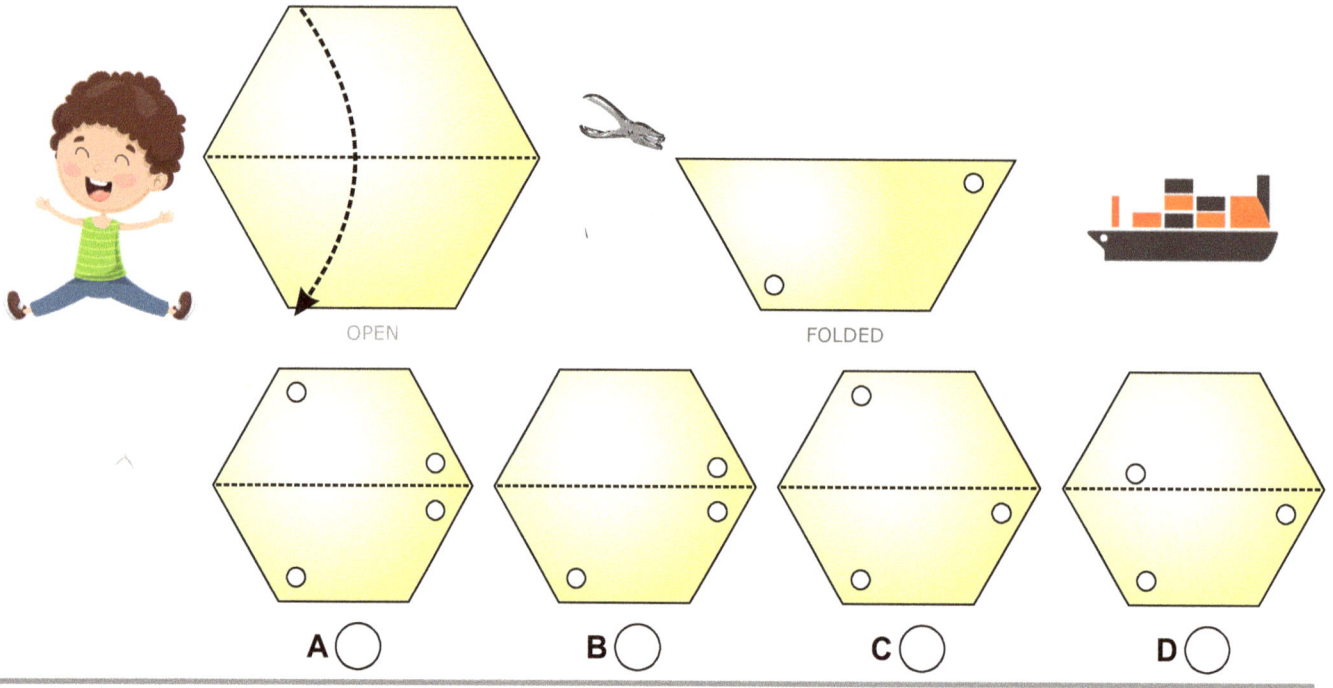

OPEN

FOLDED

A ◯ B ◯ C ◯ D ◯

Q-4

Look at the question and put your finger on Aeroplane. Grace folded the paper and made holes to it as shown. When the paper is unfolded how does it look? Help her bubble the right option.

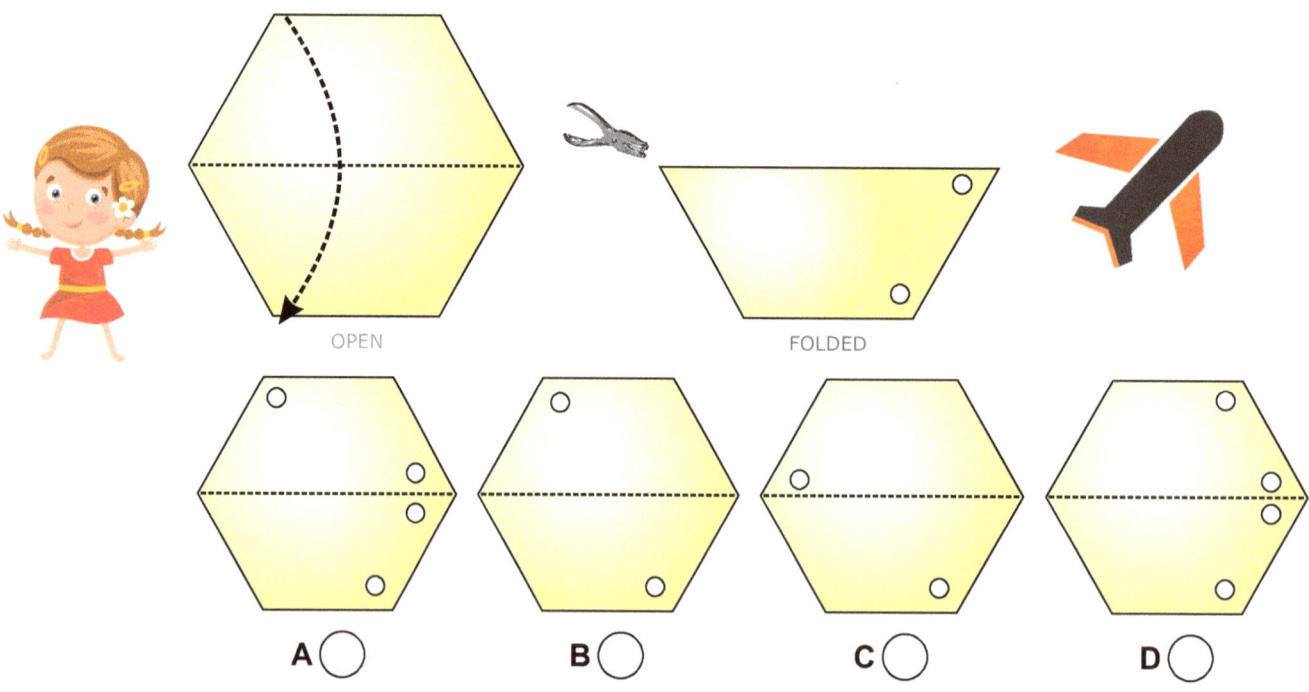

OPEN

FOLDED

A ◯ B ◯ C ◯ D ◯

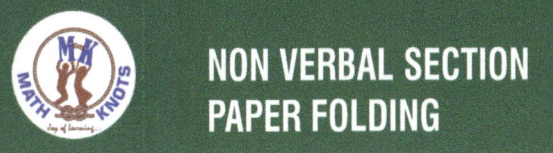

Q-5 Look at the question and put your finger on Car. Alexis folded the paper and made hole to it as shown. When the paper is unfolded how does it look? Help her bubble the right option.

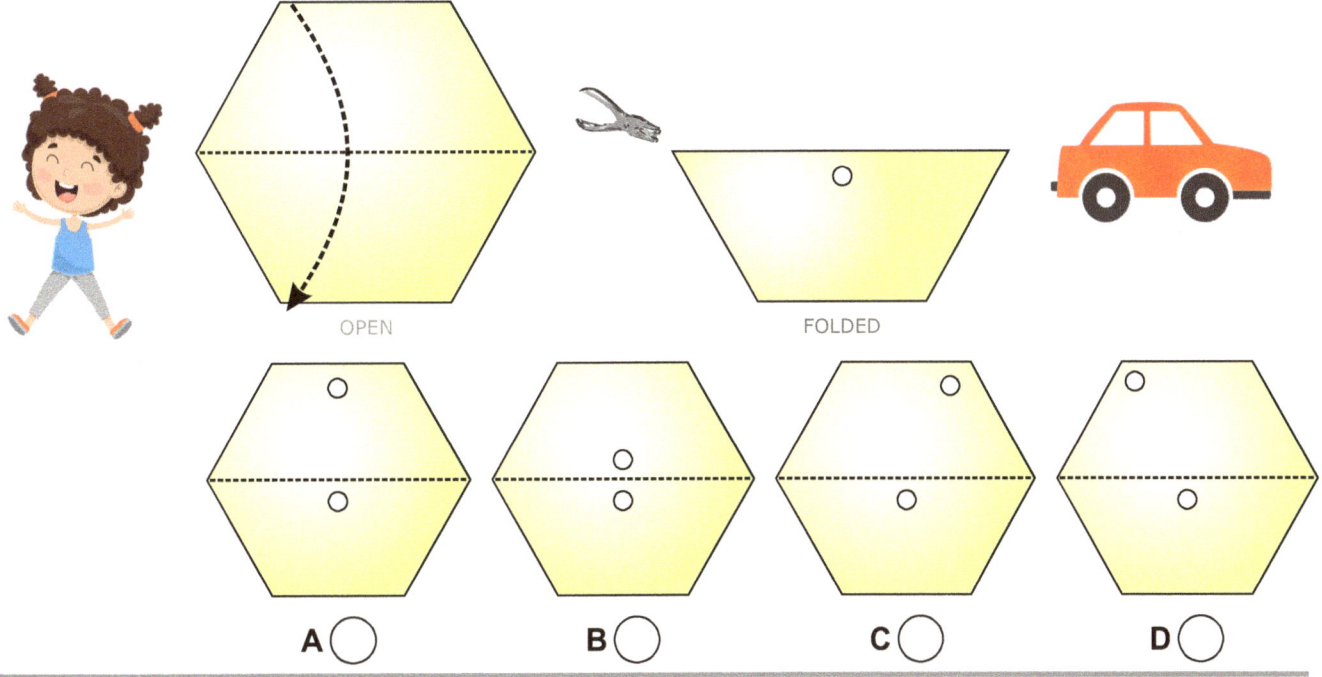

Q-6 Look at the question and put your finger on Tanker. Jacob folded the paper and made holes to it as shown. When the paper is unfolded how does it look? Help him bubble the right option.

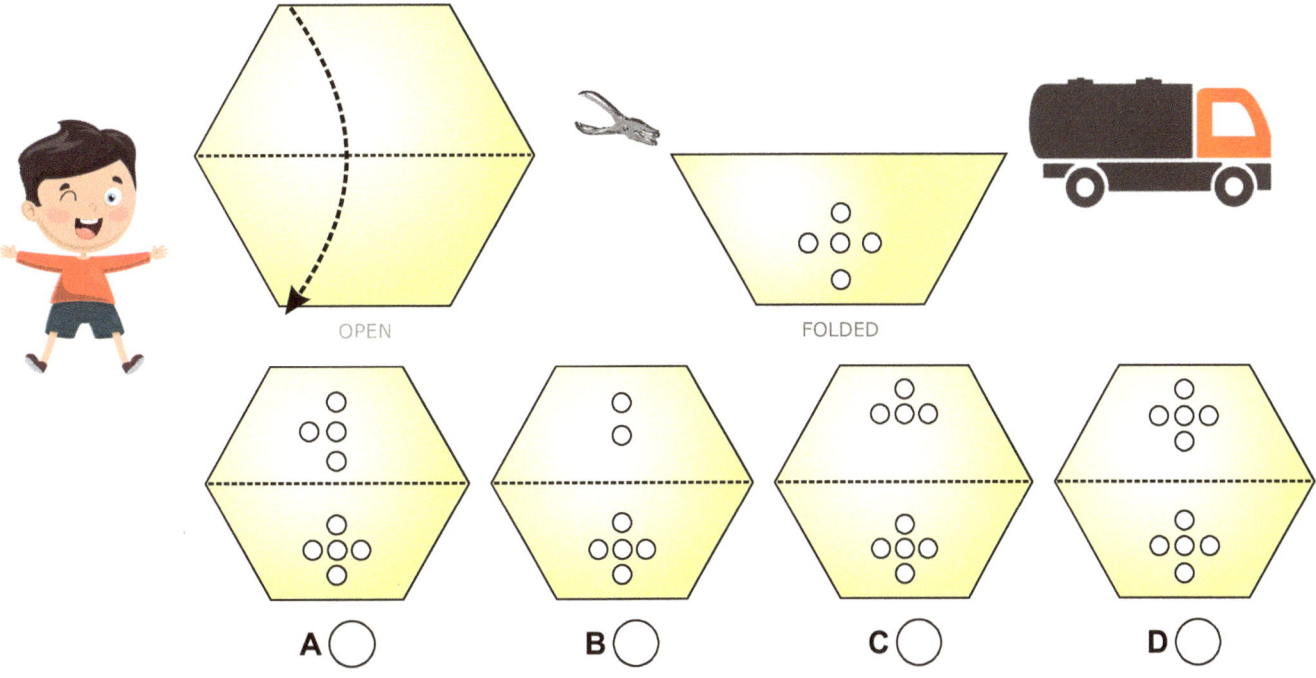

www.math-knots.com

Q-7

Look at the question and put your finger on Mini Truck. Olivia folded the paper and made holes to it as shown. When the paper is unfolded how does it look? Help her bubble the right option.

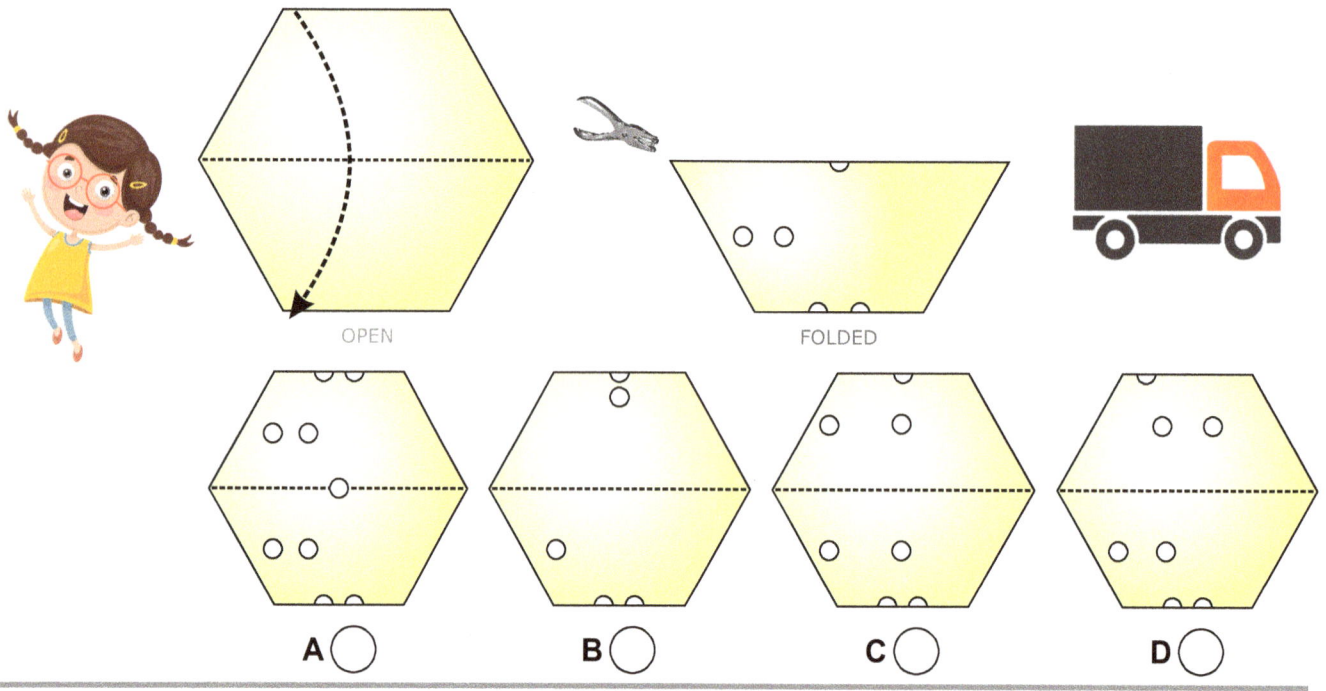

OPEN

FOLDED

A ◯   B ◯   C ◯   D ◯

Q-8

Look at the question and put your finger on Tractor. Elizabeth folded the paper and made hole to it as shown. When the paper is unfolded how does it look? Help her bubble the right option.

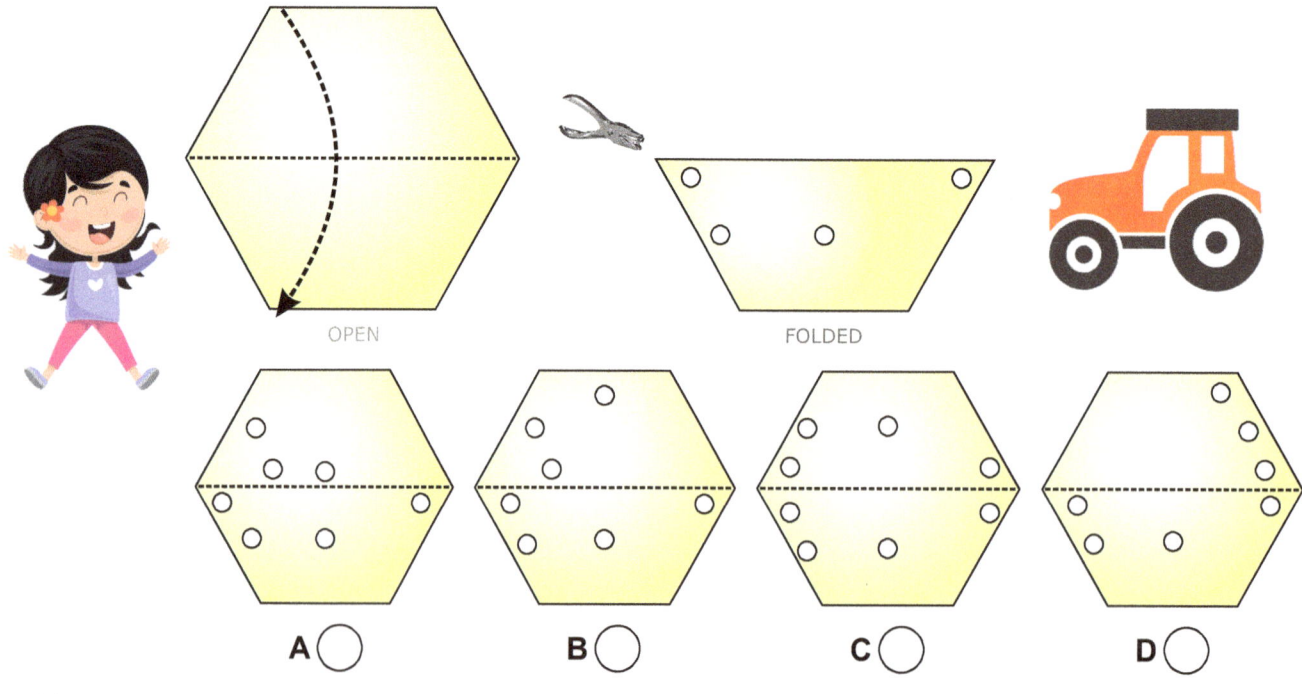

OPEN

FOLDED

A ◯   B ◯   C ◯   D ◯

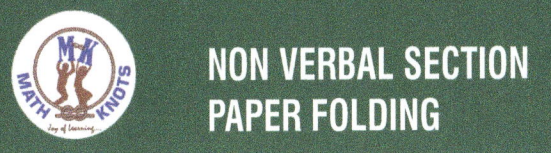

Q-9 Look at the question and put your finger on Boat. Nicholas folded the paper and made holes to it as shown. When the paper is unfolded how does it look? Help him bubble the right option.

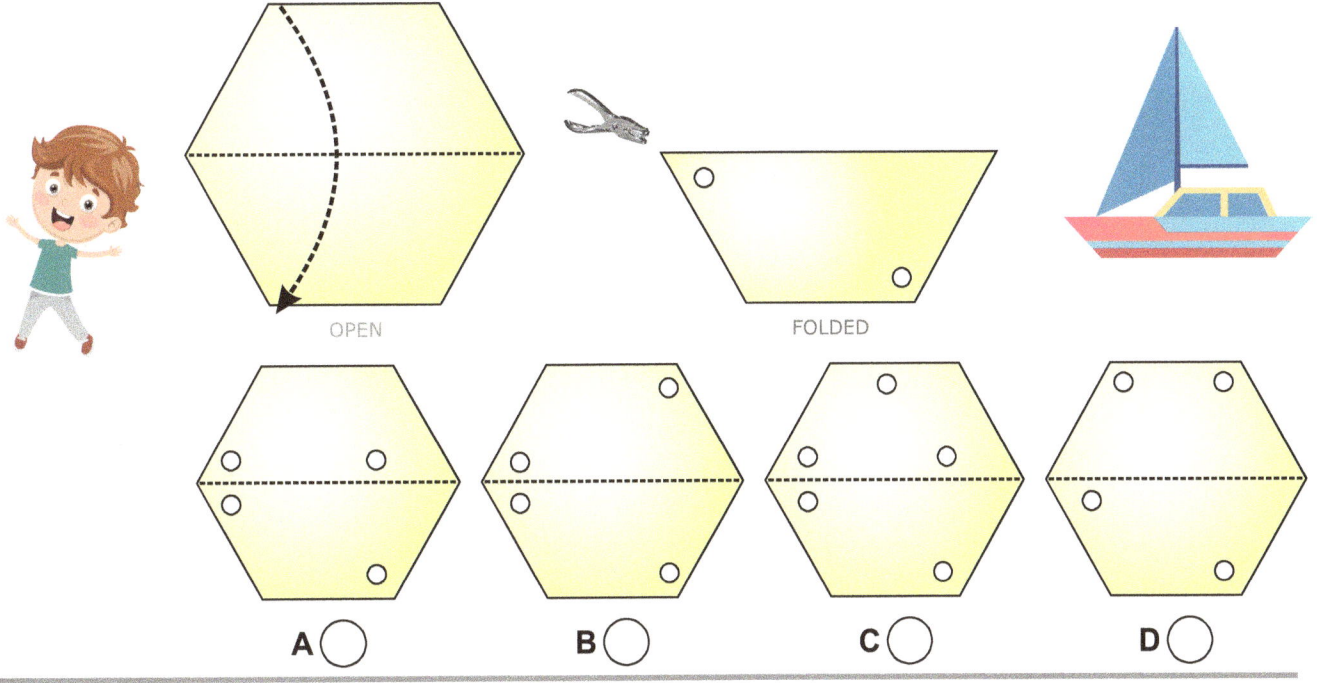

OPEN

FOLDED

A ◯   B ◯   C ◯   D ◯

Q-10 Look at the question and put your finger on Bicycle. David folded the paper and made holes to it as shown. When the paper is unfolded how does it look? Help him bubble the right option.

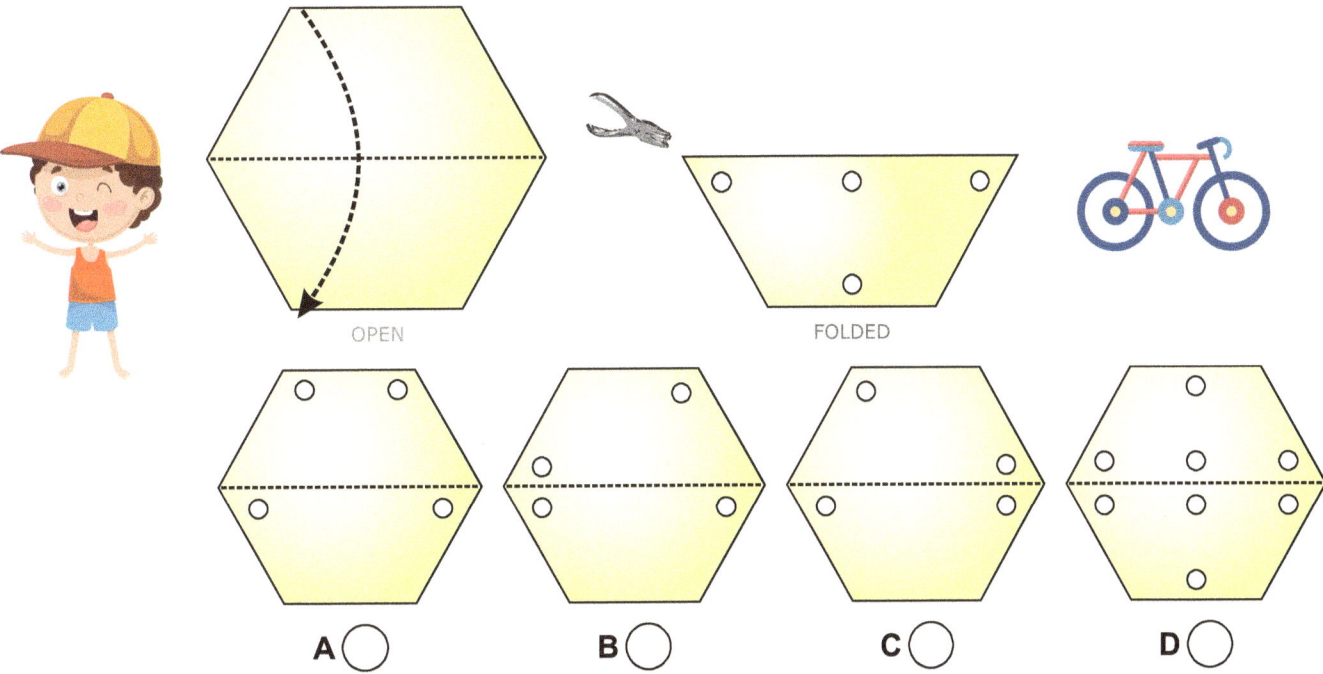

OPEN

FOLDED

A ◯   B ◯   C ◯   D ◯

Q-11 Look at the question and put your finger on Train. Benjamin folded the paper and made holes to it as shown. When the paper is unfolded how does it look? Help him bubble the right option.

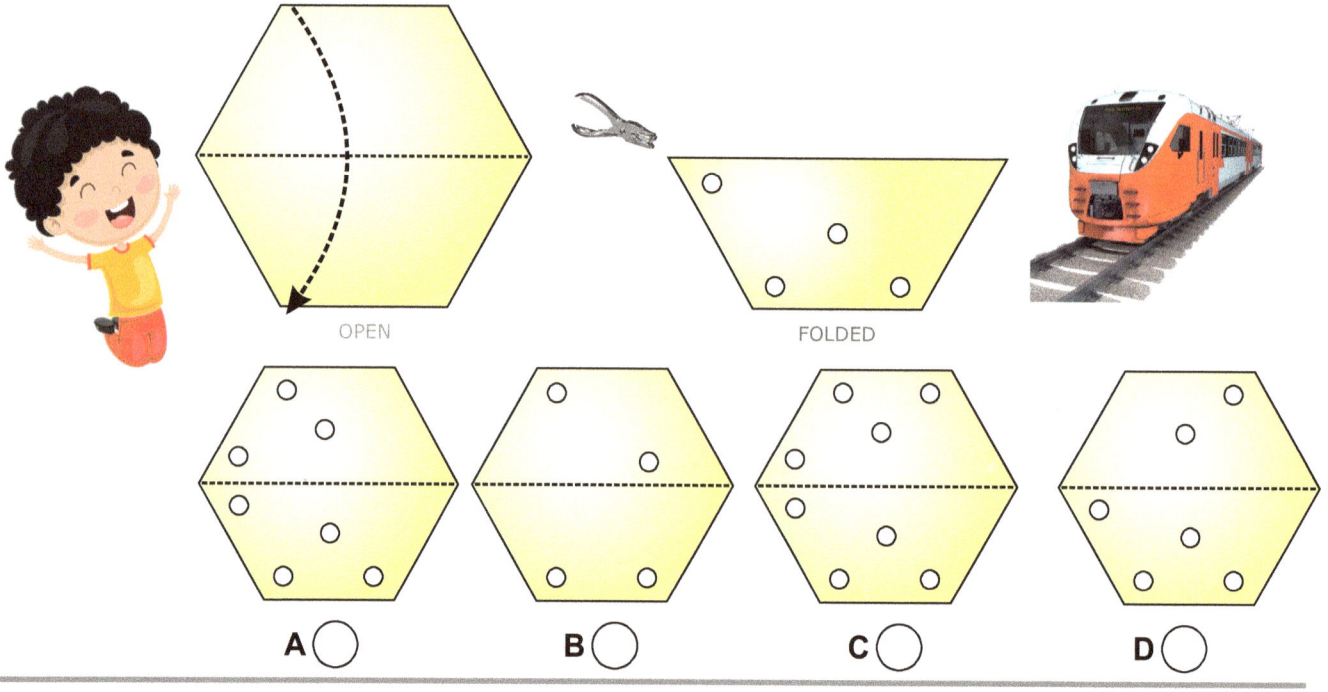

OPEN   FOLDED

A ◯   B ◯   C ◯   D ◯

Q-12 Look at the question and put your finger on Skate Board. Kristen folded the paper and made holes to it as shown. When the paper is unfolded how does it look? Help her bubble the right option.

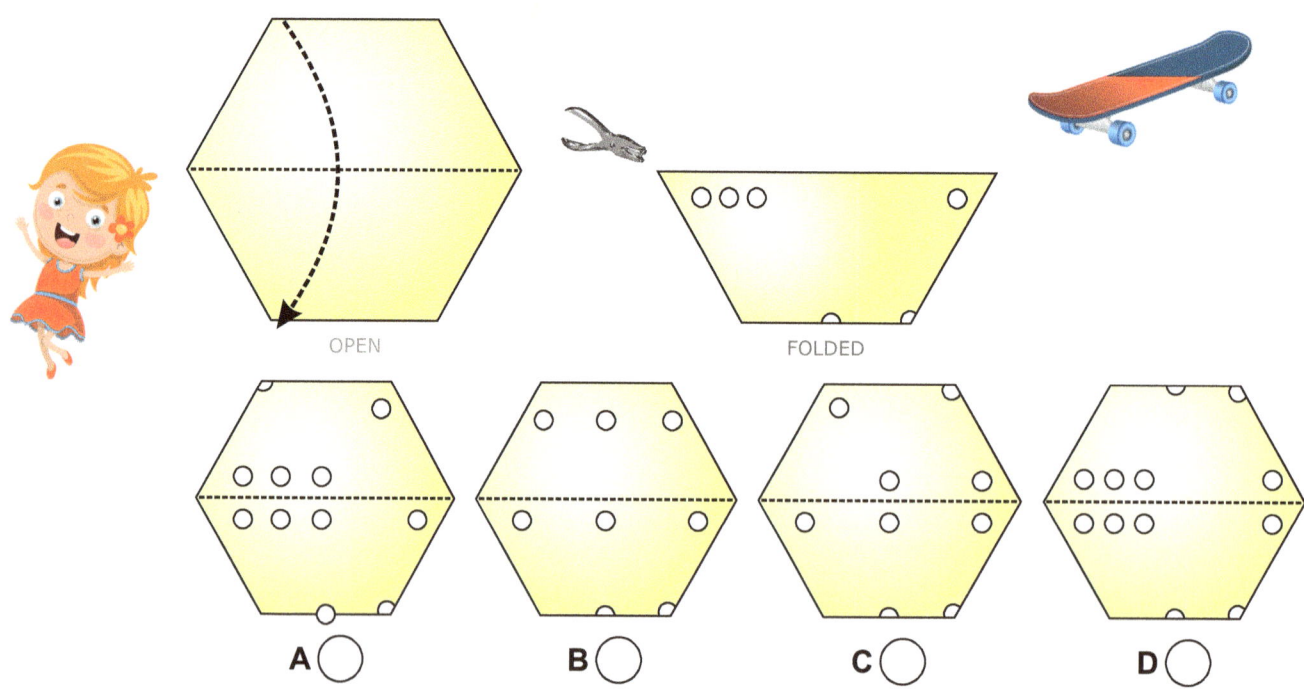

OPEN   FOLDED

A ◯   B ◯   C ◯   D ◯

Q-13

Look at the question and put your finger on Jeep. Hannah folded the paper and made holes to it as shown. When the paper is unfolded how does it look? Help her bubble the right option.

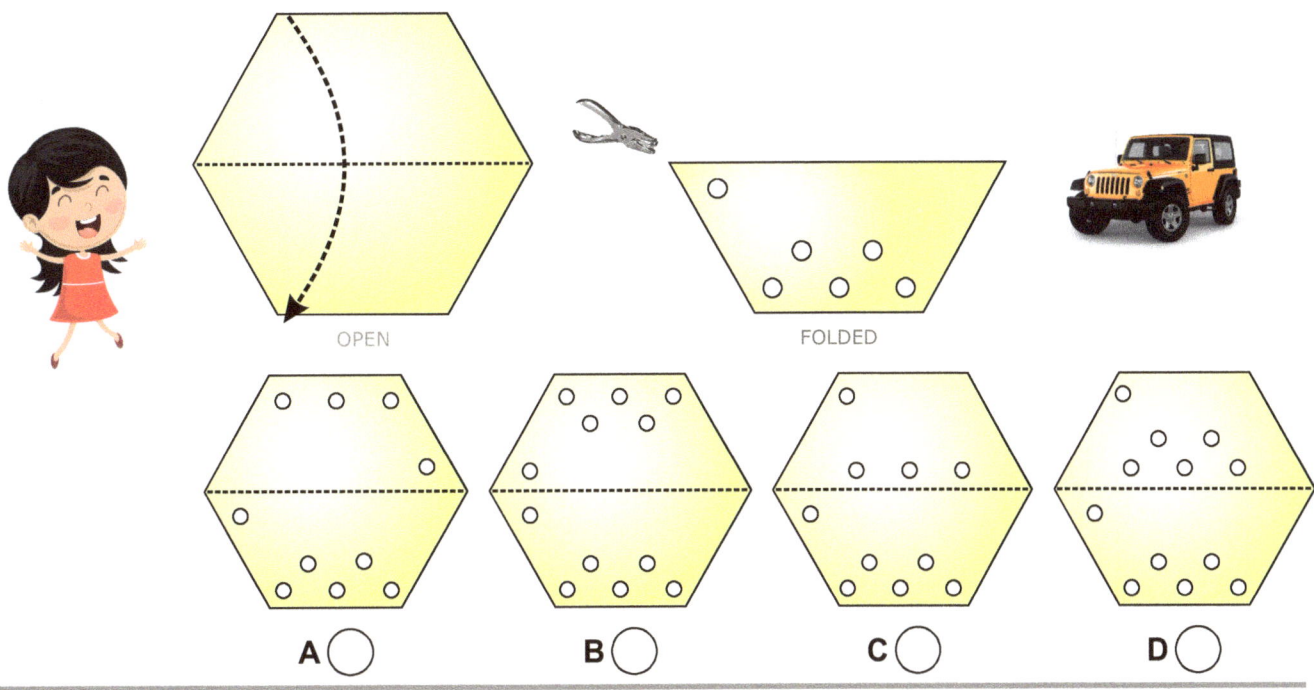

OPEN   FOLDED

A◯   B◯   C◯   D◯

Q-14

Look at the question and put your finger on Ship. Samantha folded the paper and made holes to it as shown. When the paper is unfolded how does it look? Help her bubble the right option.

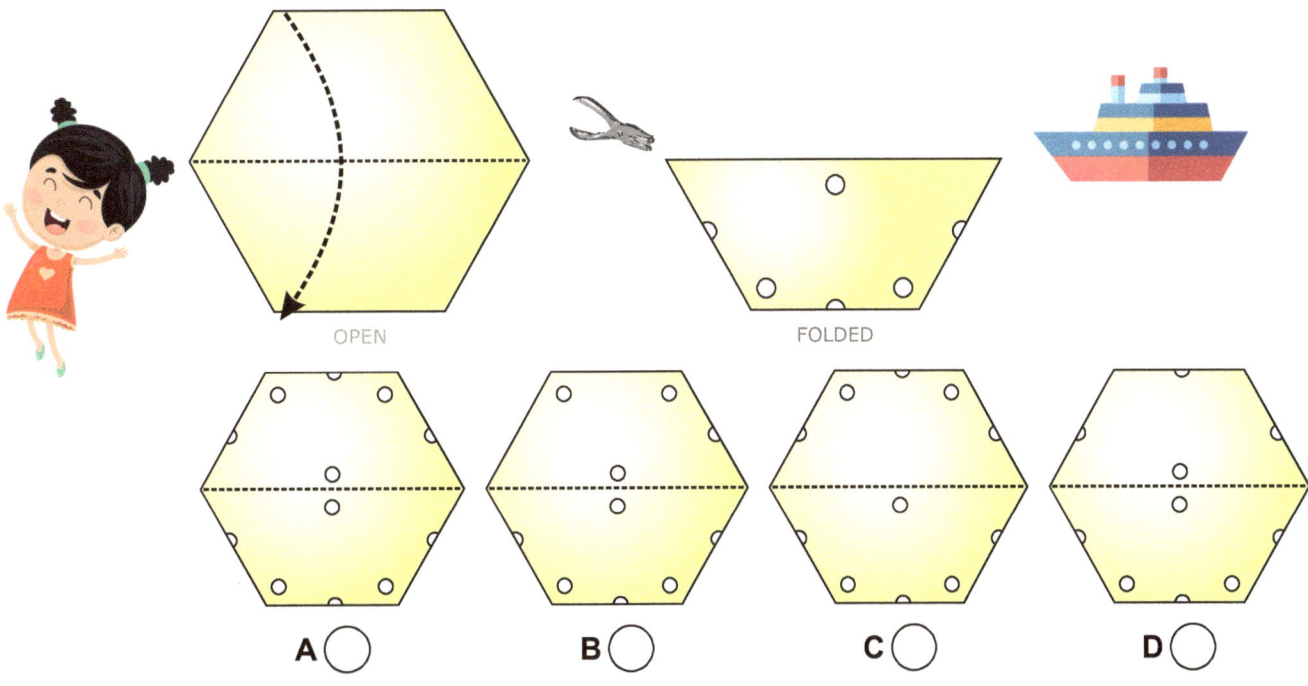

OPEN   FOLDED

A◯   B◯   C◯   D◯

Q-15

Look at the question and put your finger on Tricycle. Gabriel folded the paper and made holes to it as shown. When the paper is unfolded how does it look? Help him bubble the right option.

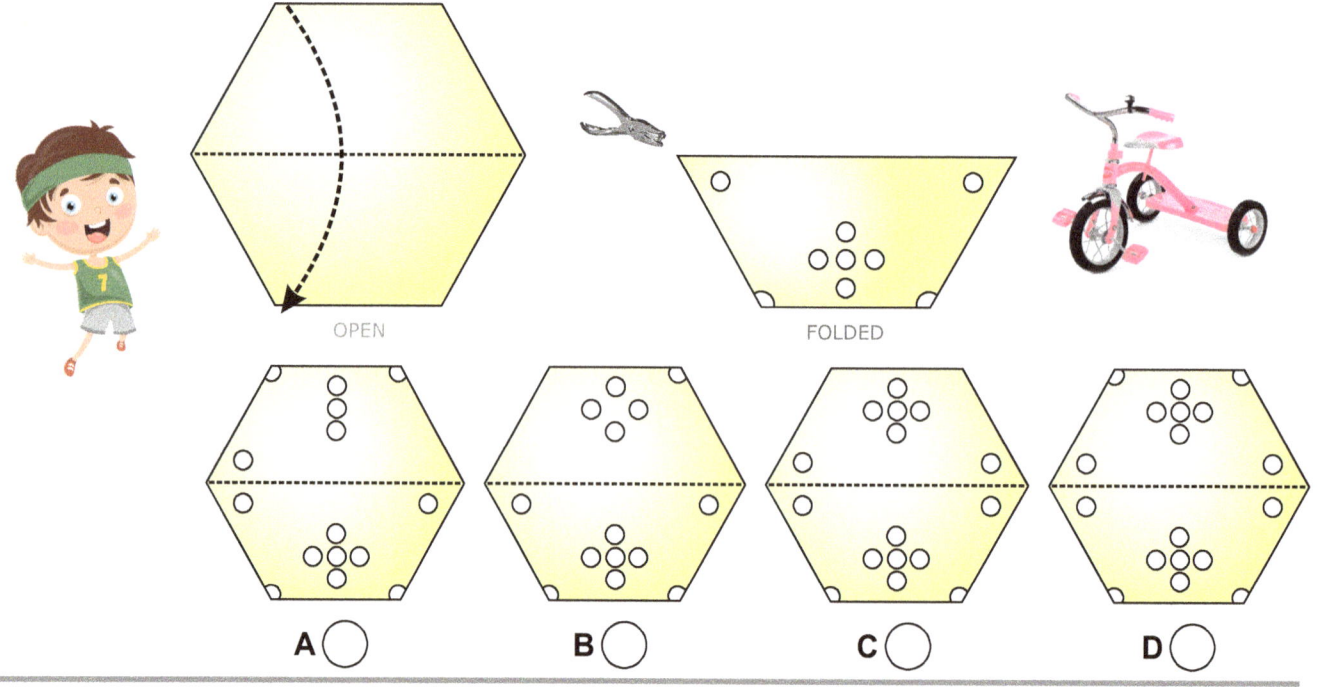

A ◯   B ◯   C ◯   D ◯

Q-16

Look at the question and put your finger on Scooter. Jessica folded the paper and made holes to it as shown. When the paper is unfolded how does it look? Help her bubble the right option.

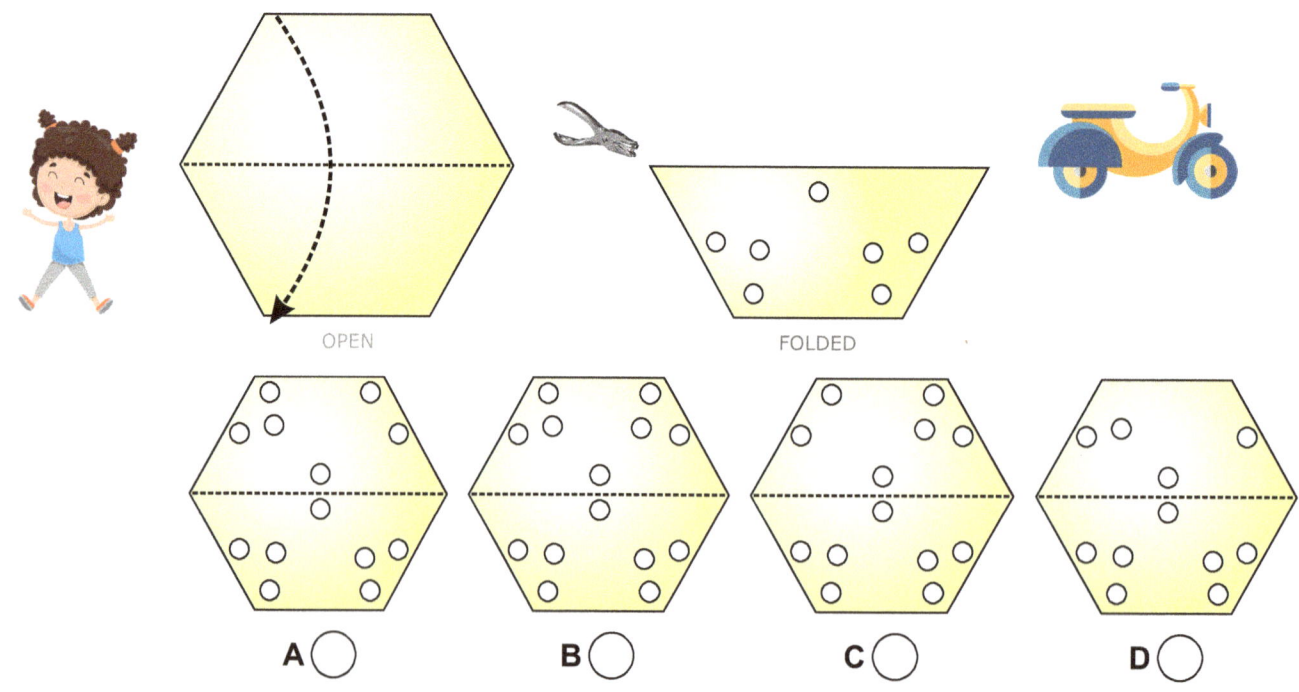

A ◯   B ◯   C ◯   D ◯

www.math-knots.com

MATH-KNOTS CHALLENGE

Q-17 Look at the question and put your finger on Van. Issac folded the paper and made holes to it as shown. When the paper is unfolded how does it look? Help him bubble the right option.

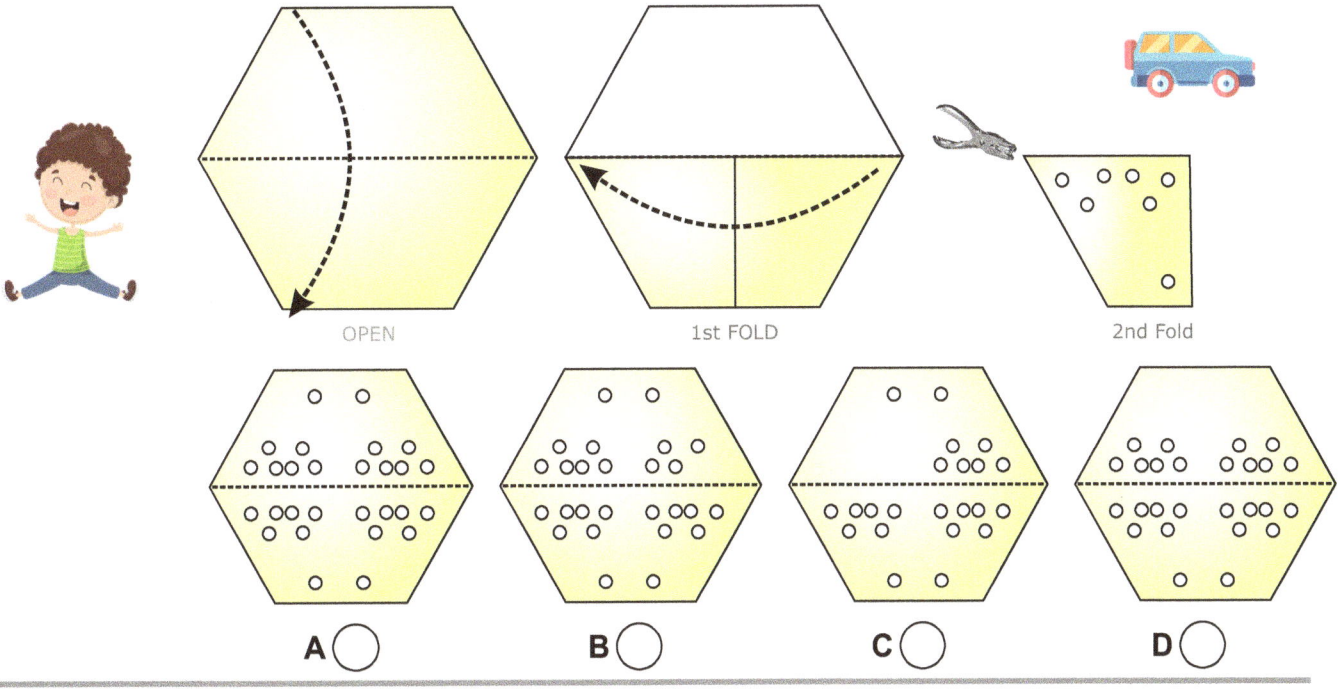

OPEN   1st FOLD   2nd Fold

A ◯   **B** ◯   **C** ◯   **D** ◯

MATH-KNOTS CHALLENGE

Q-18 Look at the question and put your finger on Bus. Victoria folded the paper and made holes to it as shown. When the paper is unfolded how does it look? Help her bubble the right option.

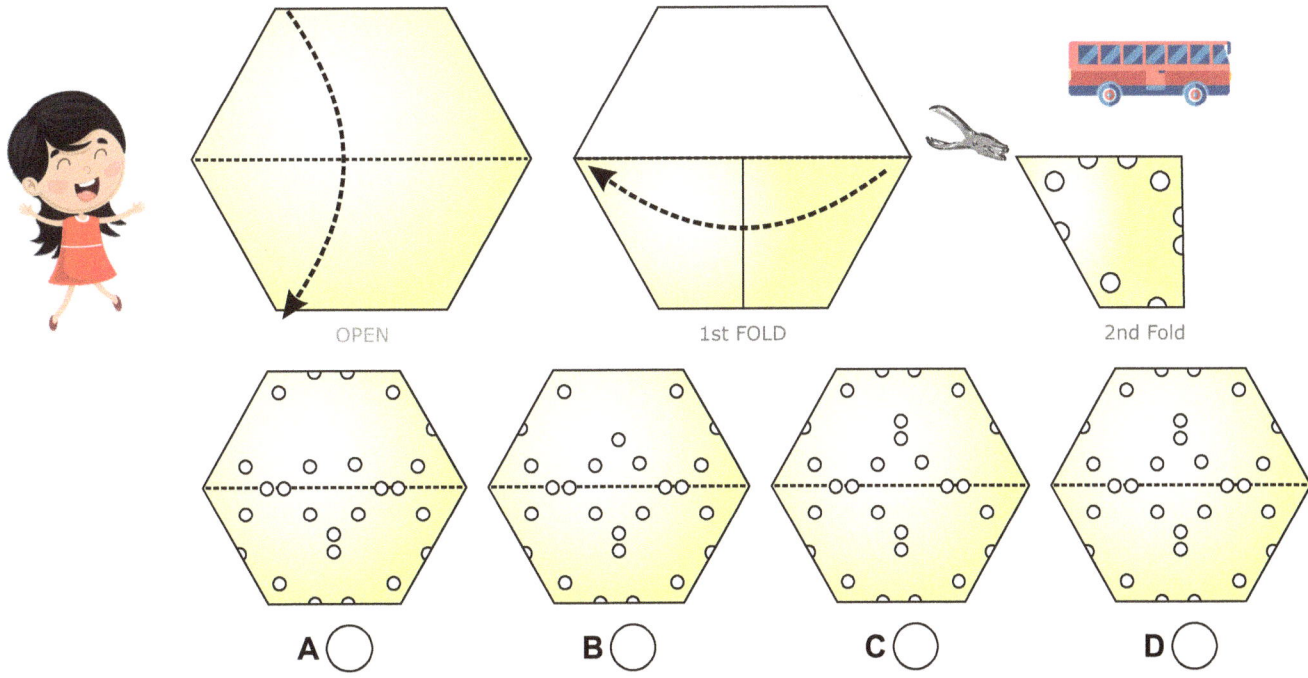

OPEN   1st FOLD   2nd Fold

A ◯   **B** ◯   **C** ◯   **D** ◯

MATH-KNOTS CHALLENGE

Q-19 Look at the question and put your finger on Swing. Anthony folded the paper and made holes to it as shown. When the paper is unfolded how does it look? Help him bubble the right option.

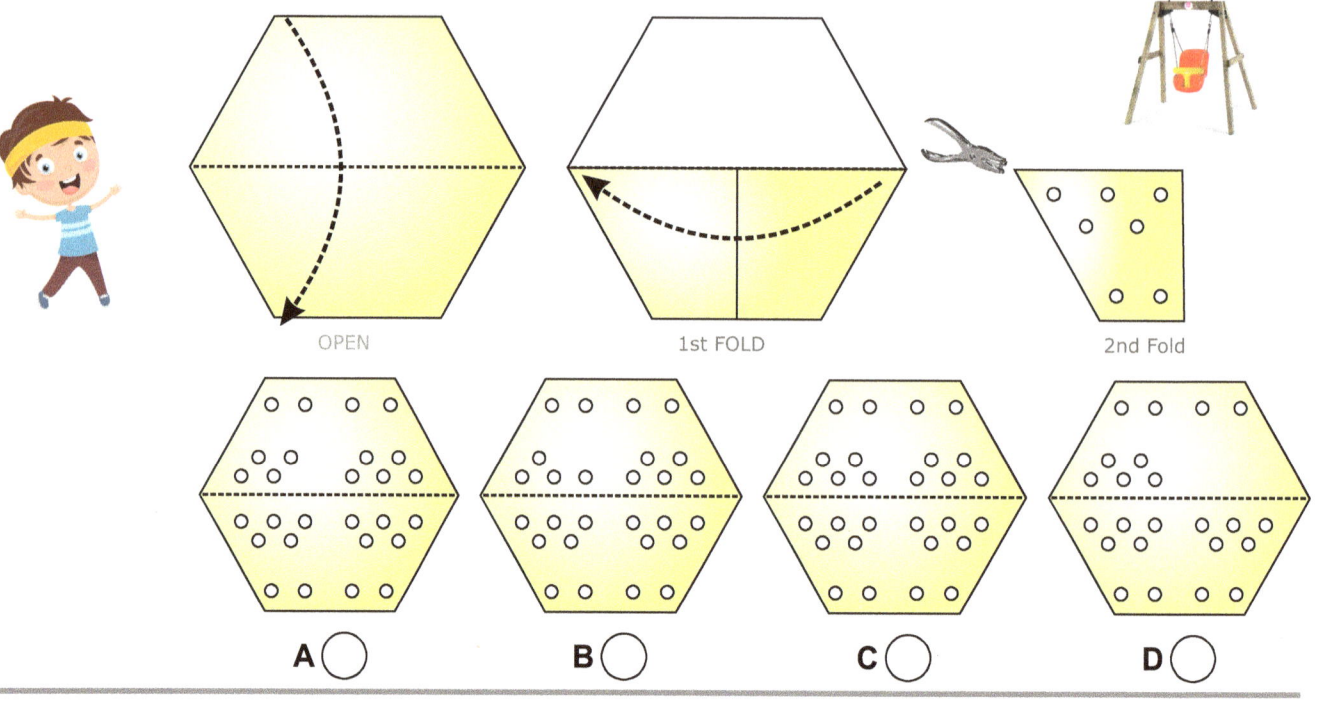

OPEN   1st FOLD   2nd Fold

A ◯   B ◯   C ◯   D ◯

MATH-KNOTS CHALLENGE

Q-20 Look at the question and put your finger on Merri Go Round . Anna folded the paper and made holes to it as shown. When the paper is unfolded how does it look? Help her bubble the right option.

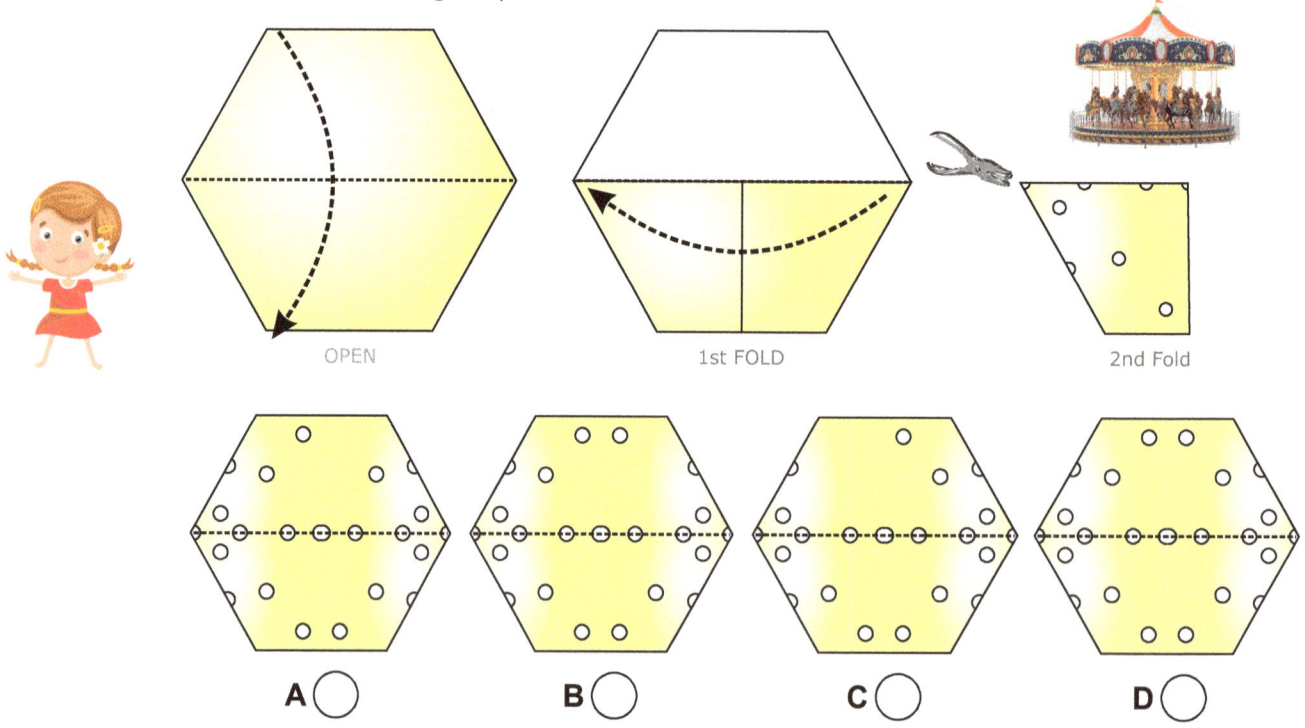

OPEN   1st FOLD   2nd Fold

A ◯   B ◯   C ◯   D ◯

www.math-knots.com

ANSWER KEYS

TEST - 1 AND 2

Lets Start the Test...

ANSWER KEY

1. A ;   Types of things we wear or Garments

2. A ;   All others are nature- bound, War is man-made

3. C ;   All others are types of color

4. D ;   All others are sense organs or related to sense organs

5. B ;   Various types of gases

6. D ;   Various expressions of joy

7. A ;   Types of solid metals

8. B ;   Various joints in human body

9. D ;   Types of various professions

10. C ;   Various types of instructors

11. B ;   Various types of string instruments

12. B ;   Various forms of running water

13. D ;   Parts of tree above ground

14. A ;   Various types of transportations

15. C ;   Types of players in various sports

16. D ;   Permission meanings

17. B ;   Things made of wood

18. A ;   Meanings of highest point

ANSWER KEY

1.   A

As the wind Blows tent is pushed aside

2.   C

Fastest way of transportation is Aero plane

3.   B

A boat is used to cross the river

4.   A

To shop we need money and money is kept in hand bag. Out of the given choices hand bag is the right option to choose

5.   D

Rita needs to dress up warmly to play in snow, otherwise she will fall sick. Option D shows winter hat and gloves

6.   B

Enclosed means surround or close off on all sides. Picture is closed by frame Circle is closed by star. Map is enclosing the area. Option B, the letter U is not surrounding anything and has an opening on the top

7.   A

Single means one. Option A, showing a Baby is the single kid

8.   D

Option D is showing all 9 planets

9.   A

Lion and cat can't fly. Dolphins swim and jump but don't fly. Aero plane is the only one which flies

ANSWER KEY

10.   C

A pair means two. Three pairs of objects mean six objects in total

11.   A

Carl needs an electric socket to charge his cell phone and laptop

12.   D

Hair band is some thing that girls use to decorate their hair on the head

13.   B

Pack means a group of wild animals like wolves, tigers etc....Pack is also a box and the items within it

14.   C

Option C, Ranch is a common tool found in tool box

15.   A

Croak sounds are made by Frogs

16.   D

Sriyan can't open the laptop as he is too young

17.   D

Violin / Viola / Guitar all belong to strings family of instruments

18.   B

From the given options Red Car is the right choice.
It same of the same color as tomato

www.math-knots.com

ANSWER KEY

1.   A

2.   D

3.   C

4.   D

5.   A

6.   C

7.   A

8.   D

9.   C

10.   B

11.   D

12.   A

13.   C

14.   B

15.   D

16.   B

17.   C

18.   A

www.math-knots.com

ANSWER KEY

1.   A

        1 --> 4 (Add 3)

        1 --> 4 (Add 3)

2.   D

        6 --> 3 (Half)

        10 --> 5 (Half)

3.   C

        4 --> 4 (Same count of objects)

        6 --> 6 (Same count of objects)

4.   A

        3 --> 6 (Double)

        2 --> 4 (Double)

5.   B

        3 --> 4 (Add 1)

        6 --> 7 (Add 1)

6.   D

        5 --> 10 (Double)

        6 --> 12 (Double)

7.   A

        4 --> 3 (Subtract 1)

        5 --> 4 (Subtract 1)

ANSWER KEY

8.   B

       7 --> 5 (Subtract 2)

       9 --> 7 (Subtract 2)

9.   A

       1 --> 5 (Add 4)

       2 --> 6 (Add 4)

10.   C

       1 --> 7 (Add 6)

       1 --> 7 (Add 6)

11.   D

       1 --> 6 (Add 5)

       1 --> 6 (Add 5)

12.   A

       8 --> 1 (Subtract 7)

       8 --> 1 (Subtract 7)

13.   D

       1 --> 2 (Add 1)

       1 --> 2 (Add 1)

14.   D

       2 --> 5 (Add 3)

       5 --> 8 (Add 3)

ANSWER KEY

15.   B

8 --> 4 (Half)

4 --> 2 (Half)

16.   C

One wheel --> 2 wheels per object

Two wheels --> 4 wheels object

17.   A

Half --> Full (Double / Twice)

2 --> 4 (Double /Twice)

18.   D

1 whole Pizza --> One slice

1 Whole cake --> One slice

www.math-knots.com

ANSWER KEY

1.   A

    6, 4, 2, 0 ; Numbers are decreasing by 2

2.   D

    2, 2, 3, 3, 4, 4 ; Each number is repeating twice and then increasing by 1

3.   D

    5, 5, 3, ?, 5, 5; Each number is repeating twice and decreasing by 2 So, answer is 5, 5, 3, 3, 5, 5

4.   B

    1, 5, 1, 5, 1, 5; 1 and 5 are repeating

5.   C

    8, 6, 4, 2 ; Numbers are decreasing by 2

6.   A

    4, 3, 3, 2, 2, 1; Alternate numbers are decreasing by 1
    4, 3, 2 are one group & 3, 2, 1 are another group

7.   C

    5, 0, 0, 5, 0, 0, 5; 5, 0, 0 is the repeating sequence

8.   D

    0, 2, 4, 6, 8; Increasing by two

9.   A

    0, 7, 0, 7, 0, 7; Repeating sequence of 0 and 7

10.   C

    4, 5, 3, 4, 2, 3; Alternate numbers are decreasing by 1
    4, 3, 2 are one group & 5, 4, 3 are another group

www.math-knots.com

ANSWER KEY

11.   B

5, 3, 1, 5, 3, 1; Repeating sequence of 5, 3 and 1

12.   D

0, 0, 6, 0, 0, 6; Repeating sequence of 0, 0 and 6

13.   A

4, 4, 3, 5, 2, 6; Alternate numbers are decreasing by 1

Alternate numbers are increasing by 1.

5, 3, 2 are one group & 4, 5, 6 are one group

14.   C

7, 6, 5, 7, 6, 5; Repeating sequence of 7, 6 and 5

15.   D

5, 4, 3, 2, 1; Numbers are decreasing by 1

16.   C

2, 2, 4, 4, 2, 2, 4; Repeating sequence of 2, 2, 4, 4 and
then 2, 2, 4, 4

17.   A

11, 9, 9, 11, 7 Alternate numbers are decreasing by 2

Alternate numbers are increasing by 2

11, 9, 7 are one group & 9, 11, 13 are one group

18.   B

1, 2, 2, 3, 3, 4; Alternate numbers are increasing by 1

ANSWER KEY

1. B

    $1 + 6 = 7$

2. A

    $3 + 5 = 8$

3. C

    $6 + 4 = 10$

4. D

    $2 + 6 = 8$

5. B

    $4 + 4 = 8$

6. A

    $1 + 3 = 4$

7. B

    $6 + 3 = 9$

8. D

    $4 + 6 + 4 = 14$

9. A

    $9 + 4 + 1 = 13 + 1 = 14$

10. C

    $2 + 5 + 3 = 7 + 3 = 10$

ANSWER KEY

11.   C

$$5 + 1 + 7 = 6 + 7 = 13$$

12.   D

$$2 + 4 + 6 = 12$$

13.   B

$$6 + 1 + 9 = 16$$

14.   B

$$10 + 0 + 0 = 10$$

15.   A

$$9 - 4 + 1 = 5 + 1 = 6$$

16.   D

$$2 + 5 - 3 = 7 - 3 = 4$$

17.   C

$$4 + 1 - 2 = 5 - 2 = 3$$

18.   D

$$6 + 5 + 0 = 11$$

19.   A

$$6 + 1 + 9 = 7 + 9 = 16$$

20.   B

$$5 + 3 + 1 = 9$$

                   www.math-knots.com

ANSWER KEY

1.	A	Figures are turning 90 degrees. The best option is A
2.	A	Three figures are overlapping
3.	D	One flower with 5 petals
4.	B	Three curves cutting the circle
5.	C	Two lines cutting in the rectangle. Red line on top of green line
6.	A	Only option A matches to the group with two stars, two circles and 7 lines
7.	B	Only picture with & ,%,@ and # in sequence is option B in
8.	D	Only option with ? , @ and X
9.	C	Only option with green half circles at one end
10.	B	Only option B has # in the center and towards ends

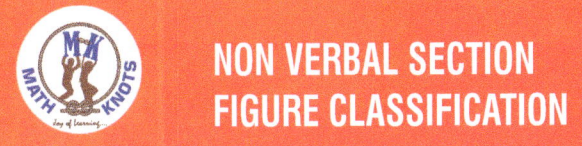
ANSWER KEY

11.	D	All three triangles are rotated together
12.	C	Green half circle has horizontal lines. Blue half circle has vertical lines
13.	A	Alphabet between two consecutive even numbers
14.	B	Two same alphabet
15.	C	Three dots in one line with closed end. Two dots in one line with open end
16.	B	Five lines originating from the same point with circles at the end
17.	A	Two stars and three triangles
18.	D	Four red circles with yellow circle on top. Looks like a flower

www.math-knots.com

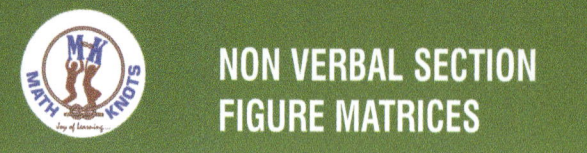

ANSWER KEY

1. A

    Angle to straight figure

2. D

    Turning 90° to right side

3. C

    Turning 90° to right side and flipping right to left.

4. A

    Flipping up to down

5. B

    Lines to checks

6. D

    One turn 90° with same petals

7. C

    Dashed lines are connecting and filling the figure

8. C

    Outside symbols on the triangle are turning anti clock wise one turn

9. A

    4 sides to 5 sides. Number sides are increasing, so 5 sides to six sides

10. D

    Dots and checks interchange in first row

    Stars and checks interchange for the second row

ANSWER KEY

11.   C

Flipping up and down

12.   D

First row: First picture has only circles. Second Picture
has two symbols (one additional)
The first picture in second row should have circles

13.   A

Size is decreasing

14.   C

First Row first picture to second picture: Flipping of top
figure in first one gives second picture of first row

15.   B

Figures in between two rays or pointed objects are
moving three slots

16.   D

Picture filled and shown transparently with shapes

17.   A

Moon inside the circle is moved to outside. So, Triangle
inside Trapezium is moved outside

18.   A

First figure above the line is moving down, while the
figure below the line is moving inside the second figure
above the line

ANSWER KEY

1.   A ;

2.   D ;

3.   C ;

4.   B ;

5.   C ;

6.   C ;

7.   B ;

8.   C ;

9.   A ;

10.   D ;

11.   C;

12.   A;

13.   D;

14.   B;

15.   A;

16.   D;

BONUS CHALLENGE QUESTIONS

17.   A ;

18.   C ;

19.   D ;

20.   B ;

ANSWER KEY

1.   C ;   Canoe is a boat ,others are resting places of birds are animals

2.   D ;   Various types of planets

3.   A ;   Various types of 2-D Pictures

4.   B ;   Various types of flying objects

5.   D ;   Various types of baby animals

6.   A ;   Various types of crawling animals

7.   C ;   Various types of vegetation

8.   B ;   Various types of indoor games

9.   B ;   Various types of payments

10.   D ;   Types of vegetables that grow under ground

11.   A ;   Various types of legal professionals

12 .   C ;   Only arrow needs a bow. Others are used by hand

13.   B ;   All months have 31 days

14.   A ;   Various types of milk Products

15.   D ;   Various meanings of foundation

16.   C ;   All are more than one in the human body

17.   B ;   Various types of outdoor games

18.   A ;   Various deserts across world

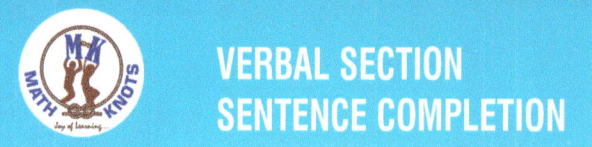
ANSWER KEY

1.   D

Alligator is the only choice that swims in water

2.   C

Pair means two. An object and two pairs meaning one object plus four objects. Total number of objects are 5

3.   C

 Lamp needs electricity to give us light

4.   A

Soccer game uses Soccer post to goal the ball. Option A soccer ball is the right choice

5.   B

Glue stick in Option B is the only correct choice

6.   D

Ella needs a measuring tape to find the dimensions of the room.
Option D, the measuring tape is the right choice

7.   A

Right choice is option A is showing wood pieces

8.   C

Option C is showing the drawing getting wiped off partially

9.   A

Cruises are big ships and is shown as option A

10.   B

Dylan needs to carry a rain poncho or an umbrella with him. Out of the given choices option B rain Poncho is the correct option

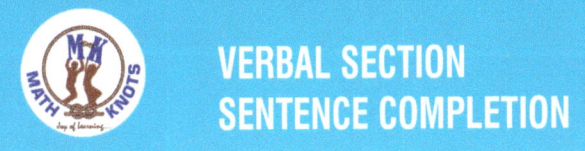

ANSWER KEY

11.   C

Gifts are wrapped up in a gift wrap or packed in a gift bag. So, option C showing gift bag is the right answer

12.   A

Double means two. Option A, showing two fruits is the correct choice

13.   D

Pair means two. Half a pair of objects is one. picture with one shoe is the correct option

14.   B

Tools are charged through an electric outlet. Option B is the right choice

15.   A

Hair clips are displayed in option A

16.   D

Flock means a group of birds or sheep

17.   C

Option C is missing the hoop

18.   A

Drums are a percussion Instrument. In percussion instruments, sound is produced by beating or striking by hand or stick

ANSWER KEY

1.   D

2.   A

3.   C

4.   A

5.   B

6.   A

7.   C

8.   B

9.   A

10.   C

11.   B

12.   D

13.   B

14.   A

15.   D

16.   C

17.   A

18.   D

www.math-knots.com

ANSWER KEY

1.   C

       5 + 2 = 7 (Add 2)

2.   A

       6 = 6

3.   A

       3 – 2 = 1 (Subtract 2)

4.   D

       4 + 1 = 5 (Add 1)

5.   B

       4 - 1 = 3 (Subtract 1)

6.   A

       3 + 1 = 4 (Add 1)

7.   C

       3 + 2 = 5 (Add 2)

8.   D

       4 - 2 = 2 (Subtract 2)

9.   C

       6 + 3 = 4 (Add 3)

10.   A

       5 - 2 = 3 (Subtract 2)

ANSWER KEY

11.   A

$2 \times 5 = 10$

12.   B

$4 / 2 = 2$ (Half)

13.   D

$3 \times 3 = 9$

14.   A

$3 - 1 = 2$ (Subtract 1)

15.   D

$5 + 2 = 7$ (Add 1)

16.   C

$8 - 3 = 5$ (Subtract 3)

17.   B

$8 + 1 = 9$ (Add 1)

18.   D

$6 - 3 = 3$ (Subtract 3)

ANSWER KEY

1.   D

    1, 5, 5, 1, 5, 5; Numbers are decreasing by 2

2.   A

    7, 5, 3, 7, 5, 3 ; Number sequence 7, 5, 3 is repeating

3.   C

    7, 5, 3, 1; Each number is decreasing by 2

4.   A

    2, 2, 5, 5, 8; Each number is repeating twice and then increasing by 3. Odd Numbers

5.   C

    4, 4, 2, 2, 0, 0; Each number is repeating twice and Numbers are decreasing by 2

6.   D

    1, 3, 1, 1, 3, 1, 1;
    Number group 1, 3, 1 is repeating

7.   B

    11, 9, 7, 5; Numbers are decreasing by 2

8.   A

    3, 0, 1, 3, 3, 0, 1, 3; Number group 3, 0, 1, 3 is repeating

9.   D

    0, 1, 3, 6, 10; 0, 0 + 1, 1 + 2, 3 + 3, 6 + 4

ANSWER KEY

10. C

6, 4, 2, 6, 4, 2; Numbers are decreasing by 2 ,and the sequence is repeating. Sequence 6, 4, 2 is repeating

11. B

8, 7, 5, 4, 2, 1; Alternate numbers are decreasing by 3

12. A

7, 6, 5, 5, 3, 4; First Alternate numbers are decreasing by 2 then next alternate numbers are decreasing by 1

13. A

1, 2, 3, 4, 5, 6, 7, 8; Numbers are increasing by 1

14. D

0, 1, 2, 0, 1, 2; Repeating sequence of 0, 1 and 2

15. B

6, 3, 0, 6, 3, 0; Repeating sequence of 6, 3 and 0

16. A

4, 4, 8, 4, 4, 8, 4; Repeating sequence of 4, 4, 8 and then 4, 4, 8

17. D

5, 5, 6, 6, 5, 5, 6; Numbers are repeating and then increasing by 1 ,repeating. Then decreasing by 1 and repeating

18. A

9, 7, 7, 9, 5, 11; Alternate numbers are decreasing by 2 . Alternate numbers are increasing by 2

www.math-knots.com

ANSWER KEY

1.   A

$$2 + 2 = 4$$

2.   C

$$6 + 1 = 7$$

3.   B

$$10 + 10 = 20$$

4.   D

$$7 + 2 = 9$$

5.   A

$$13 + 3 = 16$$

6.   D

$$11 + 0 = 11$$

7.   B

$$16 + 2 = 18$$

8.   C

$$9 + 1 + 4 = 10 + 4 = 14$$

9.   A

$$6 + 5 + 7 = 11 + 7 = 18$$

10.   C

$$2 + 7 + 1 = 10$$

ANSWER KEY

11.   D

      11 + 5 + 7 = 23

12.   B

      10 + 1 +10 = 11 + 10 = 21

13.   C

      5 + 10 + 3 = 15 + 3 = 18

14.   A

      6 + 5 + 9 = 11 + 9 = 20

15.   B

      5 + 2 + 1 = 8

16.   A

      11 + 5 + 1 = 17

17.   D

      15 + 0 + 0 = 15

18.   C

      13 + 7 + 19 = 39

19.   B

      1 + 8 + 6 =15

20.   A

      1 + 10 + 9 = 11 + 9 = 20

www.math-knots.com

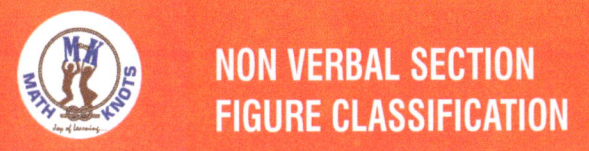
ANSWER KEY

1.	C	Leaf with a circle in the sides and on top
2.	A	Ball with the curved lines and same colors
3.	C	Water floating tube with same colors
4.	B	Multi color ball with same colors
5.	A	Two pictures joining to form a bigger shape
6.	D	Green flower with five petals with three red stars and two blue star
7.	A	Numbers in a sequential order differing by 11
8.	A	Symmetric figures (when it is cut it should be divided into two equal half)
9.	B	Wisk with three rays on top and three circles in the bottom side. Make sure the color is same
10.	D	Disk with a blue dot in the center and three white dots

www.math-knots.com

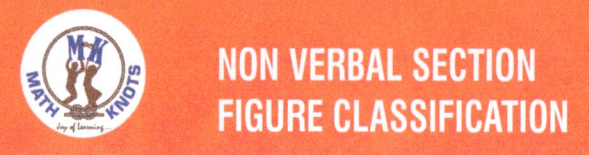
ANSWER KEY

| 11. | C | Two curves with five antennas on one curve pointing out |

| 12. | A | Numbers 123 ; 456 ;789 enclosed in the same order between two curves |

| 13. | D | Two halves in the circle. A circle on the flat side of the half |

| 14. | A | Acute angle (less than 90 degrees) |

| 15. | D | Umbrella with 5 water drops and a flower at the to With all colors being same |

| 16. | C | A line dividing 3 curves and two curves. Same color With two curves pointing to each other on both sides individually |

| 17. | A | Figure enclosing the same figure in a smaller version |

| 18. | C | Semi circle divided into white and green equal half's. White section has two red squares |

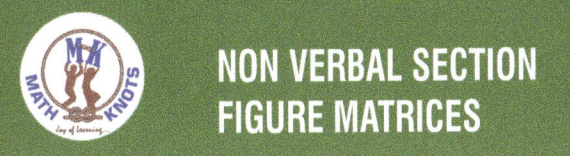
ANSWER KEY

1.   B

Turning 90° to right side

2.   D

Removing the sharp edges and make them flat

3.   A

Lines to checks

4.   C

Adding a circle to the bottom of the cone with a
different color.

5.   D

Flipping right to left

6.   B

Angular vertical lines are doubled

7.   C

Lines and Circles are interchanging from bottom to top
In the answer stars and lines are interchanging

8.   A

Dotted lines are bolded (One line is missing in.
option A on the top)

9.   C

Turning and flipping.

ANSWER KEY

10.   D

Half to full

11.   A

Two pictures forming into a complete full picture

12.   B

Adding a circle in second picture and three more symbols

13.   B

Flipping or showing other side view

14.   C

The circles are flipping to opposite side

15.   B

Figures are interchanging.

16.   D

Two equal halves making into complete picture

17.   C

Outside circles are moving to inside

18.   A

Pictures are joined in the same way as they are

ANSWER KEY

1.   A;

2.   C ;

3.   A;

4.   D ;

5.   B ;

6.   D ;

7.   A ;

8.   C ;

9.   B ;

10.   D ;

11.   C ;

12.   D ;

13.   B ;

14.   A ;

15.   D ;

16.   B ;

BONUS CHALLENGE QUESTIONS

17.   A ;

18.   D ;

19.   C ;

20.   D ;

- We have provided 16 paper folded and punched final figures.

- These pages can be tored, pictures can be cut. Student can fold the pictures along the line and understand the concept.

- This will help them in understanding their visualization of the figures.

Q1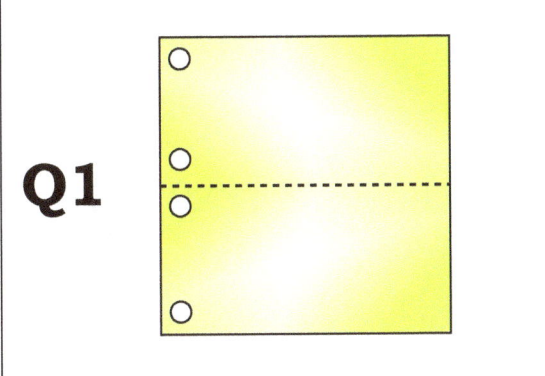

Q2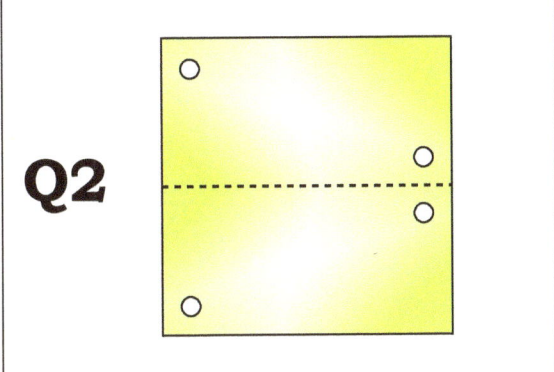

Q3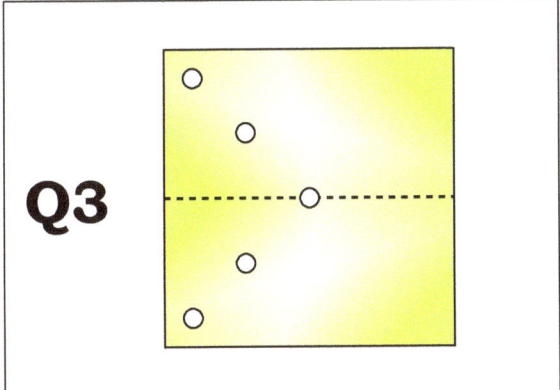

Q4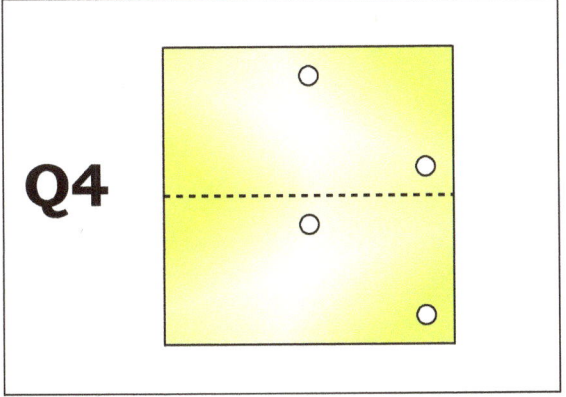

Q5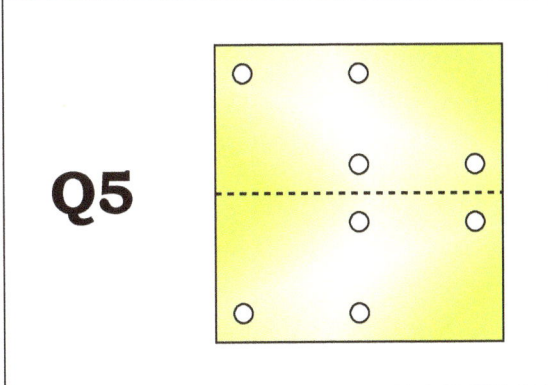

Q6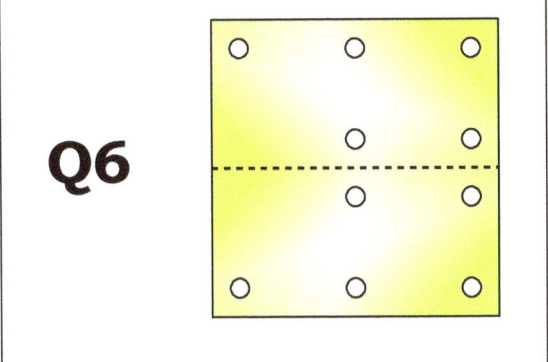

Q7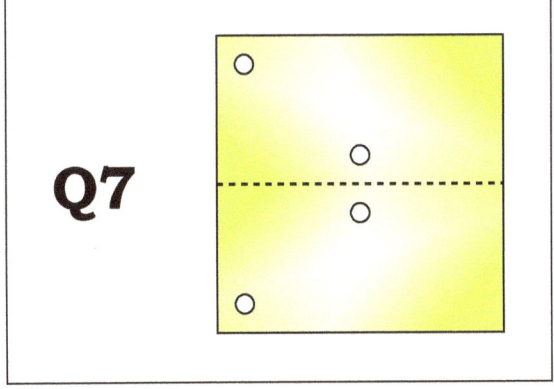

Q8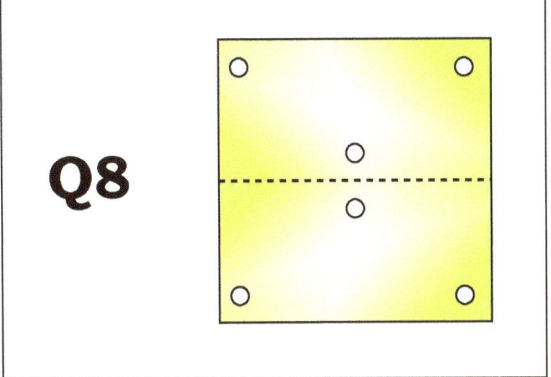

www.math-knots.com

Q9

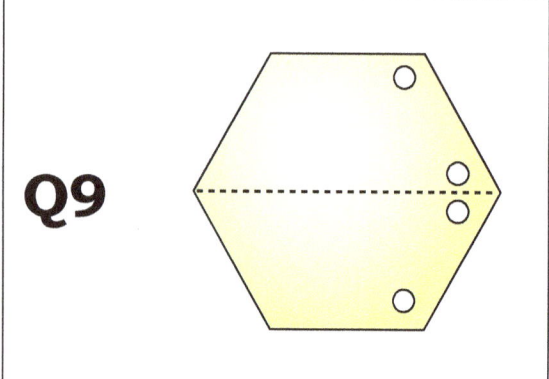

Q13

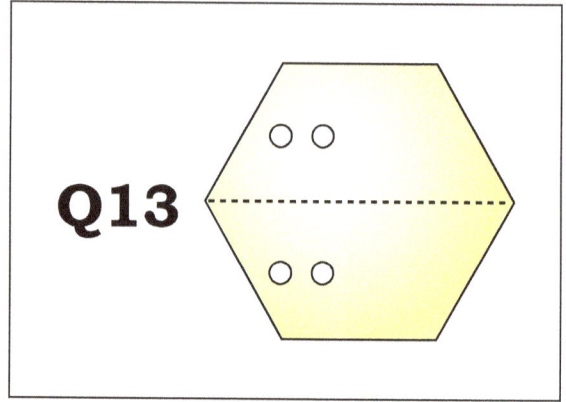

Q10

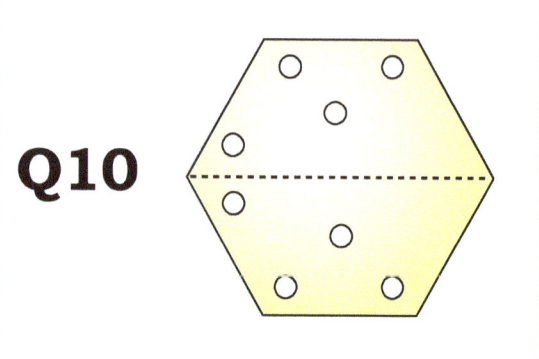

Q14

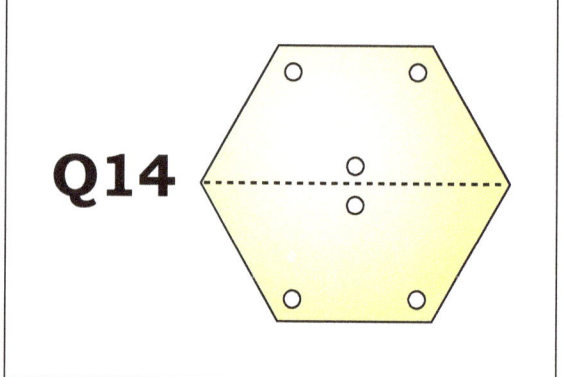

Q11

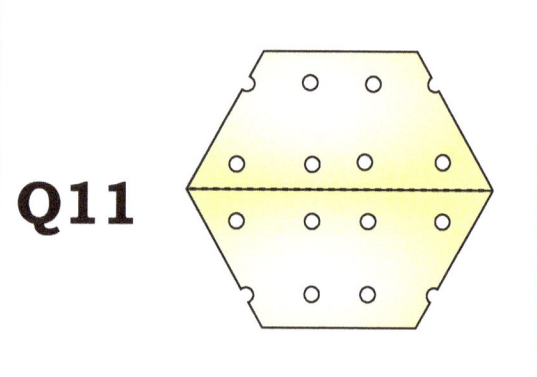

Q15

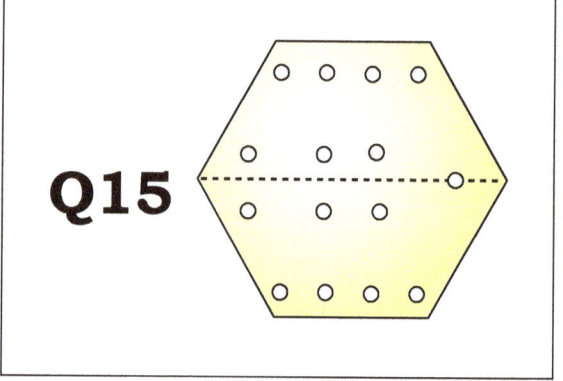

Q12

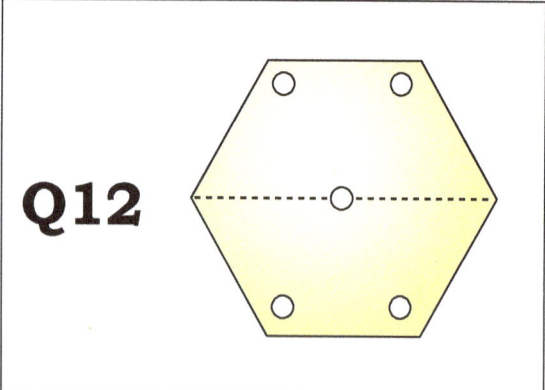

Q16

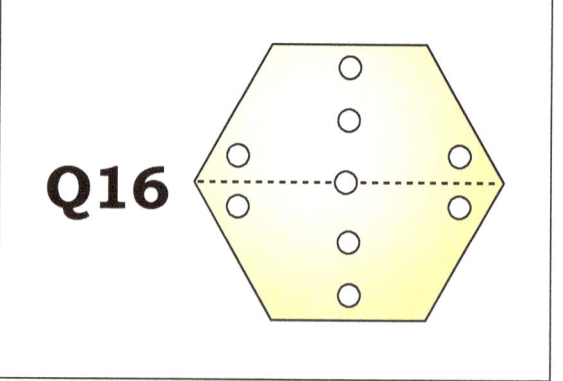

www.math-knots.com

	A	B	C	D
Q1.	○	○	○	○
Q2.	○	○	○	○
Q3.	○	○	○	○
Q4.	○	○	○	○
Q5.	○	○	○	○
Q6.	○	○	○	○
Q7.	○	○	○	○
Q8.	○	○	○	○
Q9.	○	○	○	○
Q10.	○	○	○	○
Q11.	○	○	○	○
Q12.	○	○	○	○
Q13.	○	○	○	○
Q14.	○	○	○	○
Q15.	○	○	○	○
Q16.	○	○	○	○
Q17.	○	○	○	○
Q 18.	○	○	○	○
Q 19.	○	○	○	○
Q 20.	○	○	○	○

www.math-knots.com